BISMARCK'S
FAVOURITE
ENGLISHMAN

TO MY MOTHER
Wera Frydtberg-Urbach

BISMARCK'S FAVOURITE ENGLISHMAN

Lord Odo Russell's Mission To Berlin

Karina Urbach

I.B.Tauris *Publishers*
LONDON • NEW YORK

Published in 1999 by I.B.Tauris & Co Ltd
Victoria House, Bloomsbury Square, London, WC1B 4DZ
175 Fifth Avenue, New York NY 10010
website:http://www.ibtauris.com

In the United States and Canada distributed by St Martin's Press
175 Fifth Avenue, New York NY 10010

ISBN 1 86064 438 4

A full CIP record for this book is available from the British Library
A full CIP record for this book is available from the Library of Congress

Library of Congress catalog card: available

Typeset in Baskerville 10½/12pt by The Midlands Book Typesetting Co,
Loughborough, Leicestershire
Printed and bound in Great Britain by WBC Ltd, Bridgend

Contents

Illustrations

1. Front cover: Spy Cartoon of Lord Odo Russell in Vanity Fair, July 1877.
2. Arthur, Hastings and Odo with their mother, Lady William Russell. Painting by Julius Schoppe.
3. Arthur and Odo at 17 and 13. Lithograph by Kriehuber.
4. Odo as a young diplomat.
5. Lady Emily Russell.
6. Woburn Abbey.
7. The Strousberg Palais, Wilhelmstraße. 70, in the 1860s (later to become the British Embassy). Picture by G. Heisinger.
8. Otto von Bismarck, 1874.
9. Anton von Werner's picture of the Berlin Congress ('Der Kongreß zu Berlin').

I am most grateful to Mr Cosmo Russell for his permission to reproduce pictures of his grandfather. Tony Pictures is in possession of the Spy Cartoon of Lord Odo Russell and plate 4. The picture of Woburn Abbey is reproduced by kind permission of the Marquis of Tavistock and the Trustees of the Bedford Estate. The painting of the Berlin Embassy is used by courtesy of the Landesbildstelle Berlin. The Archiv für Kunst und Geschichte, Berlin kindly gave permission to use plate 8. The Anton von Werner painting of the Berlin Congress is reproduced by permission of the Bildarchiv Preußischer Kulturbesitz.

Acknowledgements

During a lavish college dinner I was once asked by a fairly intoxicated computer scientist why anyone in their right mind would want to waste their time on one of those 'mad Russells'. My reply closed the doors of the computer lab to me forever, but I hope that readers will be more persuaded as to the need for this study. If this is the case, it will be due to the best of all supervisors, Professor Derek Beales. His wisdom, professionalism and originality have made me a devoted member of his great fan club. I would also like to thank Dr Jonathan Steinberg for his wonderful help as well as Professor T.C.W. Blanning, Professor Richard Shannon and Dr Robert Tombs. In addition, I would like to acknowledge the valuable assistance given to me by Professor Klaus Hildebrand (in person) and Professor Paul Kennedy (by letter) during the early phases of my research.

Further thanks go to the people at the German Historical Institute – financially and otherwise. Peter Carpenter from the University of Cambridge Kurt Hahn Trust and the DAAD made it possible for me to come back to Cambridge. I would also like to thank the many archivists in Britain, Germany and the US, who helped me with my research, in particular Mr Harcourt Williams and Mrs Ann Mitchell at Woburn Abbey.

Without the patience of Professor Hermann Hiery at Bayreuth University, I would not have been able to turn my thesis into book form so quickly. His enthusiasm for research on Bismarck has been a great inspiration to me. Thanks to him I met Dr Lester Crook from Tauris Academic Press who, in the true tradition of 19th century publishers, passionately cares about the books he produces.

Bayreuth, September 1998.

CHAPTER 1

Introduction

In 1990, when Germany was in the midst of its reunion, Margaret Thatcher invited Hugh Trevor-Roper, Gordon Craig, Fritz Stern, Norman Stone and Timothy Garton Ash, to a secret meeting at Chequers (which stayed secret for a whole day).[1] The idea was to quiz them about the German soul, especially its more worrying aspects. Yet despite the efforts of these historians to allay her fears, Thatcher was not satisfied. In her memoirs she describes that at first she had hoped the Soviets would stop the 're-emergence' of a powerful Germany.[2] When Gorbachev failed her, she did her best to form an Anglo-French initiative to tie down the 'German giant':[3] 'He [Mitterand] observed that in history the Germans were a people in constant movement and flux. At this I [Thatcher] produced from my handbag a map showing the various configurations of Germany in the past, which were not altogether reassuring about the future'.[4] One of these configurations was of course a picture of Germany in the 19th century. It showed the results of Prussia's ascent in Germany after its battle for dominance with Austria and its war against France in 1870.

In comparison with Mrs Thatcher, however, British politicians in the 1870s did not fear Germany. They had permitted the unity process and now looked on curiously as to what would become of this Bismarckian creation. One of these British onlookers was Lord Odo Russell. As first British ambassador to the newly united Germany, he was for 14 years constantly around the German Chancellor — from their time together at the Versailles headquarters in 1870 until Russell's death in 1884. It is the aim of this book to investigate and understand the Germany that Russell, a British Liberal, observed. The main focus will be on the period 1870–1878, when the German Reich seemed to be an unknown quantity to Russell and when he undertook his most brilliant analysis of the Chancellor. To see through Russell's 'British spectacles' gives us two advantages. First, because Odo Russell was a foreigner he did not suffer from the feelings of either deference or hatred which Bismarck's rule instilled in many Germans. Secondly, Russell's day-to-day assessments also protect us from the trap of seeing Bismarck as the great creator who guessed it all. We can learn that there were many options the Chancellor played with, and that the outcome was often quite uncertain. We will also see continuous changes in Odo's attitude towards Germany. His letters are like snaps, some taken on a bright day, some taken on a grey day or, when Bismarck seriously alarmed him, on a very dark one. For the Foreign Office (FO) and his friends in England such complexity was often difficult to handle, and they therefore just relied on the bits that appealed to their own rather vague ideas of Germany.

So who is Odo Russell? This book is not a biography but a monograph with a few biographical elements. The Victorians were of course obsessed with biographies, 'read not history, nothing but biography for that is life without theory',[5] yet even if one does not agree with this claim of Disraeli, it seems appropriate when one writes about a Victorian such as Russell to give a glimpse of his private life and political value system.

It is perhaps fortunate that Russell did not write his memoirs because he might have given us, like so many of his colleagues, a biased retrospective assessment of his time in Germany. It would have been in some instances a defensive account, glossing over the less successful episodes of his career. Instead we have his private letters, which show the 'unguarded' diplomat. Unlike his official reports (many of which have become famous and are repeatedly cited in books on German–British relations), in his private letters he openly speaks his mind about 'Zornesbock' (Bismarck) as well as the ignorance of British politicians. Russell's correspondence was not intended by his wife to survive. In true Victorian melodramatic style she was reported to have burnt a great many of her husband's letters. Amongst those destroyed there must have been numerous entertaining ones from Odo's eccentric mother who had a scathing opinion on everything and everyone in London and Berlin — certainly a great loss to social historians. Despite this brutal destruction, a great deal of material did however survive. Like his autograph collection, which was found by his daughters in the 1920s, letters to and from Odo were discovered as late as the 1970s. Together with Odo's correspondences to his many German and British friends and the material at Woburn, they constitute the foundation of this work. Yet, if we depend on Russell for guidance through the first years after German unification, we also have to live with the disadvantage that the material itself often dictates which issues are discussed in this book. The

Congress of Berlin, for example, is badly documented in Russell's official dispatches as well as in his private papers since there was no need to write to the FO when the decision makers, Disraeli and Salisbury, were in Berlin with Russell. Also, when it comes to the issue of social unrest in Germany, it is lamentable that Odo only mentions it occasionally. As with many diplomats of his generation his interest in economic problems is also greatly limited, but he was eager to learn. Fighting against his 'ignorance', he embarked on a frantic crusade of research whenever a new German crisis had to be evaluated and reported on. A wide network of friends (among them his banker Baron Bleichröder) and colleagues (like Morier, Lytton and Layard) in almost every European capital, made it possible for Russell to be *au courant* with political happenings as well as diplomatic gossip. This comradely exchange of ideas gave Odo a wide perspective on the effects that German actions had abroad. In writing about Germany he mainly focused on Prussia, and regrettably did not show much interest in what was happening in other parts of the country. He left, for example, the chargé d'affaires in Munich or the Consul General in Düsseldorf, a 'free hand' to cover their own areas.

The title of this study might at first seem confusing for readers. Did Bismarck have a 'favourite' at all and could that person be a foreigner? When one thinks of Bismarck's relationship with Englishmen, the first name that usually comes to mind is Disraeli. He was called a 'friend' by the German Chancellor, who put up a picture of the British Prime Minister next to those of his wife and the Emperor. The question is, however, whether Bismarck was actually capable of real friendship with anyone outside his family circle. It seems that the only male person he had affection for was his son Herbert, whose personality he tried to model on himself — with a doubtful outcome. The German Chancellor was probably not capable of the kind of *Seelenverwandtschaft* [a relationship of total empathy and understanding] between men that had been popularised by the German romantics. Although Bismarck admired Bettina von Arnim, who was a representative of the romantic movement, he did not share his innermost feelings with anyone. The majority of his closer friendships had deteriorated since his rise to power.[6] He had once said that he lacked the ability to admire people, and that it was a defect of his eyes that he saw human weaknesses sharper than qualities.[7] Nonetheless he did have 'favourites'. Their stock was in constant flux. The best known of these 'favourites' today is Gerson von Bleichröder, who in Bismarck's autobiography appears only once, but whose close relationship with the Chancellor was uncovered by Fritz Stern in the 1970s. Odo Russell was also becoming a favourite just like Bismarck's loyal secretaries, Bucher[8] and Abeken. As with Bleichröder, in his selective memoirs the retired Chancellor only refers to Odo once. Still, Bismarck felt as close to Russell as it was possible for him. In return, Russell himself was greatly intrigued by Otto von Bismarck. The ambassador's primary preoccupation became that of decoding Bismarck's language — a 'search for clues'.[9] This focus on Bismarck means that Russell often neglects the influence of other players on German affairs. This is certainly a great weakness of his analysis, but it does not in any way mean that he succumbs to Bismarck's 'glamour'.

A question that will of course have to be addressed in this book is why one should look at a man from the second row, or as Paul Kennedy has put it, 'the historian in retrospect may wonder whether a good or bad diplomat made much difference to the overall course of Anglo–German relations'.[10] It will, therefore, be necessary to consider whether Russell was simply an observer, informant and mediator or, alternatively, whether he had a more direct role and impact on the policies of the Whig and Tory governments that he served. Although there was a certain amount of mutual trust between the Foreign Secretaries and Russell, it will be seen that Odo was not always in accord with his government's position. The question will therefore be, how Russell managed to reconcile the divergence between his personal and political beliefs with the official stance of the FO. Although Odo was not officially a policy maker, he tried to act like one on two occasions — with very different outcomes.

To understand how Russell's analysis influenced British decision makers, we have to look at the extent to which his advice was valued by the various Foreign Secretaries and Prime Ministers he served under as well as by the Royal family. Historians have certainly treated him well. For the diplomatic historian Raymond Jones, Odo was 'brilliant'[11] and Paul Knaplund believed that '[Russell had] certain inborn personal qualities: exquisite tact, quick intelligence, and natural sympathy and kindliness'.[12] Kennedy, Hildebrand and Stern describe Odo Russell as the 'primus inter pares',[13] 'the most brilliant and successful of all ambassadorial appointments in Berlin'.[14] Winifried Taffs, who wrote a study on Odo Russell in the 1930s,[15] did not have much material to work with, but enough it seems to idealise his every move. This is not the intention of this book. It will be seen that, despite being in possession of a sharp mind, plenty of experience and good contacts, Russell frequently made mistakes in his analysis of the Bismarckian policies, as, for example, his unshakeable belief that there would be another German–Austrian war. Yet when he is at his best, his letters are irresistible.

CHAPTER 2

Odo Russell's Profile

Family Background

For a better understanding of Odo Russell's *Weltanschauung*, it is necessary to examine the political as well as the family strands of his life. Both factors are inseparable, because his family life was full of politics and British politics was full of members of his family.

One could say that Odo's outlook on things was somewhat historical as it was formed by his family's history as much as by the beliefs of his political mentors. The term 'historical thinking' has been coined by Christopher Hill to explain the psychological heritage of the decision-makers in today's Foreign Office.[1] This idea can, in part, be adapted to the case of Odo Russell and his family. Naturally the family's strong traditional value system had a direct influence on Odo's actions and ingrained him with an 'ancestral outlook'. Yet what exactly was this value system he grew up with?

The Russells owed their political and economic power to their religion. Henry VIII's break with the Catholic Church turned them into proud Protestants who loyally fought for their king. In return they were awarded vast amounts of land and, among their many titles, that of Earl of Bedford.[2] Although the achievements of the first Earls were important, the true family hero, however, turned out to be the son of the fifth Earl of Bedford — William Lord Russell. He had been involved in the Rye House plot and was seen by many of Odo's relatives as the embodiment of all their religious and political beliefs. The Russells named dozens of their sons after William and in 1820 John Russell even wrote a biography about him.[3] To the family, William Lord Russell was a martyr who had fought for a 'constitutional limitation of monarchical power'. His execution in 1683 might have been a personal tragedy for his wife, but after the Glorious Revolution of 1688, it brought the Russell family the Dukedom.

It was natural that such a rebellious heritage should arouse certain expectations in every new Russell generation. The offspring were encouraged to be politically active and to make use of their fortune for campaigning and their brains for writing. 'Whatever may be said about other families', John Russell wrote to his eldest brother:

> I do not think ours ought to retire from active exertion. In all times of popular movement, the Russells have been on the 'forward' side. At the Reformation, the first Earl of Bedford; in Charles the First's days, Francis, the Great Earl; in Charles the Second's, William Lord Russell; in later times Francis, Duke of Bedford; our father, you; and lastly myself in the Reform Bill.[4]

Such a legacy was strong enough to turn Odo into a diplomat instead of a gentleman of learning, and it also called a member of the following Russell generation, the 'radical' George, into politics. George Russell perhaps himself best expresses how his background and historical thinking made him a campaigner for Gladstone in 1878: 'To a man born and circumstanced as I was the call came with peculiar power. I had the love of Freedom in my blood. I had been trained to believe in and to serve the Liberal cause'.[5] Though the Russells were — in some ways — rightly proud of the services they had given to England, Dominic Lieven has uncovered the arrogance that lay behind their ancestral perspective. While some members of the Russell family claimed to be Liberals, they at the same time shared a feeling of superiority, the belief that they were the 'chosen ones': 'The sacred circle of the Great Grandmotherhood', Lieven writes, 'was at its core a tight aristocratic clique brought up to believe that its ancestors' successful struggle for the Protestant, free constitution against Stuart absolutism was the key to England's subsequent rise to world supremacy'.[6]

The Dukes of Bedford had to juggle a political career with the time-consuming management of their estates around Woburn and their vast London properties. It is estimated that at around 1840 they had an annual income of £100,000.[7] Their estates included rural and urban properties. In London they owned Bloomsbury and Covent Garden, which brought them enormous rents (for example, by 1880 the income from the Bloomsbury estate was £104,880 and Covent Garden brought them an extra £32,000 a year.) They also invested heavily and successfully in a variety of industries and had a very rewarding copper mine on their Cornish estate.[8] Traditionally, it fell to the less well-off Russells to prove themselves in the outside world. Lord John Russell, the younger brother of Odo's father, was of course the most prominent member of the family: 'Much of his greatness will be discovered when his dispatches are published of which the world knows but little', Odo wrote about his uncle, 'and they will add glory to the name and to the family'.[9] Although Lord John's nephews admired him, they sometimes found him to be meddlesome: 'Uncle [John] is a great man when he escapes female influence', Odo wrote to his brother Arthur, 'it is lucky for him women cannot get into the House of Commons, or aunt John would do him much harm there too, poor woman, she means well'.[10] In addition, some of John Russell's 'post-retirement' crusades were seen as embarrassing by Odo. It will be shown later that John Russell's stand on the *Kulturkampf* was, at a political level, convenient for Odo because it pleased Bismarck. However, in private Odo found it to be too radical. Also, John Russell's opinion on the Eastern Question was condemned by both Arthur and Odo. Referring to a letter John Russell had published in August 1875 in connection with the affairs in Turkey, Arthur wrote apologetically to Lady Derby: 'His [John Russell's] letter is much to be regretted. The obstinacy of old age makes it impossible to prevent him sending it to the press'.[11] Odo thought the same: 'I am glad Uncle John's pamphlet is not to appear. His letter did harm, for it was translated into every Slav dialect and given to the insurgents in Herzegowina to encourage them and was received by them with enthusiastic Zivio's'.[12] John Russell, on the other hand, must have himself often felt embarrassed by his own family, especially his benefactor the ninth Duke of Bedford. It was Odo who had first realised that 'Uncle John' had not saved anything. As a consequence, the ninth Duke of Bedford paid £3,000 to John Russell[13] and made sure that his relatives were informed about this generous donation.

It would, therefore, be a mistake to underestimate the Russells' intellectual prowess by assuming that they, privately, always agreed with each other. Their ideas of Liberalism sometimes differed considerably. At the one end of the spectrum Odo could be seen as the more conservative Whig; at the other end was George Russell who belonged to the radicals within the Liberal Party. When George campaigned for the abolition of the House of Lords, Odo's brother Hastings accused Gladstone of approving this notion and threatened to stop his support for the government as long as cousin George remained in the House.[14] Almost every Russell tried to keep some of his own identity by occasionally disobeying the head of the family. Odo's father, Lord William Russell for example (another Russell named after the family hero), for a long time resented any interference by his family in his professional and private life. It is not surprising that William Russell suffered from attacks of depression if one considers that his younger brother was Prime Minister, whereas his older brother, Francis, inherited a fortune when he became the seventh Duke of Bedford. William might have been a textbook case for psychologists who believe that the second born child often feels deprived of material goods and turns into a rebel. William did turn rebellion into his primary occupation and made the evils of primogeniture his favourite subject. It did not help much that the good-natured Francis tried to balance his brother's perspective: 'With respect to elder and younger brothers', he wrote to William, 'be assured that all positions in life have their due share of good and ill ... you are little aware of the cares and worries and plagues I have had to go through'.[15] Whereas Francis and John had found their place in life, William changed his occupation three times. At first he tried his luck in the army. He served in the Peninsular wars and — after a stint as MP for Bedford — he became aide-de-camp to the Duke of Wellington in Paris. Here he met Odo's mother, Elizabeth Rawdon, for the first time.[16] Though Elizabeth was a niece of the Marquis of Hastings, this did not put her in the 'same league' as the Russell family. Her father, The Hon. John Rawdon, was a simple minded soldier who liked to travel, spending his summers in Veneto and his winters in Vienna. As a consequence, Elizabeth had, for a British girl of her generation, an unconventional upbringing. She lived with her parents in France, Germany, Austria and Italy and in later life tried to re-enact her childhood memories by travelling the same paths with her sons. As a young girl her main capital assets were her quick wit, her intelligence and her looks. Elizabeth's outstanding beauty inspired Lord Byron in 1818 to a couple of lines in 'Beppo' ('I never saw but one — the stars withdrawn — whose bloom could after dancing dare the dawn') and the German Emperor William I would many years later confess to Odo how much he had once yearned to dance with this beautiful woman. Despite Elizabeth's Tory sympathies and the disadvantage of acquiring a mother-in-law who was described by society as 'odious', William Russell married Elizabeth in 1817.[17] Though he had wanted to live in England, his more flamboyant wife preferred the continent. They therefore spent the next years travelling and idling around Europe, until it was arranged for William to enter the diplomatic service. By then he had already three sons: Hastings, born in 1819, Arthur, in 1825 and, lastly, Odo who was born in Florence in 1829. The family seemed to have fought over Odo's name: the sixth Duke of Bedford wanted the child to be named after a king, whereas Lady William Russell thought this a highly unoriginal idea. In the end it was decided to give the infant the unusual name 'Odo'. There seem to be two possible reasons for this choice of name: the first Russell, who had, according to the incompetent family librarian J.H.Wiffen, accompanied William the Conqueror, was called Hugh or Odo, whereas in another version, which Odo Russell himself preferred, he had been named after a saint — St. Otho.[18]

Lady William Russell and her three sons. From left to right: Arthur, Hastings and Odo.
Painting by Julius Shoppe

Odo spent his early years in Italy and Germany, the countries that would later play such a great part in his career. His father had been sent to Württemberg in 1833 and in 1835 he achieved his most prestigious posting — Prussia.[19] In later years Queen Victoria was said to have congratulated Odo's mother on the great achievements of her husband and son. Odo wrote about this to Arthur:

> The story you tell me of the Queen saying to MM (his mother) 'I hope you will not mind your son having a higher rank than his father, etc., etc.,' I have heard, but do not know whether it is authentic or not. The Queen however may have done so, for she asked me at Osborne whether MM did or did not mind my rank being higher than my father's was at Berlin.[20]

After some highly dramatic years with his wife, William Russell started a much remarked on affair with a widowed lady from Frankfurt. Although the Russells never got divorced, Lord William tried his best to avoid his wife and always seemed to leave town rather hurriedly once she threatened to be *ante portas*. The Duchess of Dino summed it up succinctly: 'Anything that separates him from Lady Russell always suits his taste'.[21] The problem was that they liked to take their cures in the same spas and therefore had to make sure in advance that they would not meet. Hastings, their unfortunate go-between, probably suffered most from this situation. For years he tried to mediate between his parents, but even when William Russell was about to die in Genoa in 1846, it took a great deal of persuasion to make Lady William come and see him. Odo and Arthur felt awkward in the presence of their dying father, and Lady William Russell did not forgive him. Despite such shortcomings, Lady William's greatest achievement was her positive influence in the education of her sons: 'His [Odo's] unorthodox education had provided him with exceptional linguistic skills and far-ranging knowledge. He mixed easily, ... had charm ... his high integrity and tact were invaluable'.[22] Odo was encouraged by his mother to make friends with a variety of people including scholars, artists, the bourgeoisie and 'even' trades people.[23] As a result he would later lack aristocratic arrogance and, on the contrary, developed an unusual modesty that was to be remarked upon in Berlin.

Odo, Arthur and Hastings called their mother 'MM' and half feared, half worshipped her. Her witty writing style was one of the things they liked: 'Two of [her letters] are so full of wit' Odo wrote in the 1850s, 'that I rolled about on my sofa and laughed until I screamed all alone in my room! MM writes the best letters in the world when she chooses to do so — I make subjects of conversation of the contents of them — and I am generally found very amusing'.[24] The feared side of Lady Russell was her harsh criticisms. Her eldest son Hastings was the first target of her spite: 'I want encouragement, and not rebuff,' Hastings wrote in despair, 'without a little vanity [self-esteem] nothing would be done in this world, and to be constantly told by one's mother that one is an idiot, a coward and a liar is very disheartening'.[25] Lady William Russell was, even for the time, a very old-fashioned disciplinarian. Her sons were not allowed to sit down in her presence and had to attend to all her wishes.[26] By instilling in Odo this royal treatment towards women, Lady William equipped him with all the right ingredients to become a successful courtier.

With their French tutor,[27] Mr Drocourt, the young Russells travelled extensively through Europe. By the time they came of age, they did not have to do the grand tour any more — their whole life had already been one. They were fluent in three or four languages (the accounts vary somewhat on this point. Odo certainly spoke Italian well, and his French and German were both possibly flawless. Whether he spoke Dutch and Spanish too, as Hogarth claims, has not been proved)[28] and their love for languages was such that up to old age they used German expressions in their letters, some of them written in a Berlin dialect. Odo, especially, felt attracted by everything German and Austrian, and, by the time he joined the diplomatic service, was so germanised in his writing, that his brothers had to point out 'un-British expressions'.[29] In his youth Odo was first influenced by German authors, ploughing through Kotzebue's 42 volumes of drama as well as reading Goethe and Schiller. French and English authors (including his favourites, Carlyle and Eliot) interested him later, and for his autograph collection he only bought letters from famous German novelists and playwrights, including a letter from Goethe in which he mentions Kleist's '*Der zerbrochene Krug*'.[30] Odo's cultural memories of Germany never changed. However, after unification, he learnt to distinguish between the Germany of his youth, which had been full of poetry and music, and the 'new' Germany of the 1870s. Karl Deutsch's argument, that 'decision-making is about combining new information with old memories', in many ways fitted Odo's approach to Bismarck's Germany.

At first, the Russell family did not interfere with Lady William's upbringing of her sons abroad. They only began to become concerned about the future of Arthur and Odo once they came of age. Blakiston claims that Lady William Russell was put under pressure by her brother-in-law, John Russell, to release her sons and send them back to England.[31] At the time it was not seen as a recommendable experiment to study abroad, as Lord Acton remembered in the 1890s:

I can remember when people used to say that the Russells were heavily handi-capped because they were educated at home — or rather abroad; and that they knew foreign languages so much better than anybody else that they never could be master of their own. But the official success of one brother, and the social suc-cess of the other, deprive us of these explanations.[32]

In 1849 John Russell gave Arthur a position as his own private secretary and persuaded Odo to join the diplomatic service.[33] Arthur worked for his uncle for 5 years and then, after a 3-year break, became a member of parliament for Tavistock. Hastings' future had already been taken care of. At 19 he entered the army as a lieutenant in the Scots Fusilier Guards and then became the heir-presumptive to his cousin, the eighth Duke of Bedford. The Duke was a broody figure who suffered from melancholia and shyness. He was a hypochondriac who had already decided at Eton that he despised life and would not endure it for long. His uncle John Russell summed up the condition as 'a bad stomach, Byron and Voltaire have been the causes of the mischief'.[34] Although the Duke sat in parliament for a time, he did not have any great social or political ambitions. Politics he left to Uncle John (his favourite motto was 'Lord John is always right') and the management of the estates to his cousin Hastings. During a visit to Woburn, Disraeli commented that the eighth Duke 'fancies himself unable to encounter the world. He detests the country and country life'.[35] On his reluctance to marry and produce an heir, the Duke remarked, according to Disraeli: 'Could I have a better son than Hastings?' Disraeli was certainly a good psychologist, being one of the few people who noticed that the Duke's shyness was a common Russell family trait:

Odo Russell just arrived from Rome ... via Paris. He brought the new toy, Pharaoh's serpent. Quite a miracle! A most agreeable party, which it could not fail to be with such guests and such a host and hostess for Lady Elizabeth is quite worthy of her husband (Hastings). The predominant feature and organic deficiency of the Russell family is shyness. Even Hastings is not free from it, though he struggles to cover it with an air of uneasy gaiety.[36]

When the troubled eighth Duke of Bedford died and Hastings acceded to the Dukedom in 1872, his family was jubilant. Odo could not 'conceal his delight at the idea that your long labours are at last rewarded and that you have ascended the throne of your ancestors and can govern your Dukedom absolutely for yourself. Le Duc est mort, vive le Duc'![37] Being the brother of a Duke meant that Arthur and Odo could apply to become Lords. At first Odo pretended not to be interested in this title, but he soon found out that it would be an enormous help at the German court. Apart from enabling them to take the title, Hastings also became the financial benefactor of his brothers and their large families, a fact that made his relationship with them uneasy. From the beginning Hastings did not cope well with his newly acquired wealth and complained about what Henry James called 'the dark and merciless things which lie behind great possession'. He developed a certain meanness (which occasionally alternated with great bouts of generosity) and became cynical about his brothers', probably genuine, concern for his well being. Odo sometimes despaired that he constantly had to defend his requests for some financial support from Hastings: 'For 21 years have I struggled against the many temptations of an expensive profession, in which money is so great an element of success, to avoid the almost unavoidable debts contracted by all colleagues and never have I sought to take advantage of the wealth at your command'.[38] However, Odo's acceptance of the ambassadorship in Berlin was only made possible by Hastings' offer to support him financially.[39] A British ambassador was expected to have great private means, and it is therefore not surprising that in most of his letters to Hastings, Odo is talking about money problems:[40] 'The Congress [of Berlin] puts me to unexpected expense in this summer season. Constant receptions ... and an open house ... . When the feast of nations is over I must ask for some compensation if it is not offered by HMG'.[41] His happiness was, however, secured whenever there was a cheque from Hastings in the post: 'Thanks to Hastings' constant and most generous assistance I am financially so well off that I can meet all my representative duties largely and handsomely'.[42] Some of Odo's letters requesting financial help finish on the pathetic note: 'My widow and orphans will thank you'. Like many Victorians Odo was obsessed with mortality, and wrote about his eventual death in a rather morbid way. Although he was deeply upset when one of his children was dangerously ill, he at the same time made contingent plans for a tasteful funeral. He was also eager to help Hastings in arranging a memorial room at Woburn for his late mother. It was furnished with all her possessions, from her books to her reading glasses.

In order to receive a bonus from Hastings, Odo had to present himself as a good investment for the family. Whenever there appeared a positive article on his work in Italy or Germany, Odo immediately sent it to his brother for the family scrapbook. In 1875, for example, Hastings was proudly informed by Odo that a *Spectator* article 'of 30 January 75 headed "Lord Granville" makes honourable mention of me'[43] and in 1878 a *Times* article 'Bismarck during the war of 1870' informed its readers about Odo on 'page eight, second column'.[44] In the same year Odo advised Hastings to read Moritz Busch's book about the Franco-Prussian war, *Graf Bismarck und seine Leute während des Krieges mit Frankreich*, which in his opinion should be put in the library at Woburn 'as I am occasionally mentioned in it'.[45] Without giving away any confidential information, Odo also repeatedly mentioned how satisfied Lord Derby was with the work done at Berlin, and employing calculated understatement, Odo talked of discussions he had had with the leaders of the day, 'which may not be unsatisfactory to HMG'.[46] To have an ambassador for a brother must also have contributed to Hastings' prestige. As George Russell argues, it was a question of social status for every host to have an ambassador, whether mediocre or famous, among his dinner guests. 'I daresay that ambassador has been blundering all his life', a character in *Endymion* exclaims, 'and yet there is something in that Star and Ribbon. I do not know how you feel, but I could almost go down on my knees to him'.[47]

The impressive family seat at Woburn also proved useful for Odo's social standing in Berlin. He often asked Hastings to entertain influential German politicians and aristocrats who were travelling around England, including the Prussian Crown Princess and Herbert von Bismarck. They were all as impressed by Woburn as Disraeli had been in 1865:

> [it is] fine from its greatness and completeness, everything that the chief seat of a princely English family requires. The house, though not beautiful in its exterior, is vast. ... There are stables not unworthy of Chantilly ... a gallery of sculpture, the finest private one, perhaps, in the world. A mass of choice and rare collections of all kinds which have been accumulating for centuries.[48]

Grant Duff was less flattering in his verdict. He thought that the house itself was:

> hideous, but full to overflowing of treasures — so full that no better place can be found for the magnificent service of Sevrés, given by Louis XV to the Duke of Bedford when he was ambassador to France, than a cupboard room which is used, if I recollect rightly, for the upper servants to take tea in.[49]

Arthur and Odo were often invited to Woburn but they also had their own stamping grounds. Arthur's active social life, in particular, could have been judged equal to that of his ambassador brother. Arthur was, despite his shy nature, very clubbable and greatly valued as a listener and loyal friend. He became an enthusiastic member of numerous London clubs (the Athenaeum, the Cosmopolitan and Grillons) and co-founded the Breakfast Club in 1866.[50] To be seen in the right clubs was essential for a Russell.[51] There were political clubs like the conservative Carlton and the liberal Reform Club, but the most exclusive ones were the Athenaeum, Brooks's and the Garrick Club. Odo Russell was not

Odo (right) with Arthur, the brother he felt closest to.
Lithograph by Kriehuber.

as lucky with his club memberships as was Arthur. Short of money, he tried to leave the Marlborough Club at one point, a move that upset the Prince of Wales. His secretary Knollys wrote to Odo:

> The Prince of Wales understood that you have withdrawn your name from the Marlborough Club, and he desires me to write how sorry he is to hear of it. He would I think take it as a compliment to himself were you to reconsider the matter, as he was so anxious that you should become a member of the club in question, that he proposed you himself, a thing which, with one exception he has never done before, unless for relations.[52]

Because of his manifold club activities, Arthur's work as an MP for Tavistock suffered. In 28 years he only managed to give two speeches in the House of Commons (one was his maiden speech, the other 'a spirited defence' of Odo's work in Rome). However, for the time this was not that unusual. In Trollope's novel about an MP, *Phineas Finn*, the hero tells his sweetheart that 'not one in ten who go into Parliament ever do say anything'.[53] (Trollope, Arthur and Odo were members of the Athenaeum Club and most certainly met there. It has even been suggested that Trollope used the Duke of Bedford and the Russell family as models for his books.) According to his friend Grant Duff, Arthur was at his wittiest off stage when it came to his little apercus:

> Arthur made an excellent House of Commons answer to Simeon, who meeting him, as he came out of one of the earlier gatherings which took place at the Deanery in Westminster rushed up to him with an appearance of great embarrassment and said: 'Well, is there a God?' 'Oh yes', replied Arthur, 'we had a good majority'.[54]

However, Arthur could not be described as a 'full-blooded' politician, as Odo correctly analysed: 'in truth your mind and tendencies are "cosmopolitan", above party prejudice, philosophical, fair to all, and taking interest in the true, the good and the beautiful everywhere. *En un mot*: *ein vorherrschender Universalismus* [a universalist]'.[55] Perhaps Odo was also thinking of one of Trollope's characters when he wrote these lines. In *Phineas Finn*, the two heroes, the Whig aristocrat Palliser and the middle-class social climber Finn, represent the different 'ideals of British political life where individuals are elected to submerge their individuality in parties: for Palliser it is "service", for Phineas "independence" '.[56] Arthur was a mixture of both men, finding his independence outside his party, but feeling bound to serve the liberal cause loyally. His true talents lay more in academic work. He was an active member of the Geographical Society, and became interested in Darwinism at an early stage. Odo was intrigued by Arthur's new passion: 'Your letters have lately shown a leaning towards Darwin, here in Germany he is a Demigod, and old people wring their hands and groan to think that Goethe did not live long enough to enjoy the happiness

"Darwinismus" can give'.[57] In a conversation with a German professor about Darwinism, Odo came to the, not very scientific but from a social point of view convincing, conclusion 'that if Darwin's selection was true, humanity must degenerate, because in our society and civilisation human beings don't couple and procreate by selection, but for 'conveyance, money, position, rank, relationship etc. etc. there can be no improvement in the breed, but the contrary'.[58] After espousing such heretical ideas, Odo would never have been admitted to the inner circle of Darwinists. Their sense of humour was limited. Arthur wrote to Layard in 1890 about a scientists' club: 'I think all men of eminence get into the club in time unless they be anti-Darwinist, then the scientific men veto and nobody can venture to say a word'.[59] Such despotism was, however, against Arthur's liberal notions: 'When I see how intolerant and unforgiving Huxley and the biologists are to anyone who has dared to criticise them, I feel very grateful that Darwinism is not yet our established church'.[60] Like his close friend Matthew Arnold, Arthur was interested in education and thought about ways to reform public schools and universities. He was also a member of the Metaphysical Society, which had been founded in 1869 and met nine times a year until its disbandment in 1880.[61] Odo called its members 'the forty of the future academy', or less flatteringly, 'the atheists'.[62] Among them were Walter Bagehot, William Gladstone, Thomas Henry Huxley, Henry Edward Manning (not exactly an atheist), John Ruskin, John Seeley, Henry Sidgwick and Sir Montstuart E. Grant Duff, to name only a few. Their routine was to have dinner together at the Grosvenor Hotel and then one of them would present a paper. As Lytton Strachey put it in his, as usual, cynical and inaccurate way: 'they met once a month during the palmy years of the seventies to discuss, in strict privacy, the fundamental problems of the destiny of man'.[63] Arthur's papers for the Metaphysical Society, which are today deposited in the Cambridge University Library, show his balanced view on the opportunities and limits of scientific research. It was not surprising that he was eventually asked by his friend Grant Duff to become a fellow of the University of London, a career move that impressed Odo.[64] Yet, like his friend Acton, Arthur was so overloaded with material, as well as respect for the written word, that he suffered from writer's block. As a consequence he did not live up to his family's high expectations, feeling pestered by Odo's constant encouragements to write about certain issues. Arthur's obituary perhaps rightly summed up his life as that of a 'patron and speculator rather than a contributor',[65] whereas Noel Blakiston's more flattering judgement portrays him as a 'philosopher and savant'.[66]

Like Arthur, Odo enjoyed the company of scholars and surrounded himself at Berlin with university professors. Russell was especially fascinated by behaviourism, even before this subject was invented. His curiosity concerned not only the breeding patterns of his beloved fish but also, when he became a father himself, his children's ways of expression. The way in which his twins behaved, he sensed (despite living in a pre-Freudian world) as being dangerously peculiar. He could not tell them apart and whenever he asked for one of their names, the addressee remained silent while his twin pointed to him. They also developed their own language, which worried their parents considerably.[67] However, even Odo himself was known for his slightly eccentric behaviour. According to Blakiston he used to carry snakes and other living creatures around in his pockets when he was in the countryside. Still, he did not match the description Raymond A. Jones gives of some of Russell's colleagues. The 19th-century diplomatic service, Jones claims, 'had probably more than its fair share of eccentric and difficult personalities'.[68] Compared with David Urquhart's madness or Sir Henry Elliot's adventures, Odo's career seems uneventful. His mild peculiarities were only focused on his private life and were therefore perfectly tolerable to his chiefs.

Like their mother, who learned Hebrew in old age, the Russell sons accumulated, driven by their 'teutonic thirst for knowledge', books on every possible subject,[69] and corresponded with several museum directors about their favourite hobby-horse, the natural sciences. Even when in later life their professions hardly allowed them the time to read for pleasure, they approached their mother for advice on what books to buy: 'I want history, facts, truth, life and can no longer toil through novels,' Odo wrote in 1859 to her, knowing that she would send him the right books.[70] He shared his love for history with his uncle John Russell 'who regularly read aloud [from history books] to his family'.[71] To be interested in new inventions and academic challenges was a character trait all Russells seemed to share. The Dukes of Bedford were renowned for their modernisation, for example, being the first to introduce electricity and, today, using natural power-resources. When typewriters were developed,[72] Hastings proudly produced letters for his brothers on this latest 'printing machine': 'Your letter printing machine must be delightful', Odo wrote to Hastings, 'often and often have I wondered that Morse's telegraph had not yet been applied to letter printing'.[73] Odo naturally could not keep this latest Russell discovery to himself:

> Your printed letters are wonderful. I told the Emperor William, the Empress Augusta, the Grand Duke of Baden and his wife about them last night at dinner and they took it all for chaff and wouldn't believe me that letters could be printed like telegrams nowadays — 'Excellency *belieben wohl zu scherzen* [are joking]'.[74]

Unlike their friend, Matthew Arnold, who was so 'sensitive to the stresses of the age', the Russells welcomed the new technologies and scientific challenges wholeheartedly. They shared the Victorian belief in a rational world, facing the future with excitement and curiosity. In one instance Odo even accompanied his wife to the dentist to see her tooth being pulled out under the latest invention, 'laughing gas'. Duly he reported back to his brother: 'a horrid operation to look at, but she says she felt no pain at all'.[75] Odo's chief in later years, Lord Salisbury, was another trend-setter aristocrat who shared a similar enthusiasm for the latest technology.[76] In his leisure time, he personally supervised the installation of electric light at the family seat, Hatfield.[77] Aristocratic families such as the Bedfords and Salisburys were aware that they had to be forward looking and to set new standards of living, so that they would not become anachronistic themselves, overrun by the affluent upper-middle classes. Far from being pessimistic and backward thinking, they would have agreed with Hobsbawn's verdict that 'the long 19th century was a period of almost uninterrupted material, intellectual and moral progress'.[78]

Although Odo communicated extensively with his family, one should not assume that he had no other confidantes. He corresponded with a variety of colleagues, friends and acquaintances all over Europe. Influential English friends were, however, of particular importance to him because they could keep up his stock at the FO, in parliament and in London society while he was abroad. This does not, however, mean that Russell only recruited people who were useful to him politically. One of his closest friends, for example, was Lord Acton[79] who, despite his friendship with Gladstone, was for a long time of no political value to Odo and worked mainly as an intellectual stimulant for him. Another friend was the liberal MP William Cartwright.[80] A cosmopolitan in the true sense, he travelled to the battlefields of the Franco-Prussian war. On his way home he met the German Crown Princess in 1871, who judged him to be a defender of the German cause in England. To her mother, Queen Victoria, she wrote:

> I have made the acquaintance of a Mr Cartwright (a friend of Morier's and Lady William Russell's sons) a very agreeable and intellectual man ... He understands Germany thoroughly and is very well calculated to clear away the heap of prejudice and nonsense which has gathered in German heads about England.[81]

Not even Russell would have thought so highly of Cartwright's political judgement. Cartwright was famous for his chaotic ideas (and therefore called Cartwrong by his friends), yet his charming character appealed to Russell nonetheless. In choosing his friends, Odo followed the motto that friendship was only possible among equals. Though he socialised with his superiors, he was not a close friend of Granville or Gladstone.

His real friends were only people of the same standing, such as, for example, Morier[82] and Layard.[83] They all more or less shared the same political beliefs, were all waiting impatiently to be made ambassadors, and they all followed, apart from politics, other intellectual interests and pursuits, such as literature and science. Morier was, because of his connections with Germany, particularly close to the Russell family. He had, together with Baron Stockmar and the Prince Consort, for many years propagated a British–Prussian alliance. He was on good terms with Augusta, the Queen of Prussia, as well as with the Crown Princess — both sworn enemies of Bismarck. Together they tried to counterbalance Bismarck's influence on the King, who was in their opinion 'a mere tool of the wicked man'. Bismarck in return put Morier under police surveillance on and off during the 1860s. Morier's prospects of one day becoming British ambassador to Berlin were shattered by the spread of rumours. The irony is that he never ceased to promote a strong and united Germany — loyally defending the Prussian stance in the 1866 and 1870 wars. However, he, and many British Liberals like him, could not abide Bismarck's method of delivery for the birth of Germany — by caesarean section as it were rather than more natural means.

Odo's closest female friend was Lady Salisbury, a mentor of many rising young men.[84] Although she was a Tory, Russell seems to have owed a great deal to her intellectually and emotionally.[85] He was also in love with her. Yet, it is not clear from their letters, which have only recently been acquired by the Hatfield archive, whether theirs was more than a platonic relationship. Lady Salisbury certainly helped Russell through difficult times:

> As the sculptor models clay into shape, so have you modelled the most important, the deepest, most lasting recollections of my life and given me light in the darkness of the clay period years ago — and now, single words from you suffice to convey volumes, worlds, *Life* to my mind.[86]

Every time he had to leave her, he was desperate: '*Zwei Seelen ein Gedanke, zwei Herzen ein Schlag!* [two souls, one thought, two hearts one beat]. And my tears are dropping down on the blotting book and I must leave the Club and hide myself before anyone sees me'.[87] Odo knew that it was a hopeless love, yet through most of the 1860s he could not forget her:

> You touch on so many points that awaken thought and a longing for an exchange of ideas that your letters appear to me like your conversation. In both you exercise that mysterious fascination I call magnetism, and while I read your letter I can see your well-known eyes looking at me out of your handwriting and I can hear your insinuating voice.[88]

The relationship cooled off, however, when Lady Salisbury married Lord Derby — a move that outraged all her admirers considerably, and made her in 1874 the wife of Odo's chief.

A few words have to be said about Odo's marriage. After he had realised that Lady Salisbury could not become his wife, Odo, at the age of 40 considered marrying a 'compatible woman', Lady Emily Villiers. Emily was one of the daughters of Odo's chief, Lord Clarendon. According to the Queen of Holland, Emily was not Clarendon's favourite daughter, but she looked very much like him: 'She has a Villiers face'.[89] Odo's shyness in private affairs (which Disraeli had detected so well) became evident during the courting of his wife to be. With Lady Salisbury he discussed at length whether it was feasible at all to propose to Emily:

> I like Emily very much, but a middle-aged fat man of 40 wearing spectacles and having no money and no prospects, could not more be expected to pretend to Emily than he could to the Sun, Moon and Stars. If he did, he would be first turned out of the House for his impudence and then ridiculed for his folly and he might with a shadow of justice be called a Buffoon, a flirt, a Humbug and an affected puppy etc. ... Should I ... turn traitor to my Ex-chief who has confidence enough in me to allow me to frequent his house — and put everyone to inconvenience by making a fool of myself and casting ridicule on a young lady I esteem, love and respect? Add to that, that much as I may esteem ... E. I have no reason to believe that she cares more for me than for W.H. whom she is said to have refused.[90]

For the following month, Lady Salisbury was showered with similar letters full of self-doubt from Odo. It was only through this courting that he became acutely aware of his 'poverty':

> If I proposed and was asked what I had to live on, I could only confess in all humility that I had not enough to indulge Emily in the luxury way she is accustomed to — she little knows how simple my habits are, how small my wants — she does not know how a poor gentleman lives abroad — she scarcely knows me and would be bitterly disappointed in me, if she knew me.[91]

To his genuine surprise, Emily accepted him. As was to be expected his mother was up in arms against the match, claiming that she needed at least one son as a travel companion. Hastings was therefore instructed to make it clear to Odo that the family could not financially support such an expensive match. Tormented by this economical and emotional blackmail, Odo wrote to his confidante Lady Salisbury: 'Mama has told him [Arthur] that if I marry at all she will die next week and she must have a bachelor son and can't bear the idea'.[92]

He did marry and she did not die. How proud Odo Russell was of this match and of his wife's background is revealed in a letter he wrote to his mother after the birth of his first son, Oliver: 'Emily descending from the Chancellor Clarendon on her father's side and from Lord Bacon by her mother. Two intellectual *Ahnen* [ancestors]'.[93] Though Odo's marriage turned out to be a great social success (and brought Russell personal happiness and six children) it was not a calculated one and at first worked as a career hindrance for him. In 1869, when a position in Madrid came up, his father-in-law, Lord Clarendon, wrote to Hammond: 'Odo would be the right man but I don't venture to send him as the outbreak against nepotism would be bad for us both'.[94]

In Odo's professional life the Russell connection was a social, financial and political necessity, but it could also play a disruptive part. In 1875, Lord Derby, for example, asked Odo, at the behest of the Russells, whether he wanted 'a change'[95] from his Berlin post. Russell reacted vehemently to the suggestion: 'It would be the greatest favour if you leave me here until death or pension ends my career'.[96] It is quite likely that the Russells had grave objections against one of their members serving under a Tory ministry and — as will be shown later — in 1878 they successfully dissuaded Odo from accepting a peerage from Lord Beaconsfield. This behaviour still seemed to follow the old-fashioned perception of diplomats as being loyal to their party. However, since the 1860s a continuity was established in the Foreign Office, which transcended changes in the government: 'Foreign policy went across party lines and, for the most part, incoming administrations took on the obligations and commitments of their predecessor'.[97] Odo was also kept on by Disraeli and Derby because he was an outstanding expert on German affairs and an ideal representative for Britain. No Tory diplomat at the time could have equalled that.[98]

In his book on European aristocracy, Lieven rightly claims that 'the 19th century was a good time to be an aristocrat... The Victorian nobleman was likely to enjoy a longer, more comfortable existence'.[99] To be a member of the Russell family meant that one belonged to the elite within this aristocratic elite. Such exclusive membership offered an ideal springboard into the inner circle of Britain's decision-makers, as well as social and financial security. Odo made full use of all his political chances. He could have adopted an indulgent lifestyle like his brother Arthur,[100] but he chose instead to dedicate his life to the more glamorous, but also more demanding, public service — a commitment that was in line with the family's values: 'It was easier for someone with the family history of a Russell to play a constructive role in Victorian Europe than was the case with an aristocrat still imbued with a sense of nostalgia for his family's lost status under the old *Reich*'.[101] Odo Russell's professional success would prove that the British aristocracy was still capable of reinventing itself in a rapidly changing world.

Inside the System

When Russell joined the diplomatic service in 1849, Europe had been experiencing one of its stormiest times since the Napoleonic wars. The year of 1848 — 'the most eventful year in the history of Europe' according to *The Economist*[1]— had certainly been an 'annus horribilis' for European monarchs. A revolution had first broken out in Paris and then spread rapidly all over the continent. In England, the April 10th demonstration of the Chartists was perceived as the return of the 'Jacobian devils'.[2] Prince Albert already feared that 'European War is at our doors' and made his wife leave London.[3] In the end the 'reactionaries' triumphed, but this did not mean that the events of 1848–1849 were soon forgotten. Especially Austria, the country to which Odo was first posted,[4] would never forgive Lord Palmerston for his sympathy towards liberal movements on the continent. As a result, the British embassy in Vienna was the first target of the Austrian government's displeasure. For the first time, Odo experienced what it was like to live in a social vacuum. In the past, Austria had been a country which he had known well and in which he felt at home. As children, Hastings had been invited to shooting parties with Prince Esterhàzy and Prince Schwarzenberg, while Odo and Arthur had played with the Emperors-to-be of Mexico and Austria, Maximilian and Franz Joseph, respectively. Odo's closest friend at the time had been the son of Count Szechenyi, who would, many years later, become his colleague in Berlin. Yet, despite these excellent old contacts, Austrian society turned out to be extremely difficult for Russell to conquer in 1849. It irritated him when his old circle of friends welcomed him — half jokingly, half in earnest — as an English 'spy': 'Your mission here is as good as known to us,' Mucki Waldstein, a childhood friend claimed, 'you are here to make reports on the state of this country to Lord Palmerston'.[5] Odo told Mucki that such was the natural business of a diplomat, but this did not make him a spy. While he publicly tried to laugh off such accusations, his private letters show how concerned he was. He started to have great doubts as to whether diplomacy suited him at all, and after only a year in Vienna his worried family arranged for him to come back to London and work at the Foreign Office. In the 19th century such a return to base was quite an unusual event. It will be shown later how Russell profited from his two different experiences of the Foreign Office: as a diplomat looking at it from the outside and also when actually working within it — seeing how the despatches of his fellow diplomats were used or abused.

At the FO Russell kept in touch with Austrian politics and he was eventually sent back to Vienna again. By then, Lord Palmerston had ceased to be Foreign Secretary and anti-British feeling slowly subsided. However, in Odo's opinion, this was for the wrong reasons:

> It would be really difficult to describe the effect that Lord Palmerston's resigna-
> tion made on the population of Vienna! The coffee-houses and *Bier*-rooms were
> filled with people. Long live Queen Victoria was the general cry ... . I imagine that
> when the news of Napoleon's capture by the English after Waterloo was known to
> the world there could not have been a more sincere joy in any of the population
> of Europe as here. Their joy was foolish and showed brutal ignorance.[6]

The background to Palmerston's fall did, however, have more to do with Austria than Odo would have liked to admit. In the revolution of 1848, Kossuth had led the Hungarian uprising, which was eventually suppressed by the joint effort of Austria and Russia. For the Austrian government, Kossuth was a most wanted villain; for Palmerston, Austria's retaliation in Hungary was a monstrosity and Kossuth had to be helped. The Foreign Secretary willingly gave Kossuth asylum and in 1851 Palmerston had to be persuaded by his cabinet colleagues not to receive the Hungarian personally. Instead, he met a deputation which thanked him for his support and called the Emperors of Austria and Russia 'odious and detestable assassins'.[7] Palmerston did not seem to mind such language. The Prime Minister at the time, Lord John Russell, decided to turn a blind eye to the incident but, in December 1851, when Palmerston committed a second blunder (he expressed — without cabinet consultation — to the French ambassador Count Walewski his approval of Louis Napoleon's *coup d'etat*), he was 'released from his duties'.[8] The ousting of Palmerston by John Russell had the happy side-effect for Odo that he was welcomed into Viennese society again.

Odo's teachers during the 1850s were not only the ambassadors and the senior colleagues he worked for at the embassy, but also two men from the home front, Edmund Hammond and Austen Layard. Hammond had joined the FO in 1824 and served it for almost 50 years.[9] He supervised four political departments, including the German one.[10] From 1854 to 1873 he was Permanent Under-Secretary for Foreign Affairs and had the reputation among diplomats of being a strict 'nanny': 'He sent private warnings about high play at whist, "smuggling" in the diplomatic bag, illegible handwriting, careless docketing and consular inactivity'.[11] As far as foreign affairs were concerned, Hammond was more of a devoted bureaucrat than a visionary. He certainly did not understand the unification movements in Italy and Germany. His favourite motto — 'in quietness and confidence shall be our strength'[12] — naturally caused friction with Odo, who regretted that Britain was only playing a secondary role on the continent.[13] However, Russell learned to tolerate Hammond's position and valued him as a teacher. Sir Austen Henry Layard, Odo's other mentor, was in the early 1850s and 1860s Parliamentary Under-Secretary for Foreign Affairs and had also accumulated a vast wealth of experience as a diplomat. Craftsmanship in writing was one of the most vital skills that both Hammond and Layard tried to instil into Odo.[14] For his letters to be distinguished from those of all the other despatches that reached the FO, it was important for Odo to develop his own incisive style:

> I cannot sufficiently thank you for showing me my faults [Odo wrote to Layard] it is the act of a true friend and I am grateful to you for it. I had endeavoured to use generally plain and straightforward language and to avoid "phrasing", and I am sincerely obliged to you for pointing out to me that I have not succeeded for I shall now exert myself much more in that direction. Tell me whom you consider a really good model of despatch style? — I am most anxious to write plain, good English.[15]

Arthur also tried to influence Odo's writing style, but he was a less patient teacher than Layard: '[Your despatches] are in a strange un-English style, but with no faults of grammar ... . As your business is to write, you should do it well and the only way is to read often, daily, some of the great writers of English prose'.[16] Odo obviously succeeded in improving his style during the 1860s and proudly quoted from a letter Gladstone had sent to Clarendon: 'My dear Clarendon, whenever there is an Odo in the box, satisfaction instantly predominates'.[17] Even a Tory seemed to appreciate Odo's despatches. In 1859, Arthur passed on a surprising compliment to Odo:

> I met Disraeli walking to the House who instantly took my arm. He has done this before and it makes me very shy for when we get to the House members stare awfully. But what I wanted to say is this: he told he often had occasion to see your despatches and approved highly of them.[18]

There is a recognisable difference between Odo's despatches and those of his colleagues. Apart from his distinctive writing style, many other diplomats were not as able at condensing events as he was and often bored their readers at the FO with useless trivia. Russell had recognised this common mistake during his work at the FO. Many of the incoming despatches were, in his opinion, a sheer waste of paper, never read or used: 'I was deeply struck by the inconvenience arising from the fact that our representatives abroad are given to writing an innumerable quantity of useless dispatches which take up men's time to no purpose whatever'.[19]

Odo's thorough education made him approach his diplomatic work in a similar way to that of a scholar writing a paper. He did research on each subject, from the history of the Roman church to the problems of the Polish minority in Germany, by asking as many experts as possible for advice, reading widely on the topics and then writing everything down in as clear a form as possible.[20] This was much more than one could expect from the average diplomat. Russell himself was appalled by the way his colleagues in Rome approached their work. To Layard he wrote:

> It takes time and trouble to be really well informed in Rome as you know and I do not wish to imitate my colleagues and send you volumes of useless *on dits* which in the end only mislead the home government. I marvel at the trash the R.R. of France, Austria, Spain, Portugal, Prussia, Bavaria, etc., etc., send home and to all appearances believe in.[21]

Every minor despatch was crafted by Odo with great precision, going through several drafts. There is a similarity to Bismarck's well-honed, precise instructions to his ambassadors (which became public during the Arnim trial and impressed Odo considerably).

Another important lesson Russell learned over the years in his relations with the FO headquarters was that, although faults were tolerated, disloyalty was not. In the following chapters it will be shown that during his long career Odo, naturally, made several mistakes. The FO was most accepting of such errors, often without any great consequences for the culprit. In David Hare's play *Plenty*, the Chief Clerk at the FO makes a point that is as valid today as it was a hundred years ago:

> It's not enough to be clever, everyone here is clever, everyone is gifted, everyone is diligent. These are simply the minimum skills. Far more important is an attitude of mind. Along the corridor I boast a colleague who in 1945 drafted a memorandum to the government advising them not to accept the Volkswagen works as war reparation, because Volkswagen plainly had no commercial future ... . Unlikely as it may seem, that man has risen to the very, very top. He has forbearance. He is gracious. He is sociable ... . I am saying that certain qualities are valued here above a simple gift of being right or wrong. Qualities sometimes hard to define.[22]

These rather vague gifts are today fashionably labelled by psychologists as 'emotional intelligence'. This is the type of intelligence that makes it possible for people to survive in new social environments, to build up human relationships and a system of communication that supports them on a personal as well as on a professional level. If we look at Odo's growing social success during his postings in Rome and Berlin and his down-to-earth approach to problems, one could say that he was a master of emotional psychology, without necessarily having the most analytical head in the FO. He succeeded in giving his British and foreign colleagues the impression that he was not evasive on subjects, but sincerely willing to provide the information they were after. He perfected his uncle's advice in that direction: 'Lord Russell told me he would have given me the same instructions as Talleyrand gave a young French diplomat "parlez vous beaucoup — mais ne dites rien" '.[23]

Apart from having mentors in the FO and amongst politicians, it was also becoming increasingly important in the second half of the 19th century to be on good terms with the British press. Odo realised this vital need to keep up 'his stock' at home, and to learn to humour journalists (in Versailles he got to know his namesake, the *Times* correspondent William Russell; in Berlin he later helped the British journalist Kingston to get out of custody). Odo's friend Morier seemed to be quite jealous of these close contacts with journalists: 'to remain in such a profession is suicide — of course this does not apply to you who have the good fortune ... to be the pet of the FO, of the *Spectator*, the *Daily Telegraph* and generally of the public'.[24] Still, over the years, the press would occasionally criticise Russell's actions. In such instances, he immediately wrote defensive letters to his brother Hastings, asserting the correctness of his actions.

After his periods in Vienna and at the FO, Odo also spent some time in Paris. His first assignment to France in 1852, which only lasted a few months, was pushed for by his mother, who was a good friend of the ambassador in Paris, Lord Cowley. Odo yielded to this second experiment abroad, but was not pleased. To Arthur he wrote:

> One year at home has opened my eyes to the ... discomforts of the continent, never was I so struck by, so aware of the superiority, the greatness of England. When you [Arthur] go abroad again you will feel what I have felt — we could not before for we did not know our country. 10 days in Paris have opened my eyes again. I have seen our diplomats that I had forgotten, I have been able to compare our Statesmen with Foreign ones — I have compared the different corresponding classes with each other, the institutions and the state of society ... I feel, I understand what position I can occupy with time and by labour at home, I understand how much chance had done for me and I feel that it is my own country I must study and must know to attain my point and occupy the position that I may one day enjoy ... — I feel my ignorance more than ever and I mean to study.[25]

In France, two crises came at once for Odo: he felt homesick realising how much he missed his own country, and again he doubted whether he had made the right decision as far as his professional life was concerned. He was also deeply unhappy about his private life, which was dominated by his ever-demanding mother. In later years Odo would long for a few days holiday in Paris (even though it was a Republic by then), but in the 1850s he resented the newly established regime of Napoleon III. After the *coup d'etat* of 2 December 1851, the opposition had been suppressed and critics of Napoleon III imprisoned.[26] The majority of parties and classes quickly aligned themselves with the new man and seemed to eagerly rally around the Bonapartist sun. For Russell such 'moral insanity' was repellent:

> The state of French Society from a moral point of view, is very beastly and the only difference between the so called good and bad society that I can see is that the bad shows and gives itself as it is, while the good attempts to look virtuous, de facto they are exactly in the same state of moral development, I had a false idea of Paris corruption, it is much worse than I thought, it disgusts me![27]

A personal encounter with Napoleon did not help much either, but did at least produce a typical Russell *bon mot*. When asked how he had felt facing the French Emperor, Odo had commented: *'J'ai senti comme l'empereur, que j'etais le neveu de mon oncle'*[28] [I felt, like the Emperor, that I am my uncle's son]. Odo's estimation of monarchs was, in his younger years, quite critical. Although he made an exception as far as his own Queen was concerned, the Russell family trait to be suspicious of monarchical power was deeply rooted in him. Napoleon III was, in his opinion, a power-greedy actor and the Emperor Franz Joseph, his former playfellow, was also sceptically scrutinised. The young Franz Joseph of the 1850s was far from being the seemingly paternal father figure of the 1900s. On the contrary, to Odo he looked like a most obstinate ruler who was still unsure about his place in the world and therefore constantly tried to prove his new-won power:

> The little Emperor is full of courage and obstinacy! How can he be anything else. No one dares say a word of advice! He delights in review — and has them at a 4 hours notice once or twice a week — much to the disgust of soldiers and officers in winter. His Majesty insisted on having a review during the hard frost — he was advised against it, but uselessly — the review took place. Two *curassiers* fell and broke their necks! The Camarilla concealed this event from fear of giving pain to HM. During a review, an *anständiger Weisswaschwarenhandlungscommis* [a decent employee of a linen and washing powder shop] excited by the sight passed the Emperor smoking and forgot to take off his hat — he was taken into custody, flogged in prison and condemned to 2 years *schweren Kerker* [a severe prison sentence]. This created bad blood of course.[29]

Franz Joseph was ingrained with the reactionary beliefs of his mother Sophie and Count Grünne. Grünne was a military man, who believed that the Austrian people should be ruled with the same methods as was an army. Any form of culture (music, literature and especially theatre) sprang, according to Grünne, from subversive liberal sources and was therefore highly dangerous. Franz Joseph copied this narrow-mindedness and felt reluctant to go to see a performance of Goethe's *Torquato Tasso* on the centenary of the poet's birth because 'we have better things and people to celebrate'.[30] (It is no wonder that Franz Joseph's wife, the capricious but artistic Elisabeth, would go berserk in such an environment.) Despite his criticism of Franz Joseph, Odo also saw the tragic side in the life of this young Emperor who had to carry so many responsibilities and seemed to be alone with them. This became apparent in April 1852 when Prince Schwarzenberg, who had been Franz Joseph's greatest support, died of a heart attack. Odo, in true melodramatic style, reported home what he had heard about this from a friend at court:

> The Emperor rushed in to the room ... he flew to the Prince's bed and seized his hand and finding his best friend and faithful servant was dead, passed his hand over his eyes and nearly fainted! A second later he went down on his knees and prayed silently for quarter of an hour ... then he got up looking deadly pale, kissed the cheek of the dead man, proceeded to his writing table, opened a drawer, took some papers he seemed to know and concealed them in his pocket — then he locked carefully every other drawer, took the keys and went home. The Emperor is to be pitied, he has lost a friend to whom the House of Habsburg owes its present strength. Austria has lost a Minister, who putting aside the awful blunders he committed internally certainly understood her interests in Germany and had he lived some years longer, might, by his system have made all Germany obey Austria's will and wish 'de facto'. Prussia has lost her most dangerous, her greatest enemy — whether she will understand how to make use of her good luck is now the question.[31]

Prophetic words indeed.

In 1854 Russell was transferred from Paris to Constantinople. Both cities were at the time the only two British First Class Embassies and it seemed perfect training for him to gain experience in them. While his two short postings in 'fickle' Paris had been, in his opinion, a failure, Constantinople was an instant success. This was certainly unexpected by everyone who knew Odo's new chief. Lord Stratford de Redcliffe was called 'Buyuk Eltchi' or Elchi (the great ambassador)[32] both by the Turkish and by Odo and he was in every way charismatic. However, his management skills, as far as his staff was concerned, left something to be desired. Hammond, Lord Clarendon, Lord Cowley and Field Marshal Rose had never managed to get on with him. Yet from the moment they had first met by chance in 1852, Odo was immediately taken by Stratford: 'It is long since I have gazed upon so clever a face'.[33] Once settled in Constantinople, Odo quickly became an honorary member of the small club of people who managed to get on with Lord Stratford de Redcliffe. From the start Russell was determined to turn this posting into a success:

I was firmly resolved, on coming out here, to do all in my power and to leave no means untried to be as useful to Lord Stratford as I had tried to be to my former chiefs ... I beat about for a long time in the dark, but my resolution was always before me.[34]

It was Odo's perceptive analysis of people's character that made him react to Stratford's outbursts in the right way. He found out that though the ambassador 'boils over like a kettle',[35] he soon calmed down again and, momentarily, even felt ashamed and apologetic about his behaviour. He could also be generous as far as money was concerned, but in return he expected entire submission. Criticisms of any kind were not welcomed. Odo accepted these terms and was soon indispensable. He drafted despatches that were praised and not altered at all by his chief — a new experience that helped him to gain more self-esteem. It almost seemed as if Stratford had long waited for a soul-mate such as Odo and now could not refrain from confiding in him. The emotional dependence went so far that Odo was not even allowed to be ill: 'Eltchi won't even read his dispatches and letters if I am not by his side to listen to him; I have literally known him allow the correspondence of 4 days to accumulate unopened and unsealed because I was in bed with a headache. Quis credat'?[36] Of course, the situation at the embassy was a special one at the time and, since the outbreak of the Crimean War Stratford needed all the support he could get from his staff. The Elchi (who had romantic feelings for Poland) was a resolved enemy of Russia. The Russian threat to Turkey, and its consequences for the security of the road to India, were again and again drummed into Russell. The great ambassador wanted an absolute victory over his Russian foes and went so far as to try to undermine the Vienna conference of 1855 to which John Russell had been appointed. Instead of furnishing Lord Russell with all relevant information, Stratford seemed slow to fulfil the instructions of the FO. The obvious reason was, according to Clarendon, that: 'Stratford won't allow the Porte to make peace — on the contrary, he doesn't think we have made sacrifices enough and he wants a much more magnificent war and a guarantee for the remainder of the Turkish loan'.[37] After the end of the Crimean War, Stratford favoured a harsher peace settlement, a demand that, if it had been successful, would have prevented Russell from embarking on his famous Black Sea mission 14 years later.

Although Odo stood loyally by Stratford, he was not that much of a hawk himself. Of course, he did not feel much sympathy for Russia, either politically or emotionally. As a Whig he despised the Russian reactionary system. None of his close friends were Russians and, like the Prussian Crown Princess, he often used the word 'Russian' for everything negative. But his approach to Russia remained pragmatic. While he would successfully use Stratford's hawk-like guise to bully Bismarck during the Black Sea Question in 1870, 5 years later, during the Eastern Question of 1875, his desire for mediation in the region was greater than his dismissiveness of the Panslavists. In the 1850s, however, the male bonding between Stratford and Russell did not come to an end because of political divergences over Russia, but on rather trivial grounds. Odo fell in love with Stratford's daughter Catherine. The great Elchi, like every Victorian father would have done, forbade the marriage for pecuniary reasons.[38] After this incident, it was clear that Russell could not remain in Constantinople. In 1857 he packed his bags and left for Washington. Leaving a first-class embassy to go to a former colony seemed at the time a step backwards for a promising diplomat. In a way, this move illustrates that Russell did not have a perfect masterplan for his career; on the contrary, in the 1850s he was by no means a young man in a hurry.

In Constantinople Russell had read every Greek history book he could get hold of. In Washington, however, he read not only for educational reasons but also as a form of escapism: 'I am reading a great deal now', Odo wrote to his mother from Washington, 'it is the only thing I care for, my books and my fireside. My colleagues and society bore me to death and I avoid them like the plague'.[39] His new chief, Lord Napier, was a far less inspiring figure than Stratford. Lady Napier also failed to become a friend of Russell. The Napier children, when asked the tactful question whether they preferred their father or their mother, were quick to answer that 'the person they loved most was Odo Russell'.[40] Naturally, Lady Napier was none too happy about this and barely talked to Russell afterwards. Because the 'family embassy' at Washington turned out to be a cold one indeed, Odo turned to his natural family resources again. Arthur was invited to America and brought Russell 'civilising conversation'.[41] Together they went on an adventure trip, visiting the, at the time fairly tourist free, Niagara Falls and — always family-conscious — the site of the Battle of Brandywine, where Lady William's father had lost a leg during the Revolutionary War. It was a relief to get away from Washington for Odo, who was convinced that the 'horrid' living conditions in the capital ruined his health:

> The houses in Washington are all low and people not only live generally on the ground floor but even a good deal under ground, in what they call the basement, because it is cool in summer and warm in winter. The houses are all miserably

small, without water and without water closets, the ladies cack in pots, which the nigger carries away, and the men go to a dung hill or to the stables at the back of their houses, all this is unhealthy in hot weather for there are no drains and no sewers. ... Amongst these is the President's mansion or White House which is also thought to be unhealthy.[42]

Yet, despite all his complaints about America, Russell noted that something within society was about to change dramatically and this change interested him: 'There is, as I have said before, nothing whatever to like in this country ... but the political and social condition of the country is immensely interesting and I hope to acquire much useful knowledge here'.[43] It was obvious for him that the slave-problem, for one, had to be solved. As an experiment Russell bought a slave and tried to treat him well by paying him an extra wage. He soon realised that most of the money would go to the original slave owner and that the whole enterprise was more or less in vain.[44] He decided that the whole system was rotten and that this was mainly because the Americans had what today would be called an 'attitude problem'. Some of the highest echelons of American society seemed to think nothing of abusing Black people:

Last year a member of Congress at one of the principal hotels here ... shot the waiter with his revolver in the S*peisesaal* [dining room] because he was not sufficiently civil. The waiter was a Negro and died on the spot — everyone thought the member of Congress quite right and he is a great favourite in society here.[45]

That such a violent man was celebrated rather than condemned was, in Odo's opinion, due to the irritating gun culture that the Americans indulged in:

People in this country depend ... on their revolvers for protection. In the hotels a printed paper in every room invites you to lock your door and give money or precious objects to the Innkeeper — for nothing can be answered for and Americans who call on you for an evening visit will place their revolver in a corner with their hat and gloves as a thing of course. It takes some time to get accustomed to all this.[46]

Another thing that seems not to have changed in Washington's political society for the last 150 years is that, 'you have to be constantly on your guard when you speak to [people] for everything you say and do not say is published in the papers'.[47] Odo also could not come to terms with the darker sides of American night-life. Having lived in capitals such as Paris and London, it is surprising that this scene had escaped him before, but in America, prostitution must have been a much more obvious and straightforward profession:

The Promising Diplomat

the native American prefers hotels because he passes his day at the bar drinking spirits all day long and discussing the events of the day. At New York the hotels are excellent — but here [in Washington] they are atrocious — known to be worse than any all over the United States — indeed they are all used here by naughty women as bad houses.[48]

After such a Sodom and Gomorrah, a transfer to Rome seemed to be the only alternative for the virtuous Russell.

British relations with the Pope had not been cordial since 1534. Though Lord Melbourne had once played with the idea of sending an official envoy to the Vatican, the penalty of *Praemunire*, i.e. the 'punishment of anyone acknowledging the Pope of Rome',[49] made this a difficult endeavour. Odo would later explain to a junior diplomat that interest in accumulating information about the Vatican had increased when, in the 1820s, a British secretary of the Legation in Munich went to Italy for a cure and stayed there. Though he died despite the cure, his political reports were found useful and the FO decided to send a successor. Officially he was accredited to the British Legation in Florence and sent only as chargé d'affaires to Rome. The first one to be successfully deployed in this manner was Henry Petre, followed by Lord Minto, Lord Lyons and eventually by Russell in 1858.[50] As with his predecessors, Russell was first accredited to his town of birth, Florence. When in 1860 Tuscany was annexed, the farce continued and Odo was accredited for a while to Naples. In practice he never lived in either place and was always throughout in Rome.[51]

From the time of his arrival, Italy changed Russell both outwardly and inwardly. He was now 30 years old and had decided to grow a beard to look more mature. According to Lady Paget he succeeded in resembling 'the image of a German professor'.[52] For the first time he was the head of a mission (admittedly without any staff) and he must have felt that his early apprentice years were over. From a cultural point of view he could not have been in a more stimulating place. There was art all around him and he tried to surround himself with creative people. Over the years, for example, he got to know, and to charm, Elizabeth Browning. He not entirely truthfully praised her hero Napoleon III, which prompted another Italian tourist, Henry James, to write 'it worked in her as a malady and a doom'.[53] Unfortunately, Odo did not meet another expert of doom, Ibsen, who in the 1860s was on vacation in Italy to calm his nerves. It is not clear whether Odo got to know the interesting American visitors to Rome, W.D. Howells and Nathaniel Hawthorne. However, he was introduced to one of the most famous figures in Italy, Franz Liszt, later Abbé Liszt. Russell's good tenor voice (constantly worked on by his eccentric Italian teacher Salvi) gave him the entree to the musical scene of Rome and he was even invited to sing for the Pope.[54] He was also involved with an amateur theatre group and became a most wanted leading man. This was caused more by his nationality than by his looks. The Italian princesses who produced the plays did not under any circumstances want to include Frenchmen as actors.[55]

As usual Russell did not only mix with his class, but was also interested in what the average Italian thought. His servant 'Nazzareno', a Cavour supporter, was an entertaining yet often unreliable source. Nazzareno claimed that he knew Napoleon III personally and had once even worked for him as a spy. Whether this was true or not, Odo seemed fascinated by the idea and even learned something from his servant about the Roman criminal classes (Nazzareno seemed to be on suspiciously close terms with the pickpockets of the neighbourhood). Murders on the Corso were nothing unusual at the time and Odo, in true Victorian fashion, liked to 'revel in a good disaster'.[56] The British consuls in Rome (first Charles Newton and then Joseph Severn) had many gruesome stories with which to regale Odo. Their reports on cases of eloping British girls read today like Forster's novel *A Room with a View*. The sun and the romantic surroundings seemed to work a spell on British ladies and they ran away with Italian men on a regular basis. As Noel Blakiston shows, some very daring ones even tried to live by themselves in Rome. In one case, a newly blossomed British middle-class girl got completely out of hand and started to receive Italian men in her apartment until the police put a stop to it.[57]

As was the case during his previous posting in America, Russell again experienced a tense social and political situation. Shortly after his arrival, on 19 December 1858, he had a conversation with Cavour in Turin and listened to his plans for unification (almost half a year earlier, on 21 July 1858, Cavour had met Napoleon III at Plombières to decide on a war with Austria). In a frank discussion with Russell, Cavour predicted war within a year: 'the best campaigning season begins in May. Austria will attack us then'.[58] When Russell replied that if Piedmont were to attack Austria first, it would lose the sympathy of Europe, Cavour asserted '[we will] make Austria attack us'.[59] Although Russell dutifully passed on the details of this conversation to the FO he was, until he could be convinced otherwise, of the opinion that Cavour was a dreamer.[60] Russell's doubts should not, however, give one the impression that he was against Italian unity as such. He did welcome the idea of a united Italy (in 1866 he would write enthusiastically: 'Venetia has been ceded; Italy is made, a great fact in history'), yet remained a careful commentator — unlike his colleague in Turin, Sir James Hudson, who, as a keen Cavour supporter had overstepped his instructions. The main reason for Russell's cautiousness was of course that if he had shown too much sympathy with the unity movement his excellent contacts to the Pope and Cardinal Antonelli would have suffered. The French-friendly Cardinal Secretary of State, Antonelli, was considered to be the *eminence grise* behind the Pope and was soon a good acquaintance of Russell. Like Cardinal Manning he obtained a special dispensation from Pius to talk to Odo 'openly': 'There is a great advantage, *mon cher* Russell, in your unofficial position here. We can speak freely to each other; I can say things to you I could not say to your colleagues'.[61] According to Russell, Antonelli was in reality only 'the Pope's best servant'[62] and not as influential as many people thought. To Russell, the Pope himself, who would later be one of Bismarck's greatest adversaries, was 'of firm and independent character; his heart is charitable and benevolent and his mind is clear and logical; he means what he says'.[63] Pius IX, flatteringly, called Odo '*mio caro* Russell' and '*mio figlio*', and sometimes even displayed a great sense of humour. On one occasion, when he was displeased with the British government, he made this clear to Russell in a quite unsubtle way. Odo had come for an interview to the Pope's summer villa, Castel Gandolfo, and as usual wanted to kneel down briefly before the talk started. However, Pius kept him pressed down and Russell had to remain in that uncomfortable position during the whole conversation. It ended with Pius saying: 'Ah, my son. I wish you were a Catholic. I should send you for a fortnight's penance to the monastery at Genzano. It would do you a world of good'.[64] During another incident in July 1862, Russell, however, did not seem to get the joke. The Pope, whose position in Rome was again endangered, had asked whether he would be welcome in England. The exact words seem to have been: 'Farewell, dear Mr Russell; who knows that one day I shall not be compelled to ask you for your hospitality'.[65] The fact that Odo took this statement seriously and passed it on to the FO led to a few embarrassing diplomatic exchanges. Another utterance by the Pope was also turned to Russell's disadvantage. Members of the Pope's inner circle complained that he treated a Protestant (Russell) too well. This prompted Pius to say: 'But he is a very bad Protestant'. Jowett quoted this joke against Russell in the context of the infallibility debate: 'I doubt whether [Russell] has a comprehensive grasp of things; he is too much within ecclesiastical circles. The Pope said of him that he was not a good Catholic, but he was a bad Protestant, which I think expresses his political [point of view]'.[66] Such criticism of Russell started in 1870, after the declaration of infallibility by Pius IX. When the infallibility dogma was discussed in the Vatican Council of 1870 there was opposition to it even within the church ranks. Russell naturally took a professional interest in the Pope's declaration and the events surrounding it, but thanks to his friendship with the Catholic Acton, he also developed a personal curiosity in the spiritual uncertainties that the dogma caused for the faithful.[67] Acton himself had close ties with the church leaders of the German Catholics, who lobbied against the declaration of infallibility, one of them being his old mentor Johann Joseph Ignaz von Döllinger. When Acton had first studied in Munich at the age of 16 (the Church of England had at the time made it impossible for Catholics to study at Cambridge or Oxford),[68] Döllinger had taught him theology and encouraged his pupil's ultimately ruinous passion for collecting books (which is today the Cambridge University Library's gain). When he became ambassador to Berlin, Odo would sometimes lose patience with Acton and Döllinger's endless struggles with the Catholic Church hierarchy.[69] By then, Odo had heard all the arguments exhaustively for, after all, his Catholic friends in England had been critical of the Vatican's policies for over a decade: 'When I read Acton, ... and Henry Petre's letters I cannot but think that with such elements of discord and disobedience in the church, it was the Pope's duty to proclaim himself infallible and send them all to Hell'![70] One should not of course conclude from this remark that Odo agreed with the Pontiff's new dogma. He would always claim that the 'Pope had made his church incredulous by the proclamation ... of his own infallibility'.[71] However, this was, in Odo's opinion, of interest to the 'faithful only'.

Winifried Taffs claims that Russell was in a unique position to understand the inner life of a Catholic because his mother was one. It will be shown in the *Kulturkampf* chapter that this is incorrect. Still, after having partly grown up in Catholic countries such as Austria, Italy and France, he was not prejudiced against Catholics. This in itself was seen by some strong-minded British Protestants as a major sin. In his famous book *Eminent Victorians*, Lytton Strachey portrayed Odo as the willing puppet of the 'evil' English Archbishop (later Cardinal) Manning. For Lytton Strachey the infallibility story was a simple one to tell: Manning despised Odo's friend Acton ('such men are all vanity, they have the inflation of German professors and the ruthless talk of undergraduates'[72]) and tried to alienate Russell from Acton by getting the former under his own spell: 'soon poor Mr Russell was little better than a fly buzzing in gossamer'.[73] Here, Lytton Strachey was clearly underestimating Russell's intelligence. He is not alone. Manning's first biographer, Purcell, also seems to be under the illusion that Odo had become a great sympathiser with everything Catholic.[74] In truth, Manning, like Antonelli, was for Russell mainly an important source of information which it would have been unwise to ignore. That Manning flattered himself by thinking that he was completely supported by Russell in his fight in support of the infallibility dogma, only shows what a clever diplomat Odo could be (S. Adshead supports this theory: 'though Odo did not like "Ultramontane fanatics" he was simply good at 'drawing Manning out')'.[75] Still, he did not lead Manning on completely: 'You know that my earnest wish is to do justice to all parties', Odo wrote to the cardinal, 'and for that I require knowledge'.[76] In relation to the infallibility issue Russell advised his government not to intervene for three main reasons. First, he knew that the Pope would not waver and that the opposition, whether right or wrong, would in the end be overruled by the Italian bishops anyway. Second, at this particular juncture in world affairs, with the Pope gradually losing more and more of his temporal power, Odo saw the fight not as a religious one like Acton and Döllinger had done, but as a political one. The dogma was necessary for the immediate survival of the Church. Finally, Odo was of the opinion that after Pius IX's death, as a reaction to the dogma, a more liberal faction within the Church would gain power.[77]

Gladstone, who was kept informed about the debates in Rome by Acton, did not see matters Russell's way and pressed for a diplomatic intervention. This was successful in so far as the Cabinet decided to commission Russell to orally support the French Government's protests in Rome during April 1870. Odo followed these instructions half-heartedly. He won over Lord Clarendon who, though he personally rejected the infallibility dogma, was too much of a realist to start a quarrel with the Pope. Odo's prediction that the approval of the dogma would be passed easily turned out to be correct. Many of its critics preferred to leave Rome to avoid the humiliation of being beaten. After two months and 50 sessions the Vatican Council met for the last time on 18 July 1870. In the end, 533 members voted in favour and only two against the dogma.

The effects that this fight had on Odo's friends were mixed: Gladstone poured out his frustrations in his book on *Vaticanism*. Döllinger was excommunicated by the Pope. Acton only escaped this fate, according to his biographer Roland Hill, because he was so well connected.[78] (Here Russell's influence might have played a part too.)

Although Acton had not been pleased with Odo's 'realist approach' to the dogma, their friendship was never in serious danger. Throughout the struggle they were seen walking on the Pinicio together. On one occasion they saw Pius IX blessing kneeling people. When the Pope recognised Odo and Emily Russell he gave them a special benediction, but then noticed that Acton stood next to them: 'and suddenly [the Pope] changed his hand from the vertical to the horizontal position, he made that rapid shaking movement of the first and second fingers by which the Italian signifies negation. No blessing for you, my friend, was indicated by the gesture with painful distinctness'.[79]

Odo departed from Rome before the last Council session in July 1870. He would always remember his posting in Italy as the most fulfilled time of his life. James Rennell Rodd recounts in his memoirs a walk in Russell's garden in Potsdam:

> I [observed] to him that the miniature Dome of the Garrison Church as seen framed in the trees reminded me of the form of the dome of St Peter's, and he said that it had actually been built on those lines and that he often came and sat in that part of the garden and played with the illusion that he was once more looking from the Pinicio into the Roman sunset.[80]

Odo had once quoted Goethe to Lady Salisbury to express his love for the place: 'If you have seen Rome once you will never be entirely unhappy'.[81]

Lord Clarendon's daughter Emily Russell

CHAPTER 3

The First Encounter with Bismarck

War Clouds

Russell returned to London in the summer of 1870. His father-in-law, Lord Clarendon, had died on 27 June 1870[1] and therefore a few alterations in the higher echelons of the FO were to be expected. That summer, Odo was offered the opportunity of staying at the FO as an assistant under-secretary after he had explained his financial problems to his new chief, Lord Granville. By then Russell had already become a father for the second time and could no longer afford to live on a mediocre wage:

> Lord Granville and Hammond having volunteered to ask me what my professional wishes were, I said, promotion and if the present and future block in profession renders promotion impossible I would like some less expensive trade in some office at home as I could not go on many years carrying on a mission in a post like Rome on a secretaryship without getting into debt.[2]

Odo was convinced that Hammond and Granville wanted to promote him, 'but the ... Franco-German war will deprive us of several missions I expect'.[3] A posting to Germany always seems to have been on his mind, but in the meantime he had to be satisfied with less glittering prizes. According to Russell's incensed wife a FO job was, however, not good enough — it was even a step backwards. In her rage, Emily went so far as to patrol the FO courtyard, pressing her husband to go back to Rome with her at once.[4] Emily's fear of descending the career ladder might have sprung from the trauma of her father's death. Derby, who was related to Emily's sister, observed how much the Clarendon daughters suffered from the loss of their father — emotionally, but also socially: 'She [Constance Villiers] and her sister [Emily] also, feel very acutely the loss of social importance which belonged to them as daughters of the foreign secretary, trusted by him with his closest secrets, and acquainted with everything that passed at home and abroad'.[5] Odo tried to calm his wife's fears and, after much to-ing and fro-ing, he accepted the FO's offer and stayed in London. To Lyons he wrote: 'as the

A.U.S.ship was 1.500 Pounds p.a [instead of the 1,000 he was paid in Rome] I persuaded myself that I should learn a great deal of new and useful business in the FO'.[6] By first hesitating he might also have signalled subtly to the FO that he hoped for a more promising offer in the not too distant future. Apart from that, it was tactically useful to be at headquarters 'within reach of a mission whenever a vacancy occurs'.[7]

That year Odo Russell had to witness not only a personal but also a more general change in his profession. Lord Clarendon's death had coincided with a parliamentary enquiry into the workings of the FO. The press and a growing number of MPs had over the years developed the opinion that diplomatic agents were inefficient and overpaid. Odo's life and that of his colleagues were perceived by the public as an endless round of balls and soirées, only occasionally interrupted by short crises.[8] (John Bright had summed up such feelings by calling the Diplomatic Service 'a gigantic system of outdoor relief for the aristocracy'.) Russell himself had a direct experience of this public scepticism. While he was still in Rome, he told a Mr Reynolds that because of his growing family he might have to resign from his diplomatic career and find a 'less expensive profession'.[9] Mr Reynolds was very surprised and exclaimed: 'But do you really mean in earnest that diplomacy is not fearfully overpaid'?[10] As a direct consequence of such criticisms, Select Committees on the Diplomatic and Consular Service[11] were set up in 1861, 1870 and 1871, upsetting the equilibrium of Odo's world. Their aim was to improve the organisation of the FO and 'to strengthen the professional character of the two services by introducing a formal clarification of ranks and salaries, and a more defined system of promotion'.[12] No other department, an outraged Hammond complained, had been so severely criticised ever before, no other ministry had been so misunderstood in its dealings. (He forgot that the military had been undergoing some drastic reforms as well.) In his opinion the initiator of the 1871–1872 committee was simply 'a good-natured idiot'.[13] Though Hammond was officially a Liberal, in his politics, he was conservative in the Latin sense of the word — fighting to 'conservare' when it came to FO traditions: in his realm he would not allow any change. Hammond, therefore, needed every support and although Odo had his own reform ideas he tried to be loyal. When questioned by the committee he backed up Hammond: 'When I was at the FO 20 years ago, the Under-Secretary was Mr Addington, while I was away Mr Hammond was appointed Under-Secretary and he has certainly reformed the Foreign Office in every way'.[14] Privately, however, Odo tried to influence the committee in other ways. This was possible because his brother Arthur was a member of it. In long letters Odo briefed Arthur and lobbied for the diplomatic caste. Altogether, Odo sent Arthur 25 questions he should ask in the committee.[15] There was also advice from Odo on the right witnesses (Morier, especially, would be useful for the FO's cause) who should appear before the committee. Quite understandably however, Odo was most interested that the committee should discuss wages. From the following letter, which Odo sent in March 1870, one can see what he judged as the fiscal limitations and gains offered by a diplomatic career:

> It is my conviction that £500 or £600 is not enough to keep out of debt, for a young diplomat. I only recommend Civil Service Commissions to warn young men entering the profession that they would act more prudently if they did not attempt the career without £1,000 p.a. ... Dips. must live with the richest in the land — every attaché expects a mission in a few years — he enters Diplomacy — travels to his post ... he has already anticipated on his first quarter — journey, furniture, linen — he is not yet paid. After 2 years he is transferred — sale at a loss or carriage of furniture to the new post, journey outfit leave to go home to see his family — two journeys ... The uncertainty of expenses in diplomacy is fatal to the steadiest attaché. Five hundred Pounds is enough if he is established — or a native — but not if he is a travelling foreigner. More than three-quarters of our present body must die disappointed men, because they were enlisted under false pretences.[16]

In Odo's, admittedly, biased opinion, more money had to be invested in diplomats if they were needed to have 'talent and genius', otherwise only rich, but mediocre, men would join the service. (He did not think of himself as belonging to the category of rich diplomats.) Although ambassadors could make up to £7,000 a year, which would be about £350,000 today, they could still have financial problems as will be seen in the case of the Berlin Embassy. In order to have a continental comparison, Odo also gave his brother some statistics on expenditure from his German colleague in Rome, Arnim. Arnim spent £4,800 on house bills, and 'often feels that it would be his duty to his children to give up Diplomacy so as to save money for them'.[17] If money had to be saved by the British Treasury, Odo argued that the best way was to 'relieve diplomats of entertaining and representing'.[18] The Americans, for example, had generally not adopted a representative system yet.[19] Odo thought that 'dinners and balls are a powerful engine to acquire information',[20] but it should not be obligatory. A gifted diplomat such as Lyons, for example, did not need to entertain: 'Lyons could dismiss his flunkies and you can sell the Embassy — he could write useful reports from an entresol'.[21] If Arthur's committee reduced the salaries, no-one could, in Odo's opinion, any longer expect Great Britain to be socially represented by her impoverished diplomats.

The criticism his profession encountered was, in Odo's eyes, mainly caused by what one would call today a lack of good public relations. The FO was simply not able to sell its achievements well to the outside world. This was something that Arthur had to change. First of all, the very need for the existence of diplomats had to be explained to the people in simple terms:

> To have a policy you must have knowledge of facts and be able to distinguish between the possible and the impossible ... The principle is: that to maintain friendly relations with humanity, to promote the interchange of ideas to increase our national wealth, to develop our commercial resources, to protect our country-men, to maintain peace and to prevent war we send agents to watch over those interests and write the history of mankind.[22]

This is a fairly arrogant but, nevertheless, irresistible summary of a diplomat's importance. Of course there was, in Odo's opinion, room for improvement at the FO. It was necessary to have a better entrance examination and for the copying clerks to have more 'brain work' to do. (Hammond rejected such suggestions vehemently. He wanted gifted clerks with a 'First' who simply did copying for him. Although they naturally complained about the dullness of it, Hammond continued to ignore them.) Odo also criticised the promotion system of the diplomatic service. As an example, he cited the case of Morier, who was almost overqualified in his knowledge of Germany, but wasted his time in mediocre German states. In the FO it was naturally not opportune to ask, or apply for, promotion oneself[23] — one needed in-fluential friends 'suggesting' one's name. But even when the Queen pushed for a diplomat's promotion (as in the Morier case), the principle of seniority overruled the argument for best qualification. The aboli-tion of this seniority system was one of Odo's hobby horses. In his eyes, it would certainly 'render diplomacy more efficient and less expensive' if one was 'promoted according to the business powers or merits'.[24] (It was perhaps no coincidence that such an approach would have solved Odo's problems of getting ahead.) Russell was right in thinking that the block in his profession (before the First World War there were only 125 posts for diplomats) had a negative effect on the morale of his colleagues and that some left because of it. In the long run this did not, however, affect Odo personally. With the Versailles mission and later the ambas-sadorship to Berlin, Russell himself was promoted over the heads of many of his senior colleagues — a fact that both embarrassed and pleased him tremendously. Still, his case remained an exception.

What worried Odo most about the 1870 committee was the pos-sibility that diplomacy would take a regressive step and turn into an 'anti-Aberdeen-system', as he called it — a system in which diplomats changed 'with the Governments that have appointed them — [for example] Chelsea was dismissed by Uncle John [Russell] — and the Tories say they will dismiss Layard when they get back to Power'.[25] To Odo's relief this scenario never materialised. On the contrary, he was later asked by the Tory Lord Derby to stay at Berlin, and even Layard found a prestigious embassy under the Disraeli administration — Constantinople.[26]

One of the proposals made by the parliamentary enquiry was carried out by Odo even before the report came out: the recommendation that the 'office should be more strongly infused with diplomatic experience: that trained diplomats ... might occasionally be brought back to work permanently in the Office'.[27] Odo's second return to the FO was therefore approved of by the press (especially the *Pall Mall Gazette* and the *Telegraph*)[28] as well as by his friends, such as Hubert Jerringham:

> at last there will be at the FO someone who has lived among foreigners and learnt to appreciate them so thoroughly as to inaugurate another reign than the useless and worn out system of judging all foreign matters in an English point of view only.[29]

Russell began to see a spell among the 'pen-pushers' at the FO during a crisis like the Franco-Prussian war as a great challenge. He had a well-regulated timetable (with decent working hours from 12 noon to 7 p.m.[30]) and felt the satisfaction of being part of the circle of decision makers: 'The events are overpowering and it is a great advantage to me to be here with Gladstone and Granville deciphering the most important telegrams that Governments have ever received'.[31] Right from the start of the Spanish throne candidacy, Russell had been following the developments with keen interest, although he did not at first believe that it would become a serious issue: 'What a curious crisis the Franco-Prussian Spanish question in Paris seems to be — I read the telegrams and marvel — but I cannot but think that we shall be spared a European war'.[32] Odo was not the only one to underestimate the situation. The famous Hammond remark about a 'lull' at the FO shortly before the outbreak of hostilities, went into posterity thanks to a — rightly — disgruntled Granville.

On 19 July 1870, France declared war on Germany. At first, Napoleon III seemed to be the sole aggressor and there was great underestimation of Bismarck's role in precipitating the crisis. It has been argued that the already physically deteriorating Napoleon was pressured to provide victories for the French.[33] Whether public opinion forced the

Emperor into this war or whether it was organised groups that propagated it, is still discussed among historians. William Russell, the *Times*
correspondent, published an article on 24 September 1870 about a
conversation the Prussian King and Napoleon had had shortly after
Sedan. In this conversation Napoleon claimed that he had been rushed
into war by public opinion. William, however, rejected the argument
and said to Napoleon that ministers such as the Duc de Gramont had
instigated the masses.[34] Bismarck was outraged about William Russell's
article and denied its authenticity.[35] In many ways both countries were
determined on a conflict and had for years half-heartedly waited for
the inevitable diplomatic clash to happen and be over with. Lothar Gall
is one of the historians who supports this argument: 'Neither side
stumbled or was dragged into this war against its wishes'. (This is, of
course, true of Prussia and France, but not of the Southern German
states, 'where the governments stumbled and/or were dragged into the
war'.)[36]

Most members of the Russell family did not have any great sympathy with Napoleon III. In a letter to her daughter-in-law Kate
Amberley, Lady John Russell commented on Sedan: 'thank God that
punishment has fallen on the right head'.[37] Like his aunt, Odo had
reacted to the outbreak of war in a very emotional way: 'everybody
must necessarily think of this wicked, immoral and unjust war of the
French and I myself can think of nothing else! I want the French to
be beaten to paste, in the interest of *Geist* [esprit] and progress'.[38] Even
after Sedan, Odo could not bring himself to feel much pity for Napoleon III: 'Certainly the Emperor surrendering with 200,000 men — a
fact unparalleled in history, is one of those clever moves his Italian
nature inspires him with and which shows that he is not yet quite im-
becile as people tell us here — but Machiavellian still in regard to
Self'.[39] Given Odo's balanced character it was highly unusual for him
to show such anti-French bias, even if one takes into consideration his
disappointing postings in Paris. His mother's influence certainly played
a part — after all, she was so convincing in the role of a vengeful
Germania: 'I am *GERMANICA* to the *pineal gland,*' she wrote in her large
handwriting, 'discipline against disorder, sobriety against drunkenness,
education against *IGNORANCE*. There never was such a triumph of
intellect over brutism'![40]

For Russell the war was inevitable and he did not like to hear any
criticism that British diplomacy had not done enough to prevent it. In
his correspondence with Lady Salisbury, he persuasively argued that his
caste had not failed in July 1870, but had instead managed successfully
to postpone the problem as long as possible. Diplomacy had reached

its limits, according to Russell, when a despot like Napoleon consciously decided to cause havoc:

> You seem to accept the popular outcry that diplomacy did not foresee or prevent the war! Has diplomacy not always foretold that sooner or later a war between France and Prussia had been rendered inevitable by Sadowa and the Treaty of Prague? ... Did not Lord Stanley prevent and postpone the outbreak of war by his glorious treatment of the Luxembourg question? Did not Lord Clarendon ... bring about the disarmament of France and Prussia and was it not to his personal influence *alone* that Europe owes the Peace which lasted as long as himself?[41]

Although Russell overrated his father-in-law's influence on disarmament, he was right when he claimed that the FO had done its best to prevent the outbreak of the war. It was thanks to the British that the Spanish candidature of the Hohenzollern had been withdrawn, but even that had not been sufficient to satisfy the French. Lord Granville had simply been unfortunate to 'inherit' the Foreign Office at the moment of a continental showdown.[42] Keeping up with opponents such as Bismarck and Napoleon III seemed an enormous task for a man of Granville's calibre. (Bismarck allegedly was of this opinion. According to an anecdote he shocked Emily Russell by saying how glad he was that her father, Lord Clarendon, had died at the right moment, because he, unlike Granville, would have prevented the war.[43] This statement, if true, is probably an expression more of Bismarck's taste for morbid flattery than what he really believed.) Another, completely different version, was put forward by Morier, who had been told by the Duke of Saxe-Coburg-Gotha, a relative of Queen Victoria, that it was 'considered the greatest misfortune that Lord Clarendon should have died ... and been succeeded by a statesman of the most pronounced Napoleonic views'.[44] This, the Duke claimed, was from Bismarck's 'own lips'. As usual the great man talked in many tongues.

Whoever was Foreign Secretary at the time would have seen the exerting of damage control as his first priority. In doing so, British neutrality needed to be officially declared and then the integrity of Belgium secured. This was particularly important to Gladstone who urged Granville to get assurances from the two combatants not to violate Belgian territory. Napoleon III had already provided this on 16 July, before the declaration of war (as well as assurances respecting the territory of Luxembourg), and was followed by Bismarck a few days later. Morier, however, continued to alarm Odo over the next months with his suspicion that Germany might plan to invade Belgium, despite these assurances. In Morier's opinion, the violent German press attacks on England were a possible preparation for such an invasion: '[the German public] might then out of mere blind passion against us be induced to commit a crime from which in cold blood they would have shrunk'.[45] On the British side, however, public (although not FO) opinion at the outbreak of the war was anti-French. This was caused by the underdog factor and a propaganda trick Bismarck had used. To estrange France from Britain, he had passed on a treaty draft (written by Benedetti in 1866) to *The Times*, which gave the impression that France had, in return for a *free hand* in Belgium, offered to leave the German Southern States alone. Odo would later realise that the famous 'Benedetti treaty' had been written with Bismarck's approval and encouragement. To Acton, who was working on an article about the war and had asked for advice, Odo wrote: 'Our [FO] impression is that Bismarck dictated the draft to Benedetti so that by referring to: "the draft said to have been drawn up by Benedetti", you would imply a knowledge of the fact and give Benedetti the benefit of the doubt'.[46] In a further letter, written shortly after the war, Odo makes his annoyance with Bismarck's behaviour even clearer:

> Bismarck told me himself, in confidence, that he had led Benedetti into a trap and he dilated on the manner in which he had led him on day-after-day for months until Benedetti was ripe for reduction and accepted the ... pen and paper to draw up the fatal document. Bismarck pocketed the draft to show it to the King.[47]

The British Parliament did not play a great part in the major stages of this war. The House had ended its sittings in August and did not resume them until January/February. Gladstone and Granville, advised by their German experts, Morier in Stuttgart, Loftus in Berlin and Odo at the FO, therefore had quite a free hand in making their decisions. During the whole crisis they worked very closely together, despite the fact that the Prime Minister had an ambivalent approach to the diverse issues that this war brought up (the Alsace–Lorraine case was at the forefront of Gladstone's thinking, whereas the bombardment of Paris did not interest him as much as it did Granville). At first sight the Gladstone–Granville working relationship during this period looks ideal. They were close personal friends who exchanged their thoughts almost every day either by sending each other quick notes or in face-to-face talks. Yet this rather rare closeness between a Foreign Secretary and his chief did not culminate in a symbiosis of workable ideas. According to the editor of their correspondence, Agatha Ramm, 'Gladstone and Granville made a kind of push-forward pull backwards partnership'.[48] In other words, Gladstone's notoriously brilliant visions often overshadowed the more pragmatic solutions Granville had to offer. The Prime Minister had never claimed, however, to be an expert on foreign affairs. To Clarendon he had once confessed that he felt 'unfit' for 'sharing the responsibilities for foreign affairs'.[49] During the Franco-Prussian War his sometimes naive proposals were therefore often over-ruled by Granville and the rest of the Cabinet.[50] This process cost the decision-makers a lot of valuable time and strength.

The British Government's priority in this war was to mediate between the two combatants.[51] This was diametrically opposed to Bismarck's agenda. He tried to prevent any interference by retaliating in the usual way, with anti-British press campaigns. A scared Crown Princess wrote to Morier at the end of August: 'should England choose an unwise moment to intervene and try to force us to make a peace which is not in our eyes an advantageous one, I fear the rage will know no bounds. I have suffered more than I can say from the feeling against England — it seemed to me unjust and unfair'.[52] The first attacks on Britain had already appeared in the German press on 21 July 1870, listing the sales of British goods to France. The British cabinet had decided on 16 July that they would not be able to prevent businessmen from exporting horses, coal, uniforms and other goods to France. The German papers now argued that this could hardly be called 'neutral'. Morier thought they had a point: 'The inexhaustible storehouses of Great Britain [are believed] to support the French with ammunition for their chassepots [from Birmingham] and horses from England and Ireland'.[53] Morier advised Odo to find out whether the Americans, too, were sending weapons to France, as this would have furnished them with a good reply to the German attacks. Unfortunately, England remained the only scapegoat and German–American relations blossomed during the war. Morier and Odo were embarrassed by the weapons trade of their countrymen, yet saw no way to prevent it. A frustrated Morier wrote, 'We sit by like a bloated Quaker, too holy to fight, but rubbing our hands at the roaring trade we are driving in cartridges and ammunition'.[54] Even in later years, this arms trade episode would be used by Bismarck for emotional blackmail.[55] In 1875, Derby was surprised when the Queen mentioned to him the antipathy that existed towards Britain in Germany. Russell agreed with her:

> The Queen is quite right in thinking that the arms supplied to France by our traders produced a feeling of ill will among the [German] upper classes. ... After taking the Emperor and his army prisoners the Germans thought the war was over — then came the second part where they had to fight Gambetta's troops and every sword or bayonet, gun or cannon they captured was English, and every shot fired at them was with English powder, and every bullet extracted out of German wounds was English, so that at last they thought our neutrality less benevolent than they had expected. It is impossible to convince the Germans that HMG were strangers to the sale of arms because so many of the guns bore the Tower mark.[56]

The *Kölnische Zeitung,* an 'inspired' paper, made it clear in 1870 that except for Russia, 'the neutral powers had not manifested any good will towards [Germany] and therefore they should not try to get involved in any upcoming peace negotiations'.[57] Morier and Odo had, unlike Gladstone, understood that the moment England had declared itself neutral, it was condemned to the part of a bystander, outmanoeuvred by Bismarck:

> We must fully make up our minds [Morier wrote to Odo], that nothing less than an armed mediation will effect our object. A coalition like that made against the 1st Napoleon may do it — nothing less will. ... Mere humanitarian mediation will do no good but very much harm.[58]

However, Russell learned to understand that public opinion needed to be given the impression that the government was 'active', especially once the Germans discussed the idea of bombarding Paris. To Granville he wrote: 'The situation has changed and public opinion has undergone modifications ... . Public opinion at home and abroad ardently desires to save Paris from bombardment and thousands of Parisians from death by starvation'.[59] One could not continue to just look on because public opinion did not tolerate a 'non possumus' any longer.[60] '[The Public] will never understand why H.M.G. can do nothing but look on ... while fellow creatures are being shot down in an enclosed arena like game in a Royal Park'.[61] Russell therefore advocated the taking of a collective step by all neutral states in the form of a circular to Bismarck which would state:

> We the neutrals who are in a position to take a calm and dispassionate view of the present state of the war, beseech of you Prussia, before you cause the death of another million human beings — and you France before you sacrifice Paris and the Parisians to the apathy of the Provinces, to consent to one more meeting of Bismarck and Favre on whose renewed interchange of ideas the lives and welfare of millions depend.[62]

What had turned the tide against Bismarck was the growing awareness that this was not a restricted, defensive war any more, but had developed into a campaign of brutal conquest. The underdog had suddenly turned into an unknown quantity, announcing its future 'war atrocities' by circular. The outrage had hit all classes, including the British Royal family. Queen Victoria wrote to her daughter: 'the bombardment is a sad thing and I cannot say how I pray for the ending of this dreadful slaughter, which seems alas! so useless, for the feeling of England is becoming sadly hostile to Germany'.[63] By the time the bombardment had actually started (in January 1871) English public opinion was uniquely pro-French.[64] Apart from that, the psychological effect

Bismarck had hoped it would have on France backfired, as it turned the French people into martyrs.

On 13 September and 16 September 1870, Bismarck sent circulars to his ambassadors in which he described the necessity of new frontiers and the acquisition of French fortresses. Whether the annexation plans were Bismarck's own idea or whether they arose spontaneously in Germany, was discussed by German historians in the 1960s and is still debated today. Whereas Lipgens argued that Bismarck initiated the annexation in the press as a war objective, Kolb and Gall think that the idea arose spontaneously in different political camps in Germany, before Bismarck made the first utterances in that vein in August 1870.[65] Walker, who was with the Emperor in Versailles, later expressed the opinion that 'the forcible annexation of Alsace–Lorraine and the enormous contributions imposed on France were forced on the Emperor and his advisers by public opinion at home'.[66] In 1874 Walker wrote: 'I [will] not forget the saying of the Crown Prince in the garden of his quarter in Versailles, when discussing this question, "Colonel Walker, we dare not face the people with empty hands"'.[67]

When it became known that Bismarck wanted to annex Alsace and parts of Lorraine, Gladstone embarked on his famous 'moral crusade'. This disturbed what until then had been the relative consensus that existed between the FO and the Prime Minister. Gladstone first tried to approach Russia for cooperation, in the hope that a neutral bloc could be formed to counter Germany's annexation plans, but this failed as Gortschakoff declined to cooperate.[68] The Foreign Office, unlike Gladstone, were quicker in acquiescing to Bismarck's annexation plans. Granville's opposition to British intervention on this issue had also been strengthened by Lord John Russell, who had written to the Foreign Secretary that 'one cannot advise Germany not to demand, or France to cede Alsace'.[69] When the British cabinet failed on 30 September 1870 to back the Prime Minister's plans for intervention (only Fortescue, Goschen and Forster supported him),[70] Gladstone's last resort was to publish his views anonymously in a magazine article.[71] It turned into a bitter attack against both Germany and France, showing all the frustrations that Gladstone had suffered since the early English mediation proposals of the war. Of course, he was aware of the fact that a victorious Napoleon III would also have annexed as much territory as possible (at least, great parts of the Rhineland),[72] but in this case it would also have been Britain's duty to stop him. What upset the Prime Minister most about the annexation plan was the notion of 'wrenching a million and a quarter people from the country to which they have belonged for years'.[73] Such conduct would, in his eyes, be a violation of the principle of popular sovereignty. The inhabitants had first to be consulted by plebiscite, otherwise the newly achieved right of self-determination would be brought into question. Also, the German people had not authorised the annexation, therefore Bismarck had, in Gladstone's opinion, no right to go ahead with it. With chilling foresight the Prime Minister predicted that '[this problem] will lead us from bad to worse, and [will] be the beginning of a new series of European complications'.[74]

Gladstone's moral crusade achieved nothing but further estrangement between Britain and Prussia. The French, who had appreciated the fight for a plebiscite, also expected more from Britain than just a magazine article. After all, their conduct had been criticised as well, and it became quite obvious during the following months that French behaviour was as alien to Gladstone as that of the Germans.[75] He felt deeply torn between his sympathies for French sufferings and his disgust at the obstinacy of French politicians. France would, however, not forget Gladstone's idea of holding a plebiscite. When the new deputies of Alsace–Lorraine arrived in the Reichstag in February 1874, the first thing they demanded was a plebiscite on the Alsace–Lorraine annexation. At last the people would have a chance to express their opinion on what had been done over their heads. The Socialists, Poles and Danes voted in favour, yet the motion was lost. One reason for this was, according to Odo, that the Alsatians 'owing to their not understanding the forms of procedure, remained seated and [therefore] voted against themselves'.[76] Although Odo tried to stay neutral towards his government's Alsace–Lorraine policy as long as he was at the FO, this changed abruptly when he entered the lion's dungeon.

The Versailles Headquarters

The Franco-Prussian war had begun for Odo Russell in a rather shielded atmosphere at an FO desk in London, but in November 1870 things took an unexpected turn when he was asked to go to Versailles. This new mission would be a good promotion for him, a fact that pleased his family who already had greater plans for him: 'It is curious, isn't it,' wrote Emily Russell, 'that he should be going to grapple with Bismarck which was what he said he wished to do beyond everything — and this before he is ambassador in Berlin'.[1]

Odo Russell officially entered the stage of German–British relations at a time when they were at their lowest. By the autumn of 1870 his country had managed to alienate both combatants in the Franco-Prussian war: Prussia, by the aforementioned sales to the French as well as with unwelcomed advice, France by alleged indifference towards her struggle for survival. Similar to the Germans the French had, right from the start of the war, complained about Britain's stance; De Lavalette for example had claimed that: 'Lord Granville's attitude towards France was unsympathising and his personal manner cold, very cold'.[2] Also the British press coverage was criticised by Michael Chevalier, a friend of Gladstone. He called *The Times* 'Bismarck's official paper' and its correspondent '[a man] who covers up Prussia's cruel deeds'.[3] After Sedan, it even became dangerous to fly the Union Jack in Paris, let alone sell *The Times*. Of course the British Government could have patiently weathered this criticism until the end of the war. However, in November, Britain moved from its mediation position at the periphery of continental affairs to the centre. On 9 November 1870, Russia declared that it no longer felt bound by articles 11, 13 and 14 of the Treaty of Paris, which ensured the neutrality and demilitarisation of the Black Sea. The signatories of the treaty (Great Britain, Austria and France) had already by 1856 become sceptical about whether these clauses would be observed for long.[4] Palmerston had prophesied the annulment of the Treaty in its entirety and even businessmen in the city had seen it as a failure, predicting that Russia would, as an act of 'political self-defence', sooner or later try to shake it off.

Russia's decision to denounce these articles in 1870 had been made in a great hurry, accelerated by the armistice talks between Bismarck and Thiers at the end of October. If these talks had been successful in ending the war, there would have been no chance for Russia to get any more support from the Prussian Government. In addition, the rest of the European cabinets, no longer distracted by the Franco-Prussian War, would have been able to unite against a Russian aggressor. It is thus unlikely that Czar Alexander II would have then tried to remove the articles. The reasons he now gave sounded rather slippery to the FO: 'various changes which have taken place of late years in the transactions which constitute the balance of power in Europe'.[5] These dramatic changes were, according to the Russians, 'the admission of foreign ships of war through the Straits'.[6] Every such incident since 1856 was listed by the Russians and on top of this legal argument there was a rather polemical accusation, added for the gallery, about the whole 'unfairness' of the Black Sea clause.[7]

Denouncing the articles,[8] the Russians were however eager to point out, did not mean, that they wanted to raise the Eastern question or violate the sovereignty of the Porte. To calm British worries, the note talked of 'equal interests in the Orient ... both countries have the wish to preserve the Ottoman Empire'.[9] To the FO, this was only complimentary window dressing. In particular, it was thought that the accusation regarding '[the penetration of] the ships of war in the Black Sea' was incorrect and far-fetched.[10] Yet the British Government knew that neither legal or moral reasoning would make the Czar change his mind.

Russia's action had not come as a complete surprise to the FO. The British ambassador at St Petersburg, Buchanan, had warned a few months earlier that the Czar might try to disavow the Black Sea clauses,[11] yet it was expected by the British that this would not be done in an abrupt way, without any preliminary negotiations. The final Russian decision had, however, already been taken on 27 October. Best informed were the Prussians who had agreed with the scheme in principle.[12] To the Prussian ambassador in St Petersburg, Prince Reuss, Gortschakoff had said 'we had to watch how the treaty of 1856 was abused for 14 years' and hinted that as soon as the time was ripe, Russia would violate the clause.

The Tripartite Treaty of 30 April 1856 'guaranteed jointly and severally the independence and the integrity of the Ottoman Empire' and declared that any 'infraction of the stipulations of the said Treaty would be considered by the Powers signing the same as a *casus belli*'. Under these terms, Britain would now have been obliged to go to war with Russia. Not only did Granville not feel any enthusiasm for defending the Tripartite treaty, he regretted the fact that it had come into being in the first place. Such feelings were shared by Gladstone who already in 1856 thought that it was illusory to restrict Russia's naval strength in the Black Sea.[13] What he resented most in the Russian circular was the assumption that 'without the consent of the signatories to the treaty, Russia could release herself from its obligations'. In his opinion this was impossible, because under international law treaties were valid as long as they had not been revised by a further agreement of the co-signatories. To allow such unilateral action would lead to international anarchy. Gladstone therefore decided to 'evade the substance of the Russian document and argued solely with its verbal text'.[14] It was decided on 10 November that Granville[15] should send a sharp note to St Petersburg, criticising especially the manner in which Russia had acted but leaving the door open for negotiations.[16] Some British diplomats were not satisfied with this benevolent reply. Lytton wrote to Morier: '[Granville's] despatch is weak, wordy and ambiguous, and instead of repressing an impertinence it invites the "amiable" discussion of it'.[17] Neither Gladstone nor Granville intended for one moment to take any military steps against Russia.[18] Instead they counted on the 'common sense' of their fellow citizens. After the first shock had subsided, they would surely realise that there was no possible ally available for a war against Russia. France was 'otherwise occupied',[19] Austria could offer only moral support,[20] and Prussia was thought to have encouraged the Czar in the first place. As Britain found herself alone, Gladstone and Granville simply had no choice but to decide against military intervention.[21] 'What else could he have done?' Granville's biased biographer Fitzmaurice would ask 30 years later.[22] The only reasonable alternative was put forward, according to Fitzmaurice, by Granville's opponent Disraeli: 'Russia ought to have been told she would be left to take the future consequences of her separate action'.[23] Whether such a bluff would have worked is questionable.

The British public was left in the dark about the Russian note until 14 November. This left the government time to act without any public pressure. However, it also meant that the FO could only guess how the public would react to a conciliatory policy.[24] When the news broke, it caused a shock. Though the bloodiness of the Crimean War was still a vivid memory (as were the heavy taxes that resulted from it) and another clash with Russia was dreaded, there was also a common feeling that the government should not tolerate such an insult.[25] The newspapers already predicted war clouds and blamed the government for its pliancy and lack of foresight (the *Standard* saw the Russian circular as a 'provocation to battle' and the *Pall Mall Gazette* urged an immediate declaration of war.)[26] There was even a discussion of whether the Gladstone ministry could survive this blow — so shortly after the Franco-Prussian mediation failure. (Naturally Gladstone was unpleasantly surprised and 'much disgusted with a good deal of the language ... in the newspapers.')[27] The opposition had not been gentle with Gladstone, attacking his letter which 'had only concealed the indignity of yielding by flying the flag of international morality'.[28] Granville was also placed under great pressure by the press to react more forcefully, instead of simply criticising the Russians for their lack of 'form': 'The shells have fallen endlessly', the Foreign Secretary wrote to Lord Lyons, 'I expected it, but not in so abrupt a form'.[29]

Granville and Gladstone's policy could not be to let the matter rest just with criticising the 'form' of the Russian note. They agreed to try to insert a wedge between Prussia and Russia in order to test how close their understanding really was. For this purpose, Odo Russell was sent as a special envoy[30] to the man who was believed to have pulled the strings in the affair all along, Bismarck. The Chancellor's part in bringing about the Russian denunciation of the articles was, however, overestimated. In fact Bismarck had been, for different reasons, as upset about the Russian circular as the British. It was true that he had not discouraged the Czar from denouncing the Black Sea clauses in the 'near future' (Alexander II had already mentioned a possible renunciation during talks with William in Ems between 1 and 4 June 1870); Bismarck had also created for the Czar the suitable catch-phrase to sell his policy: 'Russia needs STRATEGICAL SECURITIES'— a slogan Alexander started to use extensively. However, Bismarck had expected to be told in advance by the Russians that the moment had arrived, so that the timing could have been coordinated. Instead, the letter from Bismarck's Russian counterpart, Gortschakoff, arrived at the worst possible moment in Versailles. On that very day, Thiers had left the German headquarters after armistice negotiations had failed. The talks with the Southern German states were also at a deadlock, and the constantly brewing rift between Bismarck and Moltke had been widened after another argument. Bismarck must have felt close to one of his physical breakdowns when he read the Russian letters, immediately realising their dangerous implications for his own campaign. Busch, however, claims that, externally, 'the chief' pretended not to be seriously worried about the English reaction. On Thursday 17 November, Bismarck read to his entourage a telegram relating to Granville's opinion about the Black Sea crisis. According to Busch, Bismarck even aped the pretentious tone of it.[31] Still, the Chancellor of the North German Confederation acted very cautiously. His first move was to grant Granville's wish for closer communication through a special envoy. 'Mr Russell will be welcome' was the wording of a telegram sent to the FO.[32] Being permitted to send a special British envoy to the German headquarters was the first diplomatic victory for Granville in weeks. It was judged by the public as a conciliatory step towards Britain, yet the over-cautious Foreign Secretary himself had no great illusions about the outcome: 'We mean to send him [Odo] tomorrow to Versailles' wrote Granville to Lord Lyons on 11 November, 'I presume there is a perfect understanding between Russia and Prussia but it is not certain'.[33] Odo's departure was rushed. In a letter to the slightly jealous Morier, Russell tried to play down being sent to Versailles: '[I] was selected because Loftus could not be spared at Berlin just at present and I was packed off in a few hours so unexpectedly that I have come here [Brussels] without warm clothing or a knowledge of my routes'.[34] The instructions the Foreign Secretary gave to Odo were rather delicate.[35] First of all, he was of course to find out whether Prussia and Russia had actually collaborated on the circular. An indication of this might be, according to the amateur psychologist Granville: 'If Count Bismarck spoke evasively on the subject, if he endeavoured to avoid giving an opinion or taking any decided steps, on the ground that the war with France engrossed his attention and his energies'.[36] If, however, Bismarck showed interest in cooperation between Prussia and Britain, Odo should ask him for advice on how to settle the dispute. In other words, Granville left — on purpose — any original thoughts on the question to Bismarck. The ball was in his court now and he was meant to feel uncomfortable with this new responsibility.

An understanding of what Russell and Bismarck knew about each other's characters and politics is helpful in assessing their first encounter. Even if Russell had not spoken German fluently, Bismarck would have been capable of negotiating with him in English. According to Moritz Busch, the 'chief' spoke with his American guests at Versailles in a 'good English'.[37] Busch had lived a cosmopolitan life, so that his praise might be expected to be accurate. The few letters that have survived from Bismarck to Russell also show how well Bismarck could write English. He was an admirer of Shakespeare and Byron and during his travels through Britain had perfected his vocabulary. When one looks at the letters the 28-year-old Otto von Bismarck wrote during his first visit to England in 1842, we do not find any particularly original observations, whether negative or positive. He enjoyed the scenery, the churches and the horses, and complained about the endless, boring Sundays. At one point, after meeting some British officers, he even toyed with the idea of doing service in India. He also had the fortune to meet an engineer from Manchester who entertained him with stories about the latest developments in the machine tool industry, complete *terra incognita* for a

Prussian Junker. However, what fascinated Bismarck's intellect most about England was its history. He had read the speeches of Peel and particularly marked one sentence: 'We should bear in mind the benefit and not the will of the people'— a motto the young Bismarck was quick to acquire. He was also an admirer of Cromwell's military skills and his pragmatic approach to life in general, slightly altering Cromwell's saying: 'pray and keep your powder dry', to: 'Pray, *but* keep your powder dry'. Naturally, Bismarck could not outwardly identify with a man who had overthrown his king and therefore chose to compare himself to Strafford instead.[38] During the constitutional crisis of 1862 he even went so far as to draw to King William's attention the parallel between their relationship and that of Charles I and Strafford. This did not exactly lift the King's spirits.

Bismarck certainly did not idealise Britain as, in his eyes, the German Liberals were doing, yet he was not its enemy either. He spoke out against the British–Prussian alliance that the *Wochenblattparty* was propagating because it would have been, unlike a Russian entente, of no military profit for Prussia. In his view, the British were unreliable allies, usually hiding behind the channel after they had achieved their own aims on the continent.[39] Over the years Bismarck would surround himself with advisers such as Lothar Bucher, who had a fairly negative perception of England. As a '48er Bucher fled to England full of idealism and high expectations about British liberalism'.[40] However, his firsthand experience caused him to become completely disillusioned and 'critical in the extreme'.[41] Although Bismarck's attitude to England was not one of such complete disillusion, nevertheless, he did tend to under-estimate Britain's strength.[42] In 1862, while he was desperately waiting to be appointed Minister-President and was tired of the uncertainty surrounding the appointment and his uselessness in Paris, he decided to make a semi-official trip to London. In the *Gesammelten Werke* it is recorded that Bismarck received a lukewarm welcome by the two most important politicians of the day, Palmerston and Russell. The most successful encounter Bismarck had was with Disraeli, at a party of the Russian ambassador to the Court of St. James's, Brunnow. Disraeli, who had seemed impressed by Bismarck's charisma,[43] was, however, not convinced that Prussia would be capable of uniting Germany.[44] Count Brunnow thought that Bismarck's trip had been a failure. The Prussian had quite obviously not invested enough time in getting to know British statesmen and they had only been willing to discuss the affairs of the day with him superficially, avoiding any kind of unnecessary theorising.[45] Bismarck himself must have been very surprised by the ignorance of his hosts. The exchange of views with Palmerston clearly showed him that British politicians had no idea whatsoever about Prussian domestic affairs. When asked, for example, about his opinion on the constitutional conflict, the Prime Minister reluctantly had to admit that he did not know anything about the Prussian constitution at all. However, he had an opinion on Prussian foreign policy: 'Don't you think', he asked Bismarck, 'that if the Prussian Liberals came to power they would work for a good cooperation with Austria?' This question revealed Palmerston's naivety about the aims of the supporters of the 'lesser German solution'. Bismarck patiently lectured the Prime Minister that, on the contrary, the Prussian Liberals, most of all, would be ready to start a war with Austria if this could bring them their yearned-for German unity. Palmerston did not seem to take this in. For him Prussia was simply 'Austria's tool and Europe's scorn', a country for which he felt nothing but contempt. Palmerston would never understand Bismarck's full potential, calling him simply the 'mad minister at Berlin', whose decision-making process remained a complete mystery. The dislike was mutual. Bismarck had already written to Gerlach in 1857 that: 'Palmerston abuses the Foreign Policy of this powerful nation, like an angry old drunkard who breaks the cutlery'. There was also no great sympathy and understanding with John Russell. The two conversed mainly about the Schleswig–Holstein problem, in which Russell defended the side of the Danes, whereas Bismarck related horror stories of oppression by the Danes. However, he assured, Prussia would have no plans of conquest in this area. Like Palmerston, Russell completely under-estimated Bismarck's cunning political skill, while his counterpart would during the Danish War poke fun at the never-ending frantic despatches from London: 'I tear them up without glancing at them'.[46]

So when Bismarck was about to meet Odo Russell, the name Russell itself must have evoked ambivalent feelings. Apart from his mixed experiences with John Russell, Bismarck had also once courted a certain Laura Russell (though no relation to the Russells).[47] Perhaps such romantic memories (Bismarck was occasionally capable of them) reminded him of his more enjoyable times in England.[48] From his visits he must have known how powerful the Russell family was, and that, in the hierarchy of the European aristocracy, it towered far above him. Bismarck could be very sensitive to such social differences and it was later rumoured that Count Arnim's slightly superior economic background had been one of many factors in bringing about his fall. Although Odo Russell could expect to be treated with due politeness, he could not expect any form of deference from the proud Bismarck entourage. In their eyes, Odo's liberal background did not speak much in his favour and it is not known how well Bismarck was informed about Russell's close friendship with Morier.

Before Russell met Bismarck, he tried to prepare himself fully for the encounter. He ascertained the views of two former Foreign Secretaries, Derby and his uncle John Russell.[49] Derby held the opinion that it was best: 'to resist any desire to go to war about Constantinople or the Black Sea [I] would go to war for the neutrality of Egypt, but not for the neutrality of the Black Sea'.[50] Odo's uncle shared this perception: 'he [Earl Russell] advised that Britain should agree to the cancellation of the article'.[51] John Russell wrote two letters to *The Times* (on 22 and 24 November) on this point: The second one is of particular interest. Here he advocated wariness of Russian expansion, but also discussed the possibility of a revision of the Paris treaty.[52] Further advice came from Sir Robert Morier who was Russell's primary source on German affairs. During the Versailles negotiations Russell would profit a great deal from Morier's psychological profile of Bismarck. After six years of his tempestuous private battle with the Iron Chancellor, Sir Robert Morier was well aware of Bismarck's cunning tactics. The only language the Chancellor would understand, in his opinion, was that of force. Already before the outbreak of the Black Sea Question, Morier had written:

> Do not forget that Bismarck is made up of two individuals, a colossal chess player full of the most daring combinations and with the quickest eye for the right combination at the right moment and who will sacrifice everything even his *personal hatreds* to the success of his game — and an individual with the strangest and still stronger antipathies, who will sacrifice everything *except his combinations*.[53]

Russell and Morier agreed that the Prussians had to be distanced from Russia's aggressiveness and be brought closer to England's point of view. Odo almost saw his mission as a 'goodwill tour' to achieve closer Prussian–British cooperation: 'My object is to remove soreness, unpleasantness, disappointment and prove that we are not so bad as we seem in the newspapers of both countries'.[54]

Thanks to Moritz Busch we know that the first conversation between Russell and Bismarck took place after a heavy lunch, at exactly 1 p.m. on 21 November.[55] Though Russell had been terribly anxious about his first interview with the 'great man', he successfully managed to suppress his nervousness, at once launching *in medias res*. The interview did not, however, go well at first. Bismarck was not willing to recognise Prussia's responsibilities as a signatory of the 1856 treaty, and only privately expressed his disapproval of the Russian circular's form and its timing. In their next session, in the evening, a desperate Russell then made his famous bluff by saying that if Russia did not withdraw the circular 'Britain would be compelled, with or without allies, to go to war'. The historian G.W. Strang sees in this behaviour a 'Palmerstonian touch'[56] and this was certainly what Odo himself had in mind. To make his threat more believable he painted a grim picture of the future, listing:

> the evil consequences to Germany of a European war before Paris was taken, the moral support the Tours Government might get from a renewal of the old Anglo-French alliance ... together with the stern fact that England must fight and that he, Bismarck, alone, could prevent it.[57]

To threaten a Russian–British war was for Odo the only way in which he could possibly get something out of Bismarck (his first interview had shown him how arduous that could be.) He later gave Gladstone six reasons for his controversial bluff:

> first, that we were bound by the Tripartite Treaty of 15th April 1856 to consider any infraction of the stipulations of the Treaty of 30th May 1856 as a *casus belli*. [The second point dealt with Gortschakoff's note which had led Russell to believe that the whole treaty was in jeopardy.] Third, that HMG had declared on the 10th last that it was impossible on their part to give any sanction to the course announced by Prince Gortschakoff. [Point four dealt with the debate in England.] Point five, that France being otherwise engaged and Austria unprepared we might be compelled to go to war with Russia even without our allies, having bound ourselves on the 15th of April to guarantee, jointly and severally, the stipulations recorded in the Treaty of the 30th March 1856... . Sixth, that not having been specifically authorised or instructed to state that the question I had been sent to submit to the Prussian Government was not in the opinion of HMG of a nature to compel us ever to go to war not withstanding our treaty engagements, I used the arguments which I believed in my conscience to be true.[58]

Thanks to his bluff, Odo argued, the Germans felt compelled to mediate and pass the threat on to the Russians, without England actually giving the Czar an official ultimatum. It took time for Bismarck to yield to Russell's acting qualities: '[the threat] gradually worked the change in his mind', Odo reported home, 'which has led him to support the cause of peace and England against Gortschakoff and his circular'.[59] Pressed for more during each interview, Bismarck offered mediation and proposed a conference to settle the question as soon as possible.[60] This was rather generous from his point of view. After all, he could well fear that at such an international conference the other powers might interfere in the 'French question'. In his instructions to Bernstorff, he would later stress this point again and again: 'We have to prevent that the conference goes beyond its task and occupies itself with other European questions, that means our conflict with France'.[61]

Odo's threats were made even more believable to Bismarck because they coincided with a war-hungry English press. 'The British papers ask for war', an irritated Bismarck told his dinner guests on 24

November, 'because of a letter, which just questions a legal interpretation'.[62] To keep Bismarck on his toes, Odo also employed the old, but always successful, methods of psychological warfare. On 26 November, for example, he demanded to see Bismarck urgently. When he was asked to wait, he stormed off and a worried Bismarck recorded: 'I asked after him 15 minutes later, but he was gone. And on *this* European peace might depend'.[63] Such calculated behaviour made Odo's 'bluff' more believable.

Despite the success of Odo's maverick gamble, he was later criticised by his own party for it. It started with Gladstone asking Odo about the details of his communication to Bismarck, a fact that Emily mistook for a compliment. It turned out to be more complex than that. When, after the publication of the Blue Book, questions were raised in the House of Commons respecting Russell's conduct, Sir J. Hay asked: '[as regards] the declaration made by O. Russell to Count Bismarck on the 21 November whether ... Odo Russell was authorised by H.M.G [to say that Britain would go to war] and what preparation H.M.G. had made in support of their threat'.[64] Gladstone did not defend his envoy's solo run:

> The argument used by Odo Russell as reported ... was not one which had been directed by HMG. In saying that, I do not imply the slightest blame attached to Odo Russell, because it is perfectly well known that the duty of H.M. diplomatic agents require them to express themselves in that mode in which they think they can best support and recommend the propositions ... . I do not therefore blame Odo Russell but such was the fact that it was not under specific authority or instructions that the argument referred to was used by him.[65]

In fact, the Prime Minister had right from the start been upset about Russell's language to Bismarck. In his eyes it was wrong that Odo had forced Bismarck to yield under false pretences 'by a representation about our going to war which really had not the slightest foundation'.[66] This verdict seems harsh if one considers what Russell had achieved. Granville therefore tried to calm down Gladstone ('I am afraid our whole success is due to the belief that we would go to war'[67]) as well as Odo. To the latter he wrote:

> Gladstone, as sometimes happens to him from his fertility of reasoning, did not answer about you [Odo] as handily as he might. I had suggested to him merely to answer that you had received no precise instructions to use the particular phrase, but that you are right in [using it]. Nobody on either side thinks you are wrong, but they try to manufacture a stick out of it with which to beat you ... us.[68]

(Note that the 'you' which was initially written by Granville was crossed out by him and replaced with 'us'.) Russell told Granville how upset he still was and started to justify his conduct in long letters to Gladstone, which he hoped would also help restore their relationship:

> I beg to assure you that when I wrote to Lord Granville that I understood you had 'snubbed me' in the House of Commons I was quoting from private letters and had not seen the newspaper reports ... . Since then *The Times* has reached Versailles and I see that what you really said was that the argument [Russell had used] was not one which had been directed by HMG, that you did not blame me for it.[69]

From Odo's private letters it becomes apparent that he had been at the brink of resignation. To his brother Hastings, he wrote a further letter in defence: 'When I heard that Mr Gladstone had disavowed me in the House of Commons I resolved to resign' (however, with the arrival of some of the English newspapers, he decided not to.)[70] 'Mr Gladstone says he does not blame me for the arguments I used, and I should say the same over again tomorrow if questioned about it. Public opinion three months ago in England threatened war if Russia violated the Treaty of 1856 — our newspapers can furnish ten thousand proofs of it. My instructions were verbal, not written'.[71]

Russell was outraged about the whole episode, which, in his opinion, could jeopardise the British (and his own stand) in Versailles. 'Count Bismarck is going to take advantage of Mr Gladstone's statement ... he fears us no longer and thinks bullying England will be popular in Germany on the principle: "hit him hard he has no friends" '.[72] The Queen also supported Russell. On her instructions Colonel Ponsonby led the pro-Russell crusade and wrote to Granville:

> I write by the Queen's commands to let you know that HM is sorry to perceive by Mr Odo Russell's letter how much he is distressed by the disavowal of his opinions by Mr Gladstone, and how he consequently finds himself placed in a very painful position. The Queen hopes you have commended him for his conduct while at Versailles, and her Majesty wishes you would communicate to him her warm approval of his tact and ability while engaged in this most difficult mission.[73]

Gladstone's failure to back Odo was a disloyalty some members of the Russell family did not forget. In a letter to his friend Layard in 1872, Arthur Russell warned him not to rely on any backing from Gladstone: 'You know the excellent Gladstone does not defend his agents with the same energy as Palmerston was wont to do'.[74] Even Lord Derby sensed the dissatisfaction of the Russells on this matter when he wrote in his diary: 'I find the Cabinet think O.R. went too far in his negotiations with Bismarck. There is no love lost between him [Odo Russell] and Lord Granville, whom he accuses of being incapable — but this only to friends, and in private'.[75]

The news of Bismarck's cooperation, however, was a great relief to Granville. When on 22 November Bismarck informed Bernstorff that Russia was willing to refer the matter to a conference, the first hurdle had been finally overcome.[76] On 25 November, Granville won the Cabinet over to support his conciliatory conference memorandum.[77] The negotiations between Russia and England over the next weeks, however, remained unpleasant. Russell was a great help in organising the details of the conference preparations[78] and the FO employed its 'new channel' extensively. The first and most basic question was where the conference should take place: Vienna, Florence and London were acceptable to the FO, St Petersburg was definitely not. Odo was also instructed to ask Bismarck about the agenda for the conference:

> If he suggests conceding all that Russia asks, get him to tell you whether he sees no objection on the part of Germany to Russia having eventually the naval command of the mouth of the Danube. If he talks of compensations ask him what they would be, sound him whether he would be inclined with Italy to join us in the Tripartite treaty.[79]

Bismarck had nothing to gain from joining this part of the treaty, but now that he had been dragged into the affair, he had to continue with his mediation efforts. In his brainstorming sessions with Russell, he brought forward many other ideas:

> On one occasion he asked whether England wished for a naval station in the Black Sea, to which he saw no objection; on another he observed that opening the Black Sea altogether might have a very civilising influence on the populations, but he committed himself to no positive opinion beyond the often repeated conviction that the sooner the conference meets the better, so that their labours may be pacifically completed before the various parliaments of Europe meet again. He would support nothing but a peace policy in the conference and seek to conciliate all parties. The sympathies of Germany and the Imperial family, and Prussia would have to support the reasonable wishes of Russia, but he would resist any exaggerated demands on her part, if she put forward any, as he had resisted her ill timed and ill advised circular.[80]

To calm the British nerves, Bismarck even brought up the idea of a Prussian–British alliance, which Granville did not take very seriously: 'Aspirations from Bismarck for an alliance with us ... seem to be an embryo, which does not at present require notice — but any such announcements are agreeable, as showing at the least, a present desire to please'.[81]

What pleased the British Foreign Secretary less were the discussions about the representatives who would attend the London conference. To Odo, Granville wrote about the matter: 'the stupid wish of the French to send a Plenipotentiary from Paris, instead of appointing Tissot, whom we all like, who would get on with Bernstorff and has knowledge of Eastern affairs'.[82] The arrival or non-arrival of a French Plenipotentiary became a never-ending saga of shrewd manoeuvres between Bismarck (who in his memoirs openly states that he had no interest whatsoever in Favre getting to London and stating his case),[83] the impatient host Granville, and a secretive Jules Favre himself. Bismarck at first denied Favre safe conduct out of Paris[84] (which naturally greatly enraged Granville). Favre, however, saved Bismarck the trouble a few days later by refusing to go to London to present his case.[85] This to-ing and fro-ing resulted in the conference sitting, after numerous postponements, without Favre on 17 January.[86]

With the decision to hold the Black Sea Conference in London, Odo's mission should, in theory, have been over.[87] But instead of being away from London for 10 days[88] his mission lasted 5 months. He was the only welcomed diplomat at the Prussian headquarters and was thus a perfect channel to Bismarck. 'Lord Granville has begged him to remain on', wrote the proud Emily Russell to her mother-in-law on 6 January 1871, 'and all the neutral Governments have asked that he should, as he is the only one the King will receive — that is very flattering I must say and the fuss that is made of him by Kings, Princes, Grand Dukes and Generals is most gratifying'.[89]

The whole Russell family approved of the prolongation of Odo's mission 'that will do much to make him famous'[90] and pushed aside Russell's complaints about his failing health. By the end of December his physical and emotional position had however deteriorated critically. He even developed symptoms which today could be classed as battle fatigue. Although Odo never actively took part in the war he was, like most civilians in the Versailles area, suffering from the noise of the shells. The endless dragging on of the war was a particular problem for participants and non-participants alike. It even became physically difficult for Odo to listen to graphic war stories: 'Ca n'est pas la guerre, c'est une St Bartheleme', he wrote to his mother.[91] Unlike the British journalists — who 'boasted of being shot at' — he did not want to develop an immunity to the cruelties:

> I cannot listen with indifference, for I know that almost every shot inflicts suffering and torture or death and misery to families. An officer told me that he had last week shot 61 Franctireurs who appeared to him to be mostly French country gentlemen. To me the idea is horrible![92]

It outraged him even more that these victims (who came 'almost' from his own class) were being brutally killed, while their English counterparts in London enjoyed themselves: 'If our gentlemen at home at ease over their 3rd edition, their salmon cutlets and champagne cup could come in close contact with the sufferings and starvation of the French as I have done, they would perhaps make an effort between luncheon and dinner to facilitate peace'.[93] On good days, however, Odo sometimes managed to regain his belief in mankind again. When he saw French and Prussian people skating together, he wondered whether the war might come to an end after all. As in every other war, cases of fraternisation also occurred in Versailles. Romances between Prussian officers and French local women at first surprised Odo: 'Some of the *belles* of Versailles skate most gracefully and like to be ogled by their Prussian enemies! Two young ladies of Versailles, well born, are already engaged to marry Prussian officers when the war is over!! Quis credat?'[94]

Russell had to handle the immense workload in Versailles all by himself. The hours of ciphering and deciphering without an assistant had already started to ruin his eyes, which would in later years fail him almost completely. He felt isolated as far as British politics were concerned and his contacts with the outside world were not always going smoothly.[95] Despite the excellent British messenger service he had to send too many telegrams, which was expensive and not well looked upon by the German authorities. Telegraphing was a way of demonstrating your important status to the people at home. Bismarck knew this and made fun of the vanity of his entourage. He had especially been irritated that the Duke of Saxe-Coburg-Gotha had taken to telegraphing: 'telegraphing should only be used for political means and not for theatrical coups'.[96]

A further burden for Odo was that his spectrum of responsibilities had widened, despite the fact that decisions on the Black Sea question were now to be made in London. Because he was the 'Diplomatic Body' personified, he was approached by every British national with problems. As would happen in later years in Berlin, Odo spent a great amount of time looking after lost compatriots. His friend Captain Hozier, for example, worked for the British Secret Service, and was arrested with other Englishmen by some German officers as spies. In the end, they were released on Odo's intervention. For the rest of the war Captain Hozier continued to send secret material via Russell. Loftus, who had found out about the existence of the correspondence, wanted to see the letters but Hozier prevented this. He did not trust Loftus and feared that such a step would make his 'position at headquarters untenable'.[97] Apart from helping out British spies, another group Odo had to support were the enthusiastic British charity workers. By August 1870, the National Society for Aid to the Sick and Wounded in War had been founded. Twenty doctors and nurses were sent to France and the longer the war lasted the more British people donated to the Society (by the end of September 1870, it had accumulated about £200,000.)[98] Although the distribution of food among starving French was 'deeply felt and acknowledged',[99] the British doctors, however, were less of a success. They could speak neither French nor German to their bewildered patients and lived 'well on the money allocated to them'.[100] All in all the British 'do gooders' in 1870 were not much good.[101] The writer Edmond Grancourt put it bluntly: 'The wounded soldier has become an object of fashion'.[102]

Further problems were created for Odo by British journalists:[103] 'All the newspaper correspondents here hate the Prussians and love the French', Odo wrote to Arthur, 'none of them know German enough to listen to and understand ... the German aspirations'.[104] Another reason why the British journalists were not capable of reporting the actual facts was, according to Odo, that 'the Prussians look upon them (British journalists) as spies and "newspaper-scribblers" and our correspondents expect to be treated as "English gentlemen" and be asked to the Royal tables, which produces a conflict. The trouble they give me is one of the reasons I want to go'.[105] Bismarck was obviously not aware of the sensitivities of the British journalists. He was used to ordering his around and it is somehow understandable that many British journalists took a dislike to such methods. A journalist from *The Times*, L. Oliphant, for example, was arrested by a 'brute [German] insisting upon taking me for a spy. He said numbers of English correspondents were spies for the French, and though I showed him my passport and your [Morier's] letter of introduction to different people, he would not believe a word I said'.[106]

Apart from such 'minor' problems, Odo had to attend many social functions, which were, despite the war, in full swing. It was rather admirable how well the British envoy managed to get on with the different factions among the Prussian decision-makers. King Wilhelm, for example, indulged in the aforementioned memories of Odo's charming mother: 'The King talked much of your extraordinary beauty and said there was nobody to compare to you and that his father and the Emperor of Russia fluttered round you so much that he could not speak to you as much as he wished which vexed him'.[107] Odo summed up the King's sympathies towards himself as follows, '*Il m'aime beaucoup*'.[108] Another person who liked him was the Chancellor of the North German Confederation. Bismarck often received Russell while lying on a sofa, ready to open his heart to him and to talk about his various grievances stemming from the King's ingratitude, Moltke's incompetence and the Crown Prince's interference. Such a conversation with the British envoy, mostly one-sided as it was, soothed 'the Chancellor's pains and worries and cheered him'.[109] Occasionally they left the living room for little excursions together: 'I took a long drive yesterday with Bismarck in the woods', Odo reported home, 'suddenly a shot was fired in the bushes (at a pheasant I think) but the great count rose and drew a long revolver and stared around him ready to defend himself — but we could not find the poacher anywhere'.[110] Apart from protecting his English guest, Bismarck was also sensitive to Odo's homesickness. During the Christmas of 1870, Bismarck gave him a box of cigars. Odo's reply is one of the few Russell letters that can be found in the Friedrichsruh Archive: 'I was extremely touched last night by your kindly recollections of, and friendly words to, the "lonely stranger" within your walls and should feel happy if my sincere wishes for your welfare could grant you many happy and glorious Christmas days in the future and in the Homeland'.[111] Russell felt courted by Bismarck and seemed to succumb to it:

> I am charmed with Count Bismarck, his soldier like, straightforward frank man-ner, his genial conversation, are truly fascinating, and his excessive kindness to me have won my heart. His foreign office staff travel with him and form his ... family. At dinner and breakfast he takes the head of the table with his under-secretaries on each side — then come the Chief Clerks — then the junior Clerks and the tele-graph clerks situated at the end of the table — everybody in uniform. When I dine there I sit between the Count and the Permanent Under-Secretary who plays the piano divinely after dinner while we smoke. The conversation is in German and the questions of the day are discussed with perfect freedom, which makes them deeply interesting and instructive.[112]

Yet Odo did not only see Bismarck's charming side: 'The demonic is stronger in him than in any man I know'.[113] The Crown Prince was, of course, of a completely different calibre. He longed to see an 'English face', which might show sympathy for his battles against everyone else. To his mother-in-law, Queen Victoria, he wrote in January 1871:

> General Walker and Mr Odo Russell hear my sorrow often enough ... Mr Odo Russell's presence here is a decision of your Government which cannot be too much praised. He understands Germany, and with his knowledge of her, and inclination for her, it is immensely important that he should stay with us here now, when our old Empire re-arises ... and that getting to know Bismarck thoroughly, he can ... smooth matters, and clear away difficulties, when otherwise it would be easy for something or another to become a new firebrand.[114]

For Granville, Odo's conversations with the Crown Prince were of particular interest. Like all British Liberals, the Foreign Secretary set great hopes on the Crown Prince: 'The character and conduct of the Crown Prince is the only reassuring point with regard to our future relations with Germany'.[115]

Because of his manifold social obligations it sometimes happened that Russell had to dine twice a day, first with Bismarck at 5 p.m. and then with the Crown Prince at 7 p.m.[116] He became the 'doyen' of the Versailles scene, not only because of his acknowledged diplomatic skills, but also for his social merits. General Walker was only one of many who were delighted about Odo: 'What a nice fellow he is. His visit appears to be by no means disliked here, at least great cordiality has been shown to him. The Crown Prince knew him well before, the King received him more than graciously at dinner'.[117] Proudly, the ever-ambitious Emily Russell recorded all the flatteries Odo had received. The Grand Duke of Weimar, for example, had at the New Year's dinner asked Russell whether he would like to become Premier of Weimar, 'governing the state as old Karl August did with Goethe,' while Mr Austin, a journalist of the *Standard* at another banquet seated between Odo and Prince Leopold of Hohenzollern Sigmaringen, flattered him in the most original way: 'I feel it is a curious event in my life sitting between the man who caused this war and the one who prevented another'.[118]

Some invitations lacked such sparkling wit. The Crown Prince's Christmas party in Versailles, for example, was one of those happenings that only the Prussian military seemed to be able to organise.[119] The intention was to create an air of 'cosiness' (to remedy the officers' homesickness); however, the atmosphere remained frightfully martial. Mulled wine and a lottery kept the 80 guests awake, and it was Russell of all people who ended up winning a Prussian Officer's *portepee* [scabbard]. Nothing could have been of less use to the war-weary intellectual. Such social gatherings were important for Odo's career, yet he also saw them as opportunities to counterbalance the voice of militarism with the voice of diplomacy:

> I think it is the duty of diplomacy to make nations reasonable by preventing war or making peace. Since I have been here I have done nothing but preach reason ... . We preached reason when war was declared and failed, we preached reason when Favre went to Ferrières, and failed, we recommended an Armistice to Prussia and a National Assembly to France and failed, but I do not regret it for that, and I think we should pounce on every opening and opportunity to preach reason to two nations killing each other.[120]

What depressed Odo during the Christmas season was the continuing unreasonableness of the French as well as the British. Many French people were under the illusion that there was still a chance that Britain might interfere militarily, as Odo records on 17 December: 'Scherer [a French friend of the Russell family] was much elated at the Luxembourg and Russian question, which he said would save France as all Europe would now go to war with Prussia!!'[121] In Versailles, Odo constantly heard wild rumours circulating among the optimistic French population that their army had won a 'series of victories', that Paris was open on the St Denis side and that Gambetta was sending up 'herds of cattle to force them into Paris'.[122] Contradicting such dreams was, in Odo's eyes, dangerous: 'they [the French] fly into a passion at once'.[123] The British were also far from facing up to the realities of the situation. Arthur, for example, agreed with Odo's argument that the cessation of Alsace–Lorraine was inevitable,[124] but he still hoped that there was a possibility for a better outcome for France. This was very similar to the opinion of the FO, were it was hoped, against hope, that Germany might see reason and ultimately act as generously towards France as it had acted towards Austria in 1866. It seemed inconceivable that Germany would intentionally create a dangerously humiliated neighbour who would one day start a war of revenge. Yet for Odo this was already a *fait accompli*. The horrors he saw had made him more and more impatient with his own government who, in his opinion, misjudged the hopelessness of the French situation completely. In letters to his brother Arthur, Odo tried to convey this feeling, without success. The following extract shows the misunderstanding between the two brothers, which was also symptomatic of that which existed between London and Versailles. On 29 December 1870 Odo wrote:

> Do not mention what follows please, because it is a secret to anyone. My opinion of the situation and of the future of Germany differs in every respect from that of the FO and the newspapers — ... FO don't like my views — and of course I may be wrong, but I see things differently from them. You know that in politics I object to illusions. Now the result of my studies is, that Germany is mistress of the situation and will be able to dictate her own terms and can and will carry on the war for years if necessary — *es ist eine Lebensfrage* [it is a question of life]. Chiefs at home want me to believe in transactions — I tell them their terms are illusions — they wouldn't believe me — I tried and got snubbed! ... I say: The declaration of war by France has made Germany, the continuation of the war will undo France. I love France and cannot bear to see her weakened, devastated, ruined, killed.[125]

Odo's argument was, clearly, 'better a horrible end than no end of the horrors!'[126] Gladstone and Granville were, however, against pressuring France to give in. Arthur shared their opinion. In his eyes diplomacy simply had not tried hard enough. He also expressed concern whether Odo might have subconsciously adopted Bismarck's argument or even perhaps come under the Prussian's spell.[127] Odo did not accept his brother's indirect accusation that his 'plea' to France to give in to German demands was showing him to be an ardent pro-German. His argument was that he urged France to give up the struggle because he loved the country:

> I advocate the cause of France only. Germany would make peace tomorrow. Not so France who wishes to continue the war for two objects — drive the enemy out of France and cede no territory. … I want to take an active part in saving France from utter exhaustion and ruin … . France is the object of my solicitude not Germany. … We have an interest in seeing her revive and regain her strength and take up her position among the great powers of Europe as soon as possible. We have therefore no interest in the continuation of the struggle. Germany has, but we haven't .[128]

A fortnight later Odo wrote, 'The people of England are urging France to fight to exhaustion — the moral weight of public opinion is on the side of a continuance of war, and when France is beaten and has lost Alsace, will the moral weight of England give them back the life, property and territory they have lost?'[129] Military honour was in Odo's eyes a weak argument to explain the French suicidal behaviour. To sacrifice life just because of military honour seemed almost obscene to him. Because of Odo's strong views one cannot blame Arthur for sometimes thinking that his brother played into Bismarck's hands, and it is true that Odo used Bismarck's words in a few of his letters. However, the point is that his analysis was correct and that the FO (as well as his brother Arthur) preferred maintaining 'illusions'.

Such fundamental questions were of course only discussed by Odo in his private letters. In everyday life his time was taken up by the immediate problems of British–German disagreements. These included, for example, putting forward unpopular demands, as in the case of the British colliers affair. These boats had been sunk accidentally by the Prussians at Rouen, and an outraged British public demanded compensation. Odo had to fight his way through to an 'ill and very bilious' Bismarck, who was in a *'Berserkerwuth'* [one of his raging bull attacks].[130] It was true heroism to bring forward such a matter but, surprisingly, Odo's charm seemed to work once again. Or, perhaps, it was more the fact that Bismarck did not want to get bad publicity at this point. The Prussian promised quick compensation, a reaction that, in particular, impressed Granville, who was used to a tight-fisted treasury at home.

Though Bismarck did show a willingness to solve such 'minor problems', he did not tolerate any outside advice on 'his' war.[131] On this point Russell did not get one inch further and he resented the FO for placing pressure on him: 'Count Bismarck replied that outside influences only encouraged the resistance of the Government of Defence and that after all the more completely France was vanquished the better in the end for Germany, and the more lasting the peace'.[132]

On 18 January 1871, William was proclaimed Emperor in Versailles. Russell at first did not understand why he was called German Emperor instead of Emperor of Germany: this was a touchy subject with Bismarck who had fought long and hard over it with William. After the ceremony, Russell continued to diplomatically convey Granville's suggestions for a fair peace settlement to an ever more irritable Bismarck.[133] According to the Germans, it was entirely up to the French to accept the peace terms that had been explained to him in September 1870 at Ferrières: 'Conditions are the same now as then', Odo recorded Bismarck's words, 'only that the amount of indemnity would increase according to the duration and expense of the war'.[134] If the advice Granville and Odo had given to the French Government on 27 December had been followed earlier, 'Paris would have been saved the horrors of bombardment and starvation and France the destruction of life and property'.[135] An armistice was worked out in the end, and on 1 March Bismarck rode into Paris.

From the periphery, Odo registered the final meeting of the London conference and the compromises resulting from it. The closure of the Straits was reaffirmed, Turkey received compensation, and the Third Republic was officially acknowledged by the European Powers after French representatives had finally attended the conference. In addition, Gladstone's demand that a treaty could not be abrogated unilaterally was discussed at length. Despite this moral success, Russia's *fait accompli* was more or less acknowledged.[136] From a diplomatic point of view this turned out to be a pyrrhic victory for England, as Russia and Germany stayed as united as ever and achieved their ends.[137]

A social butterfly by night and an industrious, often overworked, pen-pusher during the day, Odo succeeded — despite occasional hiccups — in pleasing the Foreign Office, the Prussian establishment and, what was most important for him, his family. At the beginning of March an exhausted Russell left Versailles. His return to Britain was festive, with the Queen inviting him and Emily for the weekend, quizzing him on all details of his mission. Emily, especially, was a great social success during this visit, entertaining Royalty with the 'right stories' (after Odo's death she would become a lady of the bedchamber to the Queen).[138] For the first time, the Queen seemed to take Odo as seriously as she did her greatest favourite, Morier. Before the Versailles mission Russell had been for her an entertaining singer who, at Lord Clarendon's house, had managed to draw her away from the whist table.[139] After the mission she thought him destined for something more important than a salon singer:

> I have seen and talked very confidentially to Odo Russell (who I need not praise to you as you know how clever and very charming he is) and I must say I found him most truly impressed with all that you and I can wish — completely understanding, and appreciating Germany — not blinded by Bismarck's charm of conversation, and much attached to the Emperor and beloved Fritz.[140]

His Versailles adventures also turned Odo into a London dinner party celebrity. Derby was greatly entertained by him at a feast at Portland Place and dedicated in his diary a great amount of space to one of Odo's Versailles anecdotes:

> [Russell] told us of the utter contempt in which the German officers hold the French … . A General and his staff who came to Versailles … arrived in so hopeless a state of intoxication that nothing could be done except to put them to bed. At dinner time they were roused, and invited to dine with Bismarck, but the General was in such a condition that when the soup came round he began to wash his hands in it, smiling benignly.[141]

Yet even this little story was used by Odo to show his listeners the extent to which German self-confidence, this newly acquired feeling of superiority, would change the continent in the future.

Not everyone was celebrating Odo's Versailles achievements. The Queen of Holland, although a friend of his mother, was upset that 'Emperor William fills his palace with the robberies of the French Palaces', while at the same time Gortschakoff and Bismarck were shaking hands on the 'wreck of the treaty of 1856'. To Lady Salisbury she wrote in March 1871, 'Lady William and Lady Clarendon are boasting Odo's successes. What they are, I cannot discover; Russians and Prussians have got all they coveted and Odo has been acquiescing to all'.[142] Queen Sophie might have expected too much from a diplomat and forgotten the real power behind him, the FO. Still, she guessed rightly that Russell had made himself popular at the headquarters with a long-term purpose in mind. It had been always his dream to get the ambassadorship at Berlin and he had therefore presented himself as the ideal successor to Loftus. Thanks to the propaganda of his family and friends, it was therefore only a question of when, not whether, he would be chosen as ambassador to Berlin.

CHAPTER 4

The New British Embassy at Berlin

The Social Butterfly

At the Versailles headquarters Russell had encountered Bismarck in a testing situation, fighting 'wars' on different fronts. When only half a year later Odo came to Berlin as the first British ambassador to the German Empire, he met a very different and less glamorous Bismarck.

Perhaps Odo Russell was never aware of how much his Berlin posting was due to Bismarck's manoeuvres. In later years Odo would write that he 'owed an embassy to Gladstone',[1] yet this appointment was certainly hastened by Bismarck's venomous letters in which he complained about the unpopular Lord Augustus Loftus, while at the same time praising the qualities of Odo. Bernstorff, the German ambassador in London, was showered with detailed instructions on how to discredit Loftus in the most effective way at the FO. For example, in a long despatch of 17 March 1871, Bismarck drew up a list of all the old grievances, which had probably kept him awake all night:[2]

> I have already outlined in November 1870 that the personality of Loftus is hardly appropriate for an improvement of our relationship with England. This was obvious before the war and resurfaced increasingly during the war ... . He and his staff, especially Mr Petre, have on the contrary shown their antipathy towards Germany, by siding with France and have therefore acted contrary to the concept of British neutrality. I have not confirmed by witnesses' accounts whether Lord Loftus actually did utter in diplomatic circles that England forbids the bombardment of Paris and will prevent it with the Crown Princess' influence ... . Such comments are believed to have been made, and I, after years of personal acquaintance [with Loftus] think they are credible, which shows how enormously tactless people must think he is ... . The delicate situation of the English embassy and the Crown Prince's court demands, even in peaceful times, a high degree of adroitness, delicacy and circumspection. The two previous ambassadors had these qualities. Lord Loftus' abilities, however, fall short of the mark. Mr Odo Russell, with whom I had the chance to talk about this, showed in his utterances a full understanding of my comments.[3]

Bernstorff was asked to convey these thoughts confidentially to the English side, 'without giving the impression of a complaint'.[4] Yet in

Bismarck's eyes Granville did not seem to get the hint quickly enough. As he had so often done before, the Chancellor decided to 'inspire' the press to act as his voice pipe against Loftus. The ambassador had developed into a prime target during the war and journalists were only too willing to write more articles against him.[5] As expected, when the first press attacks on Loftus appeared in May 1871, Granville complained and this was greeted by Bismarck with feigned shock. To Bernstorff he wrote:

> I cannot believe that the more discerning British public presumes that we would use the press as a tool in such a delicate situation, as the change of a diplomatic representative ... . The tone of the press is naturally conveying the unpopularity of the British embassy which unfortunately is also damaging the Crown Princess' popularity.[6]

Granville did not want to be pressured, even though he had been dissatisfied with Loftus for a long time. To the Queen he wrote on 14 November 1870, '[Lord Loftus] is wanting in tact, and a great bore, although, he has some merits'.[7] What exactly these merits were was a mystery to the Queen. She was eager that Russell should be appointed and after a further discussion with Granville, he drafted a letter for her which she could send to her friend, the German Empress:

> He [Granville] is fully aware that for this purpose [good relations] it is desirable to have a person as my representative at Berlin, who has judgement and discretion. There are considerable difficulties in the way of appointing Mr Odo Russell [according to Odo's own estimate he had to be promoted over the heads of 32 senior diplomats[8]] but Lord Granville has a very high opinion of him, and believes that, from the great kindness he received in Versailles, he would be acceptable at Berlin. I agree in Lord Granville's opinion of Mr Odo Russell's qualifications and I would not only sanction, but I would encourage him to make the proposal if I were sure that it would be agreeable to you and the Emperor.[9]

Bismarck at last got his way. Loftus packed his bags for St Petersburg, (where he continued to be an ill-informed ambassador of HMG) and on 18 September, Odo could write to Hammond, 'A thousand thanks for your solution of my difficulty! I little thought I should live to be a gazetted ambassador to Berlin in my most ambitious dreams'.[10] This was of course quite untrue. As has already been seen, in Versailles, Russell had, whether consciously or not, sold himself as the rightful successor to Loftus. Now that his greatest wish had become a reality, Odo was suddenly gripped with fear. He was scared of 'the responsibility of a mission to conciliate forty millions of Germans'.[11] It was therefore a relief to him, to be briefed not only by the FO, but also by the court: 'The Queen, the Crown Prince ... have been very gracious and given me much good advice about Berlin'.[12] To Loftus, who had left him some furniture at the Embassy House, Odo wrote that he would arrive in Berlin 'en garcon', leaving his sick children and Emily in England until they had recuperated.[13] He had to hurry because the German Chancellor could not wait to see him again: 'Bismarck has sent me a message through Petre to say that he hopes I will come soon'.[14]

The Berlin that Odo encountered in the autumn of 1871 was in a transitional stage.[15] In many ways the problems the new capital had to face in the 1870s are analogous to those of today. Within a short period of time, the capital had to cope with becoming the power centre of an extended Germany. The Imperial court, the Reichstag, the Bundesrat, all Imperial ministries, and the whole political scene in general had to be organised, while Berlin also had to establish itself as an internationally recognised trading and banking town with a growth industry.[16] Unlike the situation in the Germany of the 1990s, large funds for this undertaking were available in 1871, thanks to French reparation payments. The whole infrastructure was improved and an unprecedented housing boom attracted speculators from all over Germany (the noise Berliners suffer today must have been almost as bad in the 1870s). The notoriously ugly *Mietskasernen* (tenement houses) for the rapidly proliferating working classes[17] (during the period 1871–1875 the number of people employed in industry and commerce increased from 120,000 to 280,000) were erected at this time as well as the 'newspaper palaces', elegant shopping stores, luxury hotels such as the *Kaiserhof*, and banks[18] that 'looked like Greek temples'.[19] Stock corporations were founded[20] and the whole stock market was so enormously heated that Odo predicted that 'people (are) speculation mad ... immense fortunes are made and undone in a day — an awful crash must come a few years hence!'[21] Like his contemporary Nietzsche, who saw 'a great victor as a great danger',[22] Russell felt that the new materialism had a deplorable effect on the Germans: 'The change that has come over the Germans is very *unerquicklich* [unpleasant]. They are going for luxury and financing and no longer read their poets'.[23] Yet he also saw a new creative side that slowly emerged. Wealth had given the city a long needed cultural impetus.[24] The Lessing Theatre and the *Schauspielhaus am Gendarmenmarkt* (another Berlin theatre) were leading in the 1870s with their staging of progressive plays by Ibsen and, later, to the annoyance of William II, Hauptmann.[25] Also, Germany's finest novelist of the late 19th century, Theodor Fontane, was appointed chief theatre critic of the *Vossische Zeitung* in the summer of 1870. His novels, for example *Effi Briest* or *Stechlin*, perhaps best mirror the atmosphere of Berlin society during these years.[26] A further attraction for the British ambassador must have been the German music scene, which had improved after the establishment of the music academy in 1869. Wagner came to Berlin in the early 1870s to collect money for his Festspielhaus in Bayreuth, targeting the new class of rich speculators. The astute Baroness Spitzemberg was, however, not taken in: 'Friday night we were invited by Frau von Schleinitz, to see Richard Wagner reading the Nibelungen lyrics. Carl (Spitzemberg's husband) did not feel like it and besides, we are afraid that the whole thing will turn into a fund raising function for Bayreuth, which we don't want to take part in'.[27] However, the invention of music festivals helped Wagner, despite the disastrous *Meistersinger* premiere in March 70, to raise enough money. By 1876, even the critical Baroness was a devotee of the new German music guru.[28]

So, soon after the war, the Germans were desperately trying to enjoy themselves again. Shopping and entertainment outings became a fashionable occupation for a wider class of Berliners. New confiseries, such as *Havel* and the cafe *Bauer* with its famous marzipan cakes and ice creams, tried to introduce a Viennese cafe-house mentality. Unter den Linden, a popular Christmas market, was opened, not far from the place where Bismarck had been shot in 1866.[29] The newly acquired wealth was celebrated in the most ostentatious ways, which prompted Odo's remark that 'cette ville finira mal'.[30] In their new apartments, the Berlin upper middle-class exchanged Biedermayer furniture for nouveau riche plush sofas and fake marble columns.[31] Bismarck, though he despised pomp, took the lead in displaying this new taste to his countrymen. On his Berlin residence, the Palais Radziwill, Baroness von Spitzemberg simply commented that the rooms looked expensive, but 'truly ordinary and often tasteless'.[32]

Although Bismarck was not generally an aesthete, he did have an enormous taste for nicely decorated delicatessen foods. At Embassy functions and court balls, as well as at private soirées, he and his fellow aristocrats now demanded even more refined and expensive catering and originality: 'Politics quiet here', Odo wrote to Morier in 1875, 'but society raving mad about a fancy ball the Crown Princess is giving ... . People at sixes and sevens about costumes, petticoats, tricots. 'A' won't dance with 'B', or 'C' with 'D', quarrelling, apologies, intrigues. *Meinetwegen, meinetwegen* [fine with me]'.[33] He was not so complacent when he received the bills for *his* balls. Odo had been officially presented to the Emperor in April 1872 and was under the new etiquette obliged to give two official receptions after presenting his credentials. When the FO received the bill for poulet, caviar, champagne and flower arrangements, they answered promptly. Odo was ordered to pay most of it himself because his colleagues, Buchanan at Vienna and Loftus at St Petersburg, had coped well with £65 and £91, respectively, for such a reception extravaganza.[34] This was unfair because Russell did not only have to entertain Berlin society, but also the representatives of all German states. The FO did not accept this as an excuse; on the contrary, they wanted him to entertain more on less. Hammond himself had suggested to Odo that he should organise regular 'hops' at the Embassy house to win over the natives. These tea-time dances turned out to be so successful that they were soon followed by popular evening events. When the Emperor, who always displayed enormous stamina at balls, invited himself to one of these functions in 1873 the overworked Russell reacted rather tetchily: 'This is an unexpected honour (and expense)', Odo wrote to Hammond, 'for we thought our two little balls enough for our pockets this year, and did not look forward to a third for the Royal family with a sitting room supper of 350 persons!'[35] The situation became worse when the ball had to be cancelled:

> The death of the Empress's mother at Vienna and the consequent autograph message from the Emperor William to say that he could not come — he wished us to put off our ball — was a blow to us and to our pockets for we had to pay for the ball we did not give ... . Unable to drink the 600 cups of consomme by ourselves we sent them and all the supper to the hospitals — so that's all well that ends well.[36]

It was of course expected that the Russells would give the ball at another time.[37] However, over the years Odo learned to become more direct. When in 1881 the Empress tried to invite herself, he courageously said 'no'. The result was that she: 'looked surprised ... and turned away without saying a word ... . The Emperor and Empress are younger and younger than ever and want to be entertained and amused'.[38] Russell on the other hand seldom enjoyed great balls. Derby noted that already after a Berlin season in 1873, Odo had 'grown very unwieldy and seems out of health. They [Emily and Odo] declare that they cannot do the necessary cost of receptions, etc. at Berlin on the salary allowed, and had last year to draw £5,000 from the Duke of Bedford to meet their expenses'.[39] This became a common procedure. In 1880 Russell's yearly expenditure was £12,000. His salary amounted to £6,852 p.a., but he only received half pay when he went on leave. Thanks to his investments with the Rothschilds and Bleichröder, he also had a private income of £3,000 a year. Yet to cover all his debts he had to use the money Hastings had given him as a present.[40] This money had originally been intended for Odo's six children. They had been born in rapid succession since 1869 and his last daughter, born in 1879, was a truly German product named after her godmother, Empress Augusta. One of Odo's constant worries was not to be able to leave them enough money in his will. He wanted his four boys to go to Eton while the two young daughters should enjoy at least part of the lifestyle that their friends, the children of the Prussian Crown Princess, had: 'Christmas the joy of children and the ruin of parents is coming on', Odo wrote to his brother on one occasion, 'and I would give six pence if it was over. I hate the expense of it because the obligatory tree in Berlin is such a waste of apples and nuts and bonbons and toys and candles and you have nothing to show for it all the next day!'[41]

Odo even bought a summer house in Potsdam in order to be close to the Crown Princess and her children. That way the whole family would get some fresh air and Odo could easily commute to Berlin whenever necessary. He also went for his yearly liver cure to Karlsbad (which was an interesting gossip market for diplomats) and sometimes he accompanied Emily on holidays to recover from the stress of the season. As did the Crown Princess, Odo's wife suffered from headaches and neuralgic attacks.[42] In Emily's case, however, they were probably not hereditary but brought on by the long court receptions that were held in overheated rooms. It was becoming fashionable at the time to cure such an illness in the mountains. The Engadine Valley, with the now famous villages of St Moritz, Celerina, Samedan and Sils Maria, had in the 1870s just been discovered by the British. At first, it was academics who arrived for the sole purpose of climbing and studying every reachable mountain: 'In those days if you met a man in the Alps it was ten to one that he was a University man, eight to one ... that he was a Cambridge man'.[43] The 'steam set' soon followed and chose the Engadine as a summer retreat. Russell loved the alpine scenery. To his brother he wrote, 'No wonder you do not know Samedan which a dozen years ago no one had heard of. The Engadine valley is the highest inhabited valley of Switzerland and Europe. The air is so bracing that I often feel as if I could not breathe, like a fish out of water — but it does Emily great good'.[44] In Samedan the Russells stayed at the Hotel Bernina (which exists to this day), a rose-painted first-class hotel that no longer receives the Czar, but his Russian nouveau riche successors.

Although Russell was constantly complaining about his expensive and stressful Berlin lifestyle (which simply had to be balanced with many holidays) he never lost his sense of humour. When the Shah visited the German capital in the summer of 1873, Russell sent the FO two reports

— an official one (in which he dutifully listed the fireworks, the balls and the pleasantries that had been exchanged)[45] and a secret version of the visit:

> The impression made by the Persians in Berlin is not exactly a very favourable one. The free and easy manner of the Shah who is not yet accustomed to the society of European Ladies, has given offence to the Royal family, the disastrous effects of the Persian encampment in the magnificent apartments of the Palace have irritated the Imperial Household, and the habit of His Majesty's followers not to pay for what they order in shops has exasperated the trades-people of Berlin [The Emperor remedied this problem later on and had their bills 'charged to his own personal account]'.[46]

To Hammond, Odo wrote that the Persian ladies were not that much of a problem: 'the three wives do not appear, they are dressed as boys and are packed with the luggage'.[47] Naturally, the German Empress desired the quick departure of the 'barbarians' at once. Only the Crown Princess sympathised with the exotic guest, perhaps seeing in him a fellow outsider.[48] The Shah's next stop was England and the FO must have been wondering, after Russell's report, what was in store for them.[49]

A major disadvantage, from a social point of view, for the new British ambassador was the Embassy house in the Leipzigerstrasse itself, which belonged to Count Arnim. The Leipzigerstrasse was a cheap shopping area where one could buy 'everything from food, to toys to garden equipment'. It is possible that Odo researched the history of his new home. Hegel had for three years lived with his family at the corner of Leipziger and Friedrichstrasse. E.T.A. Hoffmann studied for his law exams here and Schopenhauer, who despised the whole place, had lived in a furnished room during 1826, in Leipzigerstr. 78. His verdict on Berlin was scathing: 'a big, overcrowded, restless city in the middle of sandhills'.[50] Compared with the newly constructed palaces around him, Odo's lodgings, which he had to share with the Turkish representative, Aristarchi Bey, looked rather plain. (Russell also was unpleasantly surprised when the elevator broke down at one point and Aristarchi Bey — without any forewarning — appeared on the British floor.) The rooms needed refurbishing, yet Hammond advised Odo not to invest too much money: 'You cannot be expected to ruin yourself for public appearance and if the Treasury will not lodge you suitably, no reproach can be attached to you for being inadequately lodged'.[51] Over the next six years a continual story of house-hunting is documented in the FO files,[52] in which the treasury played the part of the villain, while Russell seemed to feel increasingly embarrassed in trying to explain such meanness to the Emperor. This was exacerbated by the fact that the Crown Prince wanted Odo to buy a house as soon as possible for reasons of prestige. When Russell told him that this was impossible he 'was much vexed ... but I thought it best to tell him the real state of the case once and for all'.[53] The Germans did not seem pleased that the British embassy in Berlin ranked below its counterpart in Paris: 'The result is that surprise — not to say envy is keenly felt and constantly expressed by those leading statesmen of Germany ... because they fail to understand why HMG gives France a higher rank than Germany among European nations'.[54]

It was only thanks to William I[55] (and the slump) that Odo was finally allowed to rent No. 70 Wilhelmstrasse, close to the German Foreign Office, the power centre of Berlin. The lease was for 10 years, at an annual rent of 20,000 Thalers.[56] (In 1884 it was bought by the 'Commissioners of Her Britannic Majesty Works and Public Buildings in London'.)[57] The Palais had originally been owned by the entrepreneur Dr Strousberg, who had at one stage been the richest man in Germany. He had built railways in Hungary and Rumania, purchased a locomotive factory and pits, founded the newspaper *Post* and bought great estates in Prussia and Bohemia. Many members of the aristocracy took up shares in his enterprises and had to pay with heavy losses when the slump of 1873 ruined the Strousberg empire.[58] Odo's move into the Strousberg Palais was symptomatic of the change of times; the boom was long over and the British Treasury could now, slightly, profit from the decline of the hyped up grandeur. Yet despite such great changes, the young diplomat James Rennell Rodd thought that the Strousberg house remained an 'unattractive residence', and he and his colleagues, preferred working in the Chancery, which was at the Pariser Platz.[59]

Though the Russells had to compete with other, from a political point of view, more popular ambassadors, their enormous charm helped them to become a social success in Berlin society. While the French ambassador, Vicomte de Gontaut-Biron, was sometimes ignored by Bismarck, the Russian and Austrian ambassadors (Count Oubril and Count Karolyi) were very popular shortly after the war. Emily also had 'to compete' with two young, beautifully dressed ambassadoresses 'with £40,000 a year ... Mme Karolyi, a celebrated beauty, and Mme Oubril, a handsome Russian — c'est tout dire',[60] wrote Odo — obviously a connoisseur of women — to Arthur. The newspapers did, however, their best to make Russell feel as welcomed as his colleagues by portraying him as a great social asset:

> The ambassador is probably around 40 and from the outside does not look like a diplomat of English nationality ... . He [has] a slightly stout figure, his face is full and pale, rounded by a fine dark beard; his spectacles indicate short-sightedness,

yet only in a physical way. In his ... interesting features there is an artistic touch which is balanced by his decisive gestures. His character is marked by sincerity and an open, hearty and natural manner, which is most agreeable. Mr Odo Russell speaks German fluently, and German, it is said, are his sympathies.[61]

The news of Odo's social success was also well received in London. Already in 1872 Lady Derby had written to Russell: 'We hear from many quarters of your success and Emily's at Berlin. I think you will not have been above pleased at Dizzy's outburst in your praise at Manchester'.[62]

Apart from his obligations in Berlin, Russell had, in 1872, to present his credentials.[63] The German Empire was one Federal State with 25 single states. They were divided into four kingdoms (Prussia, Saxony, Bavaria, Württemberg), six grand dukedoms, five duchies, three free cities (Bremen, Hamburg and Lübeck), seven principalities and the *Reichsland*, Alsace-Lorraine. In the first round, Odo was accredited to the German Emperor as well as to the King of Prussia, the Grand Dukes of Mecklenburg-Schwerin and of Mecklenburg-Strelitz and the Duke of Anhalt. These accreditation ceremonies did not always run that smoothly. With the Duke of Mecklenburg-Strelitz, for example, Odo encountered hostile opposition: 'The old Meck [the Duke of Mecklenburg- Strelitz] says that I am too German, and should oppose Bismarck and Wilhelm and favour the course of Hannover ... Old Meck says that I must be recalled and Loftus sent back to Berlin!'[64] To Odo's relief, the Queen took his side in the Mecklenburg-Strelitz affair. When Russell visited her in 1873 he was happy to report that she did not think much of 'Meckermeckmeck' either.[65] Odo was in favour of the continuation of British representation in the smaller German states and had made this clear during a parliamentary committee hearing in 1870. With German unification approaching, the British Government had hoped to cut costs by closing down German missions. Russell's argument against this idea was that, without diplomatic ties to the outside world, these small courts would be completely dominated by Prussia. The more British influence in Germany as a whole, the better for the development of this country. However, as it turned out, the smaller German missions only provided, according to Paul Kennedy, 'additional information about German public opinion and regional politics'.[66] They would have still been useful for Russell, but eventually he did not show any great interest in them. He also did his best not to get drawn into any of the quarrels involving smaller German states. He particularly dreaded the family affairs of the duchy of Saxe-Coburg-Gotha, which occupied the Queen's mind considerably. Since Prince Albert's brother Ernest II had not produced a legitimate heir, but instead spread venereal diseases amongst his mistresses, it was clear that his nephew, the second son of Queen Victoria, would one day inherit the title. Alfred, the Duke of Edinburgh, was far from happy about this upcoming honour. Neither was his wife Marie, Grandduchess of Russia. They both seemed to dread trips to Coburg, always passing through Berlin 'in very bad humour',[67] according to Odo. He refused to give them advice on how to handle 'uncle Ernest' though — to him the court at Coburg was closer to Lessing's and Schiller's plays than to real life: 'Uncle Ernest is a womaniser and causes the family much pain. ... Coburg reminds me of the times of "*Emilia Galotti*" and "*Kabale und Liebe*" ... . The Queen, bless her, thinks I can speak to him [Ernest] which I can't and won't do. His wife, oddly enough, approves of his "escapades" and nurses his mistresses when they have the pip'.[68]

As has been shown, a great amount of Odo's time was 'misspent' at court receptions. The rigidity of these ceremonies certainly had a high purpose. Unlike Queen Victoria, who lived in semi-seclusion,[69] the Prussian monarchy was endeavouring by its ostentatious activity to enhance the aura of royalty. This was, in the opinion of Prussian, Austrian and also Russian conservatives, the only way to strengthen the power of the monarchies and to keep the 'plebeians' at bay.[70] Odo realised this intention and saw in it similarities to a church service: 'You [Arthur] and I have got over the feeling that outer forms of worship are comical. That is, they may be so, but they no longer make me laugh. Court ceremonies are equally comical, but they don't make me laugh'.[71] At these court receptions, the question of precedence was paramount. Hammond found this antiquated[72] and had to be lectured by Russell that 'precedence' did not simply mean 'a question as to the order of going into dinner', it stood for influence and power: 'Hammond [eventually] admitted that in the case of ambassadors their special right of claiming an audience of the Sovereign was important'.[73] This was not easy in Berlin. The ante-room at the Berlin FO was overcrowded by ministers who had to wait for hours and were 'kept out by the sudden arrival of an ambassador'.[74] Also, Russell did not want his embassy to lose its preferential treatment while he was away. When he left the embassy in the summer of 1872 for a short cure at Karlsbad, he wanted to put his second secretary Plunkett in charge. This caused great excitement because, as Plunkett had not been presented at court, it was feared that he would have to wait hours for an audience. It was also important for the ambassadors not to be left out of court receptions (where they could usually collect information.) Not to be on the guest list could mean that one's country was intentionally being ignored. Odo experienced this in May 1874:[75]

What misdemeanour has my embassy committed? Yesterday only one of my secretaries was invited to court. 'Where are the others', [the] Prince of Wales asked.
I would have ignored this if I had not discovered that all my Russian colleagues
had been invited. Please find out why we are not welcome at court, because I hope
we are on good terms with the government?[76]

Such problems were, however, rare. Normally, Russell received
preferential treatment at court and from Bismarck. The Chancellor had
in 1871 expressed his wish that Odo should be the 'doyen' of the
diplomatic body. Though Russell was very flattered, he also thought that
'this may create envy'.[77] Vanity succeeded and he took up this esteemed,
but at the same time demanding, position (involving as it did attendance
at every court function, being doomed to it like a member of the Royal
family.) He often regretted it. Despite the social successes, Russell felt
sometimes overworked and doubted his abilities: 'I cannot conceal from
myself that this post is more difficult than I expected and I do not feel
equal to the task. The combination of position, establishment and
correspondence with the German and English Government is often
perplexing and the duties of doyen of the Diplomatic Body delicate
and trying'.[78] In 1875 he wrote about a 'normal day' in the life of an
ambassador:

At one o'clock I drive in state to the Palace to congratulate the Emperor on his
76th birthday. At five o'clock I dine again in uniform at Bismarck's (house) with
the whole diplomatic body and propose to the health of His Majesty. At eight
o'clock 'en gala' I go to the Empress' reception and concert which lasts from 8 till
1.30 am if not 2 am. To this last affair Emily goes with me to head the circle of
the diplomatic ladies as doyenne, '*notre doyenne*' as they call her.[79]

Being the daughter of a diplomat and speaking German fluently,
Emily Russell was well trained for her position.[80] In some ways her role
was similar to that of a vicar's wife — it was expected of her to help
her husband with social work. Still, her position did have its benefits.
It was, for example, considered chic to flirt with an ambassador's wife,
according to Baroness Spitzemberg: 'There has developed an
'ambassadoress cult' among the men who want to be fashionable'.[81]
However, even such flattery cannot have been sufficient compensation
for the long hours spent in mandatory visits every day:

I find that last year 1,870 Gentlemen and 908 Ladies called ... making a total of
2,778 visits Emily had to return driving day after day to drop cards at their houses.
It is not enormous, but it takes time to accomplish and omissions are unavoidable
now and then.[82]

The Crown Princess was impressed by Emily's vitality: 'Emily Russell
can stand it [the strain of the social circuit] no better than I can. She

spends days in bed with racking headaches after these interminable dinners and soirées and yet she is a thorough "cosmopolitan" and likes society and going out so much and is always so civil and amiable to everyone'.[83] One of those successful visits was paid to Baroness Spitzemberg, who wrote about the new British ambassadoress: '[She is] a kind, pleasant and good looking woman. It is said that she is too noble and we therefore can't ask her for dinner. I think Carl [Spitzemberg] would not agree to invite such "gros bonnets" '.[84] During the 1870s, Emily was also praised by *The Times* (which called her, in connection with the Berlin Congress, an 'excellent hostess')[85] and by people so different from each other as the Prussian Crown Princess and Bismarck: 'The Crown Princess told me', Odo wrote happily, 'that Berlin had never known a Dips. wife before like her [Emily], that she was universally appreciated, that Bismarck spoke of her in the highest praise, and that I owed everything to her etc., etc., which gratified me immensely'.[86] It was expected of an 'ambassadoress' that she take an interest in her husband's career or, failing that, to keep out of sight. Emily was doubly useful because she also worked as a secretary for Odo. The 'possession' of a wife was, however, not made obligatory by the FO. Buchanan, for example, coped well without one (and therefore saved an enormous amount of money) and the German ambassador to London, Münster, employed his daughter instead.

Despite the impression of the Crown Princess that Lady Russell was cosmopolitan, Emily did not love Berlin as much as her husband did: 'Her social qualities are immense', Odo informed Arthur in 1872, 'but she does not enjoy the power she possesses, because ... foreigners are foreigners to her'.[87] In 1882 when the climate became more anti-British, Emily had more reason to feel suspicious of the 'foreigners' she had lived with for 11 years. An article by an 'unknown enemy', who was obviously aware of her close friendship with the Prussian Crown Princess, claimed that she had never made an attempt to learn German. Odo was irritated and wrote to Hastings: 'It is hard upon Emily ... when she speaks German and French better than I do'.[88] By then Odo had himself grown more critical of the average German. In a letter to his friend Morier he condemned the 'Scheissangst der Deutschen' ['shit fear' of the Germans] which made them kneel in front of Bismarck.[89] Only one class continually fascinated Russell, the German academics. After all, it had been they who had played an interesting part in the national unity movement before it was 'hijacked' by Bismarck.[90] Lord Acton provided Russell with the entrée to German academia, informing him as to who were the most interesting professors to know in Berlin. He did not think much of the famous doctor and liberal politician Virchow ('I hear [he] is a very unsympathetic individual') while Lepsius, the Egyptologist, pleased Acton. Heinrich von Friedberg, the Prussian Minister of Justice, was also an excellent source of information: both 'official and confidential' and, according to Acton, a good writer. When it came to German historians Acton was, however, more critical: 'Ranke is getting querulous and tasteless'. The same was true of Droysen whose *Geschichte der Preussischen Politik* was 'so destitute of flesh and blood that its influence has been far less than [expected]'. Mommsen's work was approved of by Acton, though not without qualification, he noted that it was 'boisterous, self-sufficient and intolerant'.[91] Odo followed Acton's advice to read all the works of these men first and then decide whether they were worth knowing. Soon, he had among his newly acquired friends in Berlin Rudolf von Gneist, Professor of Law at Berlin University, Liberal member of the Reichstag,[92] the Prussian Staatsrat and Chief of the 'Zentralverein for the benefit of the working class'; the aforementioned historian, Theodor Mommsen, Professor of Ancient History and Liberal member of the Prussian *Abgeordnetenhaus* and the *Reichstag*; the lawyer and National Liberal MP Eduard Lasker; Professor Hermann Helmholtz, who, among many other things, worked on electromagnetism; and Professor Moritz Lazarus who taught philosophy at Berlin. Together they offered a wide spectrum of subjects to assuage Odo's thirst for knowledge. However, the ambassador soon had to find out that he could not mix 'Geist' as he called his intellectual friends with other classes of the Berlin society. Military and academic people simply did not get on and so 'Geist' declined to come to an Embassy Ball 'because of the Lieutenants ... "Geist" likes Kneipe, beer and no ladies ... then they talk brilliantly ... Gneist, Helmholtz, Lepsius have social habits ... and experience of society, but Mommsen, Schulze Delitzsch belong to another world and hate the stiffness of our world'.[93]

The inner world of Berlin academics of the late 19th century,[94] to which Russell felt so attracted, has been analysed at length by Thomas Nipperdey.[95] Their ethos was idealistic, beyond materialism, and against rationalism. The idea of 'individual happiness' was seen as vulgar and trivial; what counted was the idealistic morality to achieve the common good. Matthew Arnold felt intrigued by the German aim to 'encourage a love of study and science for their own sakes; and the professors, very unlike our college tutors, are constantly warning their pupils against *Brotstudien* [bread and butter jobs]'.[96] The German academic's notion that one constantly had to work on improving one's 'culture', the spiritual and interior side of every human being, was adopted by the upper-middle and upper-classes. It became chic to go to lectures, especially those of historians such as Mommsen and the right winger Treitschke.[97] (Baroness Spitzemberg, for example, was one of these 'aristocratic lecture groupies' who demanded high entertainment. On one occasion, when she was visiting Professor Lazarus at home, she felt uncomfortable because he had also invited his students instead of 'important people').[98] Russell was less fastidious and by 1872 was already fully recognised by the academic elite of Berlin. When he was invited to a dinner at the Archaeological Society to celebrate Winkelmann, Odo proudly wrote to his brother Hastings that 'no other diplomat is invited to such a congregation of "colleagues"'.[99] He felt the same pride when he met the painter Anton v. Werner, who would later capture Odo on his famous picture of the Berlin Congress.

Although these contacts were useful and entertaining for Russell, the development of a special relationship with Bismarck was the focal point of his professional duties. From the start of his posting, Odo therefore tried to keep alive the relative closeness that had existed between Bismarck and himself at Versailles. A letter from Abeken, Bismarck's devoted secretary, who probably died of exhaustion,[100] shows that the Chancellor also enjoyed re-enacting the former 'war-bonding':

> (Bismarck) thinks ... that with the same indulgence as at Versailles you will excuse him lying on the sofa and will also kindly allow for his weakness and unfitness for much polished conversation. He is particularly anxious to reopen the personal intercourse which gave him so much pleasure at Versailles.[101]

Bismarck's habit of receiving visitors while lying on the sofa can be interpreted in two different ways. On the one hand, the Chancellor was on many occasions actually ill (his medical history — well analysed by Otto Pflanze — shows that he often suffered from nervous attacks because of his alcohol, food and tobacco abuse, as well as sheer overwork).[102] On the other hand, Bismarck was renowned for his hypochondria as well as his 'escapism', i.e. hiding for months in the countryside to show his enemies as well as his followers that he was indispensable. By pretending to be ill, it was also easier for Bismarck to establish an atmosphere of intimacy with his visitor that would not otherwise have been possible in the Chancellor's spartan office room in Wilhelmstrasse. Such a 'sofa audience' was therefore meant to appeal to Russell's tact and sensitivity not to ask difficult questions. By now, knowing the Chancellor as he did, he had learned to accept such terms. The intimacy of these sofa talks, however, does not indicate that Bismarck wanted to establish a real friendship with the British ambassador. Like many other members of the closer Bismarck entourage Odo initially felt that it would be possible to get access to the Chancellor's inner decision-making process — after all, Bismarck seemed so very generous with his opinions on the court and the ability of foreign statesmen: 'Prince Bismarck's conversations are sometimes marked by such startling frankness that to report them appears a breach of confidence'.[103] He talked with Odo about his achievements, giving the British ambassador the impression that he could become a Bismarck *confidante*. In one of these talks, for example, Bismarck revealed his superstitious side:

> Prince Bismarck on being congratulated the other day by a friend on the political lull that enabled him to take his leave this summer, replied that he felt superstitious about political lulls and Royal Christenings at Potsdam. A political lull had preceded the christening at Potsdam in 1866 and 1870 which had been immediately followed by the wars with Austria and France, and France was not acting in a manner calculated to inspire confidence.[104]

On another occasion he seemed to indulge in rather confused numerology:

> I found Prince Bismarck in one of his soft, confidential moods the other day [Odo wrote in a private letter to Derby], and he indulged me in a long talk about his own interests, past and present and perspective ... . He said that his life had been strangely divided into phases or periods of 12 years each. Born in April 1815 he had left home when he was 12 years old to begin his studies. At 24 he inherited his small patrimony and his father's debts and entered upon a life of a country gentleman. At 36 [in 1851] his diplomatic career began and he was sent to Frankfurt, St Petersburg and Paris. ... He was recalled to form the present administration which in 12 years had carried on three wars and made the German Empire. He was now 60 and worn out with the responsibility and anxieties of office, and he was resolved to enter upon a new phase [of 12 years he hoped] by resigning and retiring into private life.[105]

Russell soon realised that these 'confessions' of Bismarck were always calculated and that the Chancellor never actually said anything without a purpose. After all, Bismarck had been a diplomat himself:

> The freedom or cynicism of his language in regard to his own plans, the frankness or severity of his criticism of the Emperor and Royal Family, and of his colleagues are at all times startling, and partly no doubt serve to conceal the deep cunning of his nature, on which, when force would be of no avail, the strength of his policy is based. Even when giving vent to his violent temper he never says more than he intends, and when he wishes to please or persuade, no one can be more irresistibly fascinating than Prince Bismarck.[106]

Odo learned not to have any illusions about his relationship with Bismarck, the 'great man'. Since the Versailles days, he could not help admiring the Chancellor's intelligence and ruthlessness ('his speeches are full of wit and power'),[107] but he was never in danger of becoming a creature of Bismarck. For Odo, Bismarck was the epitome of a 'Machiavellian',[108] and in a despatch to the FO he commented that 'in following the extraordinary phases of Prince Bismarck's progress to power, I cannot but feel reminded of Wallenstein and ask myself how long will the Emperor submit to his tyranny?'[109]

Over the years it would become more difficult for Odo to get access to Bismarck,[110] a fate he and his colleagues shared with the officials of the German FO, Members of Parliament and the court. Odo wrote to Granville in 1873: 'Bismarck is such a strange creature, that no one can foretell how he will take things'.[111] When Lady Derby asked Odo whether he could arrange an interview with Bismarck for a journalist friend of hers (Edmund Dicey), he replied to Dicey:

> The great Chancellor is an unaccountable creature and no one, not even his wife can say whom he will, whom he won't receive. As a rule he is said to receive no one at Varzin, and at Berlin there is no rule by which his favours are regulated. ... My impression is, that you would not find it possible to obtain an interview while he is in the country, but when in Berlin you would have a fair chance of being received. But so much depends on the state of his nerves — you might have to wait a long time for the interview.[112]

But it was not only Bismarck who became more unreachable; secrecy also reigned in the German Foreign Office:[113]

> The other day a diplomatist asked a Clerk of the FO which department he belonged to so as to be able to send him a book he wished to read. The Clerk replied with visible embarrassment that he was not allowed to disclose the name of the department ... but that FO, Wilhelmstrasse would find him without further specification.[114]

In such a climate it became difficult for a diplomat, even of Odo's calibre, to collect information. Still, Odo received birthday greetings from Bismarck — in perfect English: 'I am unable to ascertain if really your birthday is today, but rumours being spread in that direction, at all events I will not miss the occasion, authentic or not, of sending you my best wishes for health and happiness. Lady Russell naturally being included as chief condition of the latter'.[115]

Bismarck also did receive his favourite Englishman at home more often than any of Odo's colleagues: 'You [Russell] favour me with your visit any day which you may choose, but the sooner the better. ... We dine at five and we hope ... that you will not leave us the same day of your arrival'.[116] During one of these interviews it became apparent to Odo that there was a secret system worked out by the Bismarck family to relieve the Chancellor of visitors who had overstayed their welcome:

> He [Bismarck] had devised an infallible method for terminating a tedious official interview. When his wife thought that a visitor had been with him long enough she would look in at the door and remind him that the time had come to take his medicine. On that occasion he had hardly explained the method when the Princess appeared bottle in hand.[117]

Bismarck also received straightforward treatment at Odo's house. Russell's son, the 2nd Lord Ampthill, when asked about meeting Bismarck as a child, said: 'We were in awe of nobody at the Embassy. The atmosphere in our home was so different'.[118]

The most important working relationship that Bismarck had was of course with the Emperor, which ran along rather complex lines. Though Bismarck felt contempt for the obvious intellectual shortcomings of his monarch, he initially yearned to be praised by William. In many ways, they were complete opposites: William, a man full of principles, a real military man (not just wearing a uniform like Bismarck) and conservative (unlike Bismarck, he tried to stick to his ideology and value system), with some political instinct but without a 'trained mind'.[119] It was the declining health of the Emperor that posed the greatest threat to Bismarck. In 1873, for example, rumours began to circulate that the Emperor might be going mad. Odo reacted like a seismographer trying to gauge the signals coming from the court. He noticed that 'persons connected with the court' were suddenly 'no longer at ease' and it was reported that the Emperor had had a fainting fit of several hours as well as having suffered from 'giddiness'. Odo's informants reported that worse symptoms had emerged, similar to those which 'preceded the last illness of His Majesty's brother, the late King of Prussia', which was a tactful way of describing the possibility of mental illness.[120] It turned out to be a false alarm, but the *augurs* were never far away. Again and again the Chancellor complained to Odo about the stubbornness of William, which resulted in the whole Prussian Government travelling like a 'coach with eight horses fighting for four wheels'.[121] Like Bismarck, the Emperor did not like to delegate work and resisted all attempts to diminish his workload. What must, however, have been worse for his health were the constant arguments between him, his wife and the Chancellor. Empress Augusta was in Bismarck's eyes his worst enemy at court: 'Her Majesty had the advantage over him [Bismarck] of breakfasting with the Emperor', a jealous Bismarck 'confided' to Odo:

> and of looking over the morning papers with His Majesty, when she found an opportunity to represent the views of the clericals, her spiritual and political directors, and of undermining the Emperor's confidence in him [Bismarck] whose services Her Majesty had unhappily never appreciated. When the Emperor agreed

with her views she was in the habit of saying to him: 'You never have the courage to repeat that to Bismarck'. After breakfast the Emperor of course met him prepared for resistance, and it became his laborious and wearisome duty to counteract the Empress' influence by arguments and persuasions, which often called forth the Emperor's tears, His Majesty not having really sufficiently studied or understood the requirements of his own Empire to have a practical opinion in the matter.[122]

This was the pattern of conflict with the Empress that Bismarck would tell the whole world about in his memoirs.[123] Augusta was by then dead and could not defend herself any more. In many ways she was almost a tragic figure, as all her political ambitions and religious feelings had been frustrated by the two men she lived with, Bismarck and her husband.

There were, however, fewer tussles between the Emperor and Bismarck after the end of the Kulturkampf and, as a result, William seemed to 'blossom' more and more. Odo wrote in surprise about the Emperor's 85th birthday reception in 1882: 'The old "Kaiser" ... was a glorious sight — erect, elastic, gay, amiable, conversational, energetic and as full of enjoyment as three-quarters of a century ago when he entered the army as a cadet'.[124] Two years later, when Odo himself was already feeling quite fragile, the Emperor was still in radiant health:

When I congratulated the Emperor on the 70th anniversary of his having received the order of St George for personal bravery in the field at Bar-sur-Aube before Paris in 1814, his Majesty was pleased to remind me that I had dined with him at the prefecture in Versailles on the anniversary of the same day in 1871, when the fortunes of war had brought him for the third time with a besieging army before Paris. Then shaking me warmly by the hand the Emperor said that he congratulated himself on the acquaintance made there, from which dated the cordial relations between us of the last 13 years and which had been a source of pleasure and satisfaction to him ever since.[125]

Bismarck had nothing against Russell's good relationship with the Emperor, but it is surprising that he forgave Odo his closeness to the Crown Princess, an exception no one else enjoyed. The situation in Berlin after 1871 was one of suspicion between the different generations in the Royal family. The mark of defeat would soon turn the Crown Princess and her husband into two irritable and pitiful creatures, paranoid about their enemies and constantly nagging about the lack of deference shown to them.[126] Odo later saw their struggle in a half humorous, half cynical light: 'The Royalties *in spe* are bursting to pour out their griefs and wrongs to you [Morier] and ask for advice they don't listen to in others'.[127] Despite this slight criticism, Russell always remained an admirer of the Crown Princess.[128] She had already figured in Odo's dreams before he became closer to her in Berlin. To Lady Derby (then still Lady Salisbury) he wrote in 1867: 'I dreamt I was walking with you in an unknown town, you took me to see the Princess Royal and told me she was suffering from a disease of the milk in her breast'.[129] Apart from having Freudian dreams, Odo, to his great delight, received flowers from Victoria on his 48th birthday. His wife was not pleased: 'Emily says it is ridiculous to send a bouquet to a man — but at 48 a bouquet flatters and gratifies the individual who receives it nevertheless'.[130] Naturally his chivalrous side surfaced when, shortly after his arrival, he was first confronted with the maltreatment of his Princess Royal. In October 1872 he wrote in an anxious letter to Granville:[131]

> Some days ago the Crown Prince and Crown Princess asked us to luncheon at Potsdam. They were alone with their children. The Crown Prince confided to me, for my guidance only but in the presence and hearing of the Crown Princess and of my wife, the following secret. The Emperor of Russia, he said, had told the Crown Princess that he desired to warn her most earnestly of the danger to which she was exposing herself, her husband and the cause of Royalty in Germany by her unconcealed predilection for the country of her birth. He had learnt with concern and regret that she continued in sentiment, language and manner to be more an English woman than a German, thereby causing sorrow and giving offence to the Royal family she had married into. As future Empress of Germany her anti-German tendencies would weaken her position in the estimation of her subjects — whilst her English sympathies would be thought to influence her husband in an anti-national sense and the sacred cause of Royalty must suffer from any imitation of the pernicious example given by the growing Republicanism and socialism of England. Germany, Austria and Russia should hold together to resist these dangerous and evil influences of England, and the good examples of their subjects should come from the Sovereigns and their families, if order was to be maintained in Europe.[132]

The Crown Prince had been outraged that 'the Czar [had] resumed the part of adviser and Protector of the House of Hohenzollern'.[133] Odo did not dare to tell him that he had been approached as well by another member of the Czar's family, the Duchess Helen of Russia, who feared 'the power the Crown Princess had over her husband'.[134] So looming were 'the rocks ahead', Odo concluded, that he was very worried about Victoria's future position: 'What I fear most for our beloved Crown Princess is Bismarck's intense dislike for her, which she knows and reciprocates with imprudent frankness, I regret to say'.[135] For an intelligent woman this was an imprudent thing to do. The latest one of Victoria's many biographers, Hannah Pakula, already makes it obvious in the title of her book — *An Uncommon Woman: the Empress*

Frederick, Daughter of Queen Victoria, Wife of the Crown Prince, Mother of Kaiser William — that the Crown Princess was always somebody's 'genitive', that is, she was always somebody's daughter, wife or mother — but never anyone in her own right. Of course she shared this fate with almost all women of her generation, but her upbringing, her ambition and her intelligence had equipped her for a greater role. Her fear of not playing this role was the reason for her ambivalent feelings towards Germany,[136] and for her many both real and psychosomatic illnesses. In 1881, at the age of 41, she still had to ask the Emperor for permission to go to England for a trip and, again, lacked the money for it.[137] Yet despite all the understanding one has to have for Vicky's difficult situation (and many of her biographers had too much of it), one should also keep in mind that she could be a very manipulative person herself. Bismarck was rightly angry with her in the Battenberg affair and he knew how keen she was on power for herself, much more than her husband. That Vicky also could be very self-righteous was detected by a young diplomat on Russell's staff, James Rennell Rodd. For him there was an obvious similarity between the Crown Princess and her eldest son, which made it impossible for them to get on: 'She was an idealist, lacking in worldly wisdom, and therefore often indiscreet [William II] was also an idealist, but his idealism was vitiated by a self-assurance which did not allow him to question the rightness of his own conclusion. Both were impetuous and impatient of opposition'.[138]

For both, the Crown Prince and the Princess, it was a relaxation to socialise with the members of the British embassy. Rennell Rodd describes how he was invited, shortly after his arrival in Berlin in 1884, for a game of tennis to the Neues Palais: 'Vivid still remains the impression made upon me by the Crown Prince when for the first time I saw him approaching the tennis ground with his four Italian greyhounds, a splendid figure of dignified manhood, radiating kindliness with a friendly smile'.[139] The young William was not as charming. Perhaps it is because of this and Odo's sense of tact that he does not greatly figure in Russell's private letters. To him, 'young William' only became of interest when it was discussed whether he should receive the Order of the Garter in 1877. While Queen Victoria saw this as an issue of great importance, Derby, who had to leave London to discuss the matter, was greatly irritated: 'It is difficult to suppose that anybody in England will either know or care [whether William receives the Garter]. But the loss of half a day, at a busy time, to give advice on such a matter strengthened my intention noted yesterday [to consider retirement]'.[140] Rennell Rodd, like the rest of the Embassy staff, preferred the younger brother Henry, and was not amused when the future William II hit him

The family seat of the Dukes of Bedford, Woburn Abbey.

— accidentally — with a tennis racket.[141] The other children of the Crown Princess were not very distinguished either. Vicky's eldest daughter Charlotte, who was close to her brother William, became a friend of Hastings' wife and liked to visit her in England. That in itself did not endear her to Hastings who wanted information from Odo about Charlotte's newly acquired husband, Prince Bernhard, the Hereditary Prince of Saxe-Meiningen. Nobody knew why she had been so keen on marrying him and Odo's verdict was quite diplomatic: '[Bernhard] is what people call a prig and I call "un jeune homme serieux". He loves military science ..., classics and is in politics a Tory'.[142] It is interesting to note that Odo, who usually took so much interest in young people, remained silent about the children of the Crown Princess. It had very soon materialised that there was no 'new Albert' among them and that none of them had inherited the intellectual talents of their mother. The Queen of Holland was probably the harshest in her verdict of the children. She wrote to Lady Derby about a summer holiday with the Princess Royal and her children in 1874: 'The eldest [William] is ... an ugly likeness of the Prince of Wales. He has a strange propensity to lying, inventing whole stories, which have no shadow of truth. ... In every case he will be a strange specimen of a Sovereign, perhaps the more warlike, because nature did not fit him for a soldier'.[143] It took a multitude of historians to come to the same conclusion which the sharp minded Queen Sophie had worked out during a short holiday at Skeveningen.

Though Odo could not help the Crown Princess very much by just reporting the insults she had suffered, he tried to become a good friend in other ways. When the Crown Princess had been in desperate need to find accommodation in England, Odo had offered Woburn Abbey as a place to stay: '[the Crown Prince and Princess feel the] neglect of their family and friends in England acutely. The Queen declined to lodge them, the German Embassy in London is too small and the Prince of Wales did not lend them Marlborough House!'[144]

Odo tried to persuade his shy brother to lodge them by telling him that 'it would do a world of international good and the more so as they may soon ascend the Imperial throne of Germany'. He also promised the shy and difficult Hastings that he did not need 'to come near them'.[145] In the end the Crown Princess made other arrangements, but she was very thankful for Odo's sensitivity to her problems. In 1878, when she decided to travel to some of the great English country houses, Odo was able to arrange a visit to Woburn Abbey. His brother Hastings took great pains to turn this trip into a social success by hiring an extra train for the German guests and entertaining them with lavish banquets.

A further worry of the Princess was an occasional lack of money.

She openly talked about this to her fellow sufferer Odo: 'Not long ago I heard the Crown Princess dwell with eloquence, feeling and conviction on all she could do if she had but six hundred Pounds at her disposal!'[146] Russell helped her by discreetly passing on money from her brother, the Prince of Wales. This money was paid to her confidante Seckendorff, and it is not clear from the clandestine correspondence between the two go-betweens, Lyons and Russell, how high the sum actually was. The Crown Princess was, however, not the only Royal with an occasional cash-flow problem. Her sister-in-law, the Duchess of Edinburgh, in 1878 travelled through Berlin on her way to Russia without a penny. Her mother had been taken ill and the Duchess wanted to rush to her bedside. In this rush she had forgotten her chequebook and Odo had to lend her £110 and paid for her journey.[147] Whether he got his money back is not documented.

Though Odo was close to the German Crown Princess, he had difficulties with her husband. In his private letters to Derby, he occasionally made fun of 'Fritz's ignorance' of German affairs. Of course he knew that this was not entirely the Crown Prince's fault: 'According to the traditions of the House of Hohenzollern as you know, the Queen and the Prince of Prussia are not kept informed of State Secrets, and the Emperor never speaks to the Crown Prince on foreign policy or State affairs — a fact I have heard His Imperial Highness complain of in bitter terms'.[148] Still, Russell was annoyed that the Crown Prince tried to use him as a source, but was himself not willing to make any political comments. To Morier he wrote: '[the Crown Prince] was as buttoned as ever'.[149] And in 1876: 'Bismarck must be unusually mysterious, for the Crown Prince calls every other day to ask me what is going on and what Bismarck thinks!'[150] Bismarck, of course, had strong feelings towards the Crown Prince and did not hesitate to tell Odo about them: 'A danger to which the Crown Prince would be exposed as sovereign was his love for intrigue ... the Prince was not as straightforward as he appeared, and he suffered from the weakness of obstinacy ... due to unbounded conceit and self confidence, but at least he meant well'.[151] It is hard to judge whether Russell in his judgement of Friedrich was influenced by Bismarck or whether he himself developed grave doubts about 'Fritz's' character: 'the Crown Prince, peace loving as he is', Odo wrote in 1875, 'has not sufficient independence of character to resist Bismarck'.[152] When, after the attempted assassination of the Emperor, the Crown Prince had to take over his father's responsibilities, he failed. At least, this was Odo's verdict. He reported that 'Fritz' looked tired, ill, defeated and constantly worried.

The Pen-Pusher

Accumulating information in the salons, at court soirées, from political and royal friends as well as from colleagues was Odo's prominent skill. Most of his reports were therefore not based on the rare official talks with Bismarck, or the sparse information from Bülow, but on private conversations with statesmen (some of them even taking place in railway carriages) and careful analysis of the semi-official newspapers. Spending his night hours writing, Odo already suffered from deteriorating eyesight when he arrived in Berlin: 'My eyes are growing very dim' he wrote in 1873, 'and require care. Much light makes them very dim and so I have to resort to shades, green and white'.[1] The amount of despatches Odo had to read and write during one year can be shown by an example from 1873: 'From FO: Political, 264; circulars, 16; Under-secretary of State, 15. Despatches to the FO: Political, 523, to Under-secretary of State, 26; Commercial, 77; consular, 31'.[2]

The number of despatches Odo received from the FO is, however, deceptive. Most of them were not instructions or even acknowledgements of his work, but despatches by diplomats from Petersburg or Vienna, passed on for his information. During his first years in Berlin, Russell felt acutely that he was short of instructions and general feedback from the FO. This affected not only his motivation but also his policy orientation, and he sometimes seriously doubted whether anyone at the FO bothered to read his despatches: 'Do you ever get any answers to what you write, private or official?', wrote Odo to Morier, 'I don't and suspect I am not read'.[3] Morier was not any more fortunate and Russell tried to see the humorous side of it:

> I have not a line to bless myself with — but, no, I forget and I am ungrateful. Grosstadt [their nickname for Granville] acknowledged my congratulations on the birth of his son by half a sheet of very small notepaper in Friday's bag, ... but what I mean is that I have not been able to discover whether HMG has a policy or not, so I have inaugurated one of my own, which consists in being very civil to everybody I am introduced to — and I mean to stick to it and carry it out boldly until my conduct and language are disapproved and my actions are disavowed.[4]

Unlike Granville, Odo was very attentive towards his own staff. When he came to Berlin in October 1871, he had — in contrast to his Rome and Versailles missions — plenty of secretaries around him who helped with the tiresome ciphering and deciphering of his despatches and did the translations of relevant German newspaper articles for the FO. Arthur Russell was very satisfied with Odo's human acquisitions: 'Two Roman Catholics are on the staff, Petre and Plunkett. ... Dering, son of Sir Edward, is second Secretary. Mr Bentnick (called Count Bentnick, a half Dutchman) and ... Napier complete the Staff — an excellent one'.[5] There was also Francis O. Adams who acted as first secretary (and was in 1874 replaced by Hugh MacDonnell), as well as the third secretary J. St V. Saumareg.[6]

Over the years the Berlin embassy became the starting point for many young diplomats. Some of them, such as Odo's namesake James Russell, arrived unsure as to whether they had chosen the right profession, but were so fascinated by the way Odo drew them into his work and discussed issues openly with them that they made up their minds to commit themselves to diplomacy wholeheartedly. Odo was, according to James Russell, the only man who 'could reconcile one to a career for which one never had a vocation'. Also, Arthur Nicolson, the father of Harold Nicolson, learned at Berlin to love his profession and overcome his shyness. At a ball, Odo pointed out a group of men to him including the Emperor, Roon, Moltke and Bismarck and said: 'there you can observe the makers of modern Germany'. From then on, Nicolson was hooked.[7] Unlike Hammond at the FO, Russell did not want to bore his staff with tedious copying work alone and so all of his secretaries had their own research projects: 'I am very proud of my staff', wrote Odo to Derby, 'who have produced a good history of Japan and an excellent précis of the German constitution'.[8] How much they enjoyed working for him can be seen by their letters. Most of them are addressed to 'my dear chief' and contained personal as well as professional problems. The amount of loyalty and enthusiasm the staff developed in their work for Russell is shown in a letter written by Adams on 30 August 1873:

> I have reasons to remain here. One is that I have a most excellent and kind chief, from whom ... I should be very sorry to part. Another is, that, particularly speaking, there seems to me more to be learnt here at the present moment than perhaps anywhere in Europe.[9]

Though Odo was pleased about Adams' loyalty, he also saw the dangers arising from it. When Adams rejected Guatemala, Russell thought it to be 'a great mistake. ... Fortune knocked on Adams' door over night, but he would not open — may he never regret it'.[10] Another member of Odo's staff, the military attaché Colonel Methuen, brought the embassy great honour when he became a hero in 1881: 'The Emperor after thanking Colonel Methuen in presence of the court for his act of bravery in saving a man's life from drowning, gave him a medal in token of his high sense of the Colonel's gallant deed. ... This demonstration on the part of the Emperor toward a British officer in presence of the whole court made a very favourable impression'.[11] Methuen's predecessor, Major General B. Walker, had already been considered an ideal choice as a military attaché to the embassy.[12] The Emperor liked to have familiar faces around him and Walker, as has been mentioned earlier, had been the only foreign attaché at Versailles who 'had been permitted to accompany the German armies to the field'.[13] Though Walker was appreciated in German court circles, he felt neglected by the British FO. Seeing his German counterparts becoming influential decision-makers, while not getting much recognition in England himself, irritated him.[14] Walker hoped that one day the military caste in his country would be valued as highly as in Germany:

> I may say that the fact of being a soldier is almost sufficient to bar a public man from credit [in England] and the possession of common sense and judgement. Such is not the case in this country [Germany], where military opinion is ... a not un-important influence on the public.[15]

While Walker was held in high regard at the German court, he suffered from the anti-British feeling that existed among many German officers after the Franco-Prussian War. Whereas it had been easy to exchange information about the latest military innovations before the war, this changed abruptly in 1872. 'There is such a reserve in conversation', Walker noted, 'that I have almost ceased to ask for information'.[16] Walker and Russell agreed that this was making their work awkward and that the new suspiciousness was highly unfair towards their own country, which had always been forthcoming with information.[17] Walker also suffered from the fact that the favoured nations among the Germans were now Russia and America, whereas the English were 'next to the French ... the least in favour'.[18] In his opinion the Germans showed their newly acquired superiority over the armies of Europe in a distastefully contemptuous way. This new German self-satisfaction affected all classes: 'There is no good will towards England in any class of the population ... all our shortcomings are commented on with ill-natured glee'.[19] The Germans acted like parvenus who were insecure about their newly acquired position and in return behaved boisterously. This insecurity ran through all classes of German society: 'I hear nothing of it towards myself, nothing definite, but I hear of it very frequently from country people who are passing through North Germany, and my views were emphatically confirmed by our capable consul in Danzig, Mr White, during his recent visit to Berlin'.[20] Walker attributed the 'bad feeling' between the nations to three main causes:

> 1. To the old ill-will ... which culminated at Waterloo. 2. To ignorance of the true bearing of English institutions. 3. To the extreme indiscretion and vulgarity of a too large proportion of the English Press, which has certainly done its very best to earn us the ill will of all of our neighbours.[21]

Odo never encountered as much rejection as Walker endured among the foulmouthed military men and was therefore often more lenient in his judgements about the average German's Anglophobia. Kennedy sees this as a major disadvantage: 'Russell's concentration upon the opinions of Bismarck and the gossip at court seems to have meant that his references to the more general aspects of the Anglo-German relationship — the strongly Anglophobic tone of much of the right-wing press, or the growing commercial rivalry — were only brief and fleeting'.[22] Though Odo passed on to the FO critical newspaper articles about England,[23] he would have never thought that there was an ingrained hatred of his country among the German population. The reason was probably that a worldly man like Russell simply could not understand such provincialism; his outlook on life had always been cosmopolitan and his search for harmony outweighed his anger about press attacks. Walker and Sir Joseph Archer Crowe,[24] who had been admirers of Germany in the 1860s, were much more critical in this respect and fought their own battles with German officialdom. This was because they felt the envy and competitiveness of the Germans more acutely and wanted to retaliate. This becomes evident for example in the following, on the surface harmless, story which Crowe told Odo in 1872:

> Just after Christmas a bag was received at the office of Count Bismarck addressed in Arabic character ... . It was soon apparent that no one in the *Auswärtiges Amt* [the Berlin FO] could decipher the [message]. Bismarck accordingly sent it down to the University professors for Oriental languages and after some time received it back again with the humiliating confession that no one among the Berlin Professors could read Persian.[25]

The parcel was finally sent to an expert in Leipzig and it turned out to be a '*suada* of thanks by the Shah's minister to BISIMARK, the saviour of Germany ... thanking BISIMARK for a present of a "Zündnadelgewehr" [a rifle that had been used in the Franco-Prussian war]'. 'The German press made great fun of the English FO', wrote Crowe, 'when it became apparent that no one could read Abyssinian. Our press might now return the compliment'.[26]

From the start, Crowe and Sir William Arthur White[27] were a great help to Odo in dealing with a wide variety of commercial matters. When, shortly after his arrival in Berlin, Russell had to report on the details of a commercial treaty between Germany and Britain, he turned to White for advice: 'Being rather new to things here I do not know where to get my information from and I should feel much obliged to you if you could point out to me in what books, reports ... I could get the necessary material'.[28] Crowe also often came to Berlin to help in commercial negotiations.[29] He was more than Odo's economics expert, he was, thanks to his old acquaintances such as Stosch, Roggenbach and Treitschke,[30] always well informed about all the relevant political implications too.

It is ironic that Russell, a child of the 'century of commerce'[31] did not know much about business.[32] He was, however, not at all as dismissive of it as his colleague Sir Philip Currie would be, who in the 1890s when 'asked for a general idea of the work of the Commercial Department, .. said, that, if he might put his answer in a concise form, he should say that it dealt with commercial matters'.[33] Russell had been one of the first ambassadors to support the idea of commercial attachés being appointed to the embassies. In 1879 — with the introduction of the German tariff — he suggested that a commercial expert should become a member of his staff. While Salisbury liked the proposal, it was at first 'discouraged' by the Under-Secretary at the Foreign Office who claimed that such attachés might use their 'insider knowledge' for accumulating some money on the side.[34] It took two more years (and growing economic difficulties between the two countries) until Crowe became the first commercial attaché at Odo's embassy in 1881, a role he had, unofficially, played for a long time.

The dismissiveness of the FO towards German commerce is shown in the following letter by Granville to Odo in which the appointment of a new Consul General was first discussed:

> Lord Granville is disposed to think that, in the absence of any great commercial interests in Berlin, the chief advantages of the appointment [of a Consul General] are connected with the holder of it being a person of wealth and consideration in the town of Berlin, and His Lordship would therefore wish to know whether it is advisable to find a successor to the late Baron Magnus.[35]

The candidates for the Consul Generalship were Mr Mendelssohn Bartholdy and Baron Bleichröder. The Foreign Secretary chose Bleichröder for the position. The decisive factor had been a despatch about a conversation between Odo and Bismarck.[36] Asked about Bleichröder, the Chancellor had said: 'Are you aware of the fact that Bleichröder administers my private fortune? If so, do you believe that I would mislead him?'[37] Bleichröder also advised the Emperor and the Crown Prince on financial matters as well and eventually became Odo's banker. In 1875, for example, he bought a holiday home for Russell in Potsdam (via a front man).[38] Bleichröder also helped Odo whenever he had problems 'with the mysteries of German accounting'.[39] In return Russell also did favours for Bleichröder. On one occasion he wrote several letters to the FO trying to promote a friend of Bleichröder, Albert Cohen, to become the Vice-Consul in Hannover. The FO, however, rejected this idea because they did not think that there was any need for such a position.[40]

Apart from such illustrious advisers, only one of Russell's secretaries seemed to have had a problematic character — the aforementioned Henry Dering, second secretary in Berlin from 1870 to 1873 and later secretary to Odo at the Congress of Berlin. Dering was outraged about not receiving a distinction afterwards,[41] even though he had to admit that he had not been 'charged with any special or confidential work relating to the Congress'.[42] This complaint was too much even for the patient Russell; in the only sharp letter that can be found among his staff correspondence, he replies:

> It was I and not HMG who appointed you on my own responsibility, before Lord Salisbury's arrival in Berlin, and before his sanction could even be obtained. Tell them [Dering's father and his 'condoling friends'] also that there were others who wanted the appointment and I took it upon myself to select you in preference to anyone else so as to serve your interests by bringing you into immediate [contact] with Lord Beaconsfield and Lord Salisbury. After what I have done it would be unfair ... to accuse me of not promoting your interest.[43]

Despite this rebuke, Dering stayed in Berlin until 1882. He was well aware of the fact that his chief had done everything to promote him, but the FO insisted that such a promotion was only possible after a transfer.[44] Apart from unbalanced secretaries, Russell also had to battle with unreliable servants. After a dinner with Herbert von Bismarck at the British Embassy, information reached the newspapers that his mother had been a 'difficult' guest. Odo had cut out the following newspaper article about the incident: 'If there is ill feeling between Prince Bismarck and Mr Gladstone, politics have nothing to do with it. The guilty person is the young Bismarck. At a dinner given by the British ambassador, Princess Bismarck appeared in the company of her son. Lady Russell, like all Englishwomen, likes fresh air, while Princess Bismarck despises the draught.' The article went on to explain that Emily Russell wanted all windows open while Princess Bismarck insisted on them being closed. When the servants hesitated, Herbert screamed at them so loudly that the other guests were highly irritated.[45] Such gossip naturally embarrassed Odo:

> We greatly fear, Lady Odo and myself, to judge from the enclosed article, that some of our servants may have been guilty of a want of respect to Princess Bismarck or to yourself and as my servants entirely deny there is any foundation whatever for this whole story which is going the round of the newspapers, I can only say that if unfortunately any of them should unbeknown to us have been in anyway wanting in respect to you I hope you will accept this expression of my most sincere regret.[46]

The young Bismarck did not seem to blame Russell and only a year later was his family's guest again in England (where he did, however, write letters predicting the ultimate downfall of Britain.)

Grievances about failed dinner parties were not the only petty problems an ambassador had to deal with. As in Rome, more than once Odo was confronted with British citizens who wandered about Germany, some of them slightly disturbed or, worse, penniless. Especially when they were female, Russell's chivalrous side was touched and he did everything in his power to help them. In June 1872 for example he sent to the Home Office a photograph of Mrs Stern, 'an unfortunate young English girl'[47] who, he feared, might have been the victim of a crime.[48] His 24-page-long description of her fate could have been written by a Brontë sister:

> There was something so taking about her extreme youth, her childlike innocence, her quiet ladylike bearing and the simple narrative of her sorrows that it was impossible to believe her to be a common adventuress. For the honour of womankind I almost hoped she might be mad, and as she was becoming sufficiently nervous and excitable to excuse such a step I sent her to the best mad doctor in Berlin.[49]

There she was diagnosed as suffering from hallucinations.[50] Later on it turned out that the beautiful Mrs Stern was in fact a fraud. Her 'statements were untrue' and Russell was not reimbursed for the £71 he had spent on the lady's accommodation and treatment in Germany. The reply from the FO was categorical: 'I regret that the kind and humane interest shown by Lord Odo Russell towards this person should have been thus abused, but I fear that the circumstances of the case, so far as I know them, will not warrant me in authorising the repayment of the expenses incurred by Lord Odo Russell out of public funds'.[51]

Russell also had to deal with British citizens who felt badly treated by the Prussian authorities. Since Palmerston's days the rights of British citizens abroad had been fiercely protected. Although Palmerston's successors were often less forceful in their means of protection, British ambassadors were expected to do their utmost to keep their compatriots out of continental prisons. Lord Clarendon's circular of 1 April 1870 was used by all ambassadors for guidance: 'when a case of a distressed British subject is brought under your notice, it will be your duty to cause a rigid inquiry to be made into the circumstances'.[52] It was therefore useful for Odo to be on very good terms with the Prussian Minister for Justice, Heinrich v. Friedberg. As mentioned earlier, Acton had praised Friedberg's writing and Odo soon found out that Friedberg was also very close to the Crown Prince. He befriended him and the minister helped Russell on many occasions — even in hopeless cases: 'Friedberg helped me to get a horrid miscreant out of prison in whom Lord Salisbury took an unaccountable interest', Odo wrote to Hastings in 1880. Unfortunately Salisbury had afterwards to be twice reminded to write a thank you letter to Friedberg which made Russell moan that: 'it is not easy to be an ambassador'.[53] Other cases were less complicated for the embassy staff. A Mr Hemmingway from Oxford had attempted to open a friendly conversation with German soldiers, yet was sadly misunderstood and beaten up: 'Captain Fleischmann at once hurried to the scene, but was unable to discover the offender and could do nothing more than express to Mr Hemmingway his regret at the occurrence'.[54] The culprit, a sergeant Jürgens, was brought to court yet, to Hemmingway's great outrage, not convicted.[55] For the rest of his days Hemmingway wrote letters complaining about this failure of the German legal system.

Another case was that of a Mr Stott from Dover, who seemed at the time to be considerably unbalanced. He claimed to be 'an inventor of a flying machine, which he proposed to exhibit at the Weißensee [a Berlin lake]'.[56] The exhibition never came off and he did not sell his invention to the German Government: 'The reason for this double failure', wrote Odo to the FO, 'results from the inability of Mr Stott to make his flying machine rise from the ground'.[57] Mr Stott ran up a bill of £50 at his hotel and was asked to leave. Though Russell offered to pay his travel expenses to England, the inventor refused indignantly 'as he objected to a long sea passage'.[58] Home in England, Mr Stott complained about the bad treatment he had received at the Berlin Embassy.

Further, though less bizarre, cases that needed the ambassador's intervention included for example: those of two young British boys who were severely maltreated by their employer, a circus director; the highly publicised law suit of the British emigration agent John Dyke; and the struggle of Mr Kingston, a *Daily Telegraph* journalist, with the German authorities (Kingston had dug too deeply into the Arnim case).[59] The case of Dyke in particular was difficult for Russell to handle. Because of the enormous emigration wave after the Franco-Prussian war, German authorities tried to make the life of emigration agents as difficult as possible. While some German states had between 1820 and 1860 tried to get rid of their criminal elements by making them go to the United States, by 1871, German authorities were afraid of losing young men, good farm workers and future soldiers, who were attracted 'by the Republican form of Government [in America] and the cheapness of the land'.[60] The German papers were full of articles about emigrants to Canada who had lost their German citizenship and were not entitled to a British one, living unprotected in the wilderness (both legally and figuratively).[61] Yet all these warnings did not help, according to the report of Odo Russell's chargé d'affaire: 'I have reason to believe that there is no diminution in the numbers who daily leave this country to seek a new home ... higher wages and especially freedom from military service appeal far more strongly to the mind of the German peasant or artisan than the warning voice of the Imperial authorities'.[62] The Prussian Minister of the Interior had therefore declared that he would combat the 'evils' arising from emigration (for the economy and the army) by, first, controlling emigration agents and second by trying to create 'laws to endear this country to the [would be] emigrants'.[63] This would be done by creating more jobs, developing industry, increasing construction work and extending roads and railways.[64] Yet before such plans could be set in motion, men such as Dyke had to be stopped. Dyke was a British citizen (and therefore the responsibility of the British Embassy) and an emigration agent of the Ontarian Government. The charge against Dyke was that he had unlawfully 'induced German subjects to emigrate to Ontario'. He had violated the Penal Code[65] by '[seducing] people to emigrate under false pretences'.[66] On Granville's instructions the British Embassy paid the bail for Dyke, yet Russell thought this a mistake: 'Great inconvenience may arise', he wrote to the Foreign Secretary, 'from the precedent established by your Lordship'.[67] It would encourage, in Odo's opinion, British emigration agents to come to Germany in great numbers and upset the German ruling classes.[68] Despite such misgivings about the case, Odo tried to help Dyke. He made it clear to Balan at the German FO, that Dyke had never made false promises and that his imprisonment was based on a misunderstanding. Dyke was eventually set free, but the problem of the status of emigration agents in Germany remained.

Another 'nuisance' Russell had to cope with almost daily, was the eagerness of British citizens to be presented at the German court. Together with Morier, Odo tried to change the rules for this procedure:

> In Berlin ... candidates are invited to the Balls ... where they are expected to behave properly and do honour to their nationality — which, I regret to say, is not always the case with Brown, Jones and Robinson, not to say Smith. Now, I quite agree with you that we should cover the responsibility we are supposed to incur, by written certificates and characters. ... My object in asking for a soup ticket is to make the FO share part of our responsibility in the event of Smith getting drunk at supper and not being thought 'ein feiner Weltmann'[a refined man of the world] by the natives.[69]

Such relatively minor problems were duly dealt with by the new ambassador. What Russell's mind really had to struggle with was analysing German foreign and domestic politics. His first reports in 1872 were cautious 'because I do not feel sufficiently up in the questions before me and I am extremely anxious to understand them myself before I explain them to others'.[70]

The Strousberg Palais in the 1860s before it became the British Embassy.

CHAPTER 5

Russell's Evaluation of the New German Foreign Policy

Britain and Germany

To understand the British attitude towards Germany in the years after 1871, it is useful to interrupt the chronology for a brief moment and go back in time. British politicians, especially Palmerston, had during the early stages of the German revolution of 1848 sympathised with the German professors at Frankfurt and their rather unprofessional struggle to create a united Germany. This was also true of the British Royal family, who had always shown an interest in German affairs. The Prince Consort's plan of 24 March 1848 rejected the idea of a centralised German Government and pleaded for a German Emperor elected by German princes for 10 years or for life. Queen Victoria would never forget her husband's dreams and would remain, despite her criticism of Bismarck's methods, Germany's greatest supporter. Her subjects, however, were quite indifferent about Germany. As Paul Kennedy observes in his standard work on British–German relations, the picture British people held of Germany was as heterogeneous as the country itself. During the 1850s and early 1860s, the minority of the British public that showed an interest seemed to hold a rather condescending opinion of Teutonic power politics. The many German dukedoms were looked on as quarrelling, selfish dwarfs that were trying to expand their territory and suppress liberal opposition in a reactionary way. As a consequence British politicians and newspapers, torn between shock and amusement, often played the part of the father scolding his gifted but over-active offspring. The sensitivity that had developed especially within the British–Prussian relationship can, for example, be illustrated in the rather trivial but poignant Macdonald incident. In 1860, a Captain Macdonald, who was travelling through Germany, tried to occupy a row of seats in a Prussian railway carriage by distributing his vast amount of luggage on them. He refused to take any of it away when the ticket collector appeared and both men started a heated quarrel that ended violently. Macdonald was arrested for attacking the ticket collector and, after a highly publicised trial, jailed for a couple of days. British and German papers covered the incident by calling each other's countrymen arrogant and dangerous. In parliament an MP even warned travellers not to go to Prussia because they 'were liable to dangers to which they were not subject in any other country in Europe'. Such ignorance seemed to be universal.

As has already been noted, British diplomats did not know much about Prussian affairs. Apart from Morier, who was until 1871 at the court of Hesse Darmstadt, none of Odo's Berlin predecessors showed any outstanding analytical perception about developments in Germany during the three major crises of the 1860s. Sir Andrew Buchanan, who was posted in Berlin during the Danish war, never, for example, managed to become a political, let alone a social success. He spent most of his time waiting in front of Bismarck's office and, when at last he managed to gain entry, he regularly started to quarrel with him. These arguments all took place in English (which should have given Buchanan an advantage) and all had one subject: Buchanan's great sympathy for and defence of Denmark, where he had been posted in the 1850s. The less quarrelsome Lord Napier followed in late 1864 and was condescendingly labelled as 'reliable' by Bismarck. As a consequence, Napier was recalled. After an interval Lord Loftus was appointed who, as has been shown before, was of no great help in enlightening the FO during the 1866 and 1870 wars.

As a result of the works of Mosse, Millman, Kennedy and Hildebrand, we know that Britain passively supported the process of German unification. There were several reasons for this, which Hildebrand categorised as being geographical, ideological and economic in nature. The rise of Germany meant first and foremost that there was a counter-balance to France and Russia, the two powers that Britain was at constant pains to keep in check (France in the Mediterranean, Russia in Central Asia). A strong third continental power might cause some friction for a time, but the long-term hope was that it would become a stabilising force. Given these considerations one might have expected that Gladstone's and Granville's policy towards Germany after 1871 would have been supportive. However, Gladstone had trepidations: 'Germany crowned with glory and confident in her strength, will start on her new career to encounter the difficulties of the future without the sympathies of Europe: which in my opinion no nation, not even we in our sea girthed spot can afford to lose'.[1] From this it seems that Gladstone did not place much credibility on Bismarck's post-bellum assurances that Germany was a saturated power. When the Liberal MP Cartwright carefully tried to convey to the Prime Minister the idea of an 'understanding between modern Germany and the great Liberal Party in England'[2] he failed totally: '[The PM] told him [Cartwright] that for 20 years there could be no sympathy between the Liberal party in England and Prussia and if the annexation of the new provinces necessitates severe measures the angry feeling must [grow] faster'.[3] Cartwright found that it was hopeless to argue with Gladstone: 'If for example you tell him [Gladstone] that you think Germany will become a pacific power he reminds you of Denmark, Austria and France'.[4] This opinion was shared by a lot of MPs. Arthur Russell recorded that, shortly after the war, the general atmosphere towards Germany remained hostile:

> Prussia now represents all that is most antagonistic to liberal and democratic ideas of the age: military despotism, the rule of the sword, contempt for sentimental talk, indifference to human suffering, imprisonment of independent opinion, transfer by force of unwilling populations to a hateful yoke, disregard of European opinion, total want of greatness and generosity, etc., etc.[5]

But despite this distrust, the British Government had no intention of mingling in either German or continental affairs. Gladstone was more preoccupied with his reform programmes and domestic issues than with foreign affairs (Hildebrand has shown how Britain went through an inward-looking period during the late 1860s and early 1870s, whereas Germany at the same time was in the opposite mode, fixed on its external relations.) The pressure of British public opinion had been pivotal in bringing about domestic reform, but it would soon demand a stronger focus on foreign affairs, something which Gladstone underestimated. He remained satisfied with his policy of non-intervention and had no intention of becoming the 'world's policeman'.[6] One can therefore say that after the Franco-Prussian war, British foreign policy towards the continent was almost a 'non-policy' which was detrimental to the morale of the diplomatic caste. As has already been seen in the chapter on Russell as a 'pen-pusher', Odo used to joke to Morier about the indifference of the FO towards his despatches. But of course he did not take this as lightly as he pretended. Gladstone's 'diplomatic minimalism'[7] did upset Russell. It seemed that his profession was condemned to a secondary role in British political life:

> Isn't it *spasshaft* [Odo wrote to Morier] that while 'a diplomacy' conveyed in a few dispatches or private letters to HM agents abroad might secure the peace of the world, the development of human intellect, the security, prosperity and wealth of England, at a cost not exceeding the postage of said dispatches or private letters,

the people of England should enthusiastically vote fifteen millions p.a. for the reorganisation of an army which, though undoubtedly the best and most efficient in the world, will numerically not exceed a single foreign army corps? ... I am all for a first rate army and incomparable navy — but I should like a policy besides, to render both useless.[8]

In a conversation with the Crown Prince, Odo had once said that British diplomacy ought to be organised like the Prussian army or the Society of Jesus.[9] It was imperative in his opinion that diplomats should have a creed to believe in, but this was very much missing. Odo belonged to a group of young diplomats who did not think that non-intervention combined with, as Kennedy calls it, 'appeals to moral forces'[10] would do any longer. Gladstone's moral indignation (in the Alsace–Lorraine case and even during the Bulgarian atrocities) was looked down upon by Odo. In his view a 'quasi-Palmerstonian style'[11] was needed instead: 'uncle John's policy which was an imitation of Lord Palmerston's and has been abused and called the "meddle and muddle" policy is in reality a truly national policy and will soon be missed by John Bull and Lord Stanley, non-interference will be thought weak'.[12] However, such a policy was not to be and the outcome was, as Russell explained to his friend Lady Derby, that: 'England no longer counts as her neutrality relieves all continental Powers of the necessity of consulting her, nor is her alliance of any practical use in the opinion of foreign Governments since we are not a fighting ally'.[13]

Odo seems to comment on this matter of factly, yet in reality he was desolate about Bismarck's reported lack of respect for England as an active political power. However, he would not let this show to a Tory, and therefore finished on a more patriotic note to Lady Derby (although she was a confidante, she still belonged in political terms to the 'other side' and Russell must have been aware of her love for diplomatic 'gossiping' at a high level):

> This [the neutrality] gives us a safe position and enables us to do good in a quiet way and increase our wealth and prosperity. Our neutral, pacific, conciliatory policy has not yet been well understood on the continent and is mistaken for weakness, *which it is not*. It will take time to be *pacific* and powerful and [then] we can easily make friends with her.[14]

Odo was far from enthusiastic about the subject of English isolation when he wrote to his Liberal colleagues in the diplomatic service. Here he did not have to pretend any more. In letters to Lytton, Lyons and Morier he openly deplored his Government's policy of indifference and the weaknesses it had displayed over the last years. They reciprocated wholeheartedly. Lytton, who up until 1872 had been secretary at the British Embassy in Austria, also despaired about the FO's lack of enthusiasm for even the slightest commitment on the continent. When Lytton failed to achieve a 'closer understanding' (he did not dare to use the word 'alliance' in case it might scare Lord Granville) between Austria and Britain, he had to ask himself 'whether our foreign policy is one of "non-intervention" or of absolute indifference and political nihilism',[15] It must have been increasingly frustrating for ambitious diplomats such as Lytton and Odo to operate within a Foreign Office vacuum that did not allow 'daringly' close relationships with any country except for the purpose of the usual exchanges of good wishes.[16] Not only did Gladstone not want to enter into new continental commitments, he even seemed to be hesitant about fulfilling existing ones. The PM made a speech in 1872 in which he described Britain's guarantee of Belgium as being 'optional', which upset Russell's circle considerably. Odo himself was close to desperation:

> Gladstone's speech explaining away our guarantee of Belgium ... has produced a deep impression among politicians here [in Berlin]. It is thought to mean: if France wishes for Belgium and Germany for Holland 'ce n'est pas nous' who would fight to prevent it. It is looked upon as our formal abdication as one of the great powers because everybody still thought we would fight for one thing only in Europe, and that was Belgium. The moral effect of the declaration will be deep and lasting in Europe — and probably Mr Gladstone is utterly unconscious of the importance of his declaration as regards our international position in Europe? Eh? Bismarck is reported to have said on reading Gladstone's speech: 'so Belgium has lost her only friend and parent!' I could now write a powerful despatch, on the decline and fall of British influence abroad, but it would be taken for spite against Gladstone which I really don't feel — quite the contrary ... but I cannot help feeling humiliated like Uncle John at the unnecessary weakness of our leaders. Oh! for a Palmerston, a Russell, a Clarendon during this great European crisis![17]

The Queen of Holland shared Odo's despair, sighing that 'Belgium, England's beloved baby, will now be abandoned for the next 20 years. Later, heaven knows!'[18] However, Arthur could not agree with all this. He felt annoyed by the defeatist language of his brother (who judged British foreign policy too bleakly) and Odo had to try to defend himself in long letters: 'I don't want to abuse him [Gladstone], I wish to admire him — I do admire him in most things, but some things he does I cannot comprehend. His foreign policy humiliates me, although I believe his home policy to be excellent ... Everything that lowers our moral standard at home and abroad offends and humiliates me'.[19] Odo repeated this thought a few months later, when he wrote:

I felt that [the Cabinet's] foreign policy was *weak*. I thought so equally in the Black Sea Question, and in their Alabama policy, they appeared to me to be wanting in grave and difficult questions. [Granville and Gladstone] have the best will to do what is right, but an undercurrent of *weakness*, which emboldens our neighbours to kick us with impunity. This is *weakness*, not to say self-deception, the same *weakness* and self-deception I have felt to be at the bottom of the whole of Mr Gladstone's foreign policy.[20]

Although it is beyond the scope of this chapter to go into the depths of the *Alabama* affair[21] it is important to note that it exacerbated the feeling of frustration among Odo's friends. Of course, Russell was painfully aware that the *Alabama* problem was a legacy the government had inherited from his own uncle. During the American Civil War, Britain had adopted a position of neutrality. However, Washington claimed that in providing (knowingly or not) the South with the warship *Alabama* the British had broken their neutrality. The ship had caused great damage to the Yankees, for which compensation was demanded after the war. Odo thought that the American handling of the case had been far superior to that of the British:

To me it appears that from beginning to end — from the Adams–Russell negotiations to the publication of the American case ... the American Government have ... step by step, increased their pretensions and their demands and have never gone back an iota. ... No doubt the Yankees wish to settle this much vexed question, but on their terms and not on ours.[22]

In the end the affair was settled in September 1872 in favour of the United States, which received a sum of £3,299,166 in compensation.[23] In Odo's opinion, England had again been outmanoeuvred: 'Just as we lost the withdrawal of Gortschakoff's Black Sea note, when we accepted a conference to discuss it'.[24] For Odo's circle the whole episode constituted significant evidence of the lack of backbone in the Gladstone ministry.[25] Odo was quite blunt when writing to his friend Morier about this: 'there is a most decided *Scheissangst* ['shit fear' or holy dread] of our American cousins to whom we would willingly pay 5 milliards for the sake of a quiet life'.[26]

Russell's fear that Bismarck was included amongst those not taking Britain seriously was based on the countless incidents in which the Germans had joked about British foreign politics. The Chancellor had often talked about England as a country that had 'retired from active cooperation in European affairs'.[27] This, at least, was Bismarck's perception before the war-in-sight crisis and the purchase of the Suez Canal shares. Morier reported that 'it is a favourite saying of Prince Bismarck, that he lost 5 years of his political life by the foolish belief that England was still a great power'.[28] Major General Walker had heard similar utterings from the members of the German military including that 'England is of no use as a friend and is almost harmless as an enemy'.[29] One man who was in Odo's opinion particularly active in adding fuel to such feelings was the American envoy to Berlin, Bancroft:

> To prevent a recurrence of what was called our 'benevolent neutrality' [in 1870–1871], Mr Bancroft is said to have offered the assistance of America to occupy the attention of England, and M. de Krause, the German Secretary of the Embassy in London, to have been instructed to study and report the advantages to Germany of hostilities between England and America, as proposed by Mr Bancroft.[30]

While Bancroft was almost openly intriguing against England, he wrote flattering letters to the British embassy, the hypocrisy of which defy description. Among other hyperboles, he praised Victoria as 'the best native Prince who has sat on the English throne, since the days of Queen Elizabeth'.[31] However, it was finding a way to throw her off that throne that seemed to occupy his mind most of the time. The FO was incredulous of such behaviour and Odo had to try to convince them by explaining Bancroft's character to Granville:

> In reply to your question about Bancroft's offer of American assistance to occupy the attention of England while Germany is fighting France, I will give you my reasons for this statement. I had heard from my colleagues, from Prussian officials, professors and members of parliament that Bancroft's hostility to England was a mania, and that he often predicted that Germany and America would fight England together. From the same people I heard that Bancroft Davis, his nephew, who was here last spring, told the German officials and members of parliament he spoke to that America would always be ready to act with Germany in giving England a lesson. From D. Abel, the Prussian correspondent of *The Times*, I heard incidentally that Bismarck exaggerated the value of an American alliance against England. With my own eyes I saw that Bismarck was more partial to Bancroft than to other diplomatists. ... I learnt that ... he held that America could be made a useful ally to Germany and should be treated accordingly.[32]

This was, of course, only Bismarckian game play. The Chancellor knew very well that he needed allies in Europe more urgently than in a far away continent. The British were therefore never seriously alarmed by these reports, but nevertheless remained watchful. This was also the case when in 1872 the possibility of a German invasion of England was discussed in Berlin's military circles. General Walker reported the details to Odo, but did not seem to be too concerned by such talk:

among other studies elaborated and stored up in the archives of the General Staff in Berlin the plan for the invasion of England finds a place amongst others already known ... It is in truth a mere matter of business, there is no special intention connected with it, no particular or immediate ill will towards England, though it cannot be doubted that enough of that feeling exists in more than one influential quarter.[33]

One of Walker's German friends, Colonel Boerdonsy, had travelled to England on a secret mission in 1872 and had afterwards been quite open in telling the British military attaché that the adventure of an invasion would not pay.[34] Walker was in no way an alarmist and believed his friend. Two years later he still did not think that an invasion would take place, despite the bragging of some German military men:

I believe an invasion of England to be attended with such political ... risk to the assailant, that no German statesman in the possession of his senses will attempt it, but I cannot conceal from myself the danger that the most powerful state in Europe might stand aloof from England when her distant interests were menaced, and might lend to her rival [in this case Russia] that same moral assistance which her rival lent to Germany during the French war, and which is so gratefully remembered in this country.[35]

Odo himself had quickly learned to distinguish between the bragging of officers and the Realpolitik of Bismarck:

That soldiers flushed with victory and rolling in booty should study and dream of the invasion of a country known to be richer ... and believed to be allied to an enemy preparing for a war of revenge, lies in the nature of things. Happily, however, for the peace of the world, armies are instruments in the hands of diplomacy, and the statesmen of Germany earnestly desire friendship with England rather than war.[36]

Odo was correct in believing that the views of German officers were not representative of Bismarck's foreign policy. Nevertheless, their language was irritating and could not be completely ignored. Although Russell did not fall for the bizarre idea of an invasion, his frequent conversations with Moltke reminded him again of British weakness:

When we have neither moral influence abroad, nor the means of defence at home, but plenty of wealth and weakness, the foreigner will soon find an excuse for invading us and taking our milliards — not necessarily by force of arms, but by force of arbitration, and what foreign nation ... would not chuckle to humiliate us and make us pay?[37]

Of course, Odo knew that in general Bismarck wanted to be on good terms with England. Still, the British Ambassador did not relax his guard.

Austria and Russia

In the period after 1871 Bismarck did his best to demonstrate to the world that Germany was at last a peaceful and satiated power. Yet Russell was far from convinced by these efforts:

> A man who has secretly planned three successful wars, defeated two great powers, created an Empire in the centre of Europe, and made himself the irresponsible leader of a nation of warriors, is open to suspicion and distrust ever after as no one can foretell what he may do with the power he has acquired.[1]

Odo felt that German consolidation had not yet run its full course and that a further war of unification might become necessary. However, he differed from many foreign observers on one point. The natural target for the next war would not be France but Austria.[2]

Russell was not the only foreigner who thought that Bismarck would be forced to incorporate all Germans into his Empire. Jules Favre pretended to believe in the same idea and tried to use it to divide Russia and Germany in July 1871.[3] Naturally, Bismarck was aware of these suspicions and did his best to allay them. In 1871 he had already in Gastein tried to tell a wary Beust that it would be the worst policy for Germany to gain provinces which were a hotbed of 'Catholicism'.[4] He also assured Russell personally that he would oppose such annexations 'as long as he [Bismarck] was in power, because he preferred the alliance and friendship of Austria to the annexation of provinces that would add nothing to the strength and security of Germany and the loss of which would lessen the value of Austria as an ally'.[5]

This should have sounded convincing and with the benefit of hindsight one can perhaps take the view that Russell's forecast of another German-Austrian war was rather eccentric. The question therefore is, why did Odo not trust the Chancellor's assurances when it came to the territorial integrity of Austria? Russell was not worried so much by Bismarck but by two camps which had much to gain from another war and might try to drag the Chancellor into it — the army and the National Liberals. All the anti-Austrian propaganda Odo had heard came from Bismarck's political partners at the time: 'The German National Party hold that the exclusion of Austria from the German Confederation by the war of 1866 has weakened the strategical position of the new German Empire, — because in the event of war, Austria, as a non-German power, can throw her weight either on the side of Russia, or of France, or of both against Prussia, which as a member of the German Confederation, Austria could not do before 1866'.[6] As will be shown later, Odo was already appalled by the influence the National Liberals had on the war against the German Catholics. In his opinion they now tried to exert the same power when it came to foreign policy decisions:

> The National Party, since they have defeated the Conservatives, the Particularists and the Clericals under Prince Bismarck's leadership, and have got the administration into their hands, no longer conceal their belief in the inevitable dissolution of the Austrian Empire ... They also consider the German provinces of Austria the legitimate inheritance of the German Empire, so that in the event of a war [between Russia and Austria over Turkey] the National Party would feel a greater interest in the speedy dissolution of the Austrian Empire.[7]

An anonymous letter sent from the Berlin embassy to the FO also raised fears as to the possible intentions of the National Liberal Party. Two sentences in particular make one assume that the writer belonged to Russell's circle of friends, or at least sympathised with the ambassador's ideas: '[the agenda] of the National Liberals is the completion of German unity before everything else. ... Will they be satisfied with anything less than the annexation of all the territory inhabited by German-speaking people?'[8]

As he would do with the Kulturkampf, Odo again questioned who was influencing whom (Bismarck the National Liberals, or the reverse) with regard to Austria. In Russell's view the Chancellor was politically dependent on the support of the National Liberals in so many ways, that there was a real danger it might influence his decision-making process. Whenever there was a war scare against France in the years leading up to 1875, Odo suggested to the FO that this was just a diversion to distract attention from Germany's real objective — that of attacking Austria. Derby, for one, was genuinely confused by such reports. In 1875 The Foreign Secretary wrote to his man in Vienna, Buchanan:

> Opinions agree to the extreme probability of Bismarck making war ... but they differ as to the object of attack. ... Lord Odo Russell, as you know, thinks that Austria is to be the next victim. His argument is, that France has no German provinces to lose, and that Austria has: that even Bismarck would not undertake to conquer and hold a large extent of ... French soil, while (as you also say) there are parts of the Austrian dominions in which the idea of annexation to Germany would not be disagreeable.[9]

Russell's fears with regard to Austria were taken seriously at the FO because they were confirmed by Bismarck's arch-enemy in London, the Austrian ambassador, Count Beust. Beust, who was always good for an intrigue against Bismarck, coincided with Odo in his views:[10] 'He (Beust) seemed to take Russell's view', Derby wrote, 'i.e. to think that France is only threatened and bullied, Austria attacked. I do not feel capable of deciding in such a matter'.[11] Bismarck knew very well how dangerous Beust was and tried to discredit him whenever he could, which — predictably — resulted in English newspapers taking the side of the Austrian underdog. In his memoirs Beust proudly claims that the *Standard* was of the opinion that he simply could not have had enough hands to write all the things he had been accused of by Russia and Germany.

Russell's sensitivity was often very accurate in detecting subtle plots, but he sometimes really over-estimated the complexity of situations. His prediction of a war between Germany and Austria was definitely his worst blunder.[12] First of all, he misjudged public opinion. Although there were groups in the population who were interested in a 'greater German' solution (the Catholic element was surprisingly divided about it while the socialists saw the loss of Austria as tragic),[13] Treitschke probably spoke for the majority when he described such 'dreams' as 'sentimental' and dangerous to the Empire.[14] A further reason why Odo's analysis was wrong, was that, for once, he had misjudged Bismarck and the nature of his relationship with his political partners. The Chancellor had been completely honest when he told Russell that he had no interest in destroying the Habsburg monarchy. Bismarck could have annexed parts of Austria in 1866, but he was aware of the fact that this would have resulted in a dangerous influx of Slavic and Catholic German elements into the *Reich* he was building. It would have meant the end of a well-ordered revolution from above and set the scenario for endless little wars within Europe. Also, with a dismembered Austria, Germany would have been completely dependent on Russia. With it united, however, Bismarck could keep the Czar and Gortschakoff in check.[15] Russell also under-estimated the influence that the Chancellor had on the National Liberals. Bismarck had many possible combinations of alliances up his sleeve (at different times he played with the idea of a German-British-Austrian alliance, even a German-British-Russian one or the more realistic German-Austrian-Russian one) and it was certainly not part of his make-up to allow any party to interfere with his plans.

A further reason why Odo arrived at the wrong conclusion was that he had been acutely out of touch with Austrian affairs after 1866. This was mainly the fault of his colleague in Vienna, Buchanan, who was not capable of giving any perceptive insights into Austrian affairs. Despite humouring Buchanan, Odo was deeply unsatisfied with the majority of his despatches and, in a conversation with Lady Derby mentioned 'the inefficiency of Buchanan at Vienna. Andrássy says he can do no business with him: and the old man himself evidently has no idea of retiring, but does as little as he can. In present circumstances (i.e. of the Eastern Question) this is a serious drawback'.[16] Yet it would have been too easy to place the blame on Buchanan alone. In many ways, Odo's psychological heritage was responsible for his wrong analysis too. His perception of Austria was probably too emotional, involving a nostalgic feeling of someone who was idealising his youth (and forgetting his problems as a young diplomat there.) This can be seen in a sentimental letter Odo wrote to Lytton:

> I loved the city with its foolish and lovable inhabitants, and have not been there since the houses, walks and trees, I loved have been destroyed. ... The Vienna I mean was the Vienna of Kasperl, ... Elysium und Würstelprater, ... Strauss Grand-father. I should not like to see Vienna again, - it would make me 'zu wehmütig' [too sad and sentimental] for not only has my Vienna been demolished, but the friends of my youth are dead and gone and nothing is left of the Tümmelplatz meiner Jugend [the playground of my youth].[17]

To Russell, the new role that the Habsburg Empire played in Europe after 1866 was humiliating in comparison to its past grandeur. One only has to imagine the situation of Austria at the time. After a recently lost war, the country, with its complex supranational identity, was suddenly turned into a junior partner of its former adversary, Germany.[18] At the time of Odo's assignment in Berlin, Austria had less power in its relationship with Germany than it would have in the 1890s. The exclusion from the *Reich* was strongly felt by the German population in Austria,[19] and Russell worried about the disorientation and vulnerability which his friends in the Austrian establishment seemed to suffer from. Because of their embittered reports, Odo could not believe that 'Prussia' and Austria, who had always been rivals, could be so easily reconciled by the alliance of the Three Emperors' League.

A rapprochement between Austria and Germany had, however, slowly become possible after Beust's 'abdication', and Andrássy's rise to power. Bismarck had once said to Odo that alliances often depended solely on the chemistry between the personalities who formed them. This could certainly be said of Bismarck and Andrássy's down-to-earth relationship. Although Odo acknowledged this closeness, in his eyes Andrássy's fall was always a possibility and would immediately alter Germany's policy towards Austria:

But if at any time Count Andrássy should be replaced by an anti-German or Ul-tramontane Minister with French, Catholic or Russian sympathies, the artificial ties which now hold Austria to Germany would-be rent asunder, international distrust would ensue, and the Imperial Government would have to adopt a policy calcu-lated to satisfy the National Party.[20]

So how did Russell assess the worthiness of the Three Emperors' League, this revival of the holy alliance, if he was so suspicious of the Austrian–German relationship?

The meeting of the Emperors of Austria, Russia and Germany in September 1872 had been 'orchestrated' by Bismarck to show Germany as the peaceful new power on the continent. Yet right from the start, the suspicious Russell had detected cracks in the beautifully staged Imperial gathering.[21] In his analysis of the antecedents of the meeting, he correctly showed that it had been an artificial construction right from the start, built out of a predicament, rather than real conviction on Bismarck's side:

> I believe that Prince Bismarck originally intended to form an alliance with Aus-tria, without Russia, for the promotion of German interests only, and at the same time to liberate the new German Emperor from the protectorate the Czar has ever sought to impose on the King of Prussia. Prince Gortschakoff, seeing the danger to which an Austrian-German alliance and the consequent isolation of Russia, with no other ally but bleeding France, exposed his country, persuaded his august master to travel five days and nights from the Crimea to Berlin, ... in order to neutralise the exclusive character of this Austro-German meeting, and reassert by his pres-ence ... the traditional protectorate of Russia over Prussia. The Emperor William, having accepted the Czar's unexpected and self-invited co-operation, Prince Bis-marck was obliged to make the best of an unsought for and unavoidable combi-nation, which his fertile imagination and boundless resources will readily turn to Germany's advantage.[22]

The first part of the letter shows that Odo believed that for the time being Bismarck wanted to have a strong Austria. Later, Odo added in a letter to Buchanan that although Bismarck might still want this, the National Liberals would prevent it.[23] Russell's analysis as far as Russian interference in the meeting was concerned was, however, correct. The Czar had forced himself on Bismarck. In retaliation the Chancellor made sure that no binding alliances but only a more general undertaking to consult in crisis situations was agreed on. During the whole meeting, the Emperors of Russia and Austria took great pains to show the British ambassador that they had not gathered in Berlin to conspire against Britain. Franz Joseph himself visited Odo at the embassy, assuring him that the meetings were being held to enlarge the peace and welfare of Europe.[24] Russell also had a meeting with Andrássy:

Count Andrássy, whom I had formerly known as a refugee, told me in the warmest and most eloquent terms that all his sympathies were with England. He sincerely regretted that her neutrality stood in the way of that intimate and active cooperation with Austria that had been the dream of his life. Now he felt that the existence of Austria depended on a cordial alliance with Germany.[25]

The Emperors of Russia and Germany also talked in the same soothing language to Odo, assuring him that only good would come out of the 'peace policy' which would now be inaugurated.[26] Odo summed up his impressions of the Congress in his famous secret report, which has since been referred to by many historians. It is the ideal textbook quote, colourful, accurate and to the point:

> In an after dinner conversation I had with Prince Bismarck at the Imperial Palace, the Chancellor, who was unusually cheerful, pointed to the three Emperors and made the following remarks in English, which, quaint as they were, I must endeavour to give verbatim: 'We have witnessed a novel sight today; it is the first time in history that three Emperors have sat down to dinner together for the promotion of peace. My object is fully attained, and I think your Government will approve of my work ... I wanted three Emperors to form a loving group, like Canova's three graces, that Europe might see a living symbol of peace and have faith in it. I wanted them to stand in a silent group and allow themselves to be admired, difficult as it was, because they all three think themselves greater statesmen than they are.[27]

This famous description about 'his' Imperial puppets is probably one of Bismarck's most breathtaking ones.[28] Despite England having played an outsider's role, Odo was not dissatisfied with the outcome of the meeting. To Hammond he wrote that 'England was most civilly treated in my humble person and from all sides I met with the most demonstrative international good will'.[29]

In the aftermath of the conference, Britain was, to Odo's great surprise, accused in one German paper of jealousy, and he was personally attacked for not illuminating the embassy house on the last day of the celebrations: 'The meeting of the Emperors has in fact come to pass without any representative of England, and the English embassy has made a striking – if not brilliant impression by its dark dismal seriousness during the general illumination'.[30] The accusation was untrue, but it showed that England — so shortly after the war — had to be careful about not treading on German hypersensitive nerves.

The meeting of the Three Emperors was followed by a military convention with Russia and then the Schönbrunn Convention, which finally created the Three Emperors' League in October 1873. Because Bismarck feared that England might react against this new 'Northern alliance' by becoming closer with France, he invited Gladstone to join the alliance. True to his policy, the British Prime Minister did not respond to the offer. His only concession was to eventually sign an agreement with Russia allocating spheres of interest in central Asia.[31]

The existence of the Three Emperors' League did not allay Odo's fears of a war with Austria for long. He continued to see the Habsburg Empire as the weakest partner in the fragile triangle, going so far as to call it a German or Russian vassal.[32] Odo found confirmation of his opinion, in an article in the *Allgemeine Zeitung*, where Austria was depicted as being subservient and dependent upon the 'good will of Germany and Russia'.[33] Therefore, in Odo's eyes, the outlook remained bleak for Austria: 'It appears to me ... that the very existence of the Austrian Empire depends on the submission of her statesmen to the will of her Russian and German allies and protectors'.[34]

The dual alliance Austria and Germany entered into in 1879 was of course the opposite of what Russell had predicted. He had never seriously believed in their closeness and was now being lectured that this alliance had always been a long-term plan of Bismarck's:

> Prince Bismarck's friends say that while he was cutting Austria adrift from the confederation to assert the supremacy of Prussia in Germany, the intention to make a future ally of Austria was already in his mind, and that it was to facilitate an early realisation of that intention that he so strenuously resisted his royal master's desire to annex the conquered kingdom of Bohemia during the peace negotiations which followed the seven weeks war of 1866.[35]

The British welcomed the alliance because it seemed to be directed against their foe, Russia. But Russell dampened the premature jubilation: 'I am convinced that Prince Bismarck's real object is not to quarrel or go to war with Russia, but on the contrary to compel by temporary isolation to reflect and to reenter the "Dreikaiserbund" (Three Emperors' League) on his own terms and not on those of Prince Gortschakoff which have more or less prevailed since 1875'.[36] Not a bad prediction for someone who had been wrong for so long.

Because for many years Russell did not believe in the assurances that Germany had no further territorial ambitions with respect to Austria, Hans Rothfels has accused him of playing a double game. Rothfels claims that with his despatches Odo increased English fears of German expansionism, while at the same time cunningly playing the role of the benevolent mediator with Bismarck: 'the channel through which such suspicions reached London was via Russell and ... Morier.... Bismarck was completely in the dark about Russell's part'.[37] Even if Russell had played such a double game, it would only have proved what a skilful diplomat he was. Rothfels has of course a point as far as Austria is concerned, but he is wrong in describing Odo as a war-monger. One of his accusations is that Russell took the possibility of a German annexation of the Netherlands seriously.[38] Such a view is contradicted by the fact that Odo had dutifully reported very early in 1873 a conversation he had had with Bismarck, in which the Chancellor denied any such intentions: 'even the Emperor William's insatiable desire for more territory had not led him to covet the possession of the Netherlands'.[39] The correspondence of Russell's friends also shows that Odo did not believe in the possibility of further annexations: 'Bismarck desires neither ... the cession of the Empire of Holland, Denmark or any other German country,' Lyons wrote to Bulwer Lytton after a conversation with Odo.[40] In truth, the rumour about an occupation of the Netherlands had not been initiated by Odo, but by the Queen of Holland. Because of her close friendship with Whig politicians as well as with Lady Salisbury, who was now married to Lord Derby, she had the ideal channel to the FO. To Bismarck's outrage, the Queen of Holland therefore succeeded 'during her frequent visits to England in propagating the idea that Prussia sought to annex the Netherlands with a view to acquiring colonies and a fleet for Germany. This idea was utterly unfounded'.[41] Rothfels is therefore wrong in his assertion that Russell portrayed Bismarck's foreign policy as a constantly aggressive one. Although during these first years the ambassador's reports to the FO did not exactly paint Bismarck in a favourable light, Odo usually took great pains to put Bismarck's violent language in perspective. In many important cases, before the war-in-sight crisis and during the Eastern Question for instance, Russell took Bismarck's peace assurances seriously.

Odo also had to analyse the relations between Russia and Germany as a result of the Three Emperors' League. He thought that the Germans were, at least before 1875, completely committed only to the senior partner of the League, Russia — the relationship with Austria only being of secondary importance:

> I believe myself that the alliances or understanding between Russia and Germany, Gortschakoff and Bismarck is real, intimate and sincere and that they have agreed to preserve Austria so long as she obeys and serves them, — but *weh* (oh!) to Austria if ever she attempts to be independent! Then the German and slavic elements she is composed of, will be made to gravitate towards their natural centres, leaving Hungary and her dependencies as a semi-oriental vassal of Germany and Russia.[42]

The Russian–German closeness which Russell describes here was a forced one, resulting from circumstances rather than desire. The literature on this love/hate relationship is immense and Odo's comments on it can hardly add any original thoughts. Russell never felt any need to learn Russian as this was not necessary for daily diplomatic business. (Gortschakoff and Schouvaloff both spoke French with him.) In his letters he often complained about the Russian influence at court (as the Crown Princess did), and about the close relations between the Emperor and the Russian Czar (as Bismarck did). He was also faintly aware of the complexities in the relationship between the two countries. This included of course the fact that without Russia's neutrality in the wars of 1864, 1866 and 1870–71 there would not have been a united Germany. As a consequence there was a close exchange of military information between the two countries which Russell was fully aware of.[43] Yet at the same time, Walker, possibly influenced by his German officer friends, detected an ambivalent feeling among the German military towards Russia:

> Does the rapprochement mean a real friendship between Germany and Russia? I think not, I think moreover that it is rather meant to cover the bitter aversion which the two races feel for each other, and which is only glossed over by the intimate relations which exist between the two Royal families.[44]

Odo, however, got completely different information out of Moltke. He had asked him directly whether Germany would side with Austria or Russia in case of a war in the East. Moltke's reply was straightforward: 'If compelled to take an active part (Germany) could only side with Russia in return for her offer to attack Austria if Austria had sided with France in the late war'.[45] Although Russell was aware of the fact that Bismarck often disagreed with Moltke's and the Emperor's *Nibelungentreue* to Russia, this pro-Russian statement was taken by him and the FO as being the German position up until 1875.

Bismarck's hatred of Gortschakoff from 1875 onwards, however, made the 'special relations' over the next four years appear very artificial. Although the Chancellor claimed that a statesman was simply not allowed to despise anyone ('I cannot afford either sympathies and antipathies against powers and people ... to have such feelings would constitute disloyalty against one's own ruler and country'[46]) he could not help making fun of his enemy. During a speech by Gortschakoff in 1878, Bismarck scribbled on a note: 'Pompous, pompo, pomp, po' and passed it on to Odo who pocketed it.[47] What really interested Odo as far as German–Russian affairs were concerned was, of course, how they would work together in the Balkans. As will be shown in the chapter on the Eastern Question, in this connection Bismarck often tried to exploit English–Russian differences, which worried Russell considerably.

The French Triangle

In untangling the complex triangular relationship between France, Germany and Britain from 1871 onwards, the correspondence between Lord Lyons, the British ambassador to Paris, and Lord Russell is quite enlightening.[1] Lyons and Odo had become closer friends in the 1850s. Russell looked up to the older and more experienced diplomat, seeing him as the ideal role model for his own career. He was always eager to seek advice from Lyons, yet their busy life styles did not give them a chance to meet very often: 'Odo and I gave chase to each other one whole day in London, and consequently missed each other. Had either had philosophy enough to stay quietly at home, we should have met'.[2] In their letters they were both at ease, candidly discussing the FO's mistakes as well as the follies of their 'host' countries. It was common for Odo, during his first years in Berlin, to concentrate his criticisms more on Germany's foreign policy, while Lyons judged 'Germans and French [to be] alike unreasonable'.[3] In retrospect, Lord Lyons would divide Franco–German relations during the 1870s into three phases:

> At first, rage and mortification produced a wild and unreasoning cry for revenge. This was followed by a depression almost amounting to despair. In this state of things the rumours of an intended attack by Germany in 1875 produced nearly a panic. Since that time hope and confidence have gradually returned. The general sentiment now [in 1876] is that France is safely biding her time.[4]

The second stage mentioned by Lyons, the feeling of despair, has been denied by the novelist Victor Hugo, whom Robert Tombs calls 'the self-appointed national conscience'.[5] Hugo stressed the pride of his countrymen who, despite all their suffering, looked down on the barbarous victors.[6] The fact that Hugo's view derived more from wishful patriotism than reality is shown in an account by Adams. In 1874, Sir Frances Ottiwell Adams, a former first secretary of Russell, moved from the capital of the victors, to the capital of the beaten.[7] He judged Paris to be in utter decay and not capable of solving even its most pressing problems. To his former chief, Adams sent the following impressions of post-war France: 'Upon my word I begin to think that this country is what the Americans call pretty well played out. Amongst the higher classes [there is] great discouragement and lamentation'.[8] Adams also noted that despite this depression, the desire for revenge was universal in France. Although no French Government ever officially advocated a war to recover Alsace–Lorraine,[9] rumour had it that Gambetta had coined the phrase 'Let us think of it always, let us speak of it never'.[10] This 'fantasy and mobilising myth' of *la revanche* manifested itself in museums and countless shrines all over France, which commemorated Alsace–Lorraine. Lord Lyons seemed genuinely irritated by these wasted emotions: 'The French all more or less brood over the hope of vengeance', he wrote to Odo, 'and the Germans give them credit for being even more bent upon revenge than they really are. So Germany keeps up an enormous army, and France strains every nerve to raise one — and what can diplomacy do!'[11] Odo had the same feelings of impotence. He knew that Germany and France would not find a *modus vivendi* for years to come. In August 1871, Bismarck had claimed in an interview with the French chargé d'affaires that he regretted the annexation of Alsace–Lorraine:[12] 'Alsace–Lorraine, c'est la Pologne avec la France derrière,'[13] but it remained a *fait accompli*, a millstone around his neck that from now on dictated his whole foreign policy. He had to keep France down and his methods for doing so were manifold. They included: the occupation of western regions of France which, according to the treaty of Frankfurt, would only be evacuated after the high war indemnity of five billion francs[14] was paid (an economic and psychological humiliation); an alliance system against France (which will be analysed later); occasional threats of a preventive war, and general diplomatic bullying in connection with the *Kulturkampf*. The latter included, for example, the case of the Bishop of Nancy, who had encouraged his flock to pray for the return of Strasburg and Metz. Bismarck was outraged and pressured the French Government to show 'public disapproval of the language of the Bishops and of the Ultramontane Press in France'.[15] Even Russell was involved in the unpleasant affair, having received instructions from his government to speak up for the French.[16] When the French Government renounced 'in word and deed' the Ultramontane Party, but refused to put the Bishops in jail, the *Provinzial Correspondenz* noted that this was not the end of it: 'The question how far under the circumstances and on the basis of the laws of France a further satisfaction ... for the conduct of the Ecclesiastical dignitaries themselves should be demanded, remains reserved for the further consideration of the Imperial Government'.[17] In his despatch Odo underlined these words, seeing them as a clear threat to France. After such experiences he felt that the French were entitled to revenge. In a letter to Derby he wrote:

> The French desire for revenge is natural. In Germany a similar desire lasted from 1806 to 1870. That Bismarck should provoke it by his taunts is much to be re-gretted ... The Crown Prince blamed the Chancellor severely for it.[18]

Lyons, however, still hoped in 1872 that a certain degree of harmony could be achieved between the countries by speeding up the payment of the five billion francs: 'I wish the Germans would get their milliards as fast as they can and go, 'then Europe might settle down — and they need not be alarmed about French vengeance, or grudge the French the poor consolation of talking about it'.[19] The hope that French–German relations would go back to a *status quo ante* as soon as the last payments had been received was, of course, illusory. On the contrary, the fact that France still seemed to be solvent, would be used by Bismarck to mount his many 'scare campaigns'.

The possibility of mounting pre-emptive wars against France had been discussed in Berlin ever since 1871. Yet in 1873 the situation seemed to be more serious than usual. John Russell was one of many British politicians bewildered by these constant firebrands. In May 1873, Odo tried to explain to him the complexity of the situation:

> You ask me what the opinion in Berlin is with regard to the future of France? The universal opinion seems to be that whatever Government follows that of M. Thiers, the French nation will for the next few years be intent on preparing a war of revenge. ... For that reason the Germans think it their duty to increase and improve the military defences so as to be prepared for a second attack if it should come ... In fact the so-called balance of Power in Europe is over — for Germany has become invincible and can turn out an army of one million men in 10 days. Add to that a real offensive and defensive alliance with Russia was established by Bismarck at the meeting of the Three Emperors, at Berlin ... to which Austria must be a party if she does not want to see the German population annex itself to the great Fatherland and her Slavic population side with the agents of Russia. ... The wish for peace is deep and sincere in Germany and their military preparations are merely a result of prudence and forethought, the wisdom of nations. Thanks to Lord Granville's able and skilful policy our relations with Germany are very good.[20]

This last sentence reveals that Russell withheld from his uncle some of his true opinions. As has been shown earlier, Odo was in fact not at all satisfied with Granville's 'political nihilism' and hoped for more British leadership as far as continental affairs were concerned. The whole letter seems to be full of contradictions. On the one hand, Odo describes Germany as the master of the continent; on the other, he wants to allay British (as well as his uncle's) fears by claiming that the 'wish for peace is deep'. (As will be seen in the war-in-sight crisis later, Odo spent a great amount of time calming everybody's hypersensitive nerves.) The most extraordinary aspect of this letter is perhaps that Odo, the man who thinks money should be invested in diplomacy and not in the military, actually justifies German foresight in deciding to rearm. A further statement he made to John Russell rings false: 'There is no wish whatever in Germany to interfere with the internal affairs of France'.[21] Here Odo was deliberately downplaying Bismarck's meddling in French affairs. Russell obviously tries to spare his uncle too many worries about German–French tensions,[22] of which he himself was always acutely aware.

At the end of 1873, Odo had an enlightening conversation with the Chancellor, in which he tried to worm out of him whether there was any substance behind the new threat towards France or whether it was just propaganda. He started his report by saying that Bismarck 'spoke of the French with more bitterness and contempt than usual'.[23] This was in Russell's opinion completely unnecessary, because 'France was not in a position to disturb the peace for many years to come'. Bismarck did not agree: 'Her power of making war would depend on the alliances she was able to contract.' Russell was prepared for that and countered: 'Germany has already secured the most powerful alliances of Europe.' With that Bismarck could only partly agree. He claimed he was not sure of them 'because they sometimes depended on the lives of single individuals'. That aside, it was France's duty to seek alliances of her own. The fact remained, Russell persisted, that 'France is in a weakened state, and therefore harmless at the moment'. Bismarck did not accept that: 'An excuse for war is easily found, if wanted. [I] have some experience in such matters'.[24] Whether Bismarck meant this last sentence sarcastically remains open to discussion. Russell, however, did not take it lightly. He made it clear to Bismarck that a pre-emptive war would not be tolerated. 'Germany would lose the sympathies of all the world, if she rushed into an unjust and unnecessary war'.[25] Odo had the backing of his government on this issue. The FO had specifically instructed him to impress on Bismarck the fact that France wanted to maintain peace. Looking at these despatches, it cannot be claimed that Bismarck was not repeatedly made aware of the English stand. It was part of his character (and his perception of Britain) not to take it seriously.

After such a conversation, a less experienced diplomat might have concluded that Bismarck was seriously bent on war. Although Odo was concerned, he did not over-react and waited for more indications, which duly arrived. Only a month after his talk with Bismarck, in January 1874, the 'mot d'ordre' to keep up the hostile feeling towards France was to be heard everywhere in Germany's political circles: 'I also find that he [Bismarck] has made those of his friends and agents whom he employs to carry impressions in political circles in Berlin hold similar language'.[26] Moltke, in particular, made sure that Berlin society knew that the timing for 'fighting it out with France' was now ideal.[27] However, in Odo's opinion, Moltke's influence was over-rated. Russell had come to the conclusion that the real reasons behind these manoeuvres were of a domestic nature:[28] 'by raising a cry against France on the eve of the general elections Prince Bismarck will enable his supporters to vote for the army bill which they declared themselves last session unable to render palatable to their electors in times of peace and security'.[29] A real war was not feasible at the moment, Odo argued, because the Emperor was too ill 'to consent to an unnecessary campaign' and the Crown Prince 'too pacific, too good and too wise'.[30] Odo's impression was that the agitation against France would subside as soon as the German army bill had been passed.[31] The example of 1873–1874 makes it clear why Odo reacted with a cool nerve to the war-in-sight crisis. He was used to the ups and downs in French–German relations and, after having heard so many war threats, knew not to over-react. This did not mean, however, that he was oblivious to the fact that one day a clash, stemming from German domestic problems or out of sheer military paranoia, might occur between France and Germany. He was also to be constantly reminded by the FO to stay on the lookout for signs of such trouble.

One persistent problem was Bismarck's concern about the possibility of a Franco-Russian or Franco-British alliance against Germany. Odo wrote to Lyons about it in 1872: 'The next grievance they are getting up against him [Thiers] is that he is supposed to have made offers through Le Flô to Russia against Germany'.[32] Thiers' constant 'flirtation' with the Russians did not cease to upset Bismarck. Only one year later, Russell wrote to Lyons: 'Thiers is again out of favour at Berlin because the Russian Government has warned the German Government that Thiers is working to draw Russia into the Anglo-French alliance, contrary to their wishes'.[33] The British were also under constant suspicion:

> Then again there is great jealousy at our intimacy and our sympathies with France which are believed to be as great as they were during the Empire, and I should not wonder if Bismarck was trying to estrange us from Russia so as to prevent what is much feared at Berlin, viz, a Franco-Russian alliance.[34]

The British–French commercial treaty of 1872 therefore seemed to Bismarck to be a prime example of a 'Western union' against Germany. Bernstorff was ordered to send every available detail about this newly revived French–British 'friendship' to Berlin. The *German Correspondent* wrote a vicious article about the commercial treaty, implying that this 'backsliding' was in revenge for the Three Emperors' meeting: 'As to the German people, it will hardly occur to them, we believe, to place men like Gladstone and Granville, for either good or evil, in the same rank with the Metternichs, Kaunitzes and Talleyrands. ... We Germans have for the present ceased, since English diplomacy played such an incomprehensible part in July 1870, to fear or to value England much as a power which can either hinder or further our material policy'.[35] Odo and Lyons agreed that Bismarck clearly over-estimated the whole affair. In a letter to Russell, Lyons went so far as to characterise this German reaction as a mild form of Bismarckian 'paranoia'.[36] Odo himself had hoped that the FO would have negotiated a commercial treaty with Germany first;[37] instead he now tried to calm German nerves by talking to 'leading German Pressmen', who were favourably inclined towards Britain.[38] For him, economic disagreements were more of a nuisance than a serious hindrance between the two countries.

Despite his intrigues against Thiers' foreign policy, Bismarck supported the French Republican Government as being the better of two evils.[39] With the defeat of Napoleon III, Bismarck had disposed of one of his most potent and least calculable enemies. There were two royalist parties in France now, the legitimist and the Orleanist, who, surprisingly, agreed on one candidate, the grandson of Charles X, the Comte de Chambord (called Henri V by his followers).[40] Count Arnim, the German ambassador to France, supported the Orleanists and tried to influence William I in that direction. Bismarck was, however, unlike his royal master and Count Arnim,[41] quite understandably not interested in the restoration of another Czarist personality. In order to defend his new heretical stand against the monarchist principle, Bismarck wrote to William in 1872:

> Our task for the future begins from the moment ... when France appears to the monarchical courts of Europe to be worthy of forming an alliance with them again, which it is not in its current, distraught state. ... For a united monarchical Europe the Paris crater is absolutely safe, it would burn itself out and render the rest of Europe the service of showing again as a deterrent example how France has ended under republican dominance.[42]

Although William never quite accepted this argument[43] he pretended, when Thiers was voted out of office in 1873, to regret this change. The British ambassador, however, had the feeling that the monarchical tendencies of the new MacMahon–Broglie government appealed more to William than the policies of Thiers had. As far as Bismarck's opinion about the new regime in France was concerned, the rumour was that he felt ambivalent:

> On the one hand, he hopes that the accession to power of a soldier in France may alarm the German Parliament into passing the Imperial Military Laws without opposition, ... on the other hand, he fears that the religious sympathies of the [new]

administration may encourage the hopes of the Catholic party and strengthen their opposition to the state all over Europe.[44]

Lyons, who judged the French President to have 'no political knowledge or ability',[45] could have calmed Bismarck's fears. There were many anecdotes circulating about MacMahon's stupidity. Once, when he wanted to contact the American government he ordered that a telegram should be sent to San Francisco. His private Secretary reminded him that Washington was the capital of the United States. MacMahon proudly turned to his entourage and praised his secretary: '*Il sait tout!*'[46]

The Arnim case shows that there were serious disagreements within the German FO and at court about the right policy to be adopted towards France.[47] While Bismarck had feared the coming of a French regime capable of alliances with other monarchies, Arnim, on the other hand, tried to build up contacts with the French monarchists who would, in his opinion, be the 'future masters of France'.[48] He had feared that if Thiers were to be followed by Gambetta, this would ultimately lead to a cry for *revanche*.[49] In Bismarck's eyes Arnim had become much too interfering.

Arnim had been sent to Paris by Bismarck on 23 August 1871 as an envoy extraordinary and was made ambassador shortly before Christmas 1871. Already at this stage, it had been rumoured that the Chancellor had organised this position for Arnim simply to get rid of him as a potential rival.[50] Despite constant problems with Bismarck, Arnim managed to achieve an agreement on the payment of further French reparation instalments. Bismarck was not satisfied with Arnim's results. He interrupted his ambassador's further talks in March 1873 about the last French milliard by abruptly settling the question himself with Thiers (via his ambassador Gontaut-Biron) in Berlin. This was an affront that openly showed the Chancellor's lack of confidence in his ambassador. One reason for Bismarck's annoyance had been Arnim's visit to Germany in 1872. During his stay the ambassador had had long intimate discussions with the Emperor and was also frequently invited for talks by Empress Augusta. Bismarck was at the time away from Berlin, trying to restore his health. He rightly feared that Arnim had during this visit tried to undermine his position at court.[51] Odo was well informed about the incident and wrote to Lyons:[52]

> He [Bismarck] thinks him [Arnim] a rising rival because Arnim went to Baden last autumn, and advised the Emperor behind Bismarck's back, to go in for an Orleanist monarchy and drop Thiers in opposition to Bismarck's policy who wishes to drop all pretenders and uphold Thiers as long as he lives. ... Arnim hinted [to the Em-

peror] at a readiness to take office at home if Bismarck came to grief. The Emperor is fond of Arnim and listened with complacency. [The Emperor] told Bismarck [about the talks] when he returned from Varzin. Bismarck has vowed revenge.[53]

It was also known to Odo that Arnim repeatedly had ignored the Chancellor's instructions and circumvented the Auswärtiges Amt by writing directly to the Emperor.

Bismarck could have handled the problem internally, by having Arnim either transferred or promoted upstairs, yet instead he allowed it to turn into a public scandal. He recalled Arnim from his Paris post in March 1874. At the Auswärtiges Amt the possibility of Arnim being sent to either London or Constantinople was at first tentatively discussed,[54] but it slowly became obvious that neither opportunity would materialise. As a consequence, Arnim started his revenge campaign. In the Austrian newspaper *Die Presse* he anonymously published an article entitled 'Diplomatic Revelations'. In it he quoted from a memorandum he had written in June 1870, predicting the war between the church and the German state. It was not a document showing any of Arnim's principles as far as the Kulturkampf question was concerned, but was simply an act of vanity: Arnim, the prophet, should have been listened to, and in that way domestic problems would have been avoided. It was easy for Bismarck to destroy this vanity by simply publishing some typically confused Arnim despatches in reply.[55] These made the former ambassador look like a second-rate, insubordinate amateur.[56] Odo wrote: 'Count Arnim's memo was calculated to produce an impression that he had foreseen and warned Prince Bismarck in vain of the coming dangers in Germany, ... whilst Prince Bismarck's despatches are published to prove the contrary, and perhaps also to counteract the favourable impression produced by Count Arnim's memorandum'.[57] Since it had become known to Bismarck, via the 'helpful' Holstein, that Arnim had taken documents from the Paris embassy, the ambassador had been pressed to return them. He insisted that they were private and, as a consequence, Arnim was arrested in October 1874 'in a theatrical coup'[58] at his country house near Stettin.[59] He was released after paying bail, but was apprehended again on 13 November 74 and placed under house arrest.

Odo's first secretary, Adams, was still in charge at the Berlin embassy when the first rumours had appeared about Arnim during the summer of 1874, and he immediately informed Derby in a private letter about the 'Arnim-Lindau connection'. Rudolph Lindau had been allegedly used by Bismarck to spy on Arnim in Paris and was said to be responsible for the ambassador's downfall. 'The oldest [of the Lindau

Otto von Bismarck, 1874

brothers], Rudolph ... was attached to the Embassy at Paris, ostensibly for commercial matters, but in reality, as I have reason to know, to be a spy on Count Arnim. He corresponds directly with Bismarck as he boastingly told me himself'.[60] The second brother, Richard, was a clerk at the FO, and according to Adams, an 'instrument' of Bismarck, who would do anything for his princely master.[61] Odo had already informed Lyons the previous year about this new agent of Bismarck: 'Lindau ... is a very able man and an old friend of mine. I have given him a letter to you. He might become useful some day. Let me add in confidence that he corresponds privately and secretly with Bismarck behind Arnim's back'.[62] It was also rumoured that Rudolph had 50,000 Thalers (£7,500) from the *Reptilienfonds* at his disposal to 'inspire' the French press.[63] Holstein and the journalist Emil Landsberg had also been spies in the Paris embassy, the latter being financed by Baron Bleichröder. Bleichröder despised Arnim because he had used his rival, Hansemann, to undertake the financial transactions during the war indemnity negotiations.[64] It is no wonder that Arnim became paranoid.

When Odo came back from his annual summer break on 10 October 1874, he was surprised to hear that in Berlin 'the only topic of conversation was Count Arnim's arrest and imprisonment'.[65] Even Arnim's son, Count Henning von Arnim, criticised his father's conduct privately in a conversation with Russell. Henning claimed that he himself 'had told his father about the relevant paragraphs in the penal code the previous summer, but [the Count] refused to give up his papers'.[66] The whole Arnim family seemed to be divided. Arnim's brother-in-law, Count Arnim Boitzenburg, for example, accepted the offer to become governor of Silesia — despite the affair. In Odo's opinion it was bizarre that this man wanted to work for a government that had imprisoned his relative.[67] However, the Arnims were not a close-knit family and had always competed with each other.[68] Apart from members of his own family deserting him, Arnim was also not very popular among his colleagues. The ever-bitchy Bülow describes him in his biography *Denkwürdigkeiten* as a very arrogant *Salonlöwe*. It was also noted that Arnim used too much perfume, obviously a very unmanly thing to do.[69] Odo was one of the few who had a fairly normal relationship with his German colleague.[70] He had known Arnim since the 1860s when they had both been accredited to Rome, and during the first years of his posting to Berlin had lived in a house the Arnims had leased to the British Embassy. Russell later claimed that he had been the only one to speak up for his friend in discussions with Bismarck. Though the Chancellor half-heartedly agreed that Arnim might have been a 'pleasant colleague', he claimed that this was not the case when it came to the way he treated his staff:

> If I [Odo] had known [Arnim] as he [Bismarck] did, I would agree that he was 'ripe for the rope' and ought to have been hanged long ago. ... Count Arnim was a man who would poison his own brother or steal a silver spoon without compunction, as he [Bismarck] had told the Emperor last year, but His Majesty had refused to believe it and had continued to support Arnim against himself, Bismarck. Happily the Emperor's eyes were open now at last ... and the law would deal with Arnim as he deserved, or rather not as he deserved because he would not be hanged, only imprisoned.[71]

In his memoirs Bismarck would later claim that Russell had agreed with him that Arnim was the kind of person who always asked the question: 'what can I personally gain?'[72] Russell was probably not as loyal to Arnim as he sometimes made out to be, but one also has to take into consideration that Bismarck's memory was often quite selective in such cases.

In these conversations with Odo, Bismarck also alleged that Arnim had engaged in insider trading on the stock exchange together with the Duc Decazes.[73] The Chancellor made sure that these allegations became public. Arnim refuted them in the *Deutsche Nachrichten* on 6 November 1874. Bismarck was not exactly averse to the accumulation of money himself, but he pretended to despise the trading of insider information by others.[74] The Chancellor's revelations about Arnim's 'insider dealings'[75] hardly came as a complete surprise to Russell. Arnim, as well as Odo's predecessor Loftus, had already been involved in some obscure real-estate speculation in Berlin:

> There is no doubt that Loftus went in for speculation ... and realised a fortune. I [Odo] have repeatedly been offered speculations ... to realise from 30,000 to 50,000 Thalers in a few days — which of course I decline. Arnim went in for them and offered me to join him — he merely gave his name and has realised half a million in a fortnight. Of course a diplomatist must be above these gambling gains and must never lend himself to selling his name.[76]

A year before Arnim's arrest, Odo had revealed to Lyons that Bismarck could possibly blackmail Arnim with his stock-jobbing past. Until today it has been believed that Bismarck had no proof of Arnim's manipulation, but if Odo's information is correct, this theory can no longer be upheld:

> What I have to say today grieves me to the soul because it goes against my excellent friend and landlord Harry Arnim. Said friend, it is said, could not resist the temptation of turning an honest penny in the great War indemnity loan at Paris and the ... banker he employed, called Hansemann, let it out to Bismarck who could not understand how Arnim was rich enough to buy estates in Silesia and houses in Berlin. Now Bismarck who is tired of Arnim and thinks him a rising rival will make use of this discovery with the Emperor whenever he wants to upset Arnim and send a new man to Paris.[77]

If Russell's suspicions were correct and Hansemann had indeed given Bismarck written proof, then Arnim had already been at Bismarck's mercy for quite some time.

In the first Arnim trial, Bismarck's French despatches were read out and impressed German as well as foreign observers by their foresight and clarity of language: 'Prince Bismarck's despatches were reproduced and discussed with genuine enthusiasm, both for their contents, and for their purity and clearness of style which is a new feature in German diplomatic documents,' Odo wrote home.[78] While Bismarck was hailed as a 'reformer of the German language',[79] Arnim's mental faculties were doubted. Bismarck had already speculated through his mouthpiece Bülow that Arnim might have become insane, travelling with top-secret State documents around the continent, even taking them to a spa. This could have been caused by 'the possible existence of a hereditary tendency to temporary aberration of the mind'.[80] Apart from such juicy revelations, the trial was a disappointment for the voyeuristic general public. The people, Odo wrote, had thought that Arnim would be found guilty of high treason. Instead, in this first trial, he was only sentenced to 3 months' imprisonment for not returning the despatches.[81] By then Odo had himself become impatient with Arnim's refusal to hand over the papers he had taken from the Paris Embassy. For Odo this was an 'inexcusable obstinacy in a simple question of discipline'.[82] If the press worked so well on a sceptic such as Odo, it is no surprise that the National Liberal Party celebrated their Chancellor's stand wholeheartedly. Bismarck reached an even greater height in his popularity because he had, in the eyes of the Liberals, shown sufficient 'moral courage to allow the law to take its course in the case of an aristocrat, a "Junker", an old conservative of high birth connected with the first families of Prussia'.[83] Bismarck had, with the greatest skill, neutralised a possible rival. Arnim died in exile in 1881, still feeling bitterly aggrieved.

The recall of Arnim in 1874 did not by any means lead to an improvement in communications between Paris and Berlin. Instead, German–French sensitivities came to a head in the spring of 1875 during the war-in-sight scare. This crisis has been the subject of much speculation, both by contemporaries as well as by historians,[84] and the official documents do not offer any new insights. However, it is interesting to note that at the beginning Odo did not place much importance on the crisis. The surprising fact is that the correspondence between Lyons and Russell — the two most important sources for the decision-makers at the FO — stayed relatively calm during the build-up to the affair.[85] In October 1874, Lyons and Odo met in London and in a long face-to-face talk they discussed how a French–German war could be avoided. As noted by Lyons:

> Odo confirmed the views both you [Bulwer Lytton] and I [Lyons] have always taken of the relation between France and Germany at this moment. The only safe policy for France appears to be to avoid giving Bismarck anything like a pretext which he could make appear plausible to the German People, for a fresh quarrel. Odo did not seem to think that Bismarck was absolutely seeking a fresh war, but he did think that the great Chancellor's anti-ultramontane mania or some other question of home policy might make him resolve at any moment to try a campaign against France.[86]

This opinion was also put to Derby, who seemed to agree with it: 'No expectation of war this year, as the German military organisation will not be complete till 1876'.[87] The feared pretext for war arrived when in 1875 the French Government decided to reorganise their army. Germany immediately retaliated by stopping a scheduled export of horses to France. Odo did not over-value this. Yet this export stop, combined with the famous *Post* article titled 'Is war in sight?'[88] was used by the French to alarm Russia and Britain about a possible German attack.[89] The German ambassador to the Court of St James, Münster, reported that Derby had been in an agitated mood about the *Post* article and had repeatedly stressed that the French did not intend to go to war, but simply wanted to reorganise their weak army.[90] The same panicky mood was felt among foreign diplomats in Berlin, who were as confused as Derby. On 21 April 1875, Radowitz, who had just got back from a mission to Russia (during which, as Odo guessed quite rightly, he had done his best to terminate a feared spring romance between France and Russia) attended a dinner party at the British Embassy. He was, as expected, mysteriously silent about his Russian trip, but instead made cryptic comments about a possible war between Germany and France.[91] Five days later Karolyi informed Odo that Bismarck had told him Germany had to take 'the initiative' vis-à-vis a bilious France. On top of that, Odo himself had to listen to one of Bülow's well-known conspiracy theories in which Belgium, France and Italy were as usual accused of plotting Germany's downfall. Derby, who was still worried about a possible violation of Belgium's neutrality because of Bismarck's Kulturkampf crusade, now became even more concerned.

During the whole crisis, which lasted only a few weeks, Odo Russell seemed to be the only one who was convinced that Bismarck was not bent on war:

> Bismarck is at his old tricks again [Russell wrote to Derby in April 1875] alarming the Germans through the officious press and intimating that the French are

going to attack them and that Austria and Italy are conspiring in favour of the Pope .... Now he has succeeded in making the Emperor and the Crown Prince believe that France is really meditating an invasion of Germany through Belgium ! — and not knowing better they are in despair and have ordered the War department to make ready for defence. This crisis, will blow over like so many others but Bismarck's sensational policy is very wearisome at times. Half the diplomatic body have been here since yesterday to tell me that war was imminent, and when I seek to calm their nerves ... they think that I am bamboozled by Bismarck. I do not, as you know, believe in another war with France.[92]

The Queen,[93] Disraeli and Derby, however, did. 'The Queen is eager to do something!' Derby wrote in his diary on 7 May 1875.[94] She was even thinking of sending Lord Cowley on a special mission to Berlin, which would have been a humiliation for Odo. It was only thanks to Derby, who stood by his ambassador, that it was prevented. Instead, Victoria wrote to the Czar to support his 'mediation' in Berlin. Arthur Russell was later to describe the events leading up to this Royal intervention:

the Empress Augusta wrote a heartrending appeal to Queen Victoria: 'These horrid generals', she said, 'have not had fighting enough, they are going to drag my husband and my son into war again. I appeal to you as a Queen and a mother! You can save us if you will, in God's name save me!' This Odo believed was about the tone of the letter. The Queen, deeply moved, read it to the Prime Minister. It will be remembered that Bismarck subsequently complained very angrily about political interference. In the meantime active correspondence went on and the great powers exchanged their views'.[95]

Derby agreed, however, with Victoria that Russia should become involved in the affair. He wrote to Odo: 'Is there no hope of Russian interference to maintain peace? It cannot be the interest of Russia to have France destroyed and Germany omnipotent. If the Czar were to say that a new war must not take place, and that he would not allow it, Bismarck would hardly undertake to fight Russia and France combined. I see little other prospect of averting mischief'.[96] This letter shows that Arthur Russell was completely wrong when he wrote years later that Derby was against any action: 'Lord Derby was unwilling to interfere and could not comprehend what concern it was of ours if foreigners cut each other's throats'.[97] On the contrary, at the cabinet meeting on 8 May 1875, Derby obtained approval to send a telegram to Russell instructing him to support the Czar's mediation at Berlin. Before the events of May 1875, the Prime Minister had been careful not to be manipulated by the French for their own purposes: 'He [Disraeli] wishes to encourage confidence and good will on the part of

France towards England, but sees the danger to France herself of any such appearance of a special and separate understanding as would arouse the jealousy of Bismarck'.[98] Now Disraeli saw the crisis as a chance to undermine the understanding between Russia and Germany: 'My own impression is that we should construct some concerted movement to preserve the peace of Europe, like Pam did when he baffled France and expelled the Egyptians from Syria'.[99]

Odo felt uncomfortable about carrying out his instructions.[100] To stand up to Bismarck was an entirely new experience for FO officials and British diplomats. Though he did not believe in war, Odo had written fatalistically that if Bismarck really wanted it, there was not much hope of England stopping him in any event: 'What can other Powers and particularly England do to help to preserve peace? A coalition is impossible, advice or interference adds to Bismarck's excuses for going to war — so the only course governments can follow with safety to themselves is to let him do as he pleases and submit to the consequences until he dies'.[101] Adams, writing from Paris, agreed with him: 'I confess that I can hardly bring myself to believe that if Bismarck was bent upon war, he would stop out of consideration for England. She has no battalions to work on him'.[102] Neither of them thought Bismarck would seriously fall for a show of power and they were right about this. Bismarck would finally yield in the war-in-sight crisis because of Russian, not British, pressure. But what they had not understood was that Disraeli's style of foreign policy was to be very different from what they had previously been used to.

Emperor Alexander and Gortschakoff arrived in Berlin on 10 May and the interview with Bismarck took place shortly afterwards. Odo had already by then privately delivered his FO instructions to Bismarck, and the Chancellor did not know that there was still more to come. The same day Odo was present at a conversation between Bismarck and Gortschakoff, during which he had to listen uneasily to the Russian's patronising language towards the Chancellor. Looking back on this meeting, Russell would come to view it as one of the most uncomfortable moments of his career. Shortly after the end of the crisis, he wrote to his brother Hastings: 'Versailles was an anxious affair, but I have just gone through another anxious episode in my career, with the Czar, Gortschakoff and Bismarck and delicate instructions from Uncle Derby to carry out'.[103] His brother Arthur gave a more dramatic account of the episode:

> Odo described ... the interview between the two chancellors during which he was
> present and supported Prince Gortschakoff in accordance with the instructions he

had received from the FO. Prince Gortschakoff informed Bismarck that the Czar did not desire to see France weakened any further. Bismarck was writhing under desperate efforts to control his tongue. Gortschakoff repeated, 'allons mon cher Bismarck, tranquillisez vous donc'.[104]

One day after this conversation, on 11 May 1875, it was reported that Bismarck had lost his composure completely, swearing revenge and calling Gortschakoff 'senile':[105]

> Behind our backs I hear [Odo wrote] Zornesbock swore like a maniac, and swore he would have his 'revanche' for our interference. ... He says it is Augusta's doing .... Poor old William *schlägt die Hände über den Kopf zusammen* [threw his hands up] and did not know what it all meant, for Zornesbock keeps him but very imperfectly informed of what is going on now.[106]

Although Bismarck was outraged about the humiliation he had suffered, he did not try to make Russell personally responsible for it. The Chancellor contrasted Gortschakoff's self-glorifying behaviour with the excellent British tactfulness,[107] but he was not excusing the British Government. Bismarck wrote to Münster:

> This anti-German feeling [in England] is the more striking because I am certain that Lord Odo Russell has always reported in favourable terms about things here. I think of him as a too good and truth loving observer to believe that he, who has for a long time now had experience of our peaceful policy, should have written anything different.[108]

The German official papers now made it clear to their bewildered readers that it was England and France, and not the Russians, who were under 'petticoat and ultramontane influences'. By this Bismarck meant specifically 'the Empress and the Grand Duchess of Baden ... who are supposed ... to be constantly plotting his [Bismarck's] downfall'. They had conspired against a peaceful Germany and were to blame for the latest 'diplomatic farce'.[109] Further accusations emerged and Derby noted in his diary: 'Bismarck, after laying the blame of the late panic on the shoulders of Moltke, now says that it has been got up by the press and stock jobbers. ... He ought to have added that the journals, which are at fault are those, notoriously inspired by himself'.[110] The incident ruffled English–German relations for some time, something which Odo had predicted:

> A short time after the interview [Arthur Russell recalled] Bismarck complained to Odo of the preposterous folly and ignorance of the English and all other Cabinets who had mistaken stories [set up for speculation], for the true policy of the German Government. ... The whole of Berlin society made merry over the fright of the cabinets at the simple rumours of the stock-exchange, after holding very dif-

ferent language a few months before. I recollect hearing Count Münster soon after these events complain to Odo, in the Park of Derenburg [Count Münster's
castle], of the thoughtless manner in which Lord Derby had offended Germany
by his inconsiderate support of Russia in this affair and declare that Lord Derby
had entirely misapprehended the observation he had made to him regarding the
armaments of France and the apprehensions they excited. 'As we are his guests',
observed Odo to me, 'I do not wish to contradict him'.[111]

Three years after Odo's death, in 1887, the war-in-sight scare filled the
papers again. In 1887, *The Times* commented on the 'diplomatic
indiscretions' contained in General Le Flô's memoirs about the crisis.[112]
These recollections were of course vehemently contradicted by the
German Government.[113]

Was Bismarck really intending a war against France?[114] The answer
seems to be in the negative. The majority of German historians would
agree with Odo that the whole affair was a bluff that got out of hand.
Yet, whether Bismarck meant harm or not, the war-in-sight crisis had
long-term effects. The Chancellor had been shown his limits. Also,
Austria had stood by him and his Russian partners had sent a clear sign
of their disapproval. It was evident that this had been a diplomatic
disaster for Germany. Apart from that, Bismarck's biographer Pflanze
even speculates that the crisis had a very decisive effect on the
Chancellor's personal career plans. He thinks that the affair 'may have
prolonged Bismarck's career by 15 years'.[115] According to Pflanze,
Bismarck had seriously considered resigning after his 60th birthday in
April. However, the humiliation of the war-in-sight affair made him
stay. On the British side, such marked effects on the course of German
history were not suspected at the time. Disraeli was highly satisfied with
the outcome of the crisis,[116] claiming that not since Palmerston's days
had England shown such a firm stand.[117] The mediation efforts were
undoubtedly a diplomatic success for England and showed to the world
that 'the ideological plaster'(as Hillgruber calls it)[118] of the Three
Emperors' League was not very firm.

The last stage of French–German–British diplomatic relations in the
1870s was dominated by the Eastern Question, which will be discussed
separately. During the years 1875–1878 fears surfaced occasionally at the
FO that Germany might seize the opportunity (while Russia was distracted)
to start a war with France. Lord Lyons listed for Derby the fresh French
suspicions of Bismarck after the Constantinople Conference: First of all,
Bismarck was rumoured to be jealous of the cordial understanding that
had existed at the Conference between France, England and Russia.
Furthermore, the German Chancellor was in 1876 recorded to have been

outraged about the increasing socialist votes at the last German election and saw France as the 'hotbed of socialism'.[119] According to Lyons, France's new fears seemed to be confirmed by the fact that Bismarck: 'wants a cry to make the Germans pay their taxes willingly. ... he looks with an evil eye upon the material prosperity of France. ... he considers the Exhibition of 1878 as a sort of defiance of Germany and is ready to go to great lengths to prevent its taking place'.[120]

Except for the last one, these fears were old and had all been articulated before. The upshot was, according to Lyons, that France had to tread even more carefully than usual in the minefield of Eastern affairs. While Bismarck continued to keep the French in a suppressed state, his solution for the 'Oriental Question' (as the Germans called it), as far as Great Britain was concerned, seemed more subtle. He hoped to distract the British Government's interest away from Europe, towards Egypt. He was therefore delighted and full of self-congratulation when 'his' plan seemed within reach with Disraeli's purchase of the Khedive Ismail's Suez Canal shares in November 1875.[121] Odo wrote about it to Derby: 'Prince Bismarck, who has formerly often said that in the place of HMG he would buy up the shares of the Suez Canal, feels personally flattered at the realisation of a policy that he himself has advocated and fancies he has invented, and for my part I think it prudent not to dispel this happy thought at present, which the great man has confided confidentially to his admirers'.[122] It is ironic that the British Prime Minister was at first not aware of how much this had pleased Bismarck. On the contrary, in a letter to his pen friend Lady Bradford, Disraeli indicated what he believed to be the extent of German annoyance:

> Bismarck called on Odo Russell, but the latter was unhappily not at home. Odo called at the FO and saw Bülow who handed him a telegraph from Münster, saying 'the purchase of the Suez Canal has been received by the whole English nation with enthusiasm', but not a word could be got out of Bülow himself.[123]

This is vintage Disraeli, and it seems almost prosaic that historians were to dismantle the picture of a fuming Bismarck. The letters of both Odo Russell and the Queen gave the correct picture of the situation in Germany to their PM.[124] A letter from the Crown Princess, passed on to Disraeli by her mother, shows that the positive feeling in Germany towards the purchase was genuine:[125] 'Everybody is pleased here, and wishes it may bring England good; even the great man B. expressed himself to Fritz in this sense yesterday evening'.[126]

However, Bismarck was soon disabused of any hopes he may have entertained for a new British colonial policy by an assurance from

Derby that England did not plan to 'establish authority in Egypt'. The Foreign Secretary was supported by Disraeli, who did not feel prepared for a British intervention in Egypt and 'resisted more than one such proposal'.[127] He suspected Bismarck of trying to use Egypt in order to create a wedge between Britain and France. Good French–British relations were more important for the moment.

CHAPTER 6

The German Domestic Situation

The Building of a New Empire

'No one dies before fulfilling his task, some survive the fulfilment of their task'.[1] The second part of Ernst Jünger's well-known remark has often been applied to Bismarck's domestic politics after the year 1871. With his qualities of flexibility, intelligence and innovative thinking, Bismarck seemed to have the potential to unite Germany internally, but because of his bitter battles against 'opponents' such as the Socialists, the Polish minority and his fellow Catholic citizens, Bismarck has been accused by some of having failed in this endeavour. Without Bismarck, Odo claimed in 1875, 'the Germans [left] to govern themselves would rapidly settle down to commerce, industry and science'.[2] Here Odo seems to be a useful source for historians who, to this day, draw a distinction between Bismarck's 'clever foreign policy' and his 'failed domestic one'. They argue that but for the domestic clashes and the Chancellor's turn to colonialism, Bismarck might today be universally celebrated as a great statesman. This would have been a much too simplistic interpretation for Odo. Although he thought that Bismarck failed in the Kulturkampf and had set a dangerous example in his relations with the Reichstag, he was also of the opinion that the Chancellor was doing his best to unite Germany as far as the Particularist issue was concerned: 'I think Bismarck's plan is to destroy the Prussian Particularists and germanise Prussia. However, I may be mistaken',[3] Odo wrote to Hammond. Whether in the end it was a case of Prussia being 'germanised' or vice versa has been a controversy ever since 1871.

Bismarck will again figure prominently in this and in the following chapter about the Kulturkampf, but, because Germany's internal affairs have already been analysed at length by a multitude of historians, only a selected number of issues will be briefly touched upon. Russell's interest in certain topics of the day will be the guideline for this. Naturally, his despatches on domestic affairs, although full of perceptive insights, can only give glimpses, because Odo was mainly occupied with reporting on Bismarck's foreign policy. Russell was also aware of the fact that there was not much interest in German domestic or social issues in Britain. To Morier, he wrote: 'I found in England the most utter and absolute indifference to Germany, more especially among statesmen and members of Parliament. ... Continental talk bores everybody to death'.[4] From the FO's point of view, Russell was paid to be a diplomat, not an in-depth social analyst, economist or religious affairs correspondent. Yet he still tried, step by step, to interest the successive Foreign Secretaries, particularly the receptive Derby, in the domestic problems Germany had to deal with.

Today one cannot write about Bismarckian Germany without taking into account the revolutionary studies made in the 1960s and 1970s. Yet the latest trend, set by Bismarck's biographers Gall and Pflanze, seems to indicate that these Marxist theories which Wehler used may have, at least in part, outlived their usefulness.[5] In an essay, Pflanze criticised the theories of 'negative integration' and '*Sammlungspolitik*', which were employed to explain the functioning of Bismarckian Germany. The expression 'negative integration' describes the persecution of a minority by the majority for political ends. An example would be the manipulated fear of Jesuit conspiracies, which many Germans shared during the Kulturkampf.[6] The term '*Sammlungspolitik*' applies more to the time after 1878. It postulates that Bismarck combined two power groups, the great landowners and leading industrialists who followed a 'merger movement' policy.[7] Pflanze doubts, however, whether it is possible to force the 'enigma of Bismarck' into such generalising theories. Instead, he advocates a return to the use of primary sources. If one looks at Odo's despatches relating to Bismarck's reign, it would be possible to interpret them as supporting both Pflanze's, as well as Wehler's, completely opposite arguments. During Russell's first years in Germany, his analysis of Bismarck's internal policy is perhaps closest to the Bonapartist line of approach.[8] The Caesarismus idea or Bonapartismus theory describes the governing techniques of an authoritarian political regime that achieves power in a 'revolution from above' and gradually comes to legitimise and stabilise itself.[9] 'Caesarism' is not a new theory.[10] Bismarck's contemporaries were themselves inclined towards it.[11] Arthur, for example, mentioned the very word 'Caesarism' in connection with the 'new' Germany: 'The liberal party in England has been grievously disappointed by the absence of all self-control and moderation with which philosophical Germany gratified the passion of vindictiveness upon the French — and the blindness with which he [Bismarck] introduces the evils and luxuries of *Caesarism* which have been the curse of France'.[12] Odo used the word in a similar context when he wrote to Derby: 'It is difficult to understand how a nation can give so much power to one single man who may go mad any day and fling his burning pipe into the European Powder magazine'.[13] It was this type of portrayal by Odo and Morier that gave Lord Derby the idea that Bismarck was actually suffering from the 'Napoleonic' disease:

> It seems impossible to doubt that the possession of almost absolute power, acting on a nature always impulsive and violent, has developed in the German statesman a tendency like that shown by the first Napoleon ... a tendency difficult to describe in exact terms, but which is the disease of despotism.[14]

For Odo, one trait of such an authoritarian regime was, for example, the use of Bismarck's secret financial resources with which he could, through the payment of newspaper editors, undermine any opposition. This money, the Welfenfortune (Guelph fund), originally belonged to the King of Hannover but was taken away from him by Bismarck in the aftermath of the 1866 war. Russell wrote to Granville about these funds:

> Sixteen million Thalers of His Majesty's property were handed over by the Prussian Parliament to Prince Bismarck as a secret service fund for his irresponsible use, so that he is extremely hostile to anyone who proposes to persuade the King of Hannover to give up the attitude he has assumed and be reconciled to the House of Hohenzollern and the German Empire.[15]

The Chancellor's opponents in parliament had been as suspicious about the money as Russell. The question had been raised whether the Government used the Guelph fund to corrupt journalists and finance secret undertakings. In his answer Bismarck implied that the funding of espionage was a fact of life for any state: 'I am not born to be a spy, but I think we should be grateful that they chase vicious reptiles'.[16] As a result of Bismarck's speech, the Guelph fund and those newspapers which were secretly financed by it were now called 'Reptile'.[17] There were a great number of these papers in circulation, together with other semi-official papers, such as the *Norddeutsche Allgemeine Zeitung*[18] or the official *Provinzial-Correspondenz*, which Odo read frequently. In 1884, he explained to the young diplomat Rennell Rodd what had by then become the very elaborate Bismarckian press system: 'The Bismarckian method was to have articles written and inserted by such means as were open to him in the press of all nations. These articles were then quoted in German official papers as expressing the feeling of the country in which they had been published'.[19]

The newspaper propaganda irritated Russell, but these were not the only 'Bonapartist traits' to be detected in Bismarck's Germany. For Odo the new German Empire was a place where the Chancellor used his 'irresponsible power' on a regular basis;[20] parliament was forced to yield to the wishes of the army; and a great portion of the country's inhabitants (such as Catholics and Socialists) were criminalised by obscure laws.[21] These problems increasingly worried Russell and in October 1874, after 3 years of working in Germany, Odo gave a damning summary of his perception of Bismarck's domestic manoeuvres. The aim of this long report to the FO was, in Russell's own words, to enlighten the English and to change their misguided perceptions about German affairs.[22] Only the blunt truth could prepare the people for the 'future surprises [Bismarck's] genius may create'.[23] Odo started by explaining the basics. In his view the pillars of Bismarck's power were the liberal National Party and the army. Both had profited from the Chancellor's wars and both relied on him for further victories. However, in order to maintain his power Bismarck had to overcome numerous enemies. It was the crown, the aristocracy and the church that had the greatest potential to undermine his plans:

> The crown because the Emperor could simply dismiss his Chancellor whenever it pleased him.[24] The aristocracy because the German Princes naturally supported particularisation, which was diametrically opposed to Bismarck's unity movement. And lastly, the German church, because it placed God before Bismarck [and its Centre party was a threat to the notion of a secularised new Germany].[25]

In Odo's eyes the manner in which the Chancellor ousted these enemies resembled a *coup d'état*, which went completely unnoticed by anyone outside Germany. First of all, Bismarck had over the years managed to estrange the Emperor from his family by portraying the Crown Prince as impatiently awaiting his succession and the Empress as a brainwashed victim of the Catholic Church. Secondly, the Chancellor successfully diminished the influence of the aristocracy by undermining their loyalty to the House of Hohenzollern:

> He [Bismarck] prevented the Emperor from creating a German House of Peers that their voice might not be heard in the Councils of the nation, and he invented the Bundesrath to take their place, which he composed of representatives of the minor German states selected from the liberal national party more or less subservient to his will and trained them to obey him implicitly. ... Through the Prussian House of Deputies he abolished the last remnants of feudal rights and privileges to which the aristocracy attached vital importance. ... Disgusted at their Sovereign's ingratitude, the old Conservatives, powerless and heartbroken, abandoned Berlin to return to their castles, vowing to sacrifice the blood of their sons no more for the House of Hohenzollern.[26]

Lastly, in order to 'paralyse' the disobedient German Catholic Church, and its powerful satellite, the Centre Party, Bismarck invented a whole movement — the Kulturkampf: 'This was calculated to alienate the orthodox aristocracy and the loyal clergy from a Sovereign they had hitherto looked up to as the patron of religious toleration'.[27] The outcome of all these intrigues was, for Odo, that Bismarck had managed to make himself as 'indispensable to the Emperor William as to his immediate successor, who will find it impossible to form a lasting administration without him'.[28] Russell rightly sensed that the Crown Prince's regime, despite the hopes in England, simply could not alter the direction Bismarck had chosen for Germany. He foresaw very clearly the problems which Bismarck's successors would ultimately face.

A common strategy of Bismarck's to get his way was to threaten to resign, usually at the most critical moments. One could actually write the whole story of crisis situations in the 1870s in terms of one long chain of threatened resignations by the Chancellor. In 1872, Odo witnessed, however, a quite unusual resignation scenario. A cabinet crisis had emerged in Prussia and Bismarck called on the British ambassador for a 'heart to heart talk'. During this session, the Chancellor pretended that he was eager to give up his position as Prussian Minister-President:

> Ten years of constant mental exertion, had entitled him [Bismarck] to some rest besides which his health could no longer stand the labour entailed upon him by the responsibility attaching to the many high offices he held of Chancellor of the German Empire, Prussian Premier, minister for Foreign affairs for Prussia and Germany, responsible minister for Alsace–Lorraine, Minister for Lauenburg etc.[29]

He had therefore decided to give up 'the Presidency of the Prussian Ministry and the internal administration of the kingdom'.[30] The Chancellor also claimed that if he unloaded this burden by making Roon Prussian Minister-President, it would enable him 'to devote himself to Imperial interests and his work as Foreign Secretary'.[31] Odo did not believe this explanation, and also observed that the Chancellor, far from looking exhausted, seemed to be in radiant health (Pflanze thinks, however, that Bismarck was genuinely ill at the time). It therefore did not surprise Russell when only a few days later Bismarck visited the British Embassy again, this time offering to tell 'the truth of what was going on':[32]

> He had told me on former occasions that he could not carry on the government of Germany with his present colleagues who were not equal to the situation, that he had asked the Emperor to let him form the administration the country required, but that his Majesty, with advancing years suffered from hesitation ... and could not make up his mind to part with the ministers he was accustomed to. Besides which His Majesty liked to be his own Premier, to deal with each department separately and to work one Minister against each other.[33]

Such Machiavellian methods must have reminded Odo more of his guest than of the less ingenious Emperor. To outsiders it seemed that Bismarck now retreated from Prussian domestic affairs, biding his time and playing the role of an uninterested observer. Part of the German public[34] therefore came to the conclusion that Bismarck's resignation was a personal defeat for him. Odo, however, never for one moment believed that Bismarck wanted to separate the office of Chancellor from that of Prussian Minister-President. In October 1873 Roon had to resign because of ill health and Bismarck returned (according to Pflanze, 'reluctantly') to his duties as Prussian Minister-President. It remains open to doubt whether Bismarck had guessed right from the start that the separation of the two offices would not work or whether it just eventuated that way.

Not all of Bismarck's resignation threats were related to political issues. Sometimes the great Chancellor was simply greedy. This was Odo's opinion when at the end of 1874, rumours of Bismarck's resignation circulated again: 'I now learn that his [Bismarck's] wife and daughter are on their knees before him to make him resign. His physician told him he cannot live three years in office, but may live to 100 if he will give up work'. Odo however did not think this would happen: 'He cannot leave his work in its unfinished state'.[35] To Morier he wrote that 'the great Bismarck is full of the idea of retiring into private life, and so is the "Princeps" — but nobody believes them'.[36] The reason this time was, according to Odo, the Dukedom of Lauenburg which the Chancellor had been fighting over with the Crown Princess. Odo wrote about this feud to Derby:

> After the war with France he [Bismarck] wanted to be made Duke of Lauenburg, and was much disappointed at only getting a portion of the estate ... and he knows that the Crown Princess stood in his way, who wanted the Emperor to give the Duchy of Lauenburg to her second son Prince Henry. If he [Bismarck] cannot persuade the Emperor to give the Duchy of Lauenburg to him, he will never get it from the Crown Prince. ... Bismarck's private ambitions are not yet satisfied.[37]

Derby, a wealthy man himself, could not believe this explanation. But although Odo admitted that there might be some further motive, he insisted that many people thought Bismarck simply wanted more payment and therefore played the 'prima-donna' part:

> Bismarck, who began life as a poor country gentleman with a few hundred a year, and now owns the forests of Lauenburg with 15,000 a year, has taken such a passion for buying fields and farms to 'round off' his new property that he has spent more than he could, and now wants a donation to make up the deficiency and re-establish his balance.[38]

Not surprisingly, the Chancellor eventually got more forests. Still, Lauenburg did not seem to love the Bismarck family. When Herbert von Bismarck ran there for a Reichstag seat in 1878, he lost.[39]

Such matters were of course trivial by comparison to Bismarck's condescending opinion of the parliament. For the Chancellor the *Reichstag*, with its different ideologies, was simply a toy to be played around with. In conversations with Odo, Bismarck occasionally claimed that he preferred the English parliamentary system to the German one. Odo wrote to Arthur about such attacks by the Chancellor on the parliament: 'the great Bismarck said to me the other day: "Happy England that possesses two parties able by turns to govern the country. ... poor me [Bismarck], I see no hope of an opposition capable of turning me out and giving me a little rest — I am worn out with work, etc" '.[40]

It had soon become obvious to Odo that Bismarck would try his best to reduce the influence of the Reichstag. Rennell Rodd later summed up Russell's analysis of the problem:

> The constitution of the Reichstag, against which Bismarck used frequently to in- veigh in his conversations with my chief [Russell], had been one of his admitted political miscalculations. He had made up his mind that under the Empire the German Princes would still remain Particularists, and he had therefore recom- mended universal suffrage in elections for the Diet, believing that the mass of the people, favourable to imperial union, would act as a counterpoise. Experience, however, showed that while the Princes rallied loyally to the new order, the weapon which he had devised to neutralise their anticipated opposition was constantly di- rected against himself.[41]

In 1874, Odo gave the FO a particularly glaring example of how Bismarck handled the Reichstag and its deputies. Emperor William and Count Roon had wanted to obtain 'the sanction of Parliament to a peace establishment of four hundred thousand men in perpetuity'.[42] Such a bill would have made the German nation pay indefinitely for its army with taxes.[43] For a British observer, the prospect of such a large amount of military expenditure was of course far from comprehensible. Odo himself did not value the army very highly (in his opinion, it was an unfortunate necessity for every country). In a conversation with Moltke, before the army bill negotiations took place, he made clear, that 'we [the British] were not a military nation as our press and our public debates on military matters sufficiently proved — besides which our system of Government and of public life were not favourable to a development of military institutions'.[44] In discussing the army bill with Bismarck, Odo pointed out that the majority in the Reichstag did not seem inclined to support this bill. Bismarck's reply was forceful — whether they liked it or not, the Chancellor exclaimed, they had to accept the Government's judgement: 'The army was essential to the existence of the state, and Parliament was not, and he [Bismarck] would *"send Parliament and its members to hell if they trifled with the safety of the Empire"*'.[45] When Odo tentatively suggested that this would be quite unconstitutional, Bismarck retorted with a long monologue. Russell recorded it in every detail and, contrary to his usual minimalistic writing style, he even described Bismarck's gestures. For example, Odo seemed to see it as symbolic that Bismarck was puffing away on a pipe while he talked about 'blowing up the constitution':

> He would blow up the constitution if it stood in the way of the Empire, and that, if he were to die any and every conscientious minister of the Crown would do the same, since the maintenance of peace, order and progress depended on the army and not on the constitution.[46]

To Odo, these words sounded almost revolutionary. If one took Bismarck seriously (which Odo wisely did not always do) it seemed that this man was ready to launch a *coup d'état* to solve his problems at home if he felt it necessary.[47] Still, Bismarck — despite this strong language to Odo — used, as usual, much more peaceful methods to achieve his ends. By mid-March he took to his bed, awaiting the storm. Odo detected the farcical elements of the situation when he wrote to Derby: 'Bismarck is feeling better, yet not out of bed. ... There is confusion in Parliament. His [Bismarck's] numerous followers appear somewhat at a loss how to vote when they no longer have the word of command of their great leader'.[48] The Reichstag did not function and again everything depended on the arbiter Bismarck. After the Emperor made it clear in his birthday speech on 22 March that he was deeply unsatisfied with the parliament for refusing to pass such an important bill, Bismarck received worried members of the National Liberal Party at his sick bed. The result of this unusual meeting was that the army's budget for the next 7 years (the so-called 'septennat') was decided on, for which, to Odo's disbelief, the Liberals were terribly thankful to Bismarck.

However, there were problems within Germany that even a Bismarck could not solve so quickly. One of these problems was the economic slump of 1873, which had followed the great boom after the reparation payments. At first, the Viennese banking crash seemed to be too far away to affect the Berlin bourse. This at least was the Emperor's hope, who did not comprehend the knock-on effect of international banking disasters.[49] Of course the economic recession was a psychological shock after a 'golden period'. It has, however, been recently argued by historians that this so-called great depression of the early 1870s was not as severe as some have thought. This would explain why Odo did not refer to it in great detail:

> No doubt the influence of the five milliards led to over speculation and the conse-quent loss of money reacted heavily on commerce and industry which has produced a great deal of distress but not discontent as might be supposed, because the realisation of national Unity fills the great majority of Germans with pride and hope for the future. Still, discontent will increase because Bismarck does nothing towards the improvement of Commerce, Industry and Finance, subjects he admits himself he does not know much about and which he thinks at present less important than political and military power.[50]

In the end, both Bismarck and Russell relied on the expertise of other people to analyse such economic problems and their possible remedies.

Another pressing issue that interested Russell, but about which he did not have too many original ideas, was the social question. Russell knew how much the pursuit of state socialism dominated Bismarck's thinking. In 1883, Odo wrote to Salisbury: 'Bismarck is himself much more occupied with social questions, than with foreign policy since he has ensured the peace of Europe by the creation of a peace league open to all corners, and he says himself that his last and greatest work will be the elaboration of working men's insurance laws'.[51] Odo also thought that he himself understood the working classes:

> You [Lady William Russell] did me an immense service, when you so wisely al-lowed me in my young days to associate frankly with the Karlsbad trades-people, for it has given me a practical insight into the honest portion of the working-classes, which are totally unknown to the class I live in and belong to, and who only judge them by ... sharpers they have been deceived by. Hundreds of times I have been able to apply the experience sucked in at Karlsbad to the wants and requirements of the working classes of other countries and in the end my impressions have proved more correct than those of my fellow dips.[52]

However, Russell's sympathy for poor people stopped when it came to their radical elements. In the summer of 1872, Plunkett, who was standing in for Russell, wrote in great detail about four days of rioting in the Blumenstrasse, which was in his eyes symptomatic of the problems the overcrowded Berlin had to face. The riots had started off with a carpenter who had been evicted by his landlord. A crowd, which had gathered around him and his piled-up furniture, decided to take sides and smashed the landlord's windows. After damaging more property the rioters were dispersed and met again in the evening to continue the battle against the police for the next four days. Plunkett's verdict was, that:

... although these disturbances are not very serious, for there is no doubt the Government can put them down the moment it chooses to make use of the troops, nevertheless they are not without significance as a proof of the lawless spirit which is gradually cropping up in this city, and which to a certain extent arises from the sudden increased prosperity of the Nation. Stragglers from all parts crowd into Berlin expecting ... to get some share in that great wealth which Germany has extracted from France. Once here, they find that although wages are much higher than in their country villages, everything else also is so much dearer that they get but little benefit from the change and when finally they find themselves unable to pay the enormous and preposterous rents which are now demanded ... their discontent breaks forth against the landlord who to them appears the representative of all that is ... grasping.[53]

The revolutionary element seemed to be on the increase and this frightened Russell. The attempt to kill the Emperor in 1878 was in his opinion another worrying foreboding: 'The second attempt on the Emperor's life has produced anxious days here. Bad times are coming — a conflict between the monarchical and socialistic parties has become inevitable'.[54] If the Socialists were to force their politics on to the leaders of the day, Odo argued, one would have a 'democracy, which is exclusive and dictatorial'.[55] For Russell, socialism, communism and nihilism were all the same.[56] But he could not think of a workable way to prevent people from leaving the liberal path and becoming radicals. When his brother Hastings, who was not exactly a socialist, suggested that more money should be spent on the welfare of the people than on the expansion of the army in order to assuage the growing radicalism, Odo all of a sudden defended the German system:

No doubt the standing armies of Europe are too large, but Emperors and archdukes do not keep them solely to shoot down their subjects. They are obliged to keep them, to keep order among their subjects and to protect life and property. The revolutionary element is very strong on the continent and without armies, we should have anarchy. Continental people cannot be kept in order by a police force as in England. If England were not an island and had frontiers to protect against hostile and ambitious neighbours, we should also require soldiers to support the police at home and resist foreign invasion abroad.[57]

Of course, this surprising defence does not mean that Odo wholeheartedly agreed with the draconian methods that Bismarck used against the Socialists. He was still a believer in civil rights and condemned witch hunts. But when it came to the use of such methods, his sympathy was more with the first victims of Bismarck, the Catholics, than with their successors, the socialists. A war against the Catholic Church was after all bound to fascinate Russell, this old expert of Roman affairs.

Bismarck's Fourth War: The Kulturkampf

Similar to the McCarthyism of the 20th century, the *Kulturkampf* [war of cultures] was a war of ideologies. However, whereas McCarthyism engendered the cult of the informer, the *Kulturkampf* created martyrs. This battle between the church and the state has to this day left its imprint on Germany.

German historians are divided in their interpretation of the *Kulturkampf*. Whereas, for example, Thomas Nipperdey is cautious in condemning it, Wolfgang J. Mommsen gives the most critical and detailed description of the discrimination the Catholics had to suffer, showing how step-by-step they were 'legally' turned into second-class citizens.[1] If one looks at Russell's impressions of this 'cold war', they tend to correspond more with Mommsen's interpretation.

While in Versailles Odo had noted that Bismarck 'does not wish to quarrel with the Pope and his Prussian Roman Catholic subjects',[2] this changed abruptly when the Catholic Centre Party (which had been founded in December 1870)[3] unexpectedly started to develop into a political rival that had to be reckoned with. It has been shown that Bismarck was afraid of the cosmopolitan aspect of the party, its 'secret agitation and its international side'.[4] He feared that the party would offer a 'conservative alternative' and that its press organs would outweigh his influence on German minds. What Bismarck particularly detested about this party was the support it received from 'protesting and isolated minorities'.[5] These included the Southern Particularists, the Poles, the MPs from Alsace–Lorraine and, the Welfen faction.

Why did a man who was a political and strategic master not use more clever methods to oppose a party, rather than starting an internal struggle at the worst possible moment? One would have thought that, in the aftermath of the Franco-Prussian war, Bismarck would have been more than busy enough with the immense task of uniting a culturally divided country. In Russell's opinion, one of the psychological explanations for this was that Bismarck, the successful tactician, simply could not exist without the excitement of a crusade: 'Great as Bismarck is in war, political combination and national danger he evidently lacks the less exciting qualities of [running] an administration in times of peace — he loves a conflict for its own sake and the triumph over his adversaries'.[6] It would be, of course, too simplistic to say that Bismarck embarked on his 'fourth war' because of his cantankerous character. Such an explanation would, after all, clash with the perception of

Bismarck as a *Realpolitiker*. It is, however, surprising how much emotion 'the great man' invested in this crusade and how little *ratio*. Russell, who was thrown back into his passive role of a bemused spectator whenever it came to German domestic affairs, was from the start surprised that a man like Bismarck sincerely believed he could fight a world religion. It was especially flabbergasting to him how much the Chancellor under-estimated his adversary — a serious error, which contradicted Odo's high estimation of Bismarck's intelligence.[7] In 1868, Odo had described the Pope's power as so 'enormous' that he could, at any time, rule over an army of 'disciplined Priests, of Laymen and women commanded by faith, ready to obey their spiritual head before they will obey their temporal rulers'.[8] Already, when he was in Rome, he had written to Lady Salisbury that nothing good could come out of taking measures against the Catholic Church: 'We cannot destroy the papacy, scarcely weaken it, is it not more prudent to be on good terms than to live like cat and dog and do no good thereby to humanity?'[9] There had to be some hidden agenda behind Bismarck's war, otherwise Russell simply could not see what could be gained from it:

> Bismarck is so great a genius [Odo wrote to his brother Hastings] and knows so well what he wants that I withhold my judgement until I see the results of his policy, but being by birth and instinct a liberal as well as by conviction my private im-pression is that freedom and religious toleration are more powerful weapons against Ultramontanism than prosecution.[10]

These few lines display Russell's strong belief in the values of fair play and decency, even to a political opponent — an old-fashioned notion which had nothing in common with the new convictions of the German Liberals. In Odo's opinion they lacked some of the most important requisites of a Liberal — common sense and toleration. To Arthur he wrote:

> For my part I fail to see the advantage of abolishing the Roman Church, so ardently desired by the Kulturkämpfer, I ... ask myself, *et aprés?* Humanity will always worship something, and the Roman church affords millions of people comfort, which nothing else can supply for years to come. Liberty and tolerance are to my mind the most powerful weapons against the abuses of the Church.[11]

Odo did not believe in the idolisation of the state and detested the growing control Bismarck and the National Party gained over the Germans with the *Kulturkampf* laws. In many ways, Russell's sympathies for the German Liberals died during the *Kulturkampf*. He saw them as an evil force behind the laws, as dogmatic warmongers:

> The Liberals here think that you can overcome these societies [the Roman church and the International] by throwing Bishops into prison ... *Erreur fatale!* The idea

that you can prevent Bishops from excommunicating their flocks is puerile. Excommunication is a matter of conscience and not of policy enactments. The more you interfere, the more you make the excommunication efficacious. German Liberals do not appear to me to know what Liberty means — they are no better than Italians in their notions of freedom. Bunsen, Gneist, Lazarus, Lasker, Helmholtz, Mommsen, etc., etc., are ever so many Gordinis in regard to church.[12]

Although Bismarck himself initiated the *Kulturkampf*, Odo had detected that the liberal National Party had encouraged the Chancellor to launch this ideological war. To this day there is disagreement as to who manipulated whom in this relationship. Lothar Gall calls Bismarck the *Zauberlehrling* [sorcerer's apprentice], and if one understands this in the sense of Goethe's poem and applies it to the *Kulturkampf*, then the Chancellor had lost control over his 'creatures'. Russell, for one, held the opinion that Bismarck had acted on this issue mainly in order to please his political partners, the Liberals: 'The political neutralisation of the churches has always been ardently desired by the liberals but Prince Bismarck [has] given an irresistible national impulse to the movement and a new proof of his genius as a political and national leader'.[13]

Apart from party political reasons, in a small way Bismarck's vanity played a part in his motivation to carry out the fight. Although Odo naturally exaggerated when he claimed that Bismarck 'thinks of himself as infallible and that he could not endure two infallibilities',[14] there was certainly an element of personal competitiveness. Bismarck tried to outdo his new parliamentary rivals, as well as his old acquaintances. He wanted to show his former friends among them, the Gerlachs, and Karl Friedrich v. Savigny, one of the founders of the Centre-Party, that he could take on this challenge. He also wanted to prove himself against the Centre leader Windthorst[15] who, according to Golo Mann, was 'the greatest Parliamentarian genius Germany ever had'.[16] Windthorst's excellent debating talents were celebrated by, among others, Empress Augusta's secretary Brandis. On one occasion he wrote happily to Morier: 'What do you say about Bismarck's and Windthorst's duel? We rather think that Windthorst has had the best of it. He has become a giant, having been a lilliputian and Bismarck is diminished in size and power'.[17] Of course, Bismarck knew of such comments. Another reason, if one personalises the origins of this war, was that he tried to fight the Empress and her Catholic circle.[18]

Bismarck's motives were personal, political and national, but certainly not religious, as Russell seemed to think at one point: 'Bismarck is an orthodox low churchman', wrote Odo in 1875, 'and believes in his *divine* mission to destroy the Pope'.[19] The use of the phrase 'divine mission' can easily cause one to be deceived about Bismarck's true religious beliefs. He was not fighting for the Protestant cause or any other denomination, but for the increase of power for the state. Although the Chancellor was full of anti-Catholic prejudices, he did not feel a particular *missionary* commitment against the Catholics.[20] In his opinion, it was simply a question of loyalty to the state being paramount. By framing the fight in terms of the old feud between the state and the church he helped to legitimise the *Kulturkampf* and to engender a feeling of communal spirit, a 'togetherness' for the fighters involved.[21]

The National Liberals helped Bismarck to turn his fight into a legal one. They achieved the promotion of Adalbert Falk[22] to the Prussian Ministry of Culture in 1872, a step that brought them closer to Bismarck then ever before. Falk was an 'experienced anti-cleric, a rationalist of the best type, a committed civil servant'.[23] He was now in a position to function as Bismarck's legislative arm, and he readily welcomed his new master's orders to '[re-establish] the rights of the state against the church ... with the least possible noise'.[24] Important steps had already been taken. On 10 December 1871 the 'Pulpit paragraph'[25] proposed by, of all states, Bavaria was attached as an amendment to the penal code. It made the abuse of religion for political aims illegal — it was an offence, punishable by two years imprisonment, for clergy to discuss or even allude to politics in their sermons. A few months later on 11 March 1872 a further area of church power was undermined. The Prussian school inspection bill prohibited both Catholic and Protestant clergy from being appointed to teaching posts without remuneration. The state now controlled the curriculum in all schools. With the school inspection bill, Bismarck also damaged Protestant institutions. For Odo, this bill was not the enlightened measure which it is viewed as today.[26] He thought that it was of a 'repressive character', and was simply a further way of increasing the state's spheres of influence: 'absolute power is given to the State over all and every public or private educational establishment throughout the kingdom'.[27] The enthusiasm with which the new law was welcomed therefore surprised Russell. According to the papers, every town sent congratulatory addresses to the Chancellor, who seemed to be 'at the height of his popularity and has become the acknowledged leader of the Great National Party'.[28]

Odo's first, rather flippant reaction to this new Bismarckian war in 1872 had been to 'look forward to it with childish delight'.[29] However, with the implementation of more and more anti-Catholic measures, Russell's amusement soon vanished. He simply despised the inequality (and later the brutality) of the fight.[30] Two-thirds of the German population, the Protestants, were fighting against one-third, the Catholics. The obvious unfairness of this aroused Russell's conscience.[31] He pointed out the harshness of the *Kulturkampf* laws in almost every despatch he sent relating to German domestic affairs. Yet, despite wholeheartedly condemning the laws, Russell also realised that in a paradoxical way they increased the strength of the Church: 'The Church will thrive the more it is persecuted. The great danger to the Roman Church in my mind is [equality] in the State and "indifference" in the people, then the church vegetates and sickens'.[32]

David Blackbourn points out that the *Kulturkampf* had to be fought from above, because there was no great support base among the Germans for its prosecution. This is correct for the later stages of the fight, when the public was tired of it, but it was not the case at the beginning. Odo certainly experienced it in a different way. In the course of interviewing members of all classes, it seemed to him that the war was welcomed by them wholeheartedly. Odo wrote to Lyons in 1872 that: 'It is surprising to see with what enthusiasm the Germans have responded to Bismarck's declaration of war against the Vatican'.[33] This observation shows that at first, Bismarck's hope of uniting the majority of Germans in a common ideological war worked as much as it had done during his 'real' wars. In the long run, however, as has already been mentioned, he underestimated the impact of the passive resistance of the Catholics and their power at the polls. Even within his own trusted circles there were dissenters. By 1872, Bismarck must have hoped that the Emperor would back him in this fight, yet Odo's private correspondence reveals that this did not happen. In December 1872, Russell was approached for advice by an intermediary of the Emperor, the historian and diplomat Professor Johann Heinrich Gelzer, who was about to embark on a mediation mission to the Vatican (Professor Gelzer had already worked there before, as an observer for William I during the Vatican Council). It is not clear whether Bismarck knew, via his many agents, about the Emperor and Gelzer's plan. Professor Gelzer himself doubted whether he was suited to take up this difficult task.[34] He had contacted Odo in the hope that the British ambassador could tell him which members of the Roman Curia to approach in Rome. After a long conversation, Odo encouraged Gelzer to take up the mission because it was his duty to the Emperor. He reminded him, however, that it was extremely difficult, especially for people who were not accredited, to get access to any reliable sources of information in Rome: 'The influential people of the Roman Curia never tell the truth ex officio'.[35] Real success would only be possible, Odo claimed, if Bismarck supported Gelzer's mission. By this statement

Odo made it clear that he did not want to get involved in any intrigue against the Chancellor. Although he could have used his contacts with Cardinal Antonelli and given Gelzer access to many Vatican officials, he knew that Bismarck would detect such an intrigue very quickly. Naturally, Russell could not risk his position by interfering actively in Bismarck's German domestic affairs without suffering diplomatic repercussions.

The Jesuits had the dubious pleasure of becoming the first official outcasts of the new Reich (soon to be followed by the Socialists). The year 1872 saw the expulsion of all Jesuits — a measure that was enthusiastically received by the prejudiced public and also by the Old Catholics. Döllinger for one thought that this was a reason to celebrate. Odo wrote to Arthur about such shortsightedness: 'All newspapers are delighted with his [Döllinger's] lecture on the Jesuits in which he proves that all their establishments and missions all over the world have crumbled and failed ... Fool!'[36] Odo disapproved of the Jesuit bill and the means by which it had been brought about:

> By raising the cry against the 200 Jesuits who dwelt in Germany, Prince Bismarck persuaded his supporters to vote for laws, which give the Government the unrestricted, irresponsible and everlasting power ... to imprison anyone, anywhere at any moment on the mere suspicion or accusation of being anyhow connected with the order of Jesus — a power the liberal party may some day regret to have handed over unconditionally to a military administration.[37]

Bismarck was extremely adept at personalising the *Kulturkampf* through his conspiracy theories involving Jesuits, who were caricatured as being the incarnation of evil itself. This was very effective in playing on the inherent prejudices of the masses. As during the economic crisis of 1873, they turned their hatred towards the visible scapegoats: in the case of the *Kulturkampf* the Jesuits, and during the economic crisis, the Jewish population. The propaganda worked so well that when the German Minister in Brussels, von Balan, died in 1874 there was serious speculation that he had been poisoned by Jesuits. For Odo this was a clear sign of universal hysteria:

> It makes the public see a Jesuit conspiracy in every death or disaster that occurs. Sometime since a lion died in the Zoological Gardens, who was a favourite of the Berliners. A reward of 1,000 Thalers was offered in the newspapers to anyone who could discover the cause of his sudden death, and the public jumped to the conclusion that the Lion had been poisoned by the Jesuits.[38]

It is difficult to judge whether Bismarck really believed in his Catholic conspiracy theories or whether they were simply a useful tool for manipulating the masses. He certainly tried to win over Odo with his propaganda tricks, through the years telling him numerous stories about the intrigues of the Centre Party:

> Among the papers in question [seized by the Prussian police during a raid at a priest's home] was a letter from a prominent member of the Centre faction to a canon ... in which were the words 'send just now no more petitions to the Reichstag! But you may continue the petitions at fixed intervals, ... only do not address them to the Reichstag, but directly to the German Princes'.[39]

Talk about conspiracies now became a common feature at the Auswärtigen Amt briefings. In London, Münster was pestering Granville with stories about conspiracies between refugee Jesuit priests in Belgium and Roman Catholics in Germany.[40] In Berlin, Bülow was always well prepared for his conspiracy lectures to the foreign diplomatic corps. In 1874 he told Odo that 'every day brought new proofs of the vast and powerful organisation of the Ultramontane conspiracy against the German Empire'.[41] One of these 'fully proved' stories related to a meeting of Jesuit priests in Belgium who, it was alleged, were in constant contact with their Catholic co-conspirators in Germany. They had done something very subversive and then dispersed again, finding refuge in England and America. What exactly had happened during this meeting Bülow was not willing to tell Odo, but it was definitely all part of a 'vast conspiracy of the church against the state'.[42]

Belgium, in particular, was again and again accused by Bismarck and his entourage of being a 'hotbed of Ultramontane intrigue'. Naturally, such strong language reawakened English fears of possible German interference with Belgium's neutrality under the pretext of an Ultramontane conspiracy (and eventually sobered British enthusiasm for the *Kulturkampf*). Odo, as has been shown earlier, felt that he was in a position to soothe such fears with respect to most of these cases. In his opinion, Germany herself was only scared that France and Belgium would become too involved with each other, a dangerous development for Bismarck's foreign policy: 'The independence of Belgium, from 1830 to 70 of British interest only, has [now] become by the creation of the new Empire a German interest as well, for which Germany must ... fight to prevent the aggrandisement of France'.[43]

However, it was neither the foreigners nor the Jesuits who caused the next sensation in the conspiracy saga, but a German. In 1874, Bismarck was slightly wounded during an assassination attempt. Adams was in charge at the embassy when Bismarck was attacked in Bad Kissingen by a 'fellow-German', as the shattered journalists wrote. His name was Heinz Kullmann and he was a Catholic. Naturally the 'vicious deed' was immediately connected with the 'fanaticism of the uneducated Catholics'.[44] In his first conversation with Bülow after the attack, Adams was lectured on the great conspiratorial background behind the deed:

> Several Priests had been observed during the preceding days near the house where the Chancellor is lodging, that one of these priests had been seen in the morning with Kullmann; that the statement of so uneducated a man, in answer to the Prince, that he wished to kill him on account of the new Ecclesiastical Laws seemed to indicate [the] instigators of the crime.[45]

During the next months Adams would grow tired of listening to the constantly repeated 'outbreaks of this ... fuss against Catholics': 'Whatever happens, whether it is an attempt on Prince Bismarck's life, or the shooting of a German subject by the Carlists, is put down in chorus to the same cause with increasing bitterness'.[46]

Of course, it was to be expected that Bismarck would use Kullmann for his propaganda purposes. Odo was again impressed by the Chancellor's skill at turning phrases into household words. Thanks to Bismarck's oratorical skills, the Catholics were now seen almost as a 'revolutionary party': 'You may try to disown this assassin, but none the less he is clinging to your coat tails',[47] the Chancellor declared in the Reichstag. All Catholics were capable of criminal deeds such as those of Kullmann, and the war with France had been the Pope's fault anyway. Odo wrote that:

> These declarations are calculated to strengthen the growing conviction of the National Party that the Papacy is the greatest living danger to the Unity and freedom of Germany, and that there will be no safety or peace at home and abroad until the Catholic Church is abolished.[48]

Odo noticed that Bismarck blossomed during these Reichstag confrontations: 'The great man B. tells me that he wants the opposition to attack him again about Kullmann because he has "more cartridges in his pouch" for them which it would be a pity not to fire off'.[49] Bismarck also visited Emily Russell, telling her about his latest confrontations:

> When the Catholic Party cried 'shame' and shook their fists at him, his [Bismarck's] first impulse was to take the ink stand before him and fling it at them — his second impulse was to measure the distance, spring upon them and knock [them] down ... his third impulse overcame the two first and he merely told them that 'he felt contempt for them but was too civil to say so'.[50]

Kullmann gave the enactment of the 'May Laws' of 1873 as the reason for his attack on Bismarck.[51] The May Laws, which were introduced by

Falk, made the Evangelical and Catholic churches 'subject to the laws of the state and to the legally established supervision of the state'.[52] In other words, the state took over 'the education, employment and dismissal of clergymen'.[53] One now had to pass a newly created state exam if one wanted to get a church office (or ecclesiastical position). Church officials who did not obey the laws were fined and imprisoned. The May Laws also made it easier for both Protestants and Catholics to cease being church members. In a letter to Hammond, Odo showed that he was far from impressed by these Bismarckian schemes:

> He [Bismarck] appears to think that church questions and religious matters can be regulated by police measures, and I, for one, shall be very curious to see him carry out his Church policy. He is not the man to shrink from any difficulty and is not hampered by religious scruples so that if anyone can grapple with the papacy it is he![54]

In his despatches, Odo now increasingly mentioned the excesses of the ecclesiastical laws. In the Catholic parts of Westphalia, for example, the brutality of the authorities in carrying out the laws caused demonstrations. A carpenter, who had to remove the furniture of the fined Bishop of Münster to bring it to auction, was threatened by the mob. The situation got quickly out of hand and the police soon had to face an enormous crowd loyally fighting for their bishop. Similar episodes occurred all over the country and confirmed Odo's predictions that 'The German Government do not appear to me to be aware of the power of passive resistance of the Roman Catholic Clergy. ... They will never accept the Falk laws'.[55] His predictions turned out to be correct. Already in 1873, two archbishops had happily gone to prison as a demonstration of their faith and 1300 parishes were without a vicar.[56] Every arrest and trial was the occasion for a public display of sympathy by the faithful. They accompanied their priests to the prison gates and celebrated the released ones like war heroes.[57] As well as undertaking passive resistance, the Catholic Church also fought against the discrimination by protesting publicly. Odo wrote to Hammond: 'I am rather amused at the fury of Bismarck ... because I always told him they would resist his decrees'.[58] Bismarck did not want to learn from Odo and continued in his inflexible way. In March 1874, civil marriage was made obligatory and to this day a church wedding alone is not legally binding in Germany. For Odo this law was a further sign that German morals and values were in utter decay, and that the only religion which counted was nationalism:

> Now, I am told by all competent judges that more than three-quarters of the population will only be too glad to dispense with marriage in church and Baptism alto-

gether, so highly civilised are the Germans in regard to religion. Few nations could say as much and it shows that rationalism is the real religion of Germany. The Prussian code admits 14 causes of divorce! One being madness, however slight.[59]

According to Odo's information, these 14 causes of the Prussian code were subject to great abuse. Husbands now had ideal excuses to get rid of their inconvenient wives and could easily justify 'shutting ... her up in an asylum and marrying another one instead'.[60] The Civil Marriage bill did not unleash as great a storm as had the May Laws and Odo had to admit that Bismarck's speech in defence of it was full of 'wit and power'. However, in Odo's opinion the decline of other values soon ensued. Even in Russell's circle it had become chic to look down on religion in general: 'It has become very much the fashion for Germans to smile at Christianity'.[61] Catholics were at the bottom of the list because they were poor, uneducated creatures who laboured on farms and could hardly keep up with the pace of their upwardly mobile Protestant counterparts.[62]

The Old Catholics, of course, were an exception to this.[63] Their establishment as a second religious group (which still exists in Germany today) was a further, very German development, in the fight between the state and the Catholic Church. Any enemies of the church were friends of Bismarck, and he gladly supported the 'disobedient Catholics'. In Odo's opinion, the Old Catholics were only pawns that Bismarck used to try to divide the Catholic Church:

> By offering pecuniary assistance and the spoils of the Ultramontane Clergy to the new 'old Catholic' sect in return for their support of the Falk laws, he [Bismarck] created an element of religious discord in the Roman Church, which he can turn to account or not in the future according to circumstances.[64]

Although his friends Acton and Döllinger had been involved with the Old Catholics at the beginning, Odo's opinion of the movement was quite negative.[65] He saw them as a sect that had gone far beyond 'what Döllinger and Acton intended'.[66] Russell distinguished here 'between the originators of the movement, who dreamt of a literary schism only' (such as Döllinger, and Acton the 'Ultra-Catholic') and 'the men of action [such as] Reinkens, Friedrichs [the Old Catholics]'.[67] Whether Old or Ultra, the movement did not have a great future in Odo's eyes. To Arthur, he wrote that he had strong doubts whether the Old Catholics would ever be able to attract a great number of believers. Their creed was simply too complicated and unappealing for the average German:

> because the Old Catholic rejects the Council of the Vatican and its new dogma [but] he accepts older Councils, older dogmas, and the earlier teachings of the

Roman Catholic church. Now you cannot make the ... Protestant German understand why an Old Catholic while he is about it won't reject the whole of the falla-
cies of Popery and that every refusal destroys the confidence of the people in the
Old Catholics movement. Old Catholics will continue as a respectable sect — but
it cannot become the Catholic Church in Germany without a Pope ... and an Anti-
Pope is impossible in Germany without the sanction of the state and the parliament which is absurd.[68]

In addition, Odo did not think that it was possible for the Protestants
and Old Catholics to get together and found a state church, equivalent
to the Anglican State church — an illusion that some of his English
friends still maintained:

Whether this great and important movement which Prince Bismarck has seen fit
to call forth with so much energy and political skill is calculated, as some people
predict, to bring about the establishment of a German National Church or not,
few can yet foretell. ... I doubt whether there is religion enough in Germany to
create a new one.[69]

In 1874, Odo himself became a victim of the Catholic witch-hunt
through a press campaign that was mounted against him. It still remains
a mystery whether it was his privately expressed criticism about the
Kulturkampf that was responsible for this, or whether the Catholics just
used his case for their own propaganda purposes. The articles that
appeared in October 1874 accused Odo's deceased mother and himself
of having converted to Catholicism: 'Vienna papers announce my
conversion as well as poor MMs [Lady William Russell] to Roman
Catholicism, which the Cölner Zeitung contradicts'.[70] Lady William
Russell had always enjoyed swimming against the tide and her
purported conversion to Catholicism had probably only been motivated
by a desire to upset the strong Anglican feelings of the Russells. The
wife of the American sculptor Story was sure that in 1862 Odo's mother
had become a Catholic:

She had more than once spoken to me of her having lately embraced the Catholic
faith ... She was at the same time never narrow or violent in her faith, and when
once Mrs. H., in her presence, began to use arguments to convert me, Lady William reproved her and said 'Don't meddle with her beliefs, they are what she needs,
probably better than any you can supply'.[71]

Mrs Story makes several mistakes in her memoirs (such as, for example,
claiming that Lady William Russell's father had been British Ambassador
to Vienna) and her version is therefore not very reliable. Whether Lady
William Russell actually went through the whole conversion ceremony
is therefore far from clear. Her son Arthur denied it and wrote about his

mother's religious odyssey to Lady Derby: 'She [Lady William Russell] never formally joined the Roman Catholic Church. It is now scarcely possible to expect that the Roman Catholics will not claim her for their church — it is disagreeable there should be any controversy'.[72] To have a Catholic mother (even a dead one) was not exactly a social asset in those days. At first, Odo had been worried that English papers might copy this story, but he came to the conclusion that the best policy would be for the whole Russell family not to interfere and let the matter die a natural death. Odo himself also pretended to have no interest in finding out about the origin of the campaign.

While his mother's religious vacillations might have caused Odo embarrassment, his uncle's anti-Popish campaign had only a few months earlier made a good impression on the *Kulturkämpfer*. John Russell had expressed his moral support in a letter to the leaders of the German fight,[73] ('the cause of the German Emperor is the cause of liberty')[74] and Bismarck was overwhelmed with joy that there should be British sympathisers for his campaign. Odo wrote to John Russell about the Chancellor's reaction: 'I showed Prince Bismarck privately your letter ... the Emperor's letter to you is making the greatest sensation in Germany — it is even preferred to the one he wrote to the Pope'.[75] Bismarck forgot all the disagreements he had had with John Russell in the 1860s: '[I] need hardly say how much I am gratified by the active interest the Nestor of European statesmen is taking in our defensive warfare against the priesthood of Rome. I quite agree with the idea which seems to underline this letter: that in clerical government there is always a seed of international conflict, and that a great deal less of that seed will be thrown out, if England and Germany are agreed to stand up for religious liberty'.[76]

Although Russell profited socially from his uncle's crusade, he did not agree with it privately. To Arthur, Odo had written earlier: 'The much admired letter of [Emperor] William to Uncle John is in my private opinion a bad stroke'.[77] In a letter to the FO he tried to explain that this correspondence simply played into Bismarck's hands by providing him with the ammunition to draw the Emperor even further into the swamp of the *Kulturkampf*:

> By prevailing on the Emperor to sign the letters, instead of signing them himself, he had composed and addressed to the Pope and to Earl Russell on the religious question, he committed the sovereign personally to an anti-church policy which did not represent the Emperor's real feelings.[78]

It is ironic that the *Kulturkampf*, which Odo so strongly disapproved of, brought his country and Germany closer together for a while.[79]

British sympathy widened on the basis of the genuine but mistaken belief that Bismarck was simply demanding more tolerance from the church. The British did not know that his regime had in fact terminated the once proverbial Prussian religious toleration.[80] Even Granville, who should have been better informed by Odo's despatches, saw nothing negative about this German movement.[81] When the German Empress, who was admittedly biased in the matter, visited London in 1872 and talked to Lord Granville about the religious persecution that divided her country, she did not receive much comfort.[82] Of course Granville had only a faint idea of the successive destruction of civil liberties that was being carried out in Germany. Even Gladstone, who could distinguish between the advantages and disadvantages of Bismarck's crusade (and who could not be accused of being pro-German), wrote to Odo in 1874 that the idea behind the *Kulturkampf* deserved approval:[83]

> Bismarck's ideas and methods are not ours; they spring out of other traditions, but my sympathies though they do not go with him they are more with him than against him. I cannot but say that the present doctrines of the Roman church destroy the title of her obedient member to the enjoyment of civil rights.[84]

This comment shows, despite its reservations, that Bismarck had, even if only briefly, managed to obtain the approval of his liberal opponents in England.[85] Gladstone's two books on the Papal subject: *The Vatican Decrees in their Bearing on Civil Allegiance*[86] and *Vaticanism*[87] were, allegedly, cherished by the German Chancellor. This must have flattered Gladstone. However, Odo was not impressed:

> Gladstone has sent me his *Vaticanism* for which I must thank him, although I cannot quite agree. I hold that every attack on the Vatican unites the clergy against us. — If we Protestants left the Council alone, ignored its dogmas, the Catholics would fight and quarrel amongst each other about it, at which we could afford to smile, as Grant Duff says. Unhappily when one man declares himself to be infallible everybody else feels 'le besoin' to do the same, and there is not one infallible, but many infallibles.[88]

Many British MPs were blinded by their own anti-Catholicism and, together with other British *Kulturkampf* enthusiasts, organised meetings to express their sympathy for the Protestant 'culture warriors'. Addresses were sent from Britain to Bismarck, which the Chancellor received with 'deep gratitude'. In one of them, the MP Arthur Kinnaird, a well-known Evangelical, praised the Germans enthusiastically for their exemplary crusade. The letter was signed by, among others, Odo's uncle John Russell as well as many high-ranking churchmen, including the President of the Wesleyan Methodist Conference, Wisemann, and Duff, the Professor of Evangelistic Theology, at New College, Edinburgh. Further meetings took place in England and they were always welcomed thankfully by the Germans. The 'No Popery' meeting held on 27 January 1874 in St James Hall had, according to Odo:

> ... a beneficial influence on the feelings and sympathies of the great National Party in Germany towards England. Their newspapers are overflowing with exultation at the commencement of a new era, the alliance of the people against Priestcraft ... to unite with Germany in the interest of peace, progress and civilisation, etc., etc. Prince Bismarck ... is more deeply satisfied than words can tell at the prospect of an international understanding founded on common interest.[89]

The Germans showed their gratitude by holding another meeting in return. Among the committee members were Odo's friends Gneist, Helmholtz and Mommsen, as well as entrepreneurs such as Dr Siemens. The *German News* reported the speeches in detail, starting off with Professor Gneist's gratitude to the English ('God save old England') followed by the addresses of his fellow committee members.[90]

Bismarck answered each British address enthusiastically and the Emperor felt the same gratitude as his Chancellor for this unexpected cooperation in the church question from England. On the celebration of his 76th birthday, William told Odo how pleased he was having HMG as 'an ally in the war he was unhappily obliged to carry on against the Roman Catholic Bishops'.[91] To the Emperor's surprise Odo could not agree with him. Instead, the British ambassador gave a courageous statement of his convictions: 'The love of freedom and toleration was so great with us [the British] now, that we were not likely to imitate the policy so popular with the Liberals of Germany at the present moment of placing the clergy of all denominations under military discipline'.[92]

With this statement, Odo had clearly distanced himself from his uncle and many English MPs at home. Such harsh criticism irritated the Emperor, who could only feebly answer by repeating the arguments Bismarck had over the years programmed him to say. The 'increasing power of evil' had to be counteracted by the state, he told Odo, and to achieve this the state simply needed more power.[93]

Odo's opposition to the *Kulturkampf* did not mean, however, that he had become pro-Catholic, or wanted his government to take sides with the Catholic cause. When he was asked in March 1874, by Derby, whether HMG should establish official relations with the Pope, Odo replied:

> I could see no advantage or reason for maintaining ... relations with a Spiritual Power we neither acknowledge nor believe in. Besides which by keeping up our unofficial relations with the Pope we were encouraging resistance and the hopes of the

Ultramontanes that we had some secret future interest in the reestablishment of his temporal dominion, and by the example we were thus giving other Governments to linger on around the Vatican we were contributing to prolong the struggle.[94]

The Emperor and Bismarck were soon to find out that Russell was right in believing that the British support for the *Kulturkampf* was far from uniform. As Kennedy has shown, the brutal enforcement of the Laws irritated many British Liberals, who felt they could no longer support such methods: 'we are much more indignant at the attempt to crush the faith and the independence of any form of religious belief by state persecution and intolerance', wrote the *Edinburgh Review*.[95] Morier, who had initially agreed with the measures, also became more critical.[96] The same happened to Queen Victoria, who had lost her enthusiasm for the fight. To her daughter Vicky she wrote in 1875: '[I am] very anti-Catholic ... but with all that I think persecution very wrong and a great mistake'.[97] Apart from the increasing unease among British Protestants, British Catholics who stood up for their fellow believers also had to be reckoned with. When the Archbishop of Posen refused to pay his fines and was ultimately imprisoned in 1874, English Catholics sent letters of support to him.[98]

As with the Emperor, Russell did not hold back his opinion in conversations with Bismarck either. He liked to discuss the *Kulturkampf* issues with the Chancellor, with the pretext that 'after his long residence in Rome [he] had developed a special interest in the issue'.[99] During these discussions Odo felt that he could talk frankly, because they did not really touch on German–British foreign relations, and were more in the nature of informal exchanges between old acquaintances. Russell therefore felt entitled to warn Bismarck that 'German statesmen underrated the moral forces of Rome and the powers of resistance of the Church to the State'.[100] Completely unimpressed by this, Bismarck assured Russell that he was confident that 'it would take ten years of legislation to eradicate the cancer of Roman Catholicism out of Germany'.[101]

This was of course wishful thinking. By 1874 Bismarck had already begun to doubt whether the campaign could work. By 1879 his political priorities had completely changed. For his swing to the Conservative Party, he needed to get rid of the tiresome *Kulturkämpfer*. He could no longer face the prolongation of the battle, and the same was felt by his fellow Germans. 'Many people are growing wary of the war with the church', Odo wrote to Derby in 1875, 'they see no end to it and suffer from the family dissensions'.[102] The death of Pope Pius in 1878 seemed to be an ideal opportunity for a mediation and his successor, Pope Leo X, signalled interest.

The German Catholic Church had lost a great number of its rights during this fight, but it had also gained a fresh impetus. Odo had been right in arguing that nothing better could have happened to a church which was in a severe crisis than to have to go through this second persecution. After three years of attack, all German bishops were turned by Bismarck into the most loyal supporters of Rome, and the Catholic Church experienced an unprecedented revival:

> In Germany his [the Pope's] success has been complete [Odo wrote to Hastings in 1874] for all the bishops who voted against the new dogma in the Vatican Council now go cheerfully to prison and pay enormous fines and suffer martyr-dom for that very infallibility they voted against 3 years ago and think they will go to heaven like skyrockets when they die for their trouble.[103]

The paradox is, that although the Catholic Church ultimately benefited, the German nation did not. Crowe wrote to Odo about this:

> The social disintegration caused by the Prussian legislation against the Catholics ... is complete. ... Roman Catholics of the [middle-class], have told me that they are accused of not being patriotic; and this is true 'now'. 'I was a patriot last year', said one of the gentlemen to me, 'I am not a patriot now'.[104]

The inner gulfs widened, not only between Catholics and Protestants,[105] but also between the different generations and their value systems. The *Kulturkampf* had been an enormously forceful movement with which Bismarck had infected all Germans, even the moderate ones. Each person had to decide whether he accepted the 'common path', or was marginalised as a non-conforming citizen.

For a man such as Bismarck who had been used to quick victories, the *Kulturkampf* was a frustrating experience. To Odo, however, this showed for a second time after the war-in-sight-scare, that the great Chancellor was not invincible after all.

CHAPTER 7

No Man's Land Revisited:
Russell and the Eastern Question

The Activist

'The most persistent source of international friction in Europe'[1] raised its familiar head again in the summer of 1875. As is the case today, Europe in the 19th century seemed unable to deal with the traumatic Eastern saga, permitting it to spread into an international crisis that dominated the work of British, Russian, Austrian, French and German politicians and diplomats for the next three years. The fight over 'no-man's land',[2] as Lord Salisbury called it, would, however, ultimately have a positive effect on British–German relations, which had by May 1875 reached a trough.

There are many standard works on the Eastern Question[3] and it is difficult to find a new approach to the subject without repeating well-established details. Accordingly, the already familiar international setting for the Eastern Question will only be briefly alluded to. The main purpose of the following discussion will be to analyse closely the nature of the British–German relationship during the events. It is also proposed to outline how Odo Russell, who initially only observed events from the periphery, rose to become an important player for HMG. The more international the crisis became, the greater was his usefulness as a channel to Bismarck. Reference will be made to Russell's private correspondence with Lord Derby to throw light on the British attitude to the actions of the Three Emperors' League.

In July 1875, Christian Hercegovinans started a rebellion in a village close to Mostar.[4] Backed by sympathisers in Serbia, Montenegro, Austria–Croatia and Dalmatia, the revolt quickly spread all over Hercegovina. The 'rebels' (to use Turkish terminology) had numerous, perhaps explainable motives for their outrage. For centuries Bosnia and Hercegovina had been under brutal Turkish rule yet, spurred by Western examples, the country suddenly 'awakened' as a nation — rediscovering its religious, linguistic and historical roots. It was a national fight that under a different power bloc situation would perhaps have been received with sympathy by the British. Yet right from the start the insurgents were judged to be Russian or Austrian tools. This was due to the FO having received reports by Elliot, which made it quite clear that the Russians supported the insurgents wherever possible. Elliot, an ardent Turcophile, had never shown much interest in the deeper causes of the uprising. For him the insurgents were 'turbulent Bosnians' who 'robbed and burnt the villages whose inhabitants refused to join them, and in this way their numbers quickly increased, though at first by unwilling recruits'.[5] Elliot argued that there was a possibility that the whole affair had been manipulated by the Russians.[6] Another theory circulating at the time was that the Austrian military party might have been involved, a view that was widely expressed in British, Russian and German diplomatic circles. Such suspicions were possibly all wrong if one believes the eye-witness of the *Manchester Guardian*, who described the revolts as long overdue, spontaneous eruptions: 'the outbreak took the Omlachia [a liberal, national movement fighting against Russian and Austrian absolutism] itself by surprise'.

To Britain it was naturally of interest to know how Germany, the third and only uninvolved party of the Three Emperors' League, would react to the situation. Odo Russell was not in Berlin at the outbreak of the revolts. It was unfortunate that his absence attracted criticism from the FO as it was simply caused by the bad timing of the summer break. As was the case during the lead-up to the First World War, politicians and diplomats enjoyed their holidays while the revolt spread to Bosnia: 'While sovereigns and statesmen are drinking mineral waters, politics come to a standstill and diplomatists take their leave', Odo wrote to his Foreign Secretary in 1875.[7] It was therefore MacDonnell, Russell's chargé d'affaires, who had to judge what part, if any, Bismarck might want to play. It soon became obvious that the German Chancellor was extremely worried by the danger of the crisis for his fragile alliance system. He made it known to MacDonnell that he was especially 'concerned' about the Austrian reaction to the uprising.[8] According to MacDonnell's information,[9] the Chancellor:

> considers the Hercegovina question very serious, information had reached him that the Austrian Government are mobilising a large body of troops to act on the frontier ... The Prince is of the opinion that the Austrian Government are not acting discreetly. Reports are current of an Austrian armed intervention.[10]

Bismarck feared that the new situation might lead to the downfall of the Andrássy administration, and with a new Austrian 'military faction' in control would escalate into a Russian–Austrian war. Because of Germany's vital interest in maintaining peace between its allies, MacDonnell rightly concluded that there were no radical moves to fear from Berlin:

> I think, I can safely venture to say, that the German Government do not wish to see any important changes effected in Turkey, and will abstain from interfering in her affairs so long as they can conveniently do so, on the other hand they would not view with displeasure any complications which might increase the difficulties by which Austria is already beset.[11]

Although the first part of this analysis turned out to be correct, MacDonnell obviously shared the misconception of his absent chief that it was only a question of time before Germany annexed the German parts of Austria. This miscalculation would blur the vision of the British decision-makers and wrongly convince them that Bismarck's loyalties to Russia were, despite the war-in-sight-crisis, unshakeable.

In August 1875 the Three Emperors' League decided to start its first mediation effort with the Turkish Government. The consuls of Austria, Germany and Russia were instructed to talk to the insurgents, informing them that they could expect no help from the said powers and that they had to refrain from hostilities and put their complaints before a commission. Britain joined in this effort reluctantly, only after the Porte itself asked them to.[12] Supported by such thinly veiled British indifference to this Western effort, Turkey did not take the delegation seriously. The Turkish ambassador in Berlin, Aristarchi Bey, openly questioned the cooperation of the Northern Powers, arguing in a conversation with MacDonnell that: '[Germany] is guided by no fixed plan of action [and is only] prompted by the desire to sow discord between Russia and Austria, which may eventually serve Prince Bismarck's purpose'.[13] Such an opinion was not yet shared by the British who believed that the three Northern Powers might still act in accord.[14]

Up to this point in late August, Odo Russell had not been involved with the problem. One of the reasons for this might have been that he was not a friend or even a correspondent of the man in charge at Constantinople, Sir Henry Elliot. For Russell, the reopening of the Eastern Question would from now on pose personal as well as professional problems. Although he had privately advocated a stronger foreign policy during the time of the Gladstone government, he could not bring himself to identify with the 'new Disraelian world order'. As he was so far removed from the London power centre, at first it seemed surprisingly difficult for Odo to find out whether HMG actually had a coherent Eastern policy. Although he was still on good terms with

Derby, Disraeli's much more decisive opinions were not conveyed to Odo properly.[15] Like Bismarck, the British Prime Minister did not value diplomats highly and the few surviving letters from him to Odo only deal with the administrative arrangements for the Berlin Congress. Grant Duff once claimed that Disraeli had in the 1860s praised the young diplomat Russell ('I think Lady William Russell the most fortunate woman in England because she has the three nicest sons').[16] However, such sympathies had evaporated by the time Disraeli had to work with Odo. In December 1876, he even went so far as to call Russell a 'Russian courtier'[17] — a rather eccentric accusation. The Prime Minister wrote to Derby about his ambassador at Berlin: 'The difficulty is to get hold of Bismarck. I counted on Odo Russell, but he might as well be at Baghdad'.[18] The accusations got worse. In 1877, Disraeli fumed: 'I think Russell the worst of all [diplomats]. He contents himself with reporting all Bismarck's cynical bravados, which he evidently listens to in an ecstasy of sycophantic wonder'.[19] Seton Watson rightly points out that Disraeli seemed to expect miracles from Russell: 'though it was even then notorious both that Bismarck rarely allowed himself to be influenced by foreigners and that Russell was one of the very few foreigners to whom he listened and attached value.' Tenterden and Salisbury [then Secretary for State for India], who completed the British decision-making quartet, would, during the next three years, be of no great support for Russell either. Considering the conflicting nature of communications between headquarters and the Berlin embassy, it is not surprising that Odo would eventually commit a diplomatic faux-pas which Disraeli almost treated as a form of treason. Up to the Berlin Congress, the Prime Minister would criticise Russell's actions repeatedly, and ignore many reports from Berlin.

When Odo returned to Berlin in August 1875, he found that Bismarck was still in seclusion, that the Emperor had not seen his Chancellor since June, and that the Crown Prince was, as usual, at a loss.[20] Not to be seen by any foreign diplomats for as long as possible was a well-known Bismarck tactic, but this time he played it to excess. To Disraeli's growing disbelief, Odo reported during the early autumn that Bismarck suffered from rheumatism in his leg and, to everybody's surprise, was affected by the death of one of his valets.[21] Without its chief, the German Foreign Office was as usual in a 'lull': 'the fact is that no one knows or can say what Prince Bismarck's views and intentions really are while he lives in seclusion at Varzin'.[22]

So what was the clandestine German position towards the Balkan problem? The now so topical Bismarck quote: '[the Balkans] are not worth the bones of a single Pomeranian grenadier' is populistic and misleading. Like Disraeli, the German Chancellor was of course concerned, yet he also hoped that the Eastern Question might provide the opportunity to score a prestigious victory in the diplomatic arena. In 1862, Bismarck had already written to Reuss that: '[the Oriental Question] is a field on which we can be useful for our friends and harmful to our enemies without being hindered in our own interests'. [23] Bismarck pointed out to his chief, Emperor William, how welcome a bit of international distraction was: 'it can be only useful for us if the public attention and the policies of the other powers are for a time directed into another direction than the German–French question'.[24] The potentially dangerous side of the Eastern crisis for Germany's future had to be brought under control. So far, Russell reported in October 1875, the Chancellor was fortunate enough not to have to decide between Austria or Russia: 'but should any important difference of opinion arise between them, and Germany should be compelled to side with either, then political and national passions may be kindled in Germany'.[25] Bismarck himself believed that if any friction was created then, public opinion would be on the side of Austria.[26] This could then drive Russia into the arms of France. If Germany, however, supported Russia, Bismarck feared that the Austrian government would go to pieces 'like a ship on a sandbank'.[27] It is surprising that it did not dawn on Russell that his theory of a planned German demolition of Austria was wrong.

To understand the reaction of the British Government to the following events in Turkey, it is important to briefly look at Disraeli's approach to the Ottoman Empire on the one hand, and the extent to which Derby carried it out in his instructions to Odo. It has been said that Disraeli's 'political opportunism'[28] as well as his geographical gaps of knowledge[29] dictated Great Britain's course in the Eastern Question. This is only partly true. Disraeli was possibly genuinely driven by the fear that the Three Emperors' League, under the thin cover of humanity, would try to violate Turkey's last sovereign rights and partition it into Austrian/Russian vassal states. All assurances to the contrary by Andrássy, Bismarck and Gortschakoff could not alter the Prime Minister's perception. He believed that an occupation of Constantinople by Russia was highly possible, and that once Russia had penetrated the region, she would eventually control the Straits and therefore, the way to India and the Eastern Mediterranean.[30] Whether this fear of Russia extending her influence towards Constantinople and the Mediterranean was at the time a correct estimation of the situation or not, remains debatable.[31] It has to be remembered, that at this early point of the crisis, Russia was still divided into two camps. One was the Moscow faction, which suffered from 'orthodox mysticism and contempt for the rotten West', [32] while the other was the more sophisticated St Petersburg group, which saw the Serbs as 'revolutionaries' and was scared of being dragged into a religious war. Inside the Russian Foreign Office this friction was personified by the charismatic hawk, General Ignatiev, the 'natural champion of the oppressed Christians of Turkey' and 'doves' like Gortschakoff who, in 1875, still advocated a safer course. In a conversation with Odo in December 1875, Gortschakoff declared himself to be a 'replasterer' (compared to Ignatiev) and he defended the other members of the Three Emperors' League as fellow replasterers who, together with France, had nothing revolutionary in mind but simply wanted to pacify the region. Gortschakoff's aim during this conversation was to calm English nerves and gently prepare them for the first pacification plan by Andrássy, which would make a 'plastering session' of the Hercegovina *a six* possible. [33]

Such assurances might have impressed Russell, but did not convince Disraeli. Since the war-in-sight crisis, Derby and Disraeli had been treating Germany with suspicion. The Foreign Secretary, in particular, resented Bismarck's assurances about Germany's saturation: 'I am sorry to hear of Bismarck's continued want of sleep', Derby wrote to Berlin in August 1875, 'until he can get his rest, Europe will have none'. [34] A suspicion of everything foreign — rather a hindrance for a Foreign Secretary — seemed to be deeply rooted in Derby: 'there can not be a complete understanding between the military despotism of Berlin and a free and pacific community such as ours', [35] he wrote in one of his many gloomy moments. While Disraeli was a visionary, Derby played more the part of a cautious, political caretaker. [36] Such opposites seemed to attract, and one could claim that the two of them in some way re-enacted the Gladstone–Granville relationship — one of vigorous dialectical discussion stemming from differing character traits. In the end, however, the 'chemistry' would result in an explosion and the resignation of Derby.

On 30 December, Andrássy had made his first mediation proposal, which was treated by the British with suspicion. [37] Tenterden argued that the measures in the Andrássy note did not take into account the 'efforts' already made by the Porte. [38] Indeed, it is correct that this note could simply be seen as a public relations coup by the Three Emperors' League. William I had earlier in December made it clear to the Turkish ambassador that his country should not publish its own reforms before the Emperors' League had come forward with their proposals. It seemed that the world should see the Northern Powers as the righteous saviours of peace, while Turkey's efforts were ignored. Although the Turkish Government promised not to reject the note, they were upset about the embarrassment caused by the fact that the note differed in one major respect from their reform plan. While the Turkish plan promised 'beneficial provisions' to the insurgents only after they had laid down their weapons, the Austrian Government made no reservations of that kind.[39] Despite this, in some ways justified complaint, Odo welcomed the Andrássy note and assumed that Derby felt the same way about it: 'The Austrian note impresses me as it does you, and the five powers having already agreed, I most sincerely hope HMG will be able to join them, as it would greatly simplify the question and facilitate the passage into the next phase'.[40] Although Derby did not view the note in a negative way,[41] Disraeli felt quite differently about it. He had found three displeasing points: first, the above quoted argument that the Porte had proposed similar reforms by themselves; second, that the whole note could be a trap by Russia and Austria to drag England into their dubious projects; and third, that if Britain became a signatory to the note, this could have effects on 'our own country; for instance, the apportionment of local taxation to local purposes and the right of the peasantry to the soil'. (It is assumed that with this last point Disraeli was referring to the situation in Ireland.)[42] Russell had therefore unrealistically hoped that the Disraeli government would be interested in a smooth solution of the Turkish problem. When he realised that the acceptance of the note was in danger, he tried to use psychological pressure: 'the excitement in Germany will be great if HMG rejects the note. [Bismarck] will chuckle at the prospect of shaking off Gortschakoff and the Russian protectorate he has groaned under since last May'.[43] Although it must have been tempting for Disraeli to cause Bismarck mischief, it was not Russell's admonitions or Derby's vacillations that made the PM change his mind. Only upon the insistence of the Turks, did Britain finally support the Andrássy note. Russell generously ignored Britain's reluctance; what counted for him was the outcome. He reported home that the news had been received with excitement and sincere satisfaction in Germany.[44]

With the Andrássy note came a further inconvenience for the FO. Bismarck had, immediately after the publication of the document, asked Odo for Lord Derby's opinion on the Austrian proposals before he (Bismarck) 'answers or deals with them', because the German Chancellor wished for a 'complete understanding with England in regard to Turkey'.[45] This sudden intimacy took the British by surprise, who had naturally assumed that Andrássy had drafted this note in agreement with Bismarck. The truth was that Bismarck by now had started to fear an Austrian–Russian closeness that might make his partners carry out 'ambitious plans'.[46] In a one-and-a-half-hour-long interview with Russell, the Chancellor claimed that, though he trusted Andrássy, it was possible that a new Austrian administration might carry out an annexation policy (which the 'Slav party was urging on the Emperor').[47] In such an event, Germany would 'join England in resisting it or not'.[48] This was a seriously meant overture to England.[49] It undermined the Andrássy note and directly accused Germany's two partners in the Three Emperors' League (quite rightly as it would later turn out) of a hypocritical policy towards Turkey:

> Alone, without the support of England, he [Bismarck] would not resist the annexing tendencies of Austria and Russia in Turkey, because he did not think either of these Powers would be strengthened by such increase of territory, or the interests of Germany be affected by it.[50]

The FO was at first at a loss as how to answer and tried to gain time.[51] Odo's expertise was now required:

> The impression left on my mind [Russell wrote to the FO] by this conversation is that Prince Bismarck means what he says, and really desires a frank and cordial understanding with England for the following reasons: When he invented the alliance of the three Northern Powers, he intended to play his two allies against each other, using both to bully Europe for his own glory. Outwitted by Prince Gortschakoff last May, he had the humiliation before all the world to be bound over to keep the peace by Russia. From that moment Russia commanded the sympathies of the peace loving powers and took the lead of the Northern Alliance — Austria grew more intimate with Russia than with Germany, Prince Bismarck felt isolated, the tripartite alliance became a burden to him, and he vowed revenge. And now he thinks he sees his way to it in Turkey.[52]

This overture to England, Russell summed up, was a well-worked-out plan by Bismarck with the intention first to play the peacemaker against Russian aggressiveness, and second to get rid of any commitments to Austria and Russia in case of a war.[53] A further reason for Bismarck to put out his feelers might simply have been to sound out England's plans.[54] He was worried that England and France might form a Western alliance against the Northern Powers, a fear that circulated through the German newspapers. A further constant worry, fuelled by the German press, was that Russia could become an even more unpredictable partner if the Czar abdicated: 'I am struck by the anxiety that the mere rumour of the possibility of such a contingency produces on the German official mind',[55] wrote Odo at the end of March. While the Czar was seen as a relatively reliable man, the Czarevitch was rumoured to have French sympathies.[56] In case of a change of leadership in

Russia, Germany would have to look for new friends, the most likely of which would be England. Whatever Bismarck's intentions were, Derby felt uncomfortable about the German overtures: 'I am a little embarrassed as to the best way of meeting Prince Bismarck's offers of friendship', Derby did not know 'how [to thank] without conveying the impression that we are proposing or accepting an exclusive alliance between the two countries which is quite inconsistent with all our modes of action?'[57] Disraeli and Queen Victoria were far more enthusiastic about Bismarck's offer and briefed Odo accordingly. In the end, however, it was Bismarck himself who lost interest and 'cooled the ardour [of his two advocates]'.[58]

During the following months of March and April, it is a question of interpretation as to whether an improvement in the Eastern Question had occurred or not. While Derby wanted to see the situation become more 'hopeful', the Russians saw it as a bad 'patchwork'.[59] Bismarck agreed with this gloomy outlook and pretended to be happy that the Russians were prepared to allow an Austrian occupation of the restless provinces. This was news to Russell, who strongly emphasised that public opinion in England would not react 'favourably to further intervention in Turkey'.[60]

However, such an intervention did occur. At the beginning of May the Czar issued an invitation for the two other League members to come to Berlin. Together with Bismarck and Gortschakoff, Andrássy drew up the Berlin Memorandum, which was in the eyes of the Northern Powers a last attempt to avert war. On Friday 13 May 1876, the agreement of the three Powers was communicated to Russell. The most worrying paragraph, in British eyes, came last:

> If however, the armistice were to expire without the efforts of the Powers being successful in attaining the end they have in view, the three Imperial Courts are of the opinion that it would become necessary to supplement their diplomatic action by the sanction of an agreement to promote the efficacious measures which might appear to be demanded in the interest of general peace.[61]

Odo now had to endure a public relations *tour de force* headed by Andrássy and Gortschakoff, who in long interviews tried to sell their memorandum to the British ambassador. Russell wanted to know from them more about one 'obscure' passage in the memorandum which he had immediately spotted: 'if the negotiations failed, other efficacious measures would follow'.[62] Andrássy was not prepared to answer what kind of measures these could be, as this was 'impossible to foretell'.[63] Russell's following interview with Gortschakoff started with the Russian giving a long and colourful description of the 'powder magazine' that

Turkey was, and which could blow up at any minute. Everything or nothing could happen there as the country was utterly in disarray. Perhaps, Gortschakoff argued, the measures of the Berlin memorandum were too mild anyway. He himself would have preferred an entente of all six states to draw them up, not just of three, but one had to act in a crisis in which every hour counted.[64] Russell asked Gortschakoff the same question that Andrássy had evaded — whether he could elaborate on the 'measures' planned? Although Gortschakoff argued that time would show what was required, behind the scenes rumours circulated that his enthusiasm for the memorandum was limited. He had already come with a plan of his own to Berlin, which was rejected by Andrássy and Bismarck, who had previously met and agreed on their own tactics. The German Chancellor now, however, preferred to stay in the background, playing down his part in the memorandum. He was 'unusually reserved and serious', Odo reported, using only Bülow as his mouthpiece, and not taking part in the selling of the memorandum.

At the official presentation of the memorandum Russell had, like his colleagues, 'expressed the hope and belief that his government would give its approval' to the document, but had put it 'ad referendum'.[65] This 'premature' assurance later outraged Disraeli and his whole hatred against Russell, the Whig diplomat, broke out:

> I do not like Lord Odo's letter, or anything so far as I can gather, he has done. He was not originally justified in offering his personal opinion that our Government would accept the Russian note — an unheard of step! And the worst of it is, it indicates such a want of abilities. He does not even seem now to comprehend the situation. I have myself no doubt that if we are stiff, we shall gain all our points.[66]

In retrospect, Odo would cynically complain about the situation HMG had put him in from the start:

> Formerly Governments used to give us instructions [he wrote to his brother Hastings] but nowadays they give none, which greatly simplifies and facilitates our duties, because we can always reply to indiscreet questions that we really do not know what our governments think, but that we will be happy to ask. That is called a diplomatic answer, or what you would call an evasive answer.[67]

It was exactly such an evasive answer that he had given to the Northern Powers by stating, on 13 May, that he had to contact his government first. Disraeli was therefore wrong in accusing him of having agreed with the memorandum in an official way. Nobody would be able to prove such a faux-pas, as Russell observed: 'My enemies have been trying to make out that I committed the government to the conference policy, but they have failed, because the accusations were unfounded'.[68]

The memorandum had reached the FO on Saturday 14 May. It remains unclear whether the Northern Powers issued their statement intentionally on a Friday. They could have played on the habit of British statesmen leaving for their country estates on Fridays (where they were hard to contact and reluctant to drum up the Cabinet for an emergency sitting.) The possibility of such a rushed meeting was what Derby wanted to avoid and it is therefore very likely that his decision not to inform Disraeli of the memorandum until Sunday night was a calculated one. At the time there was speculation as to whether the delay had been caused by Derby's fear of breaking the news to his Prime Minister, or to sheer negligence on the part of the FO. Disraeli preferred to believe the latter, blaming the incident on Derby's incompetent staff rather than on the Foreign Secretary himself. On Monday 16 May, the memorandum was discussed in the Cabinet and unanimously dismissed.[69]

Disraeli therefore ignored the advice of his ambassador in Berlin as well as the 'wise warnings' (Seton-Watson) of the Queen, who feared British isolation:

> It is true that the three Emperors have acted without taking the other powers into their deliberations. But their interests are more ... vitally connected with the welfare of Turkey. The Queen's dislike to our separating ourselves from the rest arises from a fear that Turkey will look to us to help her against the rest of Europe and that we shall thus precipitate rather than prevent the catastrophe.[70]

Odo shared such fears and bombarded Disraeli with last-minute telegrams outlining the difficulties that lay in not supporting the plan: 'The encouragement it may give the Porte to a policy of resistance or inaction. The difficulty of supporting with success a policy in Turkey in opposition to the three Powers. ... The alarm it will produce in the commercial world'.[71] Such warnings did not change Disraeli's opinion any further. It should now have been obvious to Russell that he was not properly representing the government's new confrontationalist policy. His dissatisfaction was well known, and for a while it was even rumoured in diplomatic circles that he had resigned.[72]

On 17 May, Odo was officially informed by his government that 'the proposals would not achieve pacification', and that 'HMG regrets to find themselves unable to cooperate in the policy which the three Governments have invited them to pursue'.[73] The reasons were given to Odo in a long despatch, which point by point rejected each measure put forward by the Three Emperors' League.[74] The whole despatch is remarkable for its hostility. It had the effect that the memorandum was 'dropped for the moment', and, because of the outbreak of hostilities would soon become completely outdated.[75] The Queen, who had been impressed by Odo's argument that 'serious consequences' might arise from a rejection of the memorandum, was informed by Disraeli that: 'there is nothing in Lord Odo's remarks of significance. ... What Lord Odo assumes is the fear of a repetition of a Crimean War. Mr Disraeli thinks it will all end now in Congress'.[76]

Disraeli succeeded in portraying Odo to the Queen as a hysteric. He also exacerbated the situation by snapping at Schouvaloff that 'England has been treated as though we were Montenegro or Bosnia',[77] whereas Derby, more calmly, argued to the Russian ambassador that the proposals in the memorandum '[might] encourage the rebels to expect a great power intervention'.[78] These excuses barely concealed the fact that this was a calculated British attack on the Northern triumvirate. Germany certainly understood it that way. For a third time within a year, Britain, the power that once could be relied on to be non-interventionist, had turned into an unknown quantity.

The Reluctant Conformist

Privately, Odo agreed with Bismarck's opinion that Disraeli had behaved in a far from constructive manner.[1] To his brother Hastings, Russell wrote at the beginning of November 1876 that he no longer had faith in the FO's instructions:

> Politics at present, are, to my mind *unerquicklich wie der Nebelwind, der herbstlich durch die dürren Blätter kräuselt* [unpleasant like leaves rustling in the autumn fog] — I carry out the instructions from the FO without faith or hope for I do not believe we are following the right course and think we have been wrong since May last. I hope I may be mistaken!!!! Meanwhile our enemies rejoice and 'lachen [sich] ins Fäustchen [have a good laugh at our expense]'.[2]

Odo shared Bismarck's conviction that Turkey was not worth fighting for 'since [they] can no longer pay 8%'.[3] Britain clung, in Odo's opinion, to a corpse while losing everybody's sympathy and all diplomatic flexibility. If the FO continued to act so unwisely, the Northern Powers could easily use Britain as a scapegoat for a Turkish–Russian war. In a bitter letter to Arthur, Odo poured out a further list of his frustrations:

> We rejected the Berlin memo, because we were asked in the last paragraph to engage that we would consent to efficacious measures later, if the Porte did not act on our friendly advice. Tres bien! Dans ce cas que faut — il faire? said Russia ... Russia now says: You see that without the efficacious measures of the Berlin memorandum we [Russia] can obtain no redress and we must coerce Turkey, unless you, Great Powers will agree to more efficacious measures in concert next year? Eh?[4]

These were Odo's private opinions. His official ones, however, quickly altered after May 1876. Outwardly, he became a reluctant conformist.

After the British rejection of the memorandum, wild rumours were circulating in Berlin.[5] The ingrained German fear of a 'cauchemar des coalitions' had surfaced again. William I, who habitually meddled in Bismarck's FO domain whenever it came to German–Russian relations, feared that a war between Russia and England was imminent. As a consequence, Odo had, together with Bismarck, to face the Emperor's anger.[6] Although William I valued Odo Russell personally, he had now decided to treat him almost as coldly as the unfortunate Turkish representative.[7] Russell was reproached for 'the attitude of England, the language of *The Times* and the large fleet sent to the Mediterranean'.[8] Such hostile actions 'made it even more difficult for the Czar to keep the national sympathies within bounds'.[9] The adoption by the Queen of the title Empress of India had not been too well received in Germany either. Privately Odo agreed with the Emperor that the title could be seen as a calculated power demonstration; 'How much I dislike this Empress title', he wrote to his brother Hastings, 'and how gladly I would vote against it. *Da haben sie ihren Kaisertitel aber bei Jott sie machen sich lächerlich* [there, you have your Empress title, but by God you are making yourself ridiculous] is the feeling in Germany about it'.[10] The conversation also showed that as far as William was concerned, Disraeli had again succeeded in undermining the Three Emperors' League. William's sympathies were now openly and completely pro-Russian in this crisis.[11] A real friendship between the Austrian and German aristocracy would not be possible, the Emperor argued, because the 1866 war 'could not be forgotten in his lifetime'.[12] Odo agreed with this assessment and predicted an upcoming Russian–German alliance:

> I see at all times a great many Austrians and I am struck to find that one and all are convinced that in the event of a war between Austria and Russia, Germany will take part with Russia against Austria and help to crush her. Bismarck tells me the contrary. I wonder what he tells my Russian colleague.[13]

In fact, the Chancellor's remarks had for once been sincere. William's *Nibelungentreue* to the Czar drove Bismarck almost insane.

On 30 June 1876, Prince Milan of Serbia, yielding to public pressure, declared war on Turkey. Russell left Berlin at the end of July to get instructions in England. His first visit brought him to the Queen, who seemed to be very much relieved that Odo had gradually been acquiescing in Disraeli's policy:

> Lord Odo Russell came to see me this afternoon and stayed nearly an hour. He was most sensible about Eastern affairs, thought the moment very alarming, but that we should pull through it; that Bismarck was really anxious to go with us ... that we had not been asked to join with the three other Powers [a point Disraeli had chosen to be upset about] as Mr Gladstone's policy had really made it appear as though England would never hold her old place again [with this comment Odo was flattering the Queen's and Disraeli's new policy of confrontation]. Bismarck was amazed and fascinated by Mr Disraeli's wonderful quickness and his large views on foreign affairs.[14]

With such comments, Odo could be sure he would be able to win over the Queen again. When he visited Lord Derby a day later, Odo also showed no grudge about the Berlin memorandum incident. Derby decided to follow Russell's proposal to send him to Kissingen, to find out how far Bismarck was prepared to call upon Russia to observe neutrality in the Servian fight. The only real danger that we now have to fear is lest Russian feeling should grow so strong in the event of a Servian defeat as to lead the Czar to intervene. All accounts are unanimous in describing him averse to war.

Odo had volunteered to go to Kissingen because his intuition had told him that the timing and surroundings were right to approach Bismarck. His intuition turned out to be correct. Russell also wanted to win back his popularity with the FO and the court by achieving some breakthrough in German–British affairs. Disraeli had not forgotten the Berlin Memorandum episode and he was certainly not as easily charmed by Odo as was the Queen.

The British ambassador hoped to be received by Bismarck in Kissingen (despite the Chancellor's well-known trait of vigorously defending his summer breaks) and requested an informal audience.[15] To Odo's relief, Bismarck answered immediately, inviting Russell on a mysterious train journey to meet the Emperor at Würzburg: 'We will be by ourselves in my railway carriage, undisturbed. It is of great importance for me to see you before I meet His Majesty and I am very glad that we happen to meet'.[16] The private letter Odo would write to Derby about this journey shows how smoothly the chemistry between him and Bismarck worked when they had a common goal. Both of them did not agree with the politics of their chiefs, and both struggled to swing them into a middle ground for the benefit of their countries. That the Würeburg incident was never mentioned by Odo in his official despatches was a well-calculated step to avoid embarrassment for Bismarck by a Blue Book publication.

On 10 July, Odo waited to meet Bismarck on the platform. He had been warned by Herbert von Bismarck 'that I [Odo] would find his father far from well and very nervous and irritable from worry and want of sleep after receiving yesterday a letter of 15 pages from the Emperor which had sent up his pulses from 68 to 98 +100'.[17] During the whole journey Odo was exposed to Bismarck's grievances — a by now familiar experience: 'The Emperor might be a great general, but he certainly was the worst politician in the world. His Majesty was too young a master for him, and he was too old and broken a servant for the Emperor. To serve him any longer would be suicide'.[18]

The soliloquy went on for about an hour until Bismarck felt calm enough to recount the facts. William had during his summer break been under emotional pressure as a result of lobbying by pro-slavic and 'other hostile influences'.[19] His fears that England was highly aggressive[20] had been reinforced, and he therefore wanted to send a sharp note to HMG 'remonstrating against their policy and their injustice to Russia'.[21] Such a letter would have finally ruined Bismarck's last hopes to keep

Germany in the position of the manoeuvring mediator and, as Bismarck put it himself, 'commit Germany irrevocably to the support of Russia in the East'.[22] His [Bismarck's] policy was to watch and wait and when the time came for action,' to support England and Austria whose interests he felt sure must always be identical in European Turkey'.[23] If he could not persuade the Emperor to refrain from such a note and convince him of England's defensive attitude, he would resign. The conflict could, however, be overcome, Bismarck argued, if Odo were to accompany him to see the Emperor and explain the 'ifs' to Wilhelm: 'England will fight if Russia breaks the peace, but England will not initiate war if Russia desists from attacking Turkey'.[24]

Bismarck's tactics to 'break' the Emperor's will remind one of a modern police interview. The Chancellor gave himself the part of the 'bad policeman', threatening and accusing the 'culprit' (William), then Odo, the 'good policeman', would appear and win William over by soothing language. Yet when Odo arrived at the Crown Prince Hotel after a sightseeing tour, the Emperor still seemed 'unusually grave'.[25] He told Russell that he had just left the Czar 'broken hearted': '[Alexander] was suffering from [the stress] and it would kill him'.[26] The whole muddle was England's fault. She had sent out the largest fleet in the world to Besica Bay when all the other Powers of Europe were endeavouring to re-establish order.[27] Russell defended England against these allegations by claiming that General Ignatiev had displayed warlike behaviour in relation to the occupation of Constantinople and that the forthcoming Blue Book would prove that England did not have any aggressive intentions whatsoever. Though the Emperor rejected the Ignatiev argument as a 'silly suspicion' peddled by the 'unjust press', Odo's presence at Würzburg must have made an impression on him.[28] Back at the station, Bismarck and Russell congratulated each other on their successful crisis management: 'We have triumphed', a self-glorifying Bismarck told Odo, 'the Emperor I am happy to tell you has consented to give up his idea of a note to England, and I have consented to retain my post'.[29] On the way back to the spa, Bismarck smoked his (unhealthy) Meerschaum-pipe again and drank like a 'true born Teuton'.[30] To Münster he wrote a few days later: 'The imperial instructions ... will not reach you, after I have, with difficulties persuaded the Emperor that unasked for and unwanted advice would not increase the trust of the English Government'.[31] No mention of Russell here. Also, when in a private circle, Bismarck would later recount his 'adventure at Würzburg, leaving out Odo's support. Instead, the Chancellor blamed 'Disraeli, the warmonger', whose threatening language had forced him, Bismarck, the German Chancellor, 'to drive all the way to Würzburg!'[32] At least Odo got some acknowledgement at home. The Queen wrote in her journal that

'[Bismarck] urged Lord Odo to speak to the Emperor, which he did, succeeding in dispelling all his illusions'.[33]

While Bismarck sat contentedly in Berlin, the European Powers were conscious that it was just a question of time before new frantic despatches arrived from Constantinople. The fact that the Serbo-Turkish war threatened to expand into an international conflict, after repeated Turkish victories against the Serbs, soon forced the Northern Powers out of their complacency and into action again. With the Slavic future in danger, the Russian Pan-Slavists had increased pressure on the Czar to support them more openly. He could not afford to ignore this if he did not want to die a premature death. (Major General Walker tells the story of a cynical Russian officer who had stated that 'the present occupant of the Russian throne had nearly reached the limit beyond which no Czar had yet lived'.)[34] Russian volunteers had since the beginning of the war been pouring into Serbia, supporting their 'Slavic brothers' with arms, expertise and money. Thus Russia had unofficially become more and more involved in the war. For Alexander it was of vital importance to sound out whether his fellow League members would support *official* Russian involvement. On 8 July 1876, he approached Austria at Reichstadt, where they came to a secret understanding regarding the division of the Balkan territory. This agreement became obsolete a few weeks later and a contrite Andrássy confessed his Russian flirtation to Bismarck. To his relief, the German Chancellor was not outraged about the surreptitious Austrian–Russian rapprochement; after all Bismarck had himself suggested that only a division of the Ottoman Empire into different spheres of interest could solve the problem. Also, the German Chancellor would soon have to explain his own Russian 'escapade' to Andrássy.

The other 'bomb' that the Foreign Offices had to cope with that summer had a long fuse too. Already before the Northern Powers drew up the Berlin memorandum, the Bulgarian nationalists had, at the beginning of May, started a bloody rebellion against their Turkish oppressors. This was met by the Turks with a violent retaliation, which even Elliot could not play down forever. Approximately 15,000 Bulgarians were killed, including women and children. With almost a month's delay, from June onwards, British papers carried accounts of Bulgarian horrors. This, combined with Gladstone's passionate pamphlet — *The Bulgarian Horrors and the Question of the East*[35] — turned the public, which up until then had been fairly indifferent, into a political force to be reckoned with. With the Bulgarian agitation hanging over their heads, the British government was at pains to justify their policy to a daily increasing number of critics.[36] In a speech to a deputation of working men, Derby tried to defend the Government's course since the outbreak of the first revolts in 1875, on the basis that it has always been supported by a majority of people: 'In the three acts of the Eastern drama, so far as it has gone — in the acceptance of the Austrian note, in the rejection of the Berlin memorandum, and in the sending of the British fleet to Besika Bay — the country, as I believe, almost unanimously concurred'.[37] Such cohesion was now definitely a thing of the past, yet Derby did not see any reason to alter his foreign policy. He and Disraeli wished to stick to their policy of propping up a country, which was, in their eyes, only momentarily unpopular with the masses. Gladstone was of another opinion.[38] He continued to make fun of the incompetence of the government: 'Dizzy in answer to his [Lytton's] question about Eastern policy, stated that he understood the Eastern question in India, but was completely ignorant of the Eastern question in Europe'.[39]

While the British Government struggled with the Bulgarian agitation, the Germans were again encountering problems in their relations with Russia. In autumn 1876 the Czar's advisers had declared psychological warfare on their rebellious German partner in order to force her to give up her cosy neutral stand,[40] but Bismarck was not willing to get dragged into supporting the Russians if he could help it. However, he also could not afford Russian displeasure and had to show at least some goodwill. Odo was quick to analyse Bismarck's dilemma — that although the Chancellor mistrusted Russia after the Reichstadt meeting, he had to bow to the German Emperor's pressure on him to again re-establish the 'cordial relations' with his 'favourite' country. This led Bismarck to make a compromise by sending Count Manteuffel to Russia, who was according to Odo 'a devoted adherent of a Russian alliance'.[41] Although Odo did not know the contents of the letter Manteuffel had to deliver, he speculated that it included all that the Czar 'would desire'.[42] This was indeed the case. In this letter, William wrote to his nephew, that 'the memory of your attitude towards me and my country from 1864 to 1870/1871 will guide my policy toward Russia ... — quoi qu'il arrive'.[43] Despite this generosity, Manteuffel returned with the worrying news that Russia was still displeased.[44]

This news strengthened William's opinion that Germany had to become even more pro-Russian.[45] Bismarck replied by making it clear to Petersburg that in the event of war between Austria and Russia, Germany would have to stay neutral. If, however, the 'whole of Europe should combine against Russia, it would not be in Germany's interest to see Russia's position as a European power seriously and lastingly damaged'.[46] This retort has, together with the Kissinger Diktat, often been praised as an example of *Realpolitik* at its best.

Odo noticed Bismarck's newly regained understanding for the Czar's problems. When, for example, in October Russell tried to find out whether Germany supported an armistice between Serbia and Turkey,[47] he was rewarded with an emotional outburst by the German Chancellor. Bismarck made it known, via Bülow, that the attitude of the British since the Berlin memorandum had severely displeased him. In his view, Britain's aims were only destructive, namely to break up the consensus between the other powers.[48] Odo saw Bismarck's grievances against the British FO policies as an 'anti-replastering attitude'. This was combined with a personal grudge towards England since its rejection of the German overtures in January 1876.[49]

On 31 October 1876, the Turks, despite their victories, yielded to the Russian pressure for an armistice and eventually it was agreed that the British proposal for a conference at Constantinople should be followed. This proposal was seen as the first constructive step by Disraeli since May. It was now up to Britain to come to terms with Russia about the future of the Turkish Empire. There were not too many positive indicators to suggest that such a conference would be successful. Derby described to Russell that the feeling in Britain was anti-Turkish, but also at the same time increasingly suspicious of the Russians: 'We should not fight for the Sultan, but if necessary we would fight for Constantinople'.[50] Derby added, however, that he personally 'did not believe in an immediate [Russian] design on Constantinople'.[51]

It was out of the question to leave the conduct of the negotiations at Constantinople to the Turcophile Elliot. Instead, it was decided that the British plenipotentiary was to be Lord Salisbury. This choice was a compromise offered by Disraeli to please disgruntled cabinet members as well as the agitated public. It was certainly welcomed by both parties, as well as by Russell, who thought that 'the appointment ... is good and he [Salisbury] ought to be a match for Ignatiev'.[52] Salisbury was not considered to be pro-Turkish and was also thought to be open-minded about Russia. He had advocated in Cabinet over the last weeks that an understanding with Russia could pacify the region more easily — a fact that would endear him to Ignatiev and make him Elliot's arch-enemy within hours after arriving in Constantinople.

It was decided that Salisbury should, before starting work at Constantinople, go on a 'pilgrimage of consultation'[53] via Paris, Berlin, Vienna and Rome. Although Odo thought this to be a good political move, he felt slightly worried about the enormous Salisbury entourage: 'He brings five clerks and two private secretaries and I believe also a wife. When I went to settle the Black Sea question I went alone — but then I did not settle it. He has it in his power to settle the present question, if he chooses, but will he choose?'[54] A further point that must have worried Russell was the rumour that Salisbury had no friendly feelings towards Germany. According to Arthur Russell, Salisbury's hatred was composed not only of a political but also an intellectual distrust of everything German: 'we know how deeply Lord Salisbury hates Germany, which he accuses of having poisoned the Theology of Oxford and misled many young Englishmen. I remember ... how he rejoiced for the honour of his country, that Englishmen who sympathised with Germany could be counted on the fingers'.[55]

Irrespective of whether such attitudes were known in Germany or not, the announcement of Salisbury's visit to Berlin was well received by Bismarck.[56] During the last weeks Russell had again and again assured a sceptical Derby that Bismarck sincerely wanted peace and would support Russian–British cooperation at Constantinople:

> Bismarck is not hostile to us as you seem to think ... He tends to think that our policy prolongs the struggle whilst that of Russia tends to cut it short. ... If we convince him of the contrary, he will drop Russia and cooperate with us for the maintenance of peace.[57]

Whether it was that the FO thought Odo had gone native or that he was simply too naive to grasp Bismarck's vicious plans, nobody believed the peaceful assurances Russell had passed on. It took Salisbury's visit to the German capital to establish the fact that Bismarck was indeed interested in a cordial cooperation. After his discussions with the Chancellor, Salisbury concurred with the British ambassador's so far ignored analysis, but for different reasons:

> If Bismarck had wished us to quarrel with Russia it would have been easy to encourage a strong position at the Conference, to dwell on the importance of Turkey, to exaggerate the value of the Danube to Russia, to talk of his great friendship and to let me entrevoir without the least degree committing himself to the probability of Germany taking an active step on our side. He did the reverse of all this.[58]

While in Berlin, Salisbury talked to the Emperor, the Chancellor and the Crown Prince. Bismarck praised him, with polite flattery, for possessing 'great qualities as a statesman and a negotiator'.[59] In Odo's opinion, Bismarck and the Emperor treated Salisbury well and had given him a straightforward answer: 'We, Germany, will support you in keeping peace but cannot help you in making war'.[60] Salisbury, however, unrealistically seemed to have expected a greater commitment: 'Salisbury complains ... and HMG at home call it "unsatisfactory" — but it is the answer we should give Germany if she asked us to settle her differences with other European Powers'.[61]

Salisbury's visit to Constantinople is recounted in great detail in all studies on him and will therefore only be discussed here briefly.[62] It soon became evident that he was not willing to deal as smoothly with the different factions he encountered during his mission as Russell, had done in Versailles.[63] Salisbury did not accept the advice of the British community in Constantinople and made his dislike of Elliot more than obvious. (Nor did Salisbury like the Sultan — despite [or because] of the fact that he decorated the Marchioness with the Chastity Medal.)[64] Although this is understandable after all the blunders Elliot had committed, the extent to which Salisbury was taken in by the cunning Ignatiev is still surprising. This infatuation evaporated the moment Ignatiev visited Hatfield. Salisbury treated him like the ghost of a holiday romance that best remains forgotten. However, during the conference they worked closely together, which alarmed the Germans and Austrians.[65] Bismarck rightly feared that he would be outmanoeuvred at Constantinople and he was indeed later made partly responsible for the breaking up of the Conference. (This feeling of being 'shut out' was probably the reason for another Bismarck overture to Britain in February 1877.) Russell reported home that 'German diplomatists certainly do not like to see England and Russia on good terms — they are jealous of the influence it gives to both countries combined'. Speculation circulated that their 'common worries' seemed to bring Austria and Germany closer together. Bismarck and Andrássy saw each other frequently and it was rumoured that the Austrian inquired about the amount of support, moral or material,[66] which might be received from Germany in order to be used against Russia. Russell passed on the wild speculation that Andrássy might, with the backing of a benevolently neutral Germany, combine Austrian and Turkish forces against Russia. This rumour irritated the FO considerably, and Derby asked Schouvaloff about the latest strains on Austrian–Russian relations. Schouvaloff stuck to the story that there was an 'intimate understanding between Austria, Germany and Russia' and Odo admitted that this cooperation still existed in some ways. Odo now argued that the unity of the Northern Powers was far from being undermined: '[after the Berlin Memorandum] the understanding between them [the Northern Powers] became in consequence more intimate'.[67]

The Constantinople Conference lasted for nine sessions and was prematurely ended when the Sultan proclaimed that as he had decided on his own reforms the Conference was no longer necessary. The proposals by the 'foreigners' were rejected and all the parties consequently dispersed on 20 January 1877. Only Salisbury was, according to Palmer, brave enough to depart from Constantinople immediately, in the face of a storm at sea and thereby figuratively leaving no doubt as to British resolve.

Because of its severe economic depression, Russia was still hesitant about attacking Turkey. In the long run, however, the Czar had no choice but to give in to the Pan-Slavists. He declared war on Turkey on 24 April 1877, yet Turkish successes (including the brave defence of the fortress of Plevna) showed the deficiencies of the Russian army.[68] Despite the Emperor's pleas to go to the aid of the Czar, Bismarck stuck to his policy of neutrality. William feared for his Russian relative because every day there were new rumours about Russian military incompetence circulating all over Germany. Russell, for example, reported in his letter to Arthur: 'Both you and Baba [Hastings] express surprise at my saying that the Russian army mobilisation broke down. My authorities were: the Emperor William, Moltke, Bismarck, Lord Derby'.[69] These rumours later turned out to be wishful thinking by some German officers who had secretly hoped that their Russian friends and rivals would not become too victorious. Instead the Russian army recovered by the summer of 1877 (the very summer in which Bismarck dictated to his son his famous Kissinger Diktat): '[Germany's aim should be to be] in a situation in which all powers, except France, need us and are kept from coalitions against us as much as possible by their relations to each other'. The faster the Russians moved, the more it was feared in Britain that Constantinople and the Straits were in danger. Although Russell had met Disraeli in November 1877, he was still insecure about what the Prime Minister expected of him. Because Disraeli was convinced that the Northern Powers were no longer united (which Odo did not believe) he wanted to negotiate an Austrian alliance against the Russians. Lord Derby, Odo's direct chief, feared, however, that Bismarck wanted to drag Britain into another war with Russia, and it is no wonder that British diplomats — not for the first time — were confused about which policy should be represented abroad.

The Russian victory over the Turks was absolute and it brought an absolute verdict — the treaty of San Stefano. Disraeli's response was an even more confrontational policy against Russia. Derby, who feared another Crimean war, was at the time constantly contemplating resignation and, on 27 March 1878, after a lot of vacillation, he left to be replaced by Salisbury. Odo was confused about this new twist and regretted that he could not make 'himself scarce for dust'[70] (i.e. make a hasty retreat like Derby) as well. He did not think that Austria would fight together with England (a view shared with Moltke and Bismarck) and that it would be almost impossible to defeat the Russians:

> If I could afford it, I should prefer to resign like Lord Derby, rather than to have to support a war policy contrary to my convictions and feelings! To my mind there is no *casus belli* in the treaty of San Stefano and we can perfectly by patient negotiation get as much and even more than by war! We are not a military nation, and we undervalue the difficulties which await us in fighting the *wauwau*.[71]

Odo even quoted Napoleon III and his follies to show that one should not go 'to war without sufficient cause'.[72] His brother Hastings agreed with him and signed a petition in favour of peace and a congress. However, with their 'hard line', Salisbury and Disraeli achieved the reopening of the Russian–Turkish peace agreement of San Stefano at the Berlin Congress. Although he had not approved of the tactics, Russell was relieved with the results.

Though the Berlin Congress is well documented, Odo's role during the affair as third plenipotentiary, however, is not. His FO addressees were all in Berlin and for the most part communications between them were only verbal (most details of the Conference had already been discussed beforehand, with Odo being degraded to the position of a messenger.) Only his letters to his brothers give one a glimpse behind the facade and show one the nervousness of the participants before the opening of the Congress: 'Lord Beaconsfield seems excited, Lord Salisbury anxious, and all the other Plenipos are in a nervous state which is scarcely pleasant'.[73] Odo was so busy socially that his only original comments concern his fight for harmony at the dinner table. After his earlier clashes with Disraeli, Odo tried everything again to please the Prime Minister:

> I overwhelm Lord Beaconsfield with honours and respect and give him my place at the table as if he were the Queen or the Prince of Wales, at which he seems well pleased, for he calls me 'his dear and distinguished colleague', and assures me that one of his chief objects in coming to Berlin was to see my 'dear wife who is the most agreeable woman he ever knew'.[74]

Odo's greatest fear was to get into the same quarrels Elliot had had with Salisbury at Constantinople, for the sake of his own career and because 'the British Plenipos. must appear united before Europe'. His fears were unwarranted and to his surprise he grew to be impressed by Disraeli: 'I cannot say how much I admired Lord Beaconsfield's firmness and ability as a negotiator, and Lord Salisbury's marvellous knowledge of detail and rapidity of thought and resource in debate'.[75] It was thanks to Odo that Disraeli gave his famous Congress speech in English and not in French, which had a great effect on its listeners. (Disraeli's contemporaries saw his limited knowledge of languages as a hindrance to diplomatic brilliance. The touchy Prime Minister would, however, have liked to know that his new friend Bismarck, who was fluent in French and English, always claimed that 'foreign languages were useful for head waiters and couriers only'.)[76] According to Poschinger, Odo told Disraeli that everyone who was there was capable of giving a speech in French, but that no-one could talk English as wonderfully as Disraeli. Everyone just wanted to hear the supreme master of the English language.[77] During his short time in Berlin Disraeli had indeed a great effect on the Germans and consequently his novels became bestsellers. Even Bismarck read them, although with slight jealousy: '[The Chancellor] is deeply interested in Lord Beaconsfield's novels which he is reading once again. Prince Bismarck informed Monsieur de St. Vallier that, while he read novels, his mind enjoyed perfect rest, because it ceased to govern Germany for the time being — but that if he did not write novels, it was because the government of Germany required the whole of his undivided creative powers'.[78] Thanks to the Congress, Bismarck, in turn, was also becoming a bit more popular in England. An anonymous article in *Blackwood's Magazine* (its German translation was later published in Lindau's magazine *Die Gegenwart*)[79] portrayed the private Bismarck for the English audience as being an expert on dogs (this it was hoped would appeal to the British), a good family man and fighter against socialism. It remained a mystery who actually wrote this article. Theodor Fontane, who was researching for his own impressions of Bismarck, at first thought that the Paris correspondent of *The Times*, Herr von Blowitz, might be the author. Blowitz had, on Disraeli's wish, undertaken a two-hour interview with Bismarck — hardly enough to be so well informed about all the details of Bismarck's private life. Another possible author could have been Bucher, and if one goes a step further one could even speculate that Odo was involved by giving the author information.

The results of the Berlin Congress are well documented and its effects can still be felt today. Russia had won the war but lost the peace. England occupied Cyprus and Austria eventually took Bosnia–Hercegovina. Looking back, Odo would have mixed feelings about the Congress. On the one hand, he defended its achievements but, on the other, he condemned the whole handling of the crisis, revealing that he had only conformed outwardly:

> You [Arthur] say that at Berlin all were opposed to us — and you say that other Powers were more willing to make a lasting arrangement, but that it was our Plenipos who thwarted them. True, the Powers were ready to drop the Sultan and divide Turkey, but our Plenipos were not. They came with the avowed object to prolong for a while the existence of Turkey although all were opposed to them, they carried their policy against all Europe and gave Turkey a new, though per-

haps short lease of life. And that was Lord Beaconsfield's triumph that he successfully compelled Europe to bend before Great Britain. That is what people call a
spirited policy. Of course if our party had been in power, we should have saved
the country great expense, by accepting the Treaty of San Stefano and leaving
Turkey to be dealt with by Russia and Austria. We might have submitted our differences of opinion to the arbitration of America or Germany or France etc. which
would have led to the same result. But the people of England were tired of so reasonable a policy as that of the Gladstone–Granville administration so they turned
them out and asked Dizzy to give them a more spirited and more expensive one
and hitherto the people have voted for Dizzy.[80]

Russell's role during these three years is as complex as the whole
Eastern Question. While Odo had up to the time of the Berlin
Memorandum tried to influence the FO to cooperate with the
Northern Powers, by the summer of 1876 he quickly realised that his
position would be at stake if he did not conform. He then changed his
tune considerably, and tried to please both Disraeli and the Queen by
adopting their tougher stand against Russia. His many changes of
opinion mirror the confusion that prevailed at the time. The policies
of the Eastern Question deserve to be called *eine Politik von Fall zu Fall*
[a policy created issue by issue].[81] In none of the countries involved (not
even in the expansionist Russia) did there exist a master plan, and the
constant rearranging of personages and alliances on the chessboard
made it almost impossible to keep up, even for the best diplomat.

Anton von Werner's famous painting of the Berlin Congress. In the wings (fourth from the right) Odo Russell.

CHAPTER 8

The Last Years

The years after the Berlin Congress did not turn out to be a period of celebration for Russell. Exhausted from the expense and the social strains of entertaining, he was also under no illusion that the peace would last for long. His only hope was that, for the time being, none of the powers would have the energy to open Pandora's box again. However, the aftermath of the conference seemed to involve more work than the conference itself. The conscientious Lord Salisbury was, for example, not happy with the word '*pres*' in article 58, which prompted frantic correspondence between London and Berlin. In addition, the issue of the Greek–Turkish border (article 24) had to be worked on because everyone knew it would cause long-term trouble. Although Russell was conscientious in this work, he was, however, more interested in the possibilities that the Berlin Congress had opened up for British–German relations. In Odo's view, Bismarck's handling of the Eastern Question had proved him to be a good confidant and a possible ally for Britain. The Russians had not taken their defeat at Berlin very gracefully. This made it an ideal time for Britain to 'team up' with the eager Bismarck and thereby free him from the possibility of another Russian embrace.[1] Lord Salisbury, however, was not interested in any such proposals. He told Odo that the existence of good relations with Germany was enough, and that any more ambitious objectives would not be supported by the FO.[2] Russell later tried to describe his failure to Granville: '[Bismarck's] attempts to establish cordial and intimate relations with HMG and his repeated offers of cooperation were never met in a corresponding spirit. Personally, I regretted it, because I believe that we might have derived real and lasting advantages from an intimate understanding with Germany'.[3] Salisbury, however, remained adamant that there would be no further rapprochement, as he simply did not trust Bismarck. In addition, he did not look favourably upon Germany's swing to protectionism in 1879. In the 1870s and 1880s Germany's economy went through two upward cycles (1879–1882 and 1888–1890) and two downward ones (1873–1879 and 1883–1887.)[4] Since 1865 the reigning dogma had been that of a free-trade policy, but in 1879 newspapers started a campaign that caused the Germans to fear that their markets would be flooded by English products. Protectionism gradually became the new ideology. Even with his rather limited knowledge of economics, Odo realised that the new 'protective tariff' in Germany would be a great blow to British trade (which was already suffering as a result of depressed conditions at home): 'It is with deep regret that I notice the steadily growing agitation, not only in favour of reimposing import duties on iron generally, but also of taking such measures as may tend in particular to exclude English competition altogether from Germany'.[5] In the long run, protectionism was only one of many factors that led to a deterioration in British–German relations.

The only positive thing to come out of the Berlin Congress for Odo seemed to be the offer of a peerage to him: 'It is a great event in my life', he wrote to Hastings, 'and I am especially pleased at the manner in which the Queen has offered it. I may never again have the opportunity of accepting or refusing one, and I confess that a seat in the House of Lords is the height of my ambition if I live long enough not to die in harness abroad'.[6] But even this well-deserved honour transformed itself into a nightmare when Hastings decided to raise his patriarchal head. As a proud Whig he felt that Gladstone should first be asked whether a Russell could accept a peerage from a Tory government. When Gladstone turned out to be against it, Odo could hardly suppress his anger:

> I never thought that a reward offered to me for diplomatic services abroad could be looked upon as a party question at home, or have any importance in your [Gladstone's] eyes. Great was therefore my surprise when the Duke [Hastings] told me that in your opinion by accepting the peerage I was virtually repudiating the political principles of my family and of my party and that you held that I should defer the acceptance of the Queen's offer until our party was again in power.[7]

Gladstone defended himself by claiming '[that] the acceptance would under the circumstances have some tendency ... to hamper your political freedom'.[8] Odo of course disagreed, but he had no choice but to yield. He wrote bitterly to Hastings that: 'this is not the first time [Gladstone] has thrown me over'.[9] The rejection of the peerage served to again worsen Russell's relationship with Disraeli. Odo reported the Prime Minister's reaction:

> The crown gave peerages for various services irrespective of party, and he [Disraeli] mentioned Lord Northbroke and the Duke of Wellington. He said he could not admit the principle for which there was no precedent of a peerage being refused

because it came through an adverse political party. If such a principle were admitted it would shake the foundation of the British constitution. If I could not accept for private reasons, he would submit my decision to the Queen who would be as deeply annoyed as himself because HM took, as he did, a personal interest in it, but he could not admit any refusal on the principle I put forward.[10]

Uncharacteristically, Russell did not let the matter rest and over the next two years constantly continued to complain to Hastings that he needed compensation for this sacrifice: '[Gladstone] will owe me some reparation for past injuries to myself and to Oliver [Odo's oldest son], to transfer us to a post, where the obligatory Royal family representative does not exist as at Berlin, which is a family embassy'.[11] Of course Russell knew that he was indispensable in Berlin, but he also wanted to make it patently clear that his position there dwindled his own savings. If Oliver would not inherit enough money because the Princess Royal expected Russell to entertain on a large scale, then he wanted at least a peerage that he could pass on to his son.[12] However, once Gladstone was back in power, it took him eight months to offer Odo the long-awaited, truly Liberal peerage.[13] (Herbert von Bismarck thought that Granville and Gladstone never forgave Russell the fact that he had almost accepted a Tory peerage.)[14] Even though Russell was upset about this delay, he did not show it in his thank-you note to Gladstone: 'I can never sufficiently thank you, and your letter will always be treasured by me and mine'.[15] Now the Russell family brooded over an appropriate name for their new peer (Odo had seriously suggested to simply use his first name as his 'family name'; his brothers were however horrified at the idea). It is not clear from the correspondence who eventually suggested the name 'Ampthill' instead (Ampthill is a village near Woburn Abbey and today visitors can be driven around the area in Ampthill taxis). Odo asked his eight-year-old daughter Constance for advice and she said that 'Anthill sounded very pretty'. For Russell the lover of animals, this seemed to decide it. Apart from a proper name, the first Baron of Ampthill of course needed some money to go with it. Hastings, whom Odo called by now 'constitutionally irritable',[16] grudgingly endowed his brother with part of the Bedford estate and spoilt this 'present' by complaining that two peerages (Earl Russell had become a peer in 1861) would eventually 'break' the whole Bedford estate.[17] The grumbling Hastings was, however, persuaded to find a house for Odo and his family near Woburn. In 1884 it was decided that they should have Ampthill House in Ampthill. Odo was never to see it but his wife and daughters would live there for the next 40 years.

The new Liberal government gave Odo his peerage and the country a new foreign policy. Gladstone, in accord with his Midlothian promises, turned against the Turks and began to espouse the need for a closer relationship with Russia. Being one of the few statesman who believed in international law he also wanted to solve the Greek–Turkish question. It was because of his untimely idealism that in June 1880 the great powers had to meet again in Berlin to negotiate the terms by which Turkey could be forced to cede territory to Greece and Montenegro. Britain and Russia advocated the use of force, but they did not get any support from Austria, Germany and France — and it was only thanks to Bismarck that in the end the Montenegrins at least got Dulcigo.

With an idealist Prime Minister such as Gladstone, life in Berlin had in many ways become increasingly difficult for Russell. Bismarck complained whenever Odo passed on unpalatable messages from his government: 'the British ambassador had just made a communication to me which is the very height of tactlessness, typically Gladstone!'[18] Of course, it is well known that Bismarck and Gladstone, with their completely different philosophies of life, rejected everything the other stood for. Bismarck was, however, the more ardent hater. He revelled in his son's vicious letters from London about Gladstone's bizarre nightly excursions ('he is really wild in this respect and spends nights walking the streets like a brooding stag in September'),[19] the Irish problem, a mad British press, a violent working-class and governmental chaos. Odo, who of course was not aware of these letters, thought that the main reason behind Otto von Bismarck's outbursts was the Chancellor's deep-rooted fear that Gladstone's regime encouraged socialist ideas world-wide.[20] For, after all, Bismarck was still battling against his new enemy, the socialists and an end did not seem to be in sight.

Still, Bismarck should have been thankful to his British 'pet hate'. With his probably well-meaning but awkward foreign policy, Gladstone involuntarily brought Russia, Austria and Germany closer together (which helped Bismarck to create the second Three Emperors' League in 1881). In addition, Gladstone did Bismarck the favour of taking over Egypt in 1882 — a fact that naturally outraged the French and caused a sudden blossoming of German–French relations. Because of the problematic domestic situation in Britain, the PM was simply too busy to understand that he was playing into Bismarck's hands: 'No one in England cares for the foreign situation and Ireland will absorb public opinion', Odo wrote to Lady Derby, 'so that Bismarck can continue to direct the foreign policy of France and Austria to his heart's content while he lives'.[21] The more problems the British faced, the more important the German Chancellor's expertise and support seemed to become (especially with regard to Egypt). During these years Granville was of little help to Gladstone, and Russell was disappointed at having to work with such an incompetent Foreign Secretary again. In his opinion, Granville had become like a leaf in the wind, changing his foreign policy on a whim: 'Granville who was for neutrality and non-interference six years ago, is now bullying the Turk, connecting with the Russians, advising the French, blowing up the Austrians, admonishing the Italian, cajoling the German and remodelling the map of Europe, to satisfy the spirit of growing democracy'.[22]

Although Russell rightly criticised his chief, he himself was now beginning to make mistakes. One can say that in a very literal sense the colonial question killed Odo. He was slow to realise its dangerous potential and, in trying to remedy this, he did not go on his much-needed annual 'liver cures' to Marienbad in the summer of 1884.[23] The question is why Russell, who had been so perceptive on countless other occasions, did not sense that Bismarck was about to start a completely new and dangerous policy with regard to colonial acquisitions.

Since the early 1870s, Odo had been correct in believing that Bismarck's assurances against colonial expansion were sincere.[24] Russell had always passed on to the FO Bismarck's utterances on this subject without ever questioning them: 'Colonies in his [Bismarck's] opinion would only be a cause of weakness, because colonies could only be defended by powerful fleets. Many colonies had been offered to him, [but] he had rejected them'.[25] It would have never occurred to Odo that Bismarck would one day make a pact with, of all people, businessmen, to acquire *Schutzgebiete* [protective regions]. The Chancellor had often made it clear to Russell (and many others) that he despised 'shopkeepers' who try to interfere in politics. In 1873, he had in no uncertain terms condemned their obscure enterprises in China:

> Those blackguard Hamburg and Lübeck merchants have no other idea of policy in China but to, what they call shoot down those damned niggers of Chinese for 6 months and then dictate peace to them, etc., etc. Now, I believe those Chinese are better Christians than our vile mercantile snobs and wish for peace with us and are not thinking of war, and I'll see the merchants and their Yankee and French allies damned before I consent to go to war with China to fill their pockets with money.[26]

Odo ironically added that 'this is the language the great man was indulging in, to express his love of peace'.[27]

By 1884, if Russell had not already been so ill, he might perhaps have noticed that there was an atmosphere of change. His mistake probably was that after 14 years with Bismarck he felt convinced that he had worked out this enigma. Of course, given the Chancellor's flexible mind, Odo should have known that it was impossible to predict how he would act and that Bismarck's speciality was to reinvent himself and his policies. After all, Bismarck had on many previous occasions tried to manipulate Odo. But Russell had never before been taken in so badly as on this issue. Up until then it had not been part of the game to make the other person look ridiculous. Yet, this was exactly what now happened to Russell. The British ambassador was made to look like a starstruck fool to his FO colleagues. In some ways it was a blessing for Russell that he never realised the scale of Bismarck's 'manoeuvres'.

There is to this day much speculation about the reasons behind Bismarck's sudden interest in colonial expansion. While Marxist historians saw German imperialism as a natural continuation of capitalism, others, sensibly, looked at the various domestic factors including fear of rising emigration, social unrest and a Reichstag hostile to Bismarck. Some historians have also argued that foreign policy considerations played a pivotal part, in particular Bismarck's desire to provoke a quarrel with England. The latest theory is the 'Crown Prince hypothesis', which has been put forward by Axel Riehl. Riehl argues that in 1883–1884, as the Emperor's health was less than radiant, Bismarck feared that he would be dismissed if a new liberal regime came to power. The Chancellor's idea was that by embarking on an anti-British colonial policy he would make himself indispensable to the new Emperor Friedrich. Riehl uses Herbert von Bismarck as the key witness in support for this theory.[28] Looking back, Herbert noted that because it had been expected that the Crown Prince would soon come to power, 'we had to embark on a colonial policy, because it was popular and conveniently adapted to bring us into conflict with England at any moment'.[29] However, in the view of Odo and the Crown Princess, the colonial policy was not a conspiracy against the Crown Prince but had been started simply to gain patriotic support in the upcoming elections. Odo had always thought that the Crown Prince, unlike his wife, favoured colonial expansion: 'Neither he [Bülow] or Bismarck wish for colonies — the Crown Prince does,'[30] he wrote in 1873. This did not change over the years. In 1884 Odo noticed that the Crown Prince seemed to share the 'national craving [for colonies]'.[31] In contradiction to Riehl's theory one could therefore argue that Bismarck wanted to please, rather than control, the Crown Prince by acquiring colonies for him as a form of 'morning gift'. This view is supported by the fact that according to Holstein, in April 1884, the Crown Prince indicated to Bismarck that he was willing to work with him after William's death.[32] Of course, the Crown Prince could not like the anti-British component of the policy but he seemed to accept it as part of the new deal.

The events signalling the commencement of Bismarck's colonial policy were so seemingly unimportant to the outside world, that it is little wonder Odo overlooked them. It started off with the troublesome Adolf Lüderlitz who, in 1882, asked for consular protection to trade on the south-western African coast. Before the question could be considered another problem had to be dealt with. Lüderlitz had purchased the bay of Angra Pequenna, which prompted the arrival of an outraged British trader on the scene. The German FO now asked the British FO whether they had any sovereign rights in that area, which seemed not to be the case. However, it was necessary to consult the Cape colony and — many months later — their reply was that they were far from pleased to be getting a German neighbour. Rennell Rodd was probably exaggerating when he claimed in his memoirs that he had been one of the first to see the danger coming:

> The earliest indication of any deliberate German intention to found a colony over-seas which came under my personal experience had been a note received at the Foreign Office from the German Embassy in November 1883, which passed through my hands for preliminary treatment while I was serving in that Depart-ment. It set forth the desire of a commercial house at Bremen to establish a trad-ing station on the Bay of Angra Pequenna, which is some 280 miles south of Walfisch Bay .... I took it to the head of the Western Department and observed that it appeared to me to be one of the most important communications which had come under my cognisance at the Foreign Office.[33]

Perhaps the young Rennell Rodd was really that perceptive; his superiors however were not. Rennell Rodd thought that he knew the reason: 'It [the aforementioned note] did not seem to make any great impression on my immediate official superiors [which] was in some measure due to Lord Ampthill's reports'.[34] Odo had always reacted to such colonial hiccups in a most conciliatory way. For example, in May 1883 with regard to the German claims in Fiji, he had advised his government to deal with such matters 'gracefully and speedily' (for after all the German traders there had no intention of annexing the place).[35] Uppermost in his mind was his concern of not annoying Bismarck with such trivialities.

Though Odo did not think that the Chancellor himself wanted colonies, he was well informed about various pressure groups that favoured such a policy. He went to meetings of the German Colonisation Society and also reported on the endeavours of Carl Peters. Still, in Odo's opinion: 'there is no reason to suppose the German Government will be more disposed to lend its countenance to the efforts of the society [Peters had just founded] than it has been in the case of similar movements in the past'.[36]

In June 1884, after a Reichstag speech by Bismarck, Odo was finally forced to acknowledge that the Chancellor had changed his opinion on the subject: 'it is a remarkable fact that Prince Bismarck, contrary to his convictions and to his will, has been driven by public opinion into the inauguration of a colonial policy he has hitherto denounced as detrimental to the concentration of German strength and power'.[37] Eventually, Odo managed to get an interview with Bismarck who tried to excuse his actions by referring to the pressure that had been put on him: 'It was impossible for him [Bismarck] to say to these men "Germany is too weak and too poor for such undertakings" '.[38] While this conversation took place, Gustav Nachtigal was already on his mission to Africa. He hoisted flags all through the first part of July 1884: on 5 July in Togoland and on 14 July in Cameroon. The British Government was more irritated than annoyed by this *fait accompli*. Gladstone did not in principle mind the acquisition of colonies by Germany, but he was upset about the means which Bismarck employed.[39] What worried Odo most about this new German policy was that its anti-British component was so well received in Germany:[40] 'I am in perfect despair at Prince Bismarck's present inclination to increase his popularity before the general elections by taking up an anti-English attitude', he wrote in August 1884.[41] A war between British and German newspapers had by then erupted over the Angra Pequenna question. The *National Zeitung* claimed that Germany was strong enough to take 'what she pleases in Africa' and the *Standard* retaliated by answering that such impertinence should be returned 'blow for blow'.[42] Although Odo thought that this was all 'too stupid', he felt more and more depressed. Herbert von Bismarck claimed that he had heard remarks in London that Russell would be called back. This had prompted the German FO to send a letter to Münster who was instructed to make sure that under no circumstances was Morier to be sent to Berlin as Odo's successor.[43] It is true, that the constant stress had caused a deterioration in Odo's health. *The Times* would later write in his obituary that:

> … though always more or less suffering from an ailment which is supposed to be fatal to temper, [his liver trouble] he was always in his intercourse with the world at least, the perfection of sweet, equable spirits. But a shade of melancholy and sadness seemed to have settled on him of late, as if he already presaged an early end.[44]

On 19 August 1884 his liver pains increased and on the 25th his Berlin staff received a telegram from Potsdam, saying that he was in a very serious state. A few hours later a second one arrived stating that he had died. Odo was 55. In Germany, the reaction to Russell's death was unprecedented. Never before had a foreign diplomat been so deeply mourned by all factions of Berlin society. Apart from the usual official statement in such cases, which the German Minister for Foreign Affairs

Hatzfeldt provided, there was genuine grief. Empress Augusta, whose physician had looked after Odo, told a secretary of the British embassy that this was 'a national loss to both countries ... I wish you to repeat what I am saying in every quarter of your country. Lord Ampthill will never be forgotten by us or by Germany'.[45] The old Emperor burst into tears when he heard the news (which, admittedly, he did more frequently the older he got) and exclaimed, 'there was not one among his own personal officers whom he trusted or respected more'.[46] Only a year before William had, after the death of his brother Charles, literally cried on Odo's shoulder and had said to him, 'that he would be the next to die and that Russell should never forget their time together at Versailles'.[47] For both of them those months in France had been, in very different ways, the highlight of their careers.

Bismarck seemed to be touched by the death of his once favourite Englishman, even though his reaction was less emotional than that of the Emperor. Because of the colonial issue, the Chancellor and Odo had become slightly estranged during the last months but still Bismarck knew what he had lost. To Lord Granville he wrote that 'England might give a successor to the ambassador that she had lost, but could not expect to replace him'.[48] Bismarck himself would certainly never be on the same terms with another foreign diplomat again.

For the Crown Princess, who was in England at the time, the death of Russell seemed to be the end of an era. She had been proud of the social success of Odo and his wife because they seemed to symbolise all the good things about the British. But apart from this, she had also lost one of her most loyal (and few) friends: 'He was her dearest friend', Queen Victoria wrote, 'who was ever so kind and true to her, whose home was the only one she could go to for help and comfort'.[49] The Crown Prince expressed best his wife's despair, in what today sounds like a typically Victorian melodramatic outburst, when he told Rennell Rodd, 'You don't know what this means for the Crown Princess and myself. We shall have to begin a new life now'.[50] Odo seemed to have affected even the stiff Friedrich. *The Times* summed up well his 'art of diplomacy' when it wrote in its obituary: 'Doors were never closed in Odo Russell's face, and if they had been shut behind his back he would always have got them opened again by his gently knocking'.[51] Russell was buried at Chenies, just outside London between Watford and Amersham.

Odo's death coincided with an increasing anti-British feeling in German society. This new antipathy towards Britain was now openly expressed by the social and academic elite, the newspapers and consequently 'the man in the street'. It was the worst time to die and it was the worst time to take over the Berlin embassy. Gladstone and Granville had first thought of offering the ambassadorship to Hastings, but this never materialised. The Russells were, however, not willing to give up any of their sinecures. The post of British ambassador to Berlin had in effect become a Russell family possession. Odo's father had occupied it first and Odo himself was followed by his brother's son-in-law, Sir Edward Malet (Malet had married Hastings' daughter Lady Ermyntrude Russell.) Malet, like Odo, also had a Versailles connection with Bismarck, though a less glamorous one. In 1870, when Lord Lyons had gone to Bordeaux to be close to the French Government, Malet, at the time a relatively junior diplomat, had been left behind in Paris. He was chosen in September 1870 to carry an important letter to Bismarck, an adventurous endeavour. The outcome was the meeting of Favre and Bismarck in Ferrieres.[52]

One cannot compare the achievements of Russell with those of Malet and this is not the place for it. Malet would not have an easy time in Germany trying to cope with problems that Odo could not have imagined even in his worst nightmares.

CHAPTER 9

Conclusion

Russell's motto for solving political problems could be summed up by E.M. Forster's famous phrase: 'only connect'. For Odo, politics was simply about understanding and influencing people. He idealistically believed that people could always be reasoned with, and that having the right contacts was the key factor. Any notion that ideologies or economics could also make history would have been alien to him.

When Russell, with his strong Whig tradition and pride in British institutions, first took up his post as ambassador to Berlin he was still of the opinion that British political ideals should be adopted world-wide. However, 14 years of cultural contact with the Germans taught him that such a transfer of political values was not possible. He learnt to accept that a German Liberal had after all few things in common with a British one, and that not even Crown Prince Fiedrich would be capable of changing the tide and liberalising Germany. The military would also continue to play a central role in Germany because of the fear of enemies — whether real or imagined. Whenever Russell tried to explain these unwelcome truths to his British friends, (at first in a critical way and later more understandingly) he ran the danger of being accused of turning into a 'native'. As the Queen at one point wrote to her daughter, the Prussian Crown Princess: 'you mention Lord Odo for a possible successor to Lord Granville [as Foreign Secretary]. No one can think more highly of Lord Odo than I do — but he has a good deal that is foreign in him'.[1] Of course she was wrong. Although Russell developed an understanding of Germany, he always remained the personification of the Anglo-Saxon Whig beliefs of his time. His special gift, however, was the ability to immerse himself in the 'German soul' and to then re-emerge again to write his reports.

It could be claimed that in some ways Russell's time in Berlin was an easier period compared with what his predecessors and successors experienced. During his tenure there were no wars, no colonial race and hardly any economic competition to deal with. However, the

Germany Odo experienced was occupied with the enormous consequences of the war. To unite a country as diverse as Germany, was as trying in the 1870s as it was in the 1990s. It was inevitable that mistakes would be committed in this process and Russell was at first one of the harshest critics of them. Still, when Count Münster wrote that Russell was a friend of Germany, he was right. However, Odo knew Germany too well to be an uncritical friend.

There were two distinct phases in Russell's view of Germany's foreign policy — pre- and post-1878. In the period leading up to 1878 a recurring theme of Russell's despatches was his mistrust of the Chancellor's assurances that Germany was a satisfied power. One of the most famous quotes of Odo Russell is that: 'The two great objects of Bismarck's policy are: first, the supremacy of Germany in Europe and of the German race in the world; second, the neutralisation of the influence and power of the Latin race in France and elsewhere. To obtain these objects, he will go to any length while he lives, so that we must be prepared for surprises in the future'.[2] Klaus Hildebrand rightly claims that this quote has been overrated by historians. In writing his daily despatches, Russell's dilemma stemmed from two competing senses of obligation: on the one hand, he felt he must not unnecessarily alarm the FO, but on the other, he did not want to be negligent in reporting possible indications of a further Bismarckian crusade.

Russell when presented with a crisis usually reacted in a cool headed manner. For example, during both the war-in-sight-crisis and the Eastern Question, Russell believed that Bismarck's peace assurances were genuine and advised the FO accordingly. Putting aside Russell's mistaken belief as to the possibility of an Austro-German war, his analysis and actions during foreign crisis situations always demonstrated his belief that the Germans would not overreact. It was usually only at the *beginning* of a crisis that Odo had difficulty in predicting which faction (Bismarck, the military or the National Liberals) in Germany would gain the upper hand. For him the Iron Chancellor was never a warmonger, but a politician who had to employ certain means to stay in power. Bismarck, in Russell's view, might start a campaign in order to distract attention from his domestic problems or to get his political partners under control — but never just for the sake of conquest. The year 1878 is critical because after this Russell accepted Germany as a peaceful power.

It is clear that Russell developed extraordinary insights into Germany and its leader, but what impact did Russell's despatches have on the formation of British foreign policy? Here one has to distinguish between, on the one hand, the influence that was specifically acknowledged by the Foreign Secretary and the Prime Minister, and on the other, influence evidenced by British government action. It was not in the culture of the FO to praise its diplomats, and therefore the acknowledged influence of Russell's advice is not that frequent. There is, of course, the praise of Russell's despatches by Gladstone ('whenever there is an Odo in the box, satisfaction instantly predominates')[3] and Derby's opinion that: 'Russell is the best man we have'. Lord Tenterden, the Permanent Under-Secretary, thought the same: 'Odo Russell is the right man in Berlin'.[4] There is, however, not surprisingly, no clear instance where one of the Foreign Secretaries or Prime Ministers whom Odo served, expressly acknowledged the influence of Odo's views on one of their decisions. Still, the FO's actions provide the best evidence that Russell did influence British foreign policy. We have seen, for example, that during the Black Sea crisis (despite Gladstone's dismissiveness of Odo's methods), the FO was to a great extent dependent on Russell's suggestions to Bismarck and owed it to Odo's famous bluff that the possibility of a conference in London was first aired. Here we see Russell not just as a mediator or informant, but as a policy maker. Another — less spectacular — example of Russell's influence can be seen in relation to the complex problem of French–German relations after 1871. The FO was persuaded by Russell's argument that Bismarck's occasional war threats against the Thiers government were caused by his domestic German problems and that there would not be a war between the two nations as long as France did not 'provoke' Germany. As a result, the FO and Lord Lyons impressed on the French Government the importance of treading a careful path. However, Russell's influence on British policy towards French–German relations suddenly diminished when Disraeli decided in 1875 to break the unity of the Northern Powers and to stand up to Bismarck. The successful outcome of this concerted British–Russian action also proved to the FO that Russell's analysis of the 'special relationship' between Germany and Russia was not entirely correct. After that incident, Disraeli's new style of politics made it increasingly difficult for Russell to have a great impact on the FO decision-making process. The irony was that it was not a Whig, as Russell had hoped, but a Tory, who mapped out the strong foreign policy he had yearned for. However, Disraeli's straightforwardness initially worried Russell, as it did not fit with his approach to the Eastern Question. This is a clear instance where Russell failed to show flexibility and adaptability in the face of new developments.

A further factor that diminished Russell's influence on British decision-makers, was simply the general indifference that still existed in England towards German affairs. German–British relations were not yet at the top of the political agenda at the FO, and it was obvious to insiders that the Berlin Embassy still ranked after Paris and St Petersburg — something which the German Emperor deplored. As has already been noted, Russell and Morier often despaired about the fact that British politicians only liked to talk about Paris (which most of them had visited), and that this apart, 'continental talk' bored everyone to death. It was Russell's personal contacts, such as his friendship with Lord and Lady Derby and the MP friends of his brother Arthur, which gave him the opportunity to promote more interest in German affairs among British decision-makers.

The overall judgement must be that Russell played an instrumental role in helping Britain to understand the unknown quantity, Germany. The decisive reason for this was his special relationship with Bismarck. The Chancellor's preferential treatment of Odo is evidenced by the fact that during the *Kulturkampf*, he forgave Russell his clear opposition and continued to treat him well. Also Bismarck did not for one moment believe during the war-in-sight crisis that Odo had deceived him. The Chancellor clearly distinguished between the individual whose integrity he admired and the policies he had to represent (Herbert von Bismarck believed wholeheartedly that Odo was Germany's political friend and admired the Chancellor).[5] This was partly true. Russell saw Bismarck, the 'great man', the 'Wallenstein', 'the Zornesbock', as an irresistable phenomenon.

Notes

Notes to Chapter 1

1 Gordon A. Craig, 'Die Chequers Affäre von 1990', in *Vierteljahreshefte für Zeitgeschichte*, 39 (1991), p. 611ff.
2 Margaret Thatcher, *The Downing Street Years* (London, 1993), p. 792.
3 *Ibid.*, p. 798.
4 *Ibid.*, p. 796.
5 Disraeli's advice in *Contarini Fleming*, quoted in Roger Ellis, *Who is Who in Victorian Britain* (London, 1997), p. ix.
6 See Lothar Gall, *Bismarck. Der weiße Revolutionär* (Berlin, 1980). Gall quotes Bismarck's comment that, 'one has to give up one's private existence when one becomes an official person', p. 460.
7 Quoted in Fritz Hartung, 'Bismarck und Graf Harry Arnim', *Historische Zeitschrift*, 171, (1951).
8 Lothar Bucher's unusual career has always fascinated historians. Books about him were published by Bernhard Dammermann, Fritz Gebauer, Heinrich Poschinger, Carl Zaddach and most recently Christoph Studt, *Lothar Bucher (1871–1892). Ein politisches Leben zwischen Revolution und Staatsdienst*. Schriftenreihe der Historischen Kommission bei der Bayerischen Akademie der Wissenschaften, 47 (Göttingen, 1992). For Holstein's account of Bucher see: Norman Rich (ed.), *Die Geheimen Papiere Friedrich von Holsteins. Erinnerungen und politische Denkwürdigkeiten*. Vol. I (Göttingen, 1958), p. 58.
9 Fritz Stern, *Gold and Iron. Bismarck, Bleichröder and the Building of the German Empire* (New York, 1977), p. 321.
10 Paul Kennedy, *The Rise of the Anglo – German Antagonism 1860–1914* (London, 1980), p. 134.
11 Raymond Jones, *The Nineteenth Century Foreign Office: A Study in Administrative History* (London, 1971), p. 177.
12 Paul Knaplund, *Letters from the Berlin Embassy 1871–74 and 1880–85*. Annual Report of the American Historical Association (Washington, 1942), p. 18.
13 Stern, *Gold and Iron*, p. 336. '[Russell] was the star of the diplomatic corps at Berlin: charming and shrewd, Russell was the favourite of Bismarck and the court', p. 170.
14 Kennedy, *Antagonism*, p. 135.
15 Winifried Taffs, *Ambassador to Bismarck, Lord Odo Russell, First Baron Ampthill* (London, 1938); Alec Randall, 'Lord Odo Russell and Bismarck', *History Today*, 27 (London, 1977), pp. 240–248; Duane Niler Pyeatt, 'The Berlin Embassy. Odo Russell and Anglo-German Relations', Unpublished PhD thesis (Texas, 1992).

Notes to Chapter 2(a)

1 Christopher Hill, 'The Historical Background — Past and Present in British Foreign Policy', in Michael Smith, Steve Smith and Brian White (eds), *British Foreign Policy — Tradition, Change and Transformation* (London, 1988), p. 1f.
2 See Ray Monk, *Bertrand Russell. The Spirit of Solitude* (London, 1996), p. 4.
3 John Russell, *William Lord Russell* (London, 1820).
4 'These hereditary influences were strong'. George Russell, *One Look Back* (London, 1911), p. 179.
5 *Ibid.*
6 Dominic Lieven, *The Aristocracy in Europe 1815–1914* (London, 1992), p. 236.

7   *Ibid.*, p. 26

8   *Ibid.*, p. 120. For a discussion of the Russell estates see also F.M.L. Thompson, *English Landed Society in the Nineteenth Century* (London, 1963).

9   Odo to Arthur, 31.5.78. FO 918 84.

10   Odo to Arthur, 20.2.54. FO 918 84.

11   Arthur Russell to Lady Derby, 30.8.75. Hatfield House Papers.

12   Odo to Hastings, 14.11.75. Woburn Papers.

13   Odo to Hastings, 25.2.75. Woburn Papers.

14   See Hastings to Gladstone, undated. British Library, Gladstone Papers, 44 488, p. 256.

15   See Georgiana Blakiston, *Woburn and the Russells* (Suffolk, 1988), p. 195.

16   See Hogarth, *Lord Odo Russell's Autograph Collection. Lord Odo Russell Collection Working Paper No. 1* (held in the MSS rare books Library, University College London) (London, 1989), p. 4f.

17   Georgiana Blakiston, *Lord William Russell and His Wife 1815–1847* (London, 1974), p. 31.

18   Lady William Russell to Lord Lynedoch, 22 March 1830. In Georgiana Blakiston, *Lord William Russell*, p. 210f.

19   See Noel Blakiston, *The Roman Question — Extracts from the Dispatches of Lord Odo Russell from Rome 1858–1870* (London, 1962), p. IX.

20   Odo to Arthur, undated, FO 918 84.

21   Blakiston, *Lord William Russell*, p. 376.

22   Hogarth, *Lord Odo Russell's Autograph Collection*, p. 8.

23   *Ibid.*, p. 6.

24   Odo to Arthur, 1856, FO 918 84.

25   Quoted from Blakiston, *Woburn*, p. 211.

26   Noel Blakiston, *Roman Question*, p. xx.

27   Monsieur Drocourt was one of the tutors who stayed with the Russells for a long time. He kept a diary, which is now in the possession of the Russell family. When he died in 1880 Russell was deeply shaken: 'another link with the past gone'. Odo to Hastings, 16.11.80. Woburn Papers.

28   See Hogarth, *Odo Russell Working Paper*, p. 11.

29   Georgiana Blakiston claims that Hastings was distressed that Odo and Arthur 'spoke English with foreign accents after their long residence abroad'. Blakiston, *Woburn* p. 211.

30   Another highlight of the collection is a letter from Alexander von Humboldt. See Hogarth, *Odo Russell Working Paper*, p.1.

31   Blakiston writes that '[Their] uncles were not resigned to seeing their grown-up nephews becoming no more than "intelligent foreigners." ' Blakiston, *Woburn*, p. 213.

32   *Ibid.*, p. 220.

33   Hogarth, *Odo Russell*, Working paper p. 8. Cannadine shows that professions like the 'judiciary, the army, the church, the law and the civil service were the favourite occupations of younger sons who wanted a high status job that perpetuated their patrician position'. David Cannadine, *The Decline and Fall of the British Aristocracy* (New Haven/London, 1990), p. 14.

34   Quoted from Blakiston, *Woburn*, p. 206.

35   Disraeli on his impressions of Woburn, 31.8.65. George E. Buckle, *The Life of Benjamin Disraeli Earl of Beaconsfield (1855–1868)*, Vol. IV (London, 1916), p. 421. While waiting to become the next Duke, Hastings represented Bedfordshire from 1847 to 1872.

36   *Ibid.*

37   Odo to Hastings, 29.5.72. Woburn Papers.
38   Odo to Hastings, Rome, Christmas 1869. Woburn Papers. This independent life,
      if it had ever existed, was to change 2 years later with Odo's new posting to Berlin.
39   See Hastings correspondence with Odo, Woburn Papers.
40   In public, it was of course seen as vulgar to talk about money, as George Russell
      vividly recalled: 'In the "Sacred circle of the Great Grandmotherhood", I never
      heard the slightest reference to income. Not that the Whigs despised money. They
      were at least as fond of it as other people, and, even when it took the shape of
      slum-rents, its odour was not displeasing; but it was not a subject for conversa-
      tion'. George Russell, *One Look Back*, p. 163
41   Odo to Hastings, Woburn 19.6.78. As a consequence Hastings contributed
      £1.000 to his brother's conference expenses. *Ibid.* 17.7.78. Woburn Papers.
42   Odo to Lord Derby, October 1874, 920 DER (15) 16/1/15.
43   Odo to Hastings, 2.2.75. Woburn Papers.
44   Odo to Hastings, 11.11.78. Woburn Papers.
45   Odo to Hastings, 14.11.78. Woburn Papers.
46   Odo to Hastings, 8.12.75. Woburn Papers.
47   George Russell is quoting from a character in *Endymion*: George Russell, *One Look
      Back*, p. 154.
48   Buckle, *Disraeli*, Vol. IV, p. 421.
49   Grant Duff on a visit with Hastings to Woburn. Sir Montstuart E. Grant Duff,
      Notes from a Diary. 1851–1872, 2 Vol. (London, 1897). Entry date: 5.1.1869.
50   On Arthur's club memberships see Sir Montstuart E. Grant Duff. According to
      Duff they founded the Breakfast Club together on 13 February 1866. See also
      Jennifer Hogarth, Lord Odo Russell Collection, Working Paper No. 2 *Lord Arthur
      John Edward Russell (1825–1892): A Victorian Intellectual* (University of London,
      1990), p. 1.
51   'The social, political and personal attributes of a gentleman were reflected in the
      Clubs he belonged to'. Note on Anthony Trollope's, *Phineas Finn*, first published
      1869. Reprinted edition (London, 1985), p. 725. Footnote 2.
52   Knollys to Odo, 14.5.72. FO 918 46.
53   Anthony Trollope, *Phineas Finn*. p. 62. Unlike some MPs however, Arthur did not
      neglect his constituency where he often gave speeches. Hogarth judges his con-
      stituency speeches as 'moderate and thoughtful'. Hogarth, *Arthur Russell Working
      Paper*, p. 1.
54   Duff, *Notes from a Diary*, p. 184.
55   Odo to Arthur, January 1884, FO 918 84.
56   Introduction to *Phineas Finn* by John Sutherland p. 19.
57   Odo to Arthur, undated, FO 918 89
58   *Ibid.*
59   Arthur to Layard, 27.2.1890, British Library, Layard Papers, 39 045, p. 76.
60   *Ibid.*
61   Alan Willard Brown, *The Metaphysical Society. Victorian Minds in Crisis, 1869–1880*
      (New York, 1973), p. 80.
62   *Ibid.*, p. XI.
63   Lytton Strachey, *Eminent Victorians* (London, 1987 edn.), p. 97.
64   Odo congratulated Arthur in 1875 enthusiastically on his appointment: 'he [Grant
      Duff] had never met with a sounder judgement'. Hogarth, *Arthur Russell*, p. 20.
65   *Ibid.*, p. 26
66   Blakiston, *Roman Question*, 19, p. IX.
67   See Hastings' correspondence, Odo to Hastings, 1874. Woburn Papers.
68   Raymond Jones, *The Diplomatic Service, 1815–1914* (London, 1983), p. 170.

69 Blakiston, *Roman Question*, p. IXf..

70 *Ibid.*, p. XI.

71 Jonathan Parry, 'Past and Future', in T.C.W. Blanning and D. Cannadine (eds), *History and Biography. Essays in Honour of Derek Beales* (Cambridge, 1996), p. 146.

72 Odo to Hastings, 11.3.76. Woburn Papers. 'Your printed letters are a great triumph of science, but they are a blow to autograph collectors'. *Ibid.* 16.3.76.

73 See *Ibid.*, Odo to Hastings, 1876. Woburn Papers.

74 *Ibid.* 28.3.76.

75 Odo to Hastings, 8.8.70. Woburn Papers.

76 And in the value of creative work. Influenced by Carlyle and Ruskin, they looked for fulfilment in their work. See Charles Harvey and John Press, 'Victorian Values: William Morris-Art and Idealism', *History Today*, Vol. 46 (London, 1996), p. 18.

77 Lady Gwendolyn Cecil, 'Lord Salisbury in Private Life', in Lord Blake and Hugh Cecil (eds), *Salisbury — the Man and the Statesman* (New York, 1987), p. 39.

78 See Eric Hobsbawn, *Das Zeitalter der Extreme* (München, 1995), p. 28.

79 Acton of Aldenham or in full: Baron John Emerich Edward Dalberg Acton (1834–1902) was born in Italy like Odo. He was a Liberal MP for a time, yet his true vocation was historical research. Quoted in the *Cambridge Biographical Encyclopaedia* (Cambridge, 1994). See also the *Kulturkampf* chapter.

80 See for example Agatha Ramm, *Sir Robert Morier. Envoy and Ambassador in the Age of Imperialism 1876–1893* (Oxford, 1973), p. 4f.

81 Crown Princess to Queen Victoria, 14.4.1871. Quoted in Roger Fulford, *Darling Child. Private Correspondence of Queen Victoria and the Crown Princess of Prussia* (London, 1976).

82 Morier had been appointed 'paid attaché in Berlin in 1858 and then served (from 1866 to 1876) in turn at Frankfurt, Darmstadt, Stuttgart and Munich. Ramm, *Morier*, p. 3. His appointment to an ambassadorial post took extremely long but in 1876 he finally managed to get a first class mission. Morier's closeness to Odo is highlighted by Ramm: Russell was the only friend Morier addressed by his Christian name. *Ibid.* They also played their private games: Grosstadt was Granville, Z or Zornesbock was Bismarck, 'a great Pomeranian Giant who had no hair on his head and made everybody uncomfortable'. Morier to Odo, 5.7.75. FO 918 55.

83 Sir Austen Henry Layard (1817–1894) succeeded Elliot as ambassador to Turkey between 1877–1880.

84 She was the step-mother of the Prime Minister Lord Salisbury and married Lord Derby. Lady Salisbury's sister, Elizabeth Sackville West, was married to Odo's brother Hastings.

85 For details of her vast correspondence see W.A. Burghlere, *A Great Lady's Friendships. Letters to Mary, Marchioness of Salisbury, Countess of Derby 1862–1878*. Vol. I (London, 1926).

86 Odo to Lady Salisbury, 17.3.68. Hatfield Papers, unnumbered.

87 Odo to Lady Salisbury, 29.10.67. Hatfield Papers.

88 *Ibid.*, 13.1.68. Hatfield Papers.

89 Burghlere, *A Great Lady's Friendships*, p. 234.

90 Odo to Lady Salisbury, 18.11.67. Hatfield Papers.

91 Odo to Lady Salisbury. Rome, 13.1.68. Hatfield Papers. Despite all the family interference and his own concern, Odo was accepted at the end of January 1868 '[Emily] is the companion of the second half of my life'. *Ibid.*, 6.2.68.

92 Odo to Lady Salisbury, 15.12.67. Hatfield Papers.

93 Odo to his mother, undated, FO 918 85.

94 Clarendon to Hammond, 27.7.69, FO 391/4.

95 On Odo's reply, Derby wrote the marginal note: 'I heard this from Lord Odo's family'. 29.10.75. Derby Papers 920 DER (15) 16/1/15.

96 *Ibid.*
97 Neil Hart, *The Foreign Secretary* (Suffolk, 1984) p. 3.
98 There were not many Tory diplomats around. 'Paget, who was a Tory, complained about the effects this had on his career to Salisbury'. Paul Kennedy, *The Rise of the Anglo – German Antagonism* p. 137.
99 Lieven, *Aristocracy in Europe*, p. 1. For a European viewpoint see: Hans Ulrich Wehler (ed.), *Europäischer Adel 1750–1950* (Göttingen, 1990), p. 10ff.
100 A hard-working aristocrat seemed to be an exception. In a Vanity Fair cartoon the Marquis of Hartington was praised for his industry in the 1860s: 'His ability and industry would deserve respect even in a man; in a Marquis they command admiration'. Quoted from Patrick Jackson's article 'Skittles and the Marquis — a Victorian Love Affair', *History Today*, December 1995, Vol. 45 (12), p. 51.
101 Lieven, Aristocracy in Europe, p. 18

Notes to Chapter 2(b)

1   *The Economist*, 30.12.48.
2   See John Saville, *1848. The British State and the Chartist Movement* (Cambridge, 1987).
3   Stanley Weintraub, *Albert. Uncrowned King* (London, 1997), p. 192.
4   Great Britain, Foreign Office List and Consular Yearbook, Her Majesty's Stationary Office, 1885, p. 53–54.
5   This conversation took place as late as October 1851. Odo to his mother, Vienna 14.10.51. Woburn Papers.
6   Odo to his mother, 30.12.51 FO 918 85.
7   Quoted in: Giles St Aubyn, *Queen Victoria* (London, 1991), p. 253.
8   E.D. Steele, *Palmerston and Liberalism 1855–1865* (Cambridge, 1991), p. 18.
9   See John Tilley and Stephen Gaselee, *The Foreign Office* (London, 1933), p. 91.
10 See Mary Adeline Anderson, 'Edmund Hammond — Permanent Under-Secretary of State for Foreign Affairs 1854–1873' unpublished PhD dissertation (University of London, 1955), p. 230.
11 *Ibid.*, p. 226.
12 Hammond to Granville, 16.8.70. Granville Papers 30/29 104.
13 Hammond did not seem to esteem the diplomatic profession: 'The more I think and see of diplomacy, the more I am satisfied that neither the public nor the Office gain by making it a profession'. Hammond to Layard 26.2.62. Quoted in Anderson, 'Hammond', p. 214.
14 Bertrand Russell wrote in the preface to an edition of his own letters, that in the 19th century it was critical to perfect oneself in the art of letter writing if one wanted to succeed professionally. Bertrand Russell, *Briefe aus den Jahren 1950–1968* (Frankfurt, 1970), p. 2.
15 Layard Papers, British Library, Add. 39. 102, p. 408.
16 Quoted from Blakiston, *Woburn and the Russells*, p. xii.
17 Quoted from Noel Blakiston, *The Roman Question*, p. xxii.
18 *Ibid.*
19 Odo to Derby, 23.5.74. Derby Papers 920 DER (15) 16/1/15.
20 On average, his reports were three to four pages long.
21 Odo to Layard, Layard Papers, British Library, Add. 39.104, p. 216.
22 David Hare, *Plenty* (London, 1978), p. 71f.
23 Odo Russell to Lady Salisbury, 21.10.67. Hatfield Papers.
24 Morier to Odo. 21.4.71. FO 918 55.
25 Odo to Arthur, 22.1.52. FO 918 84.
26 Robert Tombs, *France 1814–1914* (London, 1996), p. 397.

27   Odo to his mother, undated (1852 or 53). FO 918 85.
28   Letter written by Lady Russell praising her nephew's wit, 24.6.73. Bertrand and
      Patricia Russell (eds), *The Amberley Papers. The Letters and Diaries of Lord and Lady
      Amberley*, (London, 1937), p.548
29   Odo to his mother, Vienna 23.3.52 Woburn papers.
30   Jean Paul Bled, *Franz Joseph* (Vienna, 1988), p. 95.
31   Odo to his mother, Vienna, 13.4.52 Typescript, Woburn Papers.
32   See Leo Gerald Byrne, *The Great Ambassador: A Study of the Diplomatic Career of the Right
      Honourable Stratford Canning, K.G. G.C.B., Viscount de Redcliffe and the Epoch during which he
      served as the British Ambassador to the Sublime Porte of the Ottoman Sultan* (Columbus, 1964).
33   Quoted from Blakiston, *Roman Question*, p. xx.
34   *Ibid.*, p. xxi.
35   *Ibid.*
36   Odo to Arthur, 28.5.56. FO 918 84.
37   Quoted in J.B. Conacher, *Britain and the Crimea. 1855–56. Problems of War and Peace*
      (London, 1987), p. 35.
38   Odo reporting the outcome to his mother, 11.12.56. FO 918 85.
39   Quoted from Blakiston, *Roman Question*, p. xii.
40   *Ibid.*, p. xv.
41   *Ibid.*, p. xii.
42   Odo to Arthur, 2.5.57, FO 918 84.
43   *Ibid.*
44   Pyeatt, *The Berlin Embassy* p. 33.
45   Odo to Arthur, 2.5.57, FO 918 84.
46   *Ibid.*
47   Odo to Arthur, undated. Washington 1857, FO 918 84.
48   Odo to Arthur, 2.5.57, FO 918 84.
49   Alec Randall, 'A British Agent at the Vatican. The Mission of Odo Russell', in
      Dublin Review 1960, Vol. 233, p. 40.
50   Sir James Rennell Rodd, *Social and Diplomatic Memories, 1884–1893*, 3 Vols (Lon-
      don, 1926), p. 47.
51   Alec Randall, 'British Agent' p. 41.
52   See Blakiston, *Roman Question*, p. xvi.
53   Alec Randall, 'British Agent', p. 42.
54   *Ibid.*, p. 43.
55   See Blakiston, *Roman Question*, p. xiii.
56   David Newsome, *The Victorian World Picture* (London, 1997), p. 87.
57   See Blakiston, *Roman Question*, p. xxx.
58   Rodd, *Social and Diplomatic*, p. 47.
59   *Ibid.*
60   Pyeatt, 'The Berlin Embassy', p. 39.
61   Quoted from Randall, 'British Agent', p. 44.
62   Rodd, *Social and Diplomatic*, p. 47.
63   Randall, 'British Agent', p. 49.
64   Rodd, *Social and Diplomatic*, p. 46.
65   Blakiston, *Roman Question*, p. xxiv.
66   Jowett to Morier, January 1870. Jowett Papers, IIIM, 34.
67   Unfortunately, the Acton–Russell correspondence in the University Library Cam-
      bridge hardly touches on the *Kulturkampf* question, because Acton was in Rome
      at the time. See Cambridge University Library, Acton Papers 8119 (5)/R 200–
      230. Noel Blakiston's edition of Russell's Rome despatches shows, however, Odo's
      concern for Acton's spiritual crisis. Blakiston, *Roman Question*, p. 407ff.

68 Although both Universities subsequently gave him honorary doctorates, and in 1895 he became Regius Professor of Modern History at Cambridge. His 'direct pupils [were] R.V. Laurence, J.N. Figgis, G.P. Gooch, J.H. Clapham, G.M. Trevelyan, H.C. Gutteridge'. Owen Chadwick, *Acton, Döllinger and History*, German Historical Institute Annual Lecture (London, 1986).

69 In 1872, however, Odo passed on to the FO a lecture by Dr Döllinger, during which (the papers reported) 'the faculty of theology was distinguished by its total absence'. The whole lecture was an appeal for a more humanistic approach to the issue — a notion with which Odo would have agreed. 23.12.72. FO 64 742.

70 Odo to Hastings, 23.11.74, Woburn Papers.

71 Odo to the FO, 1.4.74 FO 64 803.

72 Quoted in Lytton Strachey, *Eminent Victorians*, p. 88.

73 *Ibid.*

74 E.S. Purcell, *The Life of Cardinal Manning* (London, 1896).

75 S.A.M. Adshead, 'Odo Russell and the First Vatican Council', in *Journal of Religious History*, 1962, p. 297.

76 Winifried Taffs, *Ambassador to Bismarck*, p. X.

77 Adshead, 'Odo Russell', 75, p. 297.

78 He was, however, put under great emotional pressure by Manning, to accept the verdict of the Roman Council. Acton did not yield, but was traumatised by the whole experience. See Roland Hill, 'Macht tendiert zur Korruption. Von Bayern geprägt: Vor 100 Jahren wurde Lord Acton Professor in Cambridge', *Süddeutsche Zeitung*, 29/30.7.1995, p. III.

79 Rodd, *Social and Diplomatic*, p. 46.

80 *Ibid.*

81 Odo Russell to Lady Salisbury, 26.11.63. Salisbury Papers.

Notes to Chapter 3(a)

1 'An immense calamity indeed'. Odo to Hammond, 10.7.70. Hammond Papers. FO 391 22.

2 Odo to Hastings, 7.8.70. Woburn Papers.

3 *Ibid.*

4 Odo made his marital problems known to Granville. 11.8.70. PRO 30/29 92.

5 Diary entry: 28.10.70. John Vincent (ed.), *A Selection from the Diaries of Eduard Henry Stanley, 15th Earl of Derby (1826–1893). Between September 1869 and March 1878* Camden Fifth Series, Vol. 4 (London, 1994), p. 70. Odo also talks about Emily's unhappiness in a letter to his brother: 'I have given up Rome with deep regret because it is too expensive and prolongation appears impossible. ... Emily regrets Rome and dislikes my present post which she considers a step backwards instead of forwards in my profession'. Odo to Hastings 12.8.70. Woburn Papers.

6 Odo to Lyons, 29.8.70. Lyons Papers Box 197.

7 *Ibid.*

8 Fritz Stern sums up the public opinion that 'they [diplomats] led great lives perched in dignity on the edge of often imagined disaster'. Fritz Stern, *Gold and Iron*, p. 307.

9 Odo wrote this to Hammond in retrospect, 5.8.70. Hammond Papers FO 391 22.

10 *Ibid.*

11 See for example: First (1871) and Second (1872) Reports of the Select Committee on Diplomatic and Consular Services 1870 VII. Official Publications Room, University Library Cambridge.

12 Mary Adeline Anderson, 'Edmund Hammond — Permanent Under-Secretary of State for Foreign Affairs 1854–1873' unpublished PhD dissertation (University of London 1955), p. 212.

13   *Ibid.*
14   *Parliamentary Papers*, 1871, VII., 238, p. 260, q. 844. Odo was not very satisfied with his appearance before the committee. He had been nervous and felt that he had failed to bring his point across.
15   'Establish whether diplomacy requires training, like the army, the Navy, the Law, etc., etc. or whether professional training, knowledge of the continent and foreign languages, etc., etc. are really necessary ... You might then enquire how the efficiency of an agent can be (tested), before you select and appoint him'. Odo to Arthur, Rome, 24.3.70. FO 918 84.
16   *Ibid.*
17   Odo to Arthur, 18.4.70. FO 918 84.
18   Odo to Arthur, 24.3.70. FO 918 84. Hammond had a similar idea: 'He suggested ways of economising in social activities, as for instance, the substitution of *soirées dansantes* for full dress balls'. Anderson, 'Hammond', p. 221.
19   Odo did not have a high opinion of American diplomats: '...otherwise you can only get men unfit for the work like American Diplomatists. The American Dips. sent to London are men of private wealth like Buchanan, Adams, Motley, Dallas but they don't represent'. Odo to Arthur, 24.3.70. FO 918 84.
20   Odo to Arthur, 24.3.70. FO 918 84.
21   *Ibid.*
22   *Ibid.*
23   Though Odo claimed in a letter to White that Granville was a different chief: 'He prefers a direct communication regarding promotion'. Odo to White, 20.5.72. White Papers FO 364 8.
24   Odo to Hastings, 4.5.70, Woburn Papers.
25   Odo to Arthur, 24.3.70. FO 918 84.
26   He took over from Elliot at the height of the Eastern Question, in March 1877.
27   Such a recommendation had already been made in 1861, much to the annoyance of Hammond. The 1861 committee had recommended that 'exchanges between the two branches [the Foreign Office and the Diplomatic Service] should be encouraged and facilitated as much as possible'. John Tilley and Stephen Gaselee, *The Foreign Office* (London, 1933), p. 90. When asked by the 1861 committee for his views on such a scheme, Hammond had said that 'members of the Diplomatic Service would be of no use at all for the upper work of the office'. Anderson, 'Hammond', p. 200.
28   'I flatter myself that I have done wisely in accepting my present post. It has been well received in the office and by the Press. Vide *Pall Mall* of yesterday and *Telegraph* of today'. Odo to Hastings. 16.8.70. Woburn Papers.
29   Jerringham to Odo Russell, 25.8.70. FO 918 44. Odo's friend Lord Acton could not share this opinion: 'I do not know whether I ought to congratulate you as I do the FO on your change of scenery'. 4.9.70. FO 918 66.
30   See letter to Hastings from 23.8.70. Woburn Papers.
31   Odo to Arthur, 4.9.70. Walmer Castle. FO 918 84.
32   Odo to Lyons, July 1870. Lyons Papers, West Sussex Record Office, Chichester, Box 197.
33   For the part that mob psychology could play in a politician's decision-making process, see William L. Langer, *European Alliances and Alignments 1871–1890* (2nd edn, New York, 1950).
34   See for this episode W. Russell's source — the Crown Prince. Otto Meisner, *Kaiser Friedrich III. Das Kriegstagebuch von 1870/71* (Berlin, 1926).
35   Thomas Schaarschmidt, *Außenpolitik und öffentliche Meinung in Großbritannien während des deutsch-französischen Krieges von 1870/71*. Europäische Hochschulschriften, Reihe III, Vol. 575 (Frankfurt a.M. 1993), p. 295f.

36 Paul W. Schroeder, 'The Lost Intermediaries: The Impact of 1870 on the European System'. *The International History Review*, Vol. VI (1984), p. 27.

37 Quoted in Alistair Horne, *The Fall of Paris*, revised edn (London, 1989), p. 162f.

38 Odo to Arthur, July 1870. FO 918 84.

39 Odo to Arthur, undated, FO 918 84.

40 Lady William Russell to Layard, 18.10.70. Layard Papers, British Library, 38 998f 303. Earlier she had written to her friend Lady Salisbury, a passionate defence of the Ems telegram: 'Suppose La Valette was to meet the Queen taking a ... walk ... at Windsor [and] say to her "pray Ma'am how do you mean to settle the Alabama"'? 7.8.70. Hatfield Papers.

41 Odo to Lady Salisbury, undated (possibly before 19.8.70), Hatfield Papers.

42 See C.J. Bartlett, 'Clarendon, the Foreign Office and the Hohenzollern Candidature, 1868–1870', *English Historical Review*, 75 (1960), p. 276.

43 Klaus Hildebrand, *No Intervention. Die Pax Britannica und Preußen 1865/66–1869/70* (München, 1997), p. 346.

44 Morier to Granville, copy. 1.8.70. Morier Papers, Box 5/2. Agatha Ramm had a higher opinion of Granville. See Agatha Ramm, 'Granville', in: Keith M. Wilson (ed.), *British Foreign Secretaries and Foreign Policy: From Crimean War to First World War* (London, 1987). Knaplund calls Granville simply 'a suave diplomatist of the old school'. See Paul Knaplund, *Gladstone's Foreign Policy* (London, 1970), p. 30f.

45 Morier to Odo. 19.9.70. FO 918 55.

46 Odo to Acton, undated, Acton papers, Cambridge University Library, Add 8119 (5)/R 200–230.

47 Odo to Acton, 6.5.71. Acton Papers, Add 8119 (5)/R 200–230.

48 Ramm, 'Granville', p. 86.

49 See Knaplund, *Gladstone's Foreign Policy*, p. 30.

50 *Ibid.*, p. 31.

51 Kennedy shows that this mediation was half-hearted. Paul Kennedy, *The Rise of the Anglo – German Antagonism*, p. 23.

52 Crown Princess to Morier, 24.8.70. Morier Papers, Box 5/2.

53 Morier to Granville, 31.7.70. Morier Papers, Box 5/2.

54 Rosslyn Wemyss, *Memoirs and Letters of the Rt. Hon. Sir Robert Morier G.C.B. from 1826–1876* (London, 1911), p. 208ff.

55 See for example, Walker to Russell, Confidential, 24.12.74. FO 64 807.

56 Odo to Derby, 3.4.75. Derby Papers, 920 DER (15) 16/1/15.

57 12.9.70. Quoted from W.E. Mosse, *The European Powers and the German Question 1848–1871. With Special Reference to England and Russia* (Cambridge, 1958).

58 Morier to Odo, 22.8.70. FO 918 55.

59 Odo to Granville, 16.10.70. PRO 30/29 92.

60 *Ibid.*

61 *Ibid.*

62 *Ibid.*

63 Fulford, *Your Dear Letter*, p. 222f.

64 *The Times* published on 13.1.71 an article 'Sympathies for France' in which German barbarism was condemned.

65 See Walter Lipgens: 'Bismarck, die öffentliche Meinung und die Annexion von Elsaß Lothringen 1870', *Historische Zeitschrift* 199 (1964). L.Gall, 'Zur Frage der Annexion von Elsaß und Lothringen 1870', *Historische Zeitschrift* 206 (1968). E. Kolb, 'Bismarck und das Aufkommen von Annexionsforderungen 1870', *Historische Zeitschrift* 209 (1969).

66 General Walker to Odo Russell, 10.4.73. FO 64 770.

67   4.12.74. FO 64 807. Walker to Odo Russell, confidential. Treitschke's pamphlet 'What do we ask from France' appears to support Walker's opinion. For Treitschke see for example: G.P. Gooch, *History and Historians in the Nineteenth Century* (first published 1913), 2nd edn (London, 1952), p. 141.

68   Buchanan received a negative reply on 17.10. See Mosse, *The European Powers*, p. 341.

69   John Russell to Granville, undated, PRO 30/29/79.

70   Fitzmaurice quotes a letter from Granville to his wife: 'Quite exhausted after the longest fight I ever had against Gladstone'. 30.9.70. Fitzmaurice, *Granville*, Vol. II, p. 62.

71   See the famous *Edinburgh Review* article, Vol. CXXII, October 1870.

72   See Jean-Baptiste Duroselle, 'Die europäischen Staaten und die Gründung des Deutschen Reiches,' in Theodor Schieder and Ernst Deurlein (eds), *Die Reichsgründung 1870–71. Tatsachen, Kontroversen, Interpretationen* (Oxford, 1988), p. 391.

73   See the *Edinburgh Review*, Vol. CXXII, October 1870.

74   *Ibid.*

75   About the first negotiations between Bismarck and Favre he wrote to his wife, for example: 'The proceedings of Jules Favre are to me quite unintelligible'. Quoted from A. T. Bassett, *Gladstone and his Wife* (London, 1936), p. 179.

76   Odo to FO, 20.2.74. FO 64 80.

Notes to Chapter 3(b)

1   Emily Russell to Lady William Russell, November 1870, FO 918 85.

2   Quoted from Fitzmaurice, *Granville*, p. 39.

3   Quoted from Jean-Baptiste Duroselle, 'Die europäischen Staaten und die Gründung des Deutschen Reiches,' in Theodor Schieder and Ernst Deurlein (eds), *Die Reichsgründung 1870–71* (1st published 1936) (Oxford, 1988), p. 394. See for this also D.N. Raymond, *British Policy and Opinion During the Franco-Prussian War* (New York, 1921).

4   See Kurt Rheindorf, *Die Schwarzmeer Pontusfrage* (Berlin, 1925), p. 9.

5   Summary of FO memorandum on this issue, 18.11.70

6   *Ibid.*

7   *Ibid.*

8   Rheindorf thinks that the Russians made a tactical mistake in denouncing article 11, yet claiming to recognise the others. As these included article 8, which demanded negotiations in the case of 'dissent', they could not reject the request for a conference. Rheindorf, *Pontusfrage*, p. 99.

9   *Ibid.*

10   'The statement in the circular that ships of war had passed the Dardanelles in such numbers as to constitute whole squadrons is without foundation ... not more than nine armed vessels of war of all nations ... have passed the straits into the Black Sea since the conclusion of the Treaty of 1856 ... it will be seen ... on nearly every occasion, questions were formally raised as to the peculiar circumstances under which those vessels were allowed to pass and ... the inquiry resulted, in its being shown that the favour had been accorded by the Sultan out of respect to a friendly government.' FO memorandum 18.11.70.

11   See Werner Eugen Emil Mosse, *The Rise and Fall of the Crimean War System, 1855–71. The Story of a Peace Settlement* (London, 1963), p. 163. Russia had already tried in 1866 to raise the Black Sea question.

12   *Ibid.*, p. 161.

13   Mosse sees some ambiguity in Gladstone's Commons speech of 1856. In 1871, the PM, however, reiterated very strongly his feelings against the treaty. *Ibid.*, p. 179.

14 *Ibid*. Odo Russell himself helped to draft the reply on 9.11.70. See Odo to Granville, PRO 30/29/92.

15 Decided in cabinet meetings on 10 and 11 of November 1870. Gladstone wrote afterwards to the Queen that one could not in principle refuse Russia's demand. See Thomas Schaarschmidt, *Außenpolitik und öffentliche Meinung*, p. 377.

16 Granville wrote to Lord Russell, 'The Russians have opened their fire in a very sudden and offensive manner. We have taken a very firm ground on the form of their declaration, which is inadmissible'. Granville to Lord Russell, 13.11.70, PRO 30/29/79.

17 Lytton to Morier, 14.11.70. Morier Papers, Box 5/2. Lytton continued to argue that Austria would join Britain in a 'bold policy', only if the English asked for it.

18 No military preparations were discussed at the Cabinet meetings of 10.11 and 11.11. See Schaarschmidt, *Außenpolitik*, p. 381.

19 Alistair Horne, *The Fall of Paris*, revised edn (London, 1989), p. 245.

20 Mosse argues that it is doubtful whether the Austrians would have been 'actually willing to be dragged into hostilities'. Mosse, *Crimean System*, p. 161.

21 The British Fleet was of no use at this time of the year in the Baltic Sea, and in the Black Sea there was nothing to destroy.

22 Ramm agrees, 'Britain could not have fought Russia, without France, for geographical reasons if no others'. According to her argument it was sensible to acquiesce. Agatha Ramm, 'Granville', in Keith M. Wilson (ed.), *British Foreign Secretaries and Foreign Policy: From Crimean War to First World War* (London, 1987), p. 91.

23 Quoted in Fitzmaurice, *Granville*, p. 77.

24 Schaarschmidt, *Außenpolitik*, p. 383. See also W.E. Mosse, 'Public Opinion and Foreign Policy. The British Public and the War-Scare of November 1870,' *Historical Journal*, 6 (1963).

25 'The denouncing of the circular provoked throughout Britain an extraordinary outburst of russophobia and bellicose patriotism'. *Ibid.*, p. 38. Odo's two friends Grant Duff and Morier exchanged ideas on the subject. Grant Duff, who was an under-secretary at the India Office, wrote, 'If a Tory or other weak Cabinet had been in power here it would have been hurried along by a frenzied press'. Duff to Morier, 24.11.70. Quoted from Schaarschmidt, *Außenpolitik*, p. 371.

26 The *Pall Mall Gazette* criticised mainly Gladstone and John Bright, who were accused of being members of the 'peace at any price' party. See Schaarschmidt, *Außenpolitik*, p. 389. However, some newspapers believed in the government's determination, for example the *Illustrated Daily News*: 'Never was there a time, when Britain was less disposed to put up with insult, never a time when she was more disposed to do justice' (19 November 1870). See Raymond, *British Policy*, p. 245 and Mosse, *Crimean System*, p. 161. Derby summed up the press reaction in his diary: 'The universal reaction is "We don't wish to fight but if the announcement is meant as a challenge we can not refuse it" ... The *Standard* and *Pall Mall* are crying out for instant war: the former in the interest of France, the latter for no visible reason'. John Vincent. (ed.), *A Selection from The Diaries of Edward Henry Stanley 15th Earl of Derby (1826-93). Between September 1869 and March 1878*, Camden Fifth Series, vol. 4, (London, 1994) (to be referred to as the Derby Diaries) Diary entry: 19.11.70. *Derby Diary*, p. 70.

27 Gladstone to Granville, 19.11.70. Ramm, *The Political Correspondence of Mr Gladstone and Lord Granville 1868-1876*, (London, 1952) p. 161.

28 Ramm, *Foreign Secretaries*, p. 91.

29 Granville to Lyons, 11.11.1870. FO 362/4.

30 The idea of sending Odo to the headquarters had already been discussed before the Russian note arrived. The plan had then been 'to ascertain about what was

going on'. Granville to Gladstone, 15.10.70. Ramm, *Correspondence*, p. 147. In October 1870 Gladstone and Hammond had still opposed this, now only Hammond rejected such a mission (11.11.70). See Schaarschmidt, *Außenpolitik*, p. 379.

31 Moritz Busch, *Bismarcks Große Tage* (Landsberg, 1990), p. 164f.

32 Telegram of Bismarck to Bernstorff, 11.11.70. Quoted in Eberhard Kolb, *Der Weg aus dem Krieg. Bismarcks Politik im Krieg und die Friedensanbahnung 1870/71* (München, 1989).

33 Granville to Lyons, 11.11.70. FO 362/4.

34 Odo to Morier, 13.11.70. Morier Papers, Box 5/2.

35 Officially Odo was to deliver the British reply to the Russian circular. 'I have to instruct you to proceed to the Prussian Headquarters at Versailles and communicate to the Chancellor of the North German Confederation the following ... dispatches ... . You will tell Count Bismarck that HMG have felt regret that the circumstances of the war have hitherto prevented their having any representative who could make communications to His Excellency, as it would be inconvenient to detach Lord Augustus Loftus from ... Berlin'. 11.11.70. FO 64 737.

36 11.11.70. FO 64 737.

37 Busch, *Bismarcks Große Tage*, p. 33.

38 See Gall, 'Bismarck und England', in Paul Kluke and Peter Alter (eds), *Aspekte der deutsch-britischen Beziehungen im Laufe der Jahrhunderte* (Stuttgart, 1978), p. 48.

39 See his memoirs: 'England's constitution does not allow lasting alliances'. Bismarck, *Gedanken und Erinnerungen*, p. 441.

40 See Bernhard Dammermann, 'Lothar Bucher in England. Seine Entwicklung vom Achtundvierziger zum Gehilfen Bismarcks', *Archiv für Politik und Geschichte*, Vol. 8 (Berlin, 1927).

41 'Everything was hypocrisy and material self-interest. He [Bucher] doubted the authenticity of public opinion and therefore underestimated its power'. Bruce Waller in his *Review Article* of Studt's book. German Historical Institute Bulletin (London, 1995).

42 See Klaus Hildebrand, *No Intervention. Die Pax Britannica und Preußen 1865/66–1869/70* (München, 1997), p. 113.

43 After a dinner conversation, in which Bismarck had outlined that a war against Austria would eventually bring about German unity, Disraeli commented to Count Vitzhum, 'Take care of that man! He means what he says'. See George E. Buckle, *The Life of Benjamin Disraeli Earl of Beaconsfield (1855–1868)*, Vol. II (London, 1916), p. 75.

44 See, for example, W.H. Dawson, *The German Empire and the Unity Movement* (London, 1966), p. 282ff. British politicians were, however, impressed by certain aspects of Bismarck's commercial policies (e.g. the extending of the Zollverein). Veit Valentin, *Bismarcks Reichsgründung im Urteil englischer Diplomaten* (Amsterdam, 1937), p. 241.

45 Bismarck wrote to his wife about these talks: 'Loftus seems to write them more rubbish than I thought'. And to Roon, 'The people there [in London] are better informed about China and Turkey than about Prussia'. 5.7.62. *Bismarck, die Gesammelten Werke*, Vol. 14/II, p. 599.

46 Conversation with Leutnant Schubert on 23 April 1864. Quoted in Willy Andreas (ed.) *die Gesammelten Werke*, p.87

47 Emil Ludwig even claims that Bismarck was secretly engaged to her and broke off this commitment after he heard unpleasant rumours about her family. Emil Ludwig, *Bismarck* (Berlin, 1932), p. 26.

48 For Bismarck's interests in England, see Lothar Gall, 'Bismarck und England'. See also two further books on this subject which were published during the Third

Reich and lack any objectiveness: E.M. Baum, *Bismarcks Urteil über England und die Engländer* (München, 1936) and M.v. Hagen, *Bismarck und England* (Stuttgart, 1943).

49 Odo to Granville about the interviews. Quoted, for example, in Paul Knaplund, *Letters from the Berlin Embassy* p. 25.

50 *Ibid.*

51 See Knaplund, *Letters from the Berlin Embassy*, p. 25. Only the unpopular Otway risked his position over the Russian circular: 'Should we maintain the Treaty at the *risk* of war? Yes. For the risk may be reduced to a minimum by the success of our diplomacy. England, France, Austria, Italy and Turkey combined can be more powerful than Russia'. Otway to Granville 19.11.70. PRO 30/29/107. Otway had for a long time been unpopular at the FO and Granville was not amused. Already in June 1870 he had written, 'From Hammond's account Otway is mauvais coucheur, conceited, jealous and perfectly incapable ... the same opinion is universal among the clerks'. Derby did not think much of Otway's disloyal behaviour either: 'News that Otway has left the FO (from which he ought to have been excluded by his folly and conceit), and is replaced by Lord Enfield'. Diary entry: 27.12.70. *Derby Diary*, p. 71f.

52 'Earl Russell on the Eastern Question', in *The Times* 24.11.70, p. 3.

53 Morier to Odo, 2.9.70. FO 918 55.

54 Russell to Morier, 13.11.70, Morier Papers, BOX 5/2.

55 Busch, *Große Tage*, p. 167

56 G.W. Strang, *Britain in World Affairs* (London, 1961), p. 194.

57 Odo to Granville (in a longer version of the events of 21.11.70) written on 30.11.70. Copy among the Gladstone Papers, 44.428f., 245. Odo gave Granville the details of this second conversation: 'On returning to him [Count Bismarck] in the evening where we had two-and-a half hours more talk, I felt that I knew him better, I could express more easily all that I had ... to say to convince him'. *Ibid.*

58 Odo to Gladstone, 27.2.71. Gladstone Papers, 44 429f.

59 Odo to Granville, 30.11.70. Copy among the Gladstone Papers, 44.428f, 245.

60 Already on 22.11, Bismarck informed Bernstorff that Russia would discuss the question at a conference. See W.E. Mosse, *Crimean System*, p. 179.

61 Translation of a letter from the Politisches Archiv (PA). Bonn, PA I ABq 69, Vol. 7.

62 Busch, *Große Tage*, p. 175.

63 *Ibid.*

64 Copy of the question among Gladstone Papers, 44,428f 245. See also 3 Hansard 204 (16. February 1871); p. 318–319.

65 16.2.71. Gladstone Papers, 44,428f. 245.

66 Gladstone to Granville, 6.12.70, Ramm, *Correspondence*, p. 176.

67 Granville to Gladstone, 8.12.70, *ibid.* p. 179.

68 Granville to Russell, PRO 30/29 92.

69 Odo to Gladstone, 29.3.71. Gladstone Papers, 44 430f.

70 Odo made it clear to his brother that he could not have resigned anyway 'from a pecuniary point of view'. Odo to Hastings, 25.2.71. Woburn Papers.

71 *Ibid.*

72 *Ibid.*

73 Ponsonby to Granville, 8.3.71. George E. Buckle (ed.), *The Letters of Queen Victoria. 1870–1878*. Second Series, Vol. II. (London, 1926), p. 123.

74 Arthur Russell to Layard, 3.2.72. Layard Papers, British Library 39 000/181.

75 *Derby Diary*, 11.3.71. p. 78.

76 See Mosse, *Crimean System*, p. 172.

77 *Ibid.*

78   *Ibid.*, p. 173.
79   Granville to Odo, 2.12.70. Granville Papers, PRO 30/29 110.
80   Russell to Granville, Granville Papers, PRO 30/29 92.
81   Granville to Odo, 2.12.70. PRO 30/29 110.
82   Granville to Odo, 20.12.70. PRO 30/29 110.
83   Bismarck, *Gedanken und Erinnerungen*, p. 439.
84   Busch, *Große Tage*, p. 183.
85   Granville could not understand such a blunder: 'It is an enormous step by the Provisional Government to be recognised by Prussia, Austria, Turkey, Italy and England as capable of attending a conference and it will be very foolish of them to lose the opportunity and remain out in the cold'. Granville to Lyons, 30.11.70. FO 362 4.
86   By 13.3.1871 a French representative, the Duc de Broglie, arrived.
87   Odo to Arthur, 29.12.70, FO 918 84.
88   Odo to Morier, 13.11.70. Morier Papers, Box 5/2.
89   Emily to Lady William Russell, 6.1.71. FO 918 85.
90   Arthur Russell to Layard, 30.11.70. Layard Papers, British Library, 38 998, p. 366.
91   Odo to his mother, New Year 1871, FO 918 85.
92   *Ibid.*
93   *Ibid.*
94   *Ibid.*
95   At one stage his wife became ill and Odo was ready to leave Versailles to see her. This was, however, declared to be unnecessary by the FO, because it was not a life-threatening illness.
96   Busch, *Große Tage*, p. 151.
97   Odo reporting Hozier's fears to Hammond, 26.11.70. Hammond Papers, FO 391 22.
98   *The Times*, 27.9.70, p. 6.
99   Odo to Arthur, 1870, FO 918 84.
100 *Ibid.*
101 Caroline Moorehead, *Dunant's Dream. War, Switzerland and the History of the Red Cross* (London, 1998).
102 Roy Porter, 'Agents of Mercy', *Sunday Times Book Section*, 24.5.98, p. 5.
103 To Hammond, Odo wrote, 'But you have no idea of the jealousies among the foreign press and English correspondents at Headquarters, it is most disagreeable and regrettable'. Odo to Hammond, 26.11.70. Hammond Papers, FO 391 22.
104 Odo to Arthur, undated, FO 918 84.
105 Odo to his mother, 27.12.70. FO 918 85.
106 Oliphant to Morier, 27.10.70. Morier Papers, Box 5/2.
107 Odo to his mother, undated, FO 918 85.
108 *Ibid.*
109 Odo to Arthur, undated, FO 918 84.
110 *Ibid.*
111 Odo to Bismarck, Christmas 1870. Bismarckarchiv Friedrichsruh, FBA B102–120.
112 Odo to Hammond, 2.12.70. Hammond Papers, FO 391 22.
113 Odo to his mother, 10.2.71. FO 918 85.
114 German Crown Prince to Queen Victoria, 3.1.71. Quoted from George E. Buckle, *The Letters of Queen Victoria. 1870–1878*. p. 103.
115 Granville to Odo, 7.12.70. PRO 30/29 110.
116 Odo to Arthur, 12.12.70. FO 918 84. To Hammond, Odo wrote about these arrangements: 'I dined two days running with the Crown Prince and his Staff who

asked whether the Neutrals could do nothing to persuade the French to give in, and I replied "nothing" each time'. Odo to Hammond, 2.12.70. Hammond Papers, FO 391 22.

117 Walker to Loftus, Loftus Papers, 519/284.

118 Emily to Lady William Russell, FO 918 85.

119 For this episode see Franz Herre, *Anno 1870/71 — Ein Krieg, ein Reich, ein Kaiser* (Berlin, 1970), p. 151f.

120 Odo to Arthur, FO 918 84.

121 Odo to his mother, 17.12.70. FO 918 85.

122 *Ibid.*

123 *Ibid.*

124 Even Arthur defended Odo's argument to their cousin Amberley. Bertrand Russell, *The Amberley Papers*, p. 455f.

125 Odo to Arthur, December 1870, FO 918 84.

126 The German expression that Odo used here goes back to the Freedom fighter Schill, who used it against Napoleon on 12.5.1809. See *Geflügelte Worte*, p. 252.

127 Odo to Arthur, January 1871. F0 918 84.

128 Odo to Arthur, 11.1.71. FO 918 84.

129 Odo to Arthur, 25.1.71. FO 918 84.

130 Odo wrote to his mother about the matter: 'I am full of business, interviews and ciphers about our Colliers sunk at Rouen by the Prussians — a very bad business indeed!' New Year 1871. FO 918 85.

131 As Schaarschmidt has shown in detail, all mediation proposals failed in the end.

132 Odo to Granville, February 1871. PRO 30/29 92.

133 Thiers was much more of a realist politician than Granville. See Robert Tombs, 'The Thiers Government and the Outbreak of the Civil War in France February–April 1871', *Historical Journal*, 23(4) (1980), p. 814.

134 Odo to Granville, 3.2.71. FO 64 739.

135 *Ibid.*

136 Strang is right when he claims, 'In the Black Sea we gained the form, but not the substance'. G.W. Strang, *Britain in World Affairs* (London, 1961), p. 195.

137 Bernadotte E. Schmitt, *England and Germany 1740–1914* (Princeton, 1916), p. 128.

138 Odo was also invited by the Prince of Wales, via Knollys: '[The Prince of Wales wants to talk to you] about the very interesting scenes you have lately been witnessing'. Knollys to Odo, 18.3.71. FO 918 46.

139 Noel Blakiston, *The Roman Question* p. XV.

140 Quoted from Roger Fulford, *Darling Child. 1871–1878* (London, 1976), p. 16.

141 *Derby Diary*, 11.3.71. p. 78.

142 Queen of Holland to Lady Salisbury, 15.3.71. W.A. Burghclere, *A Great Lady's Friendship. Letters to Mary, Marchioness of Salisbury*, p. 307.

Notes to Chapter 4(a)

1 Odo to Arthur, 13.4.1872, FO 918 84.

2 The Chancellor suffered from severe sleeping disorders. At night he tended to recapitulate all the insults he had experienced during his life, sometimes going back as far as his school days. See Otto Pflanze, *Bismarck and the Development of Germany. The Period of Consolidation 1871–1880*, Vol. II (Princeton, 1990), p. 51.

3 Translated. Bismarck to Bernstorff, 17.3.71. Bonn, Politisches Archiv. Aktengruppe London 90.

4 *Ibid.* Bismarck continued to write spiteful epistles to Bernstorff, complaining about the 'hostile feeling of Mr Petre'. Petre was Secretary of the British embassy. Bismarck to Bernstorff, 21.4.71, Politisches Archiv, Aktengruppe London 92.

5   18.5.71. Politisches Archiv Bonn. Aktengruppe London 90.
6   *Ibid.*
7   Quoted from George E. Buckle (ed.), *The Letters of Queen Victoria, a Selection from Her Majesty's Correspondence and Journal Between the Years 1868 and 1878,* Vol. 1 (London, 1926), p. 85.
8   Odo to Hastings, 7.7.71. Woburn Papers.
9   Buckle, *Letters of Queen Victoria,* p. 133.
10   18.9.71, Hammond Papers FO 391/22. See also, 11.2.74. FO 918 84.
11   This was Russell's first reaction when Hammond had told him 'in strictest confidence' about the upcoming offer. Odo to Hastings, 29.6.1871. Woburn Papers.
12   Odo to Hastings, 2.8.71. Woburn Papers.
13   Odo to Loftus, 16.2.72. Loftus Papers FO 519 284.
14   Odo to Hastings, 4.11.71. Woburn Papers.
15   For a vivid description see: Fritz Stern, *Gold and Iron.* p. 160ff.
16   See Bodo Harenberg, *Die Chronik Berlins* (Dortmund, 1986), p. 231.
17   Every fourth Berliner was a member of the working classes. See: Museum für Deutsche Geschichte (ed.), *Berlin 1871–1945 — Sonderausstellung des Museums für Deutsche Geschichte Berlin* (Berlin, 1987), p. 6.
18   Georg von Siemens had led the trend by founding the Deutsche Bank on 10 March 1870.
19   See Alexander Reissner, *Berlin 1675–1945* (London, 1984).
20   In 1872 about 300 new enterprises were founded. See Harenberg, *Chronik*, p. 238.
21   Odo to Arthur 3.5.72., FO 918 84. This happened on 28.10.72, when the share prices fell at the Berlin Stock Exchange. Twenty-eight banks had to declare bankruptcy, construction enterprises and chemical factories also faced financial ruin. Harenberg, *Chronik*, p. 238.
22   Quoted from Hans Kohn, *The Mind of Germany*, Education of a Nation (London, 1961). p. 186.
23   Odo to Arthur, 9.12.72. FO 918 84.
24   Egon Friedell however argues that after 1870 German culture did not improve, while France — the beaten nation — blossomed in this respect. He concludes that there is an antagonism between the political rise of a nation and its cultural rise. Egon Friedell, *Kulturgeschichte der Neuzeit. Die Krisis der Europäischen Seele von der Schwarzen Pest bis zum Ersten Weltkrieg* (München, 1927), p. 1320.
25   In 1876 the first performance of Ibsen's play 'Der Kronprätendent' left Baroness Spitzemberg 'breathless'. See *Spitzemberg Tagebuch*, p. 159.
26   Even though it was the educated classes of Berlin society that constituted his readership, Fontane hated the 'Parvenu-Bourgeoisie of the *Gründerzeit*'. See Sebastian Haffner's essay on 'Theodor Fontane' in Sebastian Haffner and Wolfgang Venohr (eds), *Preußische Profile* (Frankfurt, 1986), p. 178.
27   17.1.73. *Spitzemberg Tagebuch* p. 138.
28   On 24.4.76 she writes: 'Half the world was in the opera today to see "Tristan und Isolde". We feel exhausted but overwhelmed'. *Ibid.*, p. 156.
29   Hans-Heinrich Welchert (ed.), *Die glückliche Straße — Geschichte und Geschichten 'Unter den Linden'* (Hamburg, 1949).
30   Odo to Arthur 8.4.72. FO 918 84.
31   'Modern' German artists in particular indulged in pomp as Stern shows. Stern, *Gold and Iron*, p. 161.
32   Quoted from Otto Pflanze, *Bismarck and the Development of Germany. The Period of Consolidation 1871–1880,* Vol. II (Princeton, 1990), p. 37.
33   Odo to Morier, 19.1.75. Morier Papers, Box 37/1.
34   24.4.72. FO 64 743.

35   Odo to Hammond, 25.1.73. Hammond Papers, FO 391/22.

36   Odo to Hammond 20.2.73. Hammond Papers, *ibid.*

37   The Emperor also made a few 'surprise calls' at the British Embassy over the years. In 1874 Russell wrote to Derby: 'their Majesties having also dined spontaneously with us last year ... never having dined in any other diplomatic house before'. Odo to Derby, 4.4.74. Derby Papers. 920 DER (15) 16/1/15.

38   Odo to Hastings, 16.2.81. Woburn Papers.

39   *Derby Diary*, p. 143.

40   Odo to Hastings, 24.11.80, Woburn Papers.

41   Odo to Hastings, 4.12.79, Woburn Papers.

42   See Roger Fulford (ed.), *Beloved Mama. Private Correspondence of Queen Victoria and the German Crown Princess, 1878–1885* (London, 1981), p. 89.

43   David Robertson, 'Mid-Victorians Amongst the Alps', in V.C.Knoepflmacher (ed.), *Nature and the Victorian Imagination* (Berkeley, 1977).

44   Odo to Hastings, 28.8.78. Woburn Papers.

45   7.6.73. FO 64 772.

46   Secret, 13.6.73 FO 64 772.

47   Odo to Hammond, 24.5.73. Hammond Papers. FO 391 24.

48   Crown Princess to Queen Victoria, 21.6.73. Fulford, *Darling Child*, p. 95

49   Hammond wrote to Odo: 'but we must hope that they will behave themselves better in this country under the supervision of persons accustomed to their way of thought and habits of oriental life'. Hammond to Odo, 11.6.73. FO 918 38.

50   See Karl Voss, *Reiseführer für Literaturfreunde — Berlin* (Frankfurt, 1980), p. 85f.

51   Hammond to Russell, 5.8.71, FO 918 38. In the future there would also be constant problems with the lease. See e.g. letter from 11.5.72. FO 64 745.

52   To Buchanan, who already had a house of his own, a desperate Odo wrote: 'I wish you would tell me your secret for persuading the Treasury to build or buy an Embassy House. All my attempts have failed, and 2 years hence, I, or my successor, will be much embarrassed to find a suitable embassy even at exorbitant prizes at Berlin'. Odo to Buchanan, 15.5.74. Nottingham, Buchanan Papers. BU 281 94.

53   Odo to Derby, 5.12.74. *Derby Papers*, 920 DER (15) 16/1/15.

54   18.5.74. FO 64 804.

55   Further help was also given by Bleichröder. Odo had asked him for some background information. 2.11.75. Bleichröder Papers Box 24 Folder 6e.

56   1.6.76. FO 64 852.

57   Laurenz Demps, *Berlin-Wilhelmstraße*. p. 303.

58   For the Strousberg episode see: Paul Wieger, *Wilhelm I. — Sein Leben und seine Zeit*, (Dresden, 1927), p. 610. Also Pflanze, *Consolidation*, p. 167 and Reisner, *Berlin*, p. 56.

59   Sir James Rennell Rodd, *Social and Diplomatic Memories, 1884–1893*, 3 Vols (London, 1926), p. 48.

60   Odo to Arthur, 8.4.72. FO 918 84.

61   Kölner Zeitung (translated), 13.4.73.

62   Lady Derby to Odo, 21.4.72. FO 918 71. The Prince of Wales was also appreciative of Odo's success. He congratulated Russell via his secretary Knollys: 'HRH desires me to let you know [how] pleased [he is] to hear of the good reception you met with at Berlin and he is delighted likewise at what you say respecting the good feeling which you have every reason to hope will soon exist between England and Germany. The Prince's sentiments towards the Crown Prince and Princess are and always have been of the most cordial and affectionate nature, and nothing would give him greater gratification than to see his feeling extended to the two countries'. Knollys to Russell, 22.5.72. FO 918 46.

63 In the case of the Duke of Mecklenburg-Schwerin, Russell did not have to travel to Mecklenburg. The duke received the ambassador at the Royal Palace in Berlin. 7.6.73. FO 64 772.
64 Odo to Hastings, July 1873. Woburn Papers.
65 Odo to Hastings, 3.8.73. Woburn Papers.
66 Paul Kennedy, *The Rise of the Anglo-German Autagonism 1860–1914*, p. 136.
67 Odo to Hastings, 27.8.80. Woburn Papers.
68 Odo to Hastings, 29.10.83. Woburn Papers.
69 See P. Guedalla, *The Queen and Mr Gladstone 1845–1879* 2 Vols, (London, 1933–1934), p. 357.
70 See David Cannadine, *Die Erfindung der Monarchie 1870–1994* (Berlin, 1994), p. 23.
71 Odo to Arthur 23.6.75. FO 918 84.
72 John Tilley and Stephen Gasele, *The Foreign Office*, (London, 1933), p. 100.
73 *Ibid.*
74 *Ibid.*, p. 101
75 It is not quite clear to whom the letter is addressed. Odo simply calls his addressee: 'Verehrtester'. 3.5.1874. FBA 102–120.
76 In a marginal note to the letter, it is explained that the whole affair is based on a misunderstanding. *Ibid.*
77 Odo to Hastings, 9.9.71. Woburn Papers.
78 Odo to Hastings, 27.1.73. Woburn Papers.
79 Odo to Hammond, 22.3.75. Hammond Papers FO 391/22.
80 As one German newspaper almost romantically described her: 'She is an English lady in the word's best sense. Tall, with a delicate complexion and the kind of hair colour, that thanks to the Venetian school has become a canon of beauty'. *Kölner Zeitung*, 13.4.73 (translated).
81 *Spitzemberg Tagebuch*, p.156.
82 Odo to Arthur, undated. FO 918 84.
83 Roger Fulford (ed.), *Beloved Mama*, p. 89.
84 28.2.73. *Spitzemberg, Tagebuch*, p.139.
85 *The Times*, 18.6.1878.
86 8.11.75. FO 918 84. See also John Russell to Odo, 27.5.72. FO 918/9.
87 Odo to Arthur Russell, 8.4.72. FO 918 84. Odo also made a point of mentioning Emily's efforts in his FO dispatches: 'Lady Odo, though suffering from neuralgia considered it to be her duty to attend the first Court reception ... because her absence, as doyenne of the diplomatic body, might have caused some inconvenience to their majesties'. 1.2.73. FO 64 767.
88 Odo to Hastings, undated 1882. Woburn Papers.
89 Odo to Morier, 20.3.81. Morier Papers Box 6/1 xii.
90 G.P. Gooch, *History and Historians in the Nineteenth Century* (London, 1952), p. 122.
91 Acton to Odo, 16.3.72. FO 918 66. Ranke was, however, later praised by Acton in his inaugural speech, see Peter Burke, 'Ranke als Gegenrevolutionär', in Wolfgang Mommsen (ed.) *Leopold von Ranke und die moderne Geschichtswissenschaft* (Stuttgart, 1988), p. 189. See also Lord Acton, 'On the Study of History' (1895), in H.R. Trevor-Roper, *Lectures on Modern History* (London, 1966), p. 22
92 He had entered the Prussian Parliament in 1861 as a member of the Fortschrittspartei, and in 1881 he became a member of the Reichstag. Quoted from Heinz Wolter (ed.), *Otto von Bismarck, Dokumente seines Lebens. 1815–1898* (Leipzig, 1886), p. 217. Gooch praises Mommsen rightly as a 'Prince of scholars'. See Gooch, *History and Historians in the Nineteenth Century* (London, 1952), p. 468.
93 Odo to Arthur, 22.1.72. FO 918 84.

94 Most of them lived in the district around the Lützowstrasse, called the 'Professoren Quarter'.

95 See Thomas Nipperdey, *Geschichte 1866–1918, Vol. I: Arbeitswelt und Bürgergeist* (München, 1990), p. 590f.

96 Quoted from R.H. Super (ed.) *Matthew, Arnold. Schools and Universities on the Continent* (Michigan, 1964), p. 262. See Keith Robbins, *Protestant Germany Through British Eyes: a Complex Victorian Encounter, Annual Lecture of 1992 held at the German Historical Institute London* (London, 1992).

97 Their popularity can be explained by the fact that these historians, especially Treitschke, 'interpreted and legitimised' the new German Empire. They analysed German history on an ideological basis and therefore helped to create a new German identity. See Nipperdey, *Deutsche Geschichte 1866—1918 Machtstaat vor der Demokratie* (München, 1992), p. 592.

98 6.3.73. *Spitzemberg Tagebuch*, p. 154

99 Odo to Hastings, 9.12.72. Woburn Papers.

100 Plunkett to FO, 10.8.72. FO 64 746.

101 Abeken to Russell, 2.12.71, FO 918 13.

102 Pflanze, *Consolidation*, p. 51.

103 See Odo to the FO, 22.12.72. FO 64 747.

104 24.5.72. FO 64 744.

105 Odo to Derby, 9.11.74. Derby Papers 920 DER (15). 16/1/15.

106 16.10.74. FO 64 806.

107 Odo to FO, 18.12.73. FO 64 777. A few days later he recorded: 'a long visit by Bismarck, he talked over the topics of the day with usual wit and cynical originality'. 22.12.73. FO 64 777.

108 See, for example, 1.11.72. FO 64 747.

109 22.12.72. FO 64 747. Odo's contemporary, Fontane, also compared Bismarck to Wallenstein: 'He has a lot in common with Schiller's Wallenstein: genius, saviour and sentimental traitor. Always me, me, me'. 'Theodor Fontane' in Sebastian Haffner and Wolfgang Venohr (eds), *Preußische Profile*, p. 179.

110 Odo to Hammond, 1.3.73. Hammond Papers. FO 391 22.

111 Odo to Granville, 28.6.73. PRO 30/29 93.

112 Odo to Edmund Dicey, 27.12.77. FO 918 71.

113 'In an age of secret diplomacy, Bismarck was exceptionally secretive, he kept his own subordinates in the dark'. Stern, *Iron and Gold*, p. 312.

114 23.10.75. FO 64 830.

115 Bismarck to Odo, 20.2.73, FO 918 12.

116 Undated, FO 918 12.

117 Rennell Rodd, *Social and Diplomatic*, p. 55.

118 Winifried Taffs, *Ambassador to Bismarck*, p. 391.

119 See Haffner, 'Wilhelm I', in Sebastian Haffner and Wolfgang Venohr (eds), *Preußische Profile*, p. 152. He argues that the King is undervalued.

120 Odo to FO, 7.6.73. FO 64 772. Odo even seemed to see parallels to the mental health problems of George III and predicted a Regency. *Ibid.*

121 22.12.72. FO 64 748.

122 22.12.72. FO 64 748. In 1873 Augusta told Emily Russell that Bismarck had only spoken to her twice since the Franco-Prussian war. See Paul Kennedy, *Antagonism*, p. 130.

123 See Otto von Bismarck, *Gedanken und Erinnerungen* p. 107.

124 Odo to Hastings, 25.3.82. Woburn Papers.

125 27.2.84. FO 64 1049.

126 On this see Röhl's excellent analysis. John C.G. Röhl, *Wilhelm II — Die Jugend des Kaisers 1859–1888* (München, 1993), p. 551.

127 Odo to Morier. Morier Papers, Box 36/2.
128 Odo to Arthur, 20.2.77. FO 918 84.
129 Odo to Lady Salisbury, 18.11.67. Hatfield Papers.
130 Odo to Arthur, 20.2.77. FO 918 84.
131 As this letter has, to my knowledge, not been used by historians before, it will be quoted here at great length.
132 9.10.72. PRO 30/29 22A/9.
133 *Ibid.*
134 *Ibid.*
135 *Ibid.*
136 Röhl analyses the ambivalent relationship of the Crown Princess towards Germany at length. Röhl, *Wilhelm II*, p. 282. See also David Cannadine, 'Kaiser William II and the British Monarchy', in T.C.W. Blanning and D. Cannadine (eds), *History and Biography. Essays in Honour of Derek Beales* (Cambridge, 1996), p. 190.
137 Odo to Hastings, 7.5.81. Woburn Papers.
138 Rodd, *Social and Diplomatic*, p. 50.
139 *Ibid.*, p. 49.
140 22.1.77. *Derby Diary*, p. 369f.
141 Rodd, *Social and Diplomatic*, p. 50.
142 Odo to Hastings, 2.5.83. Woburn Papers.
143 Queen of Holland to Lady Derby, 9.8.74. Quoted in W.A. Burghclere, *A Great Lady's Friendship*, p. 399.
144 Odo to Hastings, 12.5.74. Woburn Papers.
145 *Ibid.*
146 Odo to Hastings, 19.4.75. Woburn Papers.
147 Odo to Hastings, 12.6.78. Woburn Papers.
148 Odo to Granville, 26.1.81. Granville Papers 30/29 22A/9.
149 Odo to Morier, 15.5.75. Morier Papers, Box 37/6.
150 Odo to Derby 15.10.76. Derby Papers. 950 DER (15) 16/1/6.
151 Odo to Derby, 9.11.74. Derby Papers. 920 DER (15) 16/1/15.
152 Odo to Derby, 24.4.75. Derby Papers 950 DER (15) 16/1/15.

Notes to Chapter 4(b)

1   Odo to Arthur, FO 918 84. To Hastings he wrote: 'Since the first of January I have written over 300 despatches and 50 private letters to Lord Granville and innumerable notes to the German authorities'. Odo to Hastings, 25.5.73. Woburn Papers.
2   The number stayed fairly constant over the years. See the despatches that had been sent and received in 1871: 'From the FO: Political: 263, circulars: 30, from Under-Secretaries: 18, Commercial: 23... Slave trade: 24. To the FO: Political: 783, Despatches: 20, To Under-secretary: 52, Commercial: 60, Slave Trade:14.'
3   Odo to Morier, 22.5.73, Morier Papers BOX 36/1.
4   Odo to Morier, 25.3.72. Morier Papers Box 35/5.
5   Arthur to Hastings, 30.11.71. Woburn Papers.
6   John Tilley and Stephen Gasele, *The Foreign Office*, p. 26.
7   Harold Nicolson, *Sir Arthur Nicolson, Bart., First Lord Carnock* (London, 1930).
8   Odo to Derby, 13.1.75. Derby Papers 920 DER (15) 16/1/15.
9   Adams to Granville, 30.8.73. F0 918 46.
10 Odo to White, 20.5.74. FO 364 8.
11 10.2.1881. FO 64 979.

12   Russell's embassy also had a naval attache, Vice Admiral Ryder, whose work was in the 1870s rarely mentioned by Odo. See for example a short reference to Ryder in 1873: Letter to FO, 24.5.73. FO 64 771.

13   L. Hilbert, 'The Role of Military and Naval Attachés in the British and German Service with Particular Reference to those in Britain and London, and their Effect on Anglo-German Relations'. Unpublished PhD. thesis (Cambridge, 1954), p. 52.

14   L. Hilbert claims that at the FO, military attachés were not taken very seriously. Hammond even forgot during the questioning of the previously mentioned Select Committee whether there was a military attaché in Paris. Hilbert is exaggerating, though, when he sees here a fundamental British disinterest in military affairs. Hilbert, *ibid.*, p. 6.

15   Walker to Odo, 25.9.72. FO 64 746.

16   Hilbert, 'Military Attachés', p. 53.

17   *Ibid.*

18   30.10.72. FO 64 747.

19   Walker to Odo, 25.9.72. FO 64 746. Walker added that such comments were not made however in the society in which Russell mixed (at least not to his face). *Ibid.*

20   *Ibid.*

21   *Ibid.*

22   Paul Kennedy, *The Rise of the Anglo–German Antagonism 1860–1914* p. 135f.

23   The Germans accused the English of jealousy. The *Speyrer Zeitung*, for example, tried to find an explanation for British envy, 'because things go well with us in a commercial and political respect', Article attached to Odo's FO despatch, 26.9.72. FO 64 746.

24   Crowe (1825–1896) was a journalist and commercial attaché. In 1872 he became a Consul General for Westphalia and the Rhinish Provinces. By 1881 he had risen to be commercial attaché for the embassies in Berlin and Vienna. Kennedy values his influence very highly: 'His connection with Reichstag deputies, business and intellectual circles, and with the smaller courts ... turned him into a keen observer'. Kennedy, *Antagonism*, p. 136f.

25   Crowe to Odo, 29.4.72. FO 918 25.

26   *Ibid.*

27   White (1824–1891) was consul at Danzig from 1864–1875, later Consul General in Serbia, 1875–1878, and at the end of his career, 1886–1891, Ambassador to Turkey.

28   Odo to White, 14.6.72. FO 364 8. White, of course, did much more and equipped Russell with all the relevant information for his report. See Russell's 'thank you letter' from 20.6.72. A few months later Odo wanted information from White about trade marks. 21.10.72. *Ibid.*

29   Eg. in May 1877. White Papers, FO 298 1.

30   See Paul Kennedy, *Antagonism*, p. 136.

31   The expression was probably first used by William Morris. See Charles Harvey and Jan Press, 'William Morris — Art and Idealism', *History Today*, Vol. 46(3) May 1996.

32   Odo to Enfield, 19.12.71. FO 918 28.

33   From Tilley and Gasele, *Foreign Office*, p. 122.

34   See D.C.M. Platt, *Finance, Trade and Politics in British Foreign Policy 1815–1914* (Oxford, 1971), p. XX.

35   Granville to Odo, 24.9.72. FO 918 28.

36   Fritz Stern, *Gold and Iron*. p. 170f.

37   *Ibid.*, p. 106.
38   See letter from Russell to Bleichröder, 10.1.75. Bleichröder Collection, Box 24, folder 6e. Russell also had investments in France which were handled by the Rothschild bank and Bleichröder jointly. (Russell's French investments amounted in 1875 to 10.500 Francs or 2.834 Thalers.) 12.1.75, *ibid.*
39   Odo to Bleichröder, undated, Bleichröder Collection, Box 24, 6e.
40   See the letter from Odo to Bleichröder 30.1.75. *Ibid.*
41   Dering to Russell: 'My father writes to me: "What have you been doing ... to be passed over?"' 18.8.78. F0 918 26.
42   *Ibid.*
43   Russell to Dering, 27.8.78. FO 918 26.
44   Russell to Dering, 7.2.78. FO 918 26.
45   Friedrichsruher Bismarckarchiv, article enclosed with Russell's letter to Herbert von Bismarck. 6.5.80. FBA B 102–120.
46   *Ibid.*, FBA, B 102–120 Odo to Count Herbert von Bismarck. Berlin, 6.5.80.
47   6.6.72. FO 64 745.
48   See end of volume FO 64 744, as well as 31.5.1872 and 6.6.72, in FO 64 745.
49   *Ibid.*
50   6.6.72. FO 64 745.
51   17.7.72. FO 64 746.
52   Copy sent to Odo on 5.9.70.
53   Odo to Hastings, 18.2.80. Woburn Papers.
54   Thile's report to Russell, 20.4.72. FO 64 743.
55   *Ibid.*
56   25.11.76. FO 64 856.
57   *Ibid.*
58   *Ibid.*
59   Letter from 25.1.74. See FO 64 824.
60   26.12.72. FO 64 748.
61   See for example the *Staatsanzeiger*, 14.8.72. FO 64 746.
62   15.8.72. FO 64 746.
63   31.5.73. FO 64 771.
64   25.1.73. FO 64 767.
65   This code was entitled 'Beförderung und Auswanderung'. 19.2.73. FO 64 768.
66   5.3.73. FO 64 768.
67   18.2.73. FO 64 768.
68   *Ibid.*
69   Letter to Morier of 16.11.72. Morier Papers Box 35/5.
70   Odo to Morier, 25.3.72 Box 35/5. This 'slowness' on Odo's side was also due to ill health: 'I feel quite unfit for work and have not been able to write one single 'Situationsbericht' since I have been at Berlin. There was much to say — but I could not write for the life of me'. Odo to Morier 5.7.72. Morier Papers Box 35/5.

Notes to Chapter 5(a)

1   Arthur informed Morier about this. Arthur to Morier, 16.2.71. Morier Papers, Box 5/2. See also K A.P. Sandiford, 'Gladstone and Europe', in Bruce L. Kinzer, *The Gladstonian Turn of Mind* (Toronto, 1985), p. 185.
2   *Ibid.*
3   Arthur to Morier, 16.2.71. Morier Papers, Box 5/2.
4   *Ibid.*
5   *Ibid.*

6   Klaus Hildebrand, *No Intervention. Die Pax Britannica und Preußen 1865/66–1869/70*, p. 7.
7   K. Theodore Hoppen, *The Mid-Victorian Generation*, p. 620.
8   Odo to Morier, letter 25.3.72 Morier Papers, Box 35/5.
9   Quoted in Roger Fulford (ed.), *Beloved Mama*, p. 178.
10   Paul Kennedy, *The Rise of the Anglo–German Antagonism*, p. 25.
11   K. Theodore Hoppen, *The Mid-Victorian Generation*, p. 620.
12   Odo Russell to his mother, 2.9.68. FO 918 85.
13   Odo to Lady Derby, Easter Sunday, 1872. Hatfield Papers.
14   *Ibid.*
15   Bulwer Lytton to Odo 21.12.71, FO 918 53.
16   Gladstone had not been interested in an alliance with Austria in whatever form: 'As his (Gladstone's) dislike for Bismarck was outweighed by his animosity towards Austria, he could readily accept the new Germany as a nation which was unlikely to upset the old European traditions'. See W.E. Mosse, *The European Powers and the German Question 1848–1871. With Special Reference to England and Russia* (Cambridge, 1958), p. 317.
17   Odo to Arthur, 13.4.72. FO 918 84.
18   Queen of Holland to Lady Derby, 4.5.72. W.A. Burghclere, *A Great Lady's Friendship.* p. 336.
19   Odo to Arthur, 21.4.72. FO 918 84.
20   Odo to Arthur, June 1872. FO 918 84.
21   See Richard Shannon's account of the aftermath of the affair: Richard T. Shannon, *The Age of Disraeli, 1868–1881: the Rise of Tory Democracy* (London/New York, 1992), p. 103.
22   Odo to Arthur, 21.3.72. FO 918 84.
23   For a less scholarly account see: David Hollet, *The Alabama Affair. The British Shipyard Conspiracy in the American Civil War* (Cheshire, 1993), p. 113f.
24   Odo to Arthur, 21.3.72. FO 918 84.
25   1.2.71. *Derby Diary*, p. 74.
26   Odo to Morier, 19.10.73. Morier Papers, Box 6/1xii.
27   Erich Eyck, Bismarck, Vol.1, p. 276.
28   Morier quoted in Rosslyn Wemyss, *Memoirs and Letters of the Rt. Hon. Sir Robert Morier G.C.B. from 1826–1876* (London, 1911), p. 330.
29   Walker to Odo, 24.12.74. FO 64 807.
30   24.12.72. FO 64 748.
31   Bancroft to Russell, undated, FO 918 14.
32   Odo to Granville 11.1.73, PRO 30/29 93.
33   Walker to Odo, 24.12.72. FO 64 748.
34   Walker to Odo, 24.12.72. FO 64 748.
35   Walker to Odo, 24.12.74. FO 64 807.
36   24.12.72. FO 64 748.
37   Odo to Arthur, undated. FO 918 84.

Notes to Chapter 5(b)

1   Odo Russell quoted by Alan Sked, 'Great Britain and the German Question 1848–1890'. in: Adolf M. Birke and Marie-Louise Recker (eds), *Das gestörte Gleichgewicht. Deutschland als Problem Britischer Sicherheit im Neunzehnten und Zwanzigsten Jahrhundert.* (München,1990).
2   Odo to FO, 9.1.74. FO 64 801.
3   Pflanze, *Consolidation*, p. 249.

4   Friedrich Ferdinand Graf von Beust, *Erinnerungen und Aufzeichnugen. Aus Drei viertel-Jahrhunderten.* Vol. II. (Stuttgart, 1887).
5   Odo to Granville, 11.2.73. PRO 30/29 93.
6   30.11.74. FO 64 807.
7   30.11.73. FO 64 777.
8   Anonymous and undated. Russell file FO 918 13. Hildebrand thinks it was possibly written by Adams in 1874. Hildebrand, Großbritannien und die deutsche Reichsgründung', p. 49.
9   Derby to Buchanan, 28.4.75. Buchanan Papers, BU 29/3.
10   Ferdinand Graf von Beust, *Aus Dreiviertel Jahrhunderten,* p. 547.
11   Derby to Buchanan, 28.4.75. BU 29/3.
12   Kennedy writes about this error of judgment on the part of Odo: 'There were several occasions when his touch was less then perfect. Throughout the early-to-mid 1870s he was convinced that Bismarck intended to achieve the grossdeutsche aim of incorporating Austria as well.' Kennedy, *Antagonism*, p. 135.
13   See Pflanze, *Consolidation*, p. 251.
14   Quoted in Pflanze, *Consolidation*, p. 251.
15   For after all Germany had to keep Russia 'in check', an expression used by Hohenlohe Schillingsfürst in his memoirs. Chlodwig zu Hohenlohe-Schillingsfürst, *Denkwürdigkeiten des Fürsten Chlodwig zu Hohenlohe-Schillingsfürst,* Vol II, (Leipzig, 1907) p. 202.
16   Recorded in Derby's diary. *Derby Diary,* 6.7.76. p. 307. Under these circumstances, it sounds hypocritical of Odo to write to Buchanan, when he approached his retirement after half a century in diplomacy, in the following terms: '[it is hard] to lose my neighbour in diplomacy ... for you have always been so very kind to me during the last six years'. Odo to Buchanan, 7.12.77. Buchanan Papers, BU 32/12.
17   Odo to Lytton, 16.2.69. Bulwer Lytton Papers, D/EK 030.
18   See Helmut Rumpler, 'Das Deutsche Reich im österreichischen Urteil', in: Klaus Hildebrand (ed.), *Das Deutsche Reich im Urteil der Großen Mächte und europäischen Nachbarn (1871–1945),* (München, 1995), p. 20ff.
19   Hans A. Schmitt, 'Bismarck's Unfinished Empire', *The South Atlantic Quarterly.* (1966), p. 203.
20   30.11.74. FO 64 807.
21   A.J.P. Taylor calls the League of the Three Emperors' a 'fair weather system'. According to him 'monarchical solidarity was a luxury which was blown to the winds as soon as Russia and Austria-Hungary saw their Eastern interests at danger'. A.J.P. Taylor, *Bismarck — The Man and the Statesman.* (London, 1955).
22   12.9.72. FO 64 746.
23   Odo to Buchanan, 20.9.72. Buchanan Papers BU 27/31.
24   9.9.72. FO 64 746.
25   12.9.72. FO 64 746.
26   9.9.72 and 12.9.72. FO 64 746
27   12.9.72. FO 64 746.
28   Bismarck praised himself especially for his cunning tactics in outmanoeuvring Gortschakoff who had tried to take over at the Congress: 'But I told him [Gortschakoff] at once that if he disturbed the silent group of Peace I wished to present to the world, I should resign, and retire to Varzin, and he had the good sense to agree and swallow his disappointment'. 12.9.70. FO 64 746.
29   Odo to Hammond, 14.9.72. FO 918 38.
30   German newspaper article (*Speyrer* Zeitung) translated, 26.9.72. FO 64 746.
31   See for example, Pflanze, *Consolidation*, p. 261.

32   13.2.74. FO 64 803.
33   Article from 13.2.74, quoted in FO 64 803.
34   30.11.73. FO 64 777.
35   21.11.79. FO 64 936.
36   19.12.79. FO 64 936.
37   Hans Rothfels, *Bismarcks englische Bündnispolitik*, (Berlin, 1924), p. 15.
38   *Ibid.*
39   Odo to Granville 11.2.73., PRO 30/29 93. Bismarck found a devilish pleasure in occasionally blaming his wars on the Emperor.
40   9.10.74. Hertfordshire County Office, D/EK O30.
41   Odo to Derby about a conversation with Bismarck 27.3.74 FO 64 803.
42   Odo to Lyons, 14.3.73. Lyons Papers, Box 197.
43   Buchanan to Russell, undated. FO 918 16.
44   Confidential, Walker to Odo, 24.12.74. FO 64 807.
45   Odo to Granville, 2.3.73. PRO 30/29 93.
46   Gordon A. Craig, *Das Ende Preußens. Acht Porträts.* (München, 1984), p. 62.
47   Heinrich von Poschinger, *Fürst Bismarck und die Diplomaten 1852–1890* (Hamburg, 1900).

Notes to Chapter 5(c)

1   Parts of the correspondence can be found in the PRO (FO 918/52), and parts among the Lyons Papers at the West Sussex Record Office in Chichester, Box 197.
2   Lyons to Lytton, 18.9.74. Hertfordshire County Office. Bulwer Lytton Papers, D/EK 030.
3   Lyons to Odo, 8.4.73. FO 918 52.
4   Lyons to Derby, 26.9.76. Quoted in Lord Newton, *Lord Lyons,* 2 Vols (London, 1913), p. 102.
5   Robert Tombs, *France 1814–1914* (London, 1996), p. 427.
6   See Victor Hugo's speech before the Assemblée nationale on 1.3.71. Quoted in Wilfried Pabst, *Das Jahrhundert der deutsch-französischen Konfrontation* (Hannover, 1983), p. 48.
7   Sir Francis Ottiwell Adams was secretary of the embassy in Germany between 1872 and 1874 and was then secretary in France from 1874 to 1881.
8   Adams to Odo, undated FO 918/13.
9   See Tombs, *France 1814–1914,* p. 52.
10   *Ibid.*, p. 51.
11   Lyons to Russell, 8.4.73. FO 918 52.
12   Otto Pflanze, *The Period of Consolidation 1871,* p. 252.
13   August 1871. Later he added 'France is hopeless'. Quoted in Michael Stürmer, *Die Grenzen der Macht. Begegnungen der Deutschen mit der Geschichte* (Berlin, 1993), p. 86. See also Andreas Hillgruber, *Bismarck. Gründer der europäischen Großmacht Europa* (Göttingen, 1978), p. 65ff.
14   Tombs points out that this was the 'equivalent of two-and-a-half times the annual state budget of France'. Tombs, *France,* p. 437.
15   27.1.74. FO 64 801.
16   29.1.74. FO 64 801.
17   *Ibid.*, 28.1.74.
18   Odo to Derby, 7.3.74. Derby Papers 920 DER (15) 16/1/15.
19   Lyons to Russell, 7.5.72. FO 918 52. See also, Odo to Lyons, 11.5.72. Lyons Papers, Box 197.

20 Odo to John Russell, 5.5.73, PRO 30/22 17A and FO 918 10.
21 *Ibid.*
22 Hildebrand, who has also used this letter, quite rightly thinks that Odo did not want to offend his Uncle's pro-German tendencies. Klaus Hildebrand, 'Großbritannien und die deutsche Reichsgründung,' *Historische Zeitschrift*, (1980), p. 44.
23 22.12.73. FO 64 777.
24 *Ibid.*
25 *Ibid.*
26 2.1.74. FO 64 801.
27 *Ibid.*
28 20.2.74. FO 64 802.
29 Odo to Granville, 2.1.74. FO 64 801.
30 Odo repeated this a few months later to the new Foreign Secretary, Derby. 27.3.74. FO 64 803.
31 20.2.74. FO 64 802.
32 Odo to Lyons, 27.4.72. Lyons Papers, Box 197.
33 Odo to Lyons, 14.3.73. Lyons Papers, Box 197.
34 Odo to Derby, 3.4.75. Derby Papers, 920 DER (15) 16/1/15.
35 *German Correspondent* article attached to Odo's despatch, 27.11.72. FO 64 750.
36 Lyons to Russell, 8.4.73. FO 918 52.
37 Odo to White, 29.10.72. White Papers FO 364 8.
38 Odo to Granville, 23.11.72. PRO 30/29 92.
39 Like the French, Bismarck also saw Thiers as a stable factor. Tombs mentions the confidence this 'elder statesman' inspired, 'at home and abroad, not least in Germany'. Tombs, *France 1814–1914*, p. 439.
40 See Tombs, *France*, p. 438.
41 See also Heinz-Alfred Pohl, *Bismarcks Einflußnahme auf die Staatsform in Frankreich 1871–1877* (Frankfurt, 1983), p. 14.
42 Bismarck to the Emperor in 1872, (translation) quoted in Pohl, *Bismarcks Einflußnahme*, p. 14f.
43 William I argued in 1873 that 'the consolidation of the Republic or the support of the anarchy [in France] cannot be our aim'. Translated from Heinz-Alfred Pohl, *Bismarcks Einflußnahme auf die Staatsform in Frankreich 1871–1877* (Frankfurt, 1983), p. 14. Also in: Gr.Pol., Vol. I, no. 239. 28.12.74.
44 31.5.73. FO 64 771.
45 Lord Newton, *Lord Lyons*, 2 Vols (London, 1913), p. 100.
46 *Ibid.*, p. 101.
47 There is a great amount of literature on the Arnim case. The following is a selection: F. Hartung, 'Bismarck und Graf Harry Arnim', *Historische Zeitschrift* 171 (1951) p. 47–77. G.O. Kent, *Arnim and Bismarck* (Oxford, 1968). G. Kratzsch, *Harry von Arnim. Bismarck-Rivale und Frondeur. Die Arnim-Prozesse 1874–1876* (Göttingen, 1974). Fritz Münch, *Bismarcks Affäre Arnim. Die Politik des Diplomaten und die Verantwortlichkeit des Staatsmannes* (Berlin, 1990). E. v. Wertheimer, 'Der Prozeß Arnim', *Preußische Jahrbücher*, Vol. 222. (1930). Arnim's defence pamphlet *Pro Nihilo — Die Vorgeschichte des Arnim'schen Prozesses* (it was published under the pseudonym Wilhelm Eichhof). For Bismarck's treatment of his other ambassadors, see: Heinz Günther Sasse, *100 Jahre Botschaft in London — Aus der Geschichte einer Deutschen Botschaft* (Bonn, 1963), p. 8ff.
48 See Pohl, *Bismarcks Einflußnahme*, p. 14.
49 Hartung, *Arnim*, p. 55.
50 *Ibid.*, p. 53.

51 See Münch, *Bismarcks Affäre*, p. 55.
52 See also Stern who quotes a letter by Odo: 'Arnim was ready for any amount of intrigue to further his plan of succeeding Bismarck as German Chancellor'. Fritz Stern, *Gold and Iron*. p. 237.
53 Odo to Lyons, 18.1.73. Lyons Papers, Chichester, Box 197.
54 See Norman Rich (ed.), *Die Geheimen Papiere Friedrich von Holsteins. Erinnerungen und politische Denkwürdigkeiten*. Vol. I (Göttingen, 1958), p. 94.
55 Bismarck published, for example, Arnim's 1869 despatch from Rome, which showed the whole *Konzil* question in a very distorted light. See Hartung, *Arnim*, p. 65.
56 See, for example, Münch, *Bismarcks Affäre*, p. 12ff.
57 22.4.74. FO 64 803.
58 Münch, *Bismarcks Affäre*, p. 65.
59 Accompanied by his wife, Arnim was brought to Berlin and imprisoned. His Palais in Berlin as well as his mother's house were searched. See the *Post* article attached to the FO report. 5.10.74. FO 64 806.
60 Adams to Derby, 21.8.74. Derby Papers. 920 DER (15) 16/1/15.
61 *Ibid.*
62 Odo to Lyons, 18.1.73. Lyons Papers, Chichester, Box 197.
63 12.9.74. FO 64 806.
64 See Stern, *Gold and Iron*, Derby Papers p. 235f.
65 Odo to Derby, 10.10.74. 920 DER (15) 16/1/15. The Crown Princess wrote to the Queen: 'All Berlin is in a state of extraordinary agitation at Count Arnim's being arrested and put in prison — for (it is said) having unlawfully taken possession of certain despatches'. Fulford, *Darling Child. Private Correspondence of Queen Victoria and the Crown Princess of Prussia, 1871-1878*, London 1976 p. 155ff.
66 17.10.74. FO 64 806.
67 19.12.74. FO 64 807.
68 See Horst Kohl (ed.), *Briefe Otto von Bismarcks an die Schwester und Schwager Malwine von Arnim, geb. v. Bismarck, und Oskar von Arnim-Kröchlendorff 1843–1897* (Leipzig, 1915).
69 Bülow, *Denkwürdigkeiten*, Vol. 4, p. 179. I.
70 Odo gave a balanced psychological profile of Arnim to Granville in 1873. Odo to Granville, 19.1.73. PRO 30/29 93.
71 1.11.74. FO 64 807.
72 Bismarck, *Gedanken und Erinnerungen*, p. 395.
73 1.11.74. FO 64 807.
74 The Chancellor himself liked to put confidential information to good use on the stock market.
75 Bismarck, *Gedanken und Erinnerungen*, p. 391.
76 Odo to Arthur, 3.5.72. FO 918 84.
77 Odo to Lyons, 18.1.73. Lyons Papers, Chichester. Box 197.
78 19.12.74. FO 64 807.
79 *Ibid.*
80 17.10.74. FO 64 806.
81 19.12.74. FO 64 807. In the second court case, Arnim was sentenced to imprisonment for five years.
82 17.10.74. FO 64 806.
83 This was the way in which Odo summed up the opinion of his Liberal friends. 16.10.74. FO 64 806.
84 For example, Andreas Hillgruber, 'Die Krieg-in-Sicht Krise 1875. Wegscheide der Politik der europäischen Großmächte in der späten Bismarckzeit', in E.

Schulin (ed.) *Gedenkschrift für M. Göhring, Studien zur Europäischen Geschichten* (Wiesbaden, 1968). Also, Klaus Hildebrand, 'Von der Reichsgründung zur "Krieg in Sicht" — Krise. Preußen-Deutschland als Faktor der Britischen Außenpolitik', in Michael Stürmer (ed.), *Das Kaiserliche Deutschland. Politik und Geschichte 1870–1918.* (Düssseldorf, 1970). Klaus Hildebrand, *Das Vergangene Reich. Deutsche Außenpolitik von Bismarck bis Hitler* (Stuttgart, 1995), p. 28f.

85   One reason was of course that Lyons was not in Paris during the whole war-in-sight affair.

86   Lyons to Bulwer Lytton, 9.10.74. D/EK 030.

87   Diary entry: 18.1.75. *Derby Diary*, p. 191.

88   An article written by Constantin Rößler on 8 April 1875, possibly under the instruction of Lothar Bucher. See Norman Rich (ed.), *Die Geheimen Papiere Friedrich von Holsteins. Erinnerungen und politische Denkwürdigkeiten.* Vol. I (Göttingen, 1958), p. 116 and also Hildebrand, *Das vergangene Reich*, p. 31. The military was certainly pushing for such a step. Moltke had always propagated the effectiveness of a preventive war, which would once and for all have established Germany's superiority and, in Moltke's eyes, have forever prevented a coalition against Germany.

89   See Helga Deininger, *Frankreich-Rußland-Deutschland 1871–1891* (München, 1983), p. 34.

90   Münster reported Derby's assurance at length. See *Die große Politik der Europäischen Kabinette 1871–1914* (Berlin, 1926), p. 259.

91   On this, see also Pflanze, *Consolidation*, p. 268.

92   Odo to Derby 10.4.75. Derby Papers, 920 DER (15) 16/1/15. Derby took the letter very seriously; 'He [Russell] does not believe in war'. Diary entry: 18.4.75, *Derby Diary*, p. 208.

93   Kennedy clearly identifies the British decision-makers in the war-in-sight crisis as Disraeli, Derby and the Queen. See Paul Kennedy, *The Rise of the Anglo — German Antagonism* p. 138.

94   *Derby Diary*, p. 215.

95   Arthur Russell, 13.6.87. FO 918 80. Arthur wrote this account after Odo's death, giving his brother's side of the story to The Times, which had just published an article about the war-in-sight crisis of 1875 (*The Times* 2.6.87).

96   Derby to Odo, 3.5.75. Quoted in Lord Newton, *Lord Lyons*, 2 Vols (London, 1913), p. 75.

97   Arthur Russell to *The Times*, 13.6.87. FO 918 80.

98   Lyons to Adams, April 1874. Quoted in Newton, *Lord Lyons*, p. 73.

99   Quoted in R.T. Shannon, *The Age of Disraeli 1868–1881: the Rise of the Tory Democracy* (London, 1992), p. 272.

100   The Czar's active support for Britain surprised Russell. Only a year earlier Odo had written to Lyons: 'Do I attach any importance to the Emperor of Russia's pacific assurances? None whatever, because Bismarck is prepared to buy his co-operation with anything he pleases in the East'. Odo to Lyons, 20.2.74. Lyons Papers, Box 197.

101   Odo to Lyons, 20.2.74. Lyons Papers, Box 197.

102   Adams to Odo, 15.3.75. FO 918 13.

103   Odo to Hastings, 18.5.75. Woburn Papers.

104   Arthur Russell, 13.6.87. FO 918 80.

105   See Newton, *Lyons*, p. 79.

106   Odo to Morier, 15.5.75. Morier Papers, Box 37/6.

107   Newton, *Lyons*, p. 81.

108   Bismarck to Münster, 14.5.75. Quoted from *Die Große Politik der Europäischen Kabinette* (Berlin, 1926).

109 Diary entry date: 20.5.75. *Derby Diary*, p. 218.

110 *Ibid.*

111 Arthur Russell, 13.6.87. FO 918 80.

112 *Le Figaro* had published various accusations against Bismarck under the headline 'L'Empereur Alexander II. et la France en 1875'. 21.5.87. *Figaro*, 13 année numero 21. *The Times* took up the story and wrote on 1.6.87 about the 'Counter Revelations': 'Prince Bismarck has not been content to let General Le Flô remain in possession of the ear of Europe with respect to the war-scare of 1875, for through the *North German Gazette* the chancellor has now replied to the recent despatches of the ex-French ambassador by a series of counter-revelations, which seem calculated to dispel for ever any doubt that may have existed on the question whether warlike intentions were entertained by Germany towards France in the year referred to'. *Ibid.*

113 'The German despatches now published (June 1887), do not explain why the English Government believed in the danger of a threatened war'. Arthur Russell, 13.6.87. FO 918 80.

114 In *Gedanken und Erinnerungen* Bismarck calls the accusation laughable: 'So far was I from entertaining any such idea at the time, or afterwards, that I would rather have resigned'. Translation in Newton, *Lyons*, p. 82.

115 Pflanze, *Consolidation*, p. 278.

116 Hildebrand, Klaus, 'Großbritannien und die deutsche Reichsgründung,' *Historische Zeitschrift*, (1980), p. 46.

117 R.T. Shannon, *The Age of Disraeli 1868–1881: the Rise of the Tory Democracy* (London, 1992), p. 272.

118 Andreas Hillgruber, *Otto von Bismarck*, p. 21.

119 Newton, *Lyons,* p.108.

120 *Ibid.*

121 Originally Disraeli had opposed the building of the Suez Canal because of its 'engineering impracticability'. See George E. Buckle, *The Life of Benjamin Disraeli Earl of Beaconsfield (1855–1868)*, Vol. V (London, 1916), p. 408.

122 Odo to Derby, 13.11.75. Derby Papers. 920 DER (15) 16/1/15.

123 25.11.75. George E. Buckle, *Disraeli*, Vol. V, p. 450.

124 Odo to Derby (telegram), 29.11.75. Copy, Disraeli Papers, Dep. Hughenden 141/4.

125 To Odo, she wrote an even more ecstatic note: 'I must just write you a line to congratulate you both [Odo and his wife] on the news of the Suez Canal. I am so glad, so delighted that I quite forget how wretched I feel'. Copy of a letter to Odo and Emily Russell, 29.11.75. Derby Papers, 920 DER (15) 16/1/15.

126 Crown Princess to Queen, 30.11.75. Buckle, *Disraeli*, Vol. V, p. 452.

127 See Seton Watson, *Disraeli, Gladstone and the Eastern Question: a Study in Diplomatic and Party Politics* (London, 1935), p. 515.

Notes to Chapter 6(a)

1 'Ernst Jünger — Gegen die Zeit', *Focus* 13 (March, 1996), p. 145f.

2 Quoted in Klaus Hildebrand, 'Großbritannien und die deutsche Reichsgründung', *Historische Zeitschrift*, (1980), p. 37.

3 Odo to Hammond, 21.12.72. Hammond Papers FO 391 22.

4 Odo to Morier, 19.10.73. Morier Papers, Box 8/4.

5 Wehler certainly revolutionised the study of Bismarckian Germany. In the 1960s he was right to criticise his colleagues for being uninterested in the economic and sociological explanations relating to the creation of the Empire. H.U. Wehler, *Das deutsche Kaiserreich. 1871–1918* (Göttingen, 1980, 4th edn).

6 The expression was introduced by Wolfgang Sauer, 'Das Problem des deutschen Nationalstaats', in Helmut Böhme (ed.), *Reichsgründungszeit* (München, 1967).

7 Hans Ulrich Wehler, *Das deutsche Kaiserreich*, p. 100f.

8 Wehler calls the 'Bismarckian rule a Bonapartist dictatorship', and even Gall, who claims to dismiss the idea, has been accused by Mommsen of espousing Bonapartist theories. Wolfgang J. Mommsen, *Imperial Germany 1867–1918. Politics, Culture and Society in an Authoritarian State* (London, 1995), p. 22.

9 For this definition, see Otto Pflanze, *Bismarcks Herrschaftstechnik als Problem der gegenwärtigen Historiographie* (München, 1982), p. 25.

10 Wolfgang J. Mommsen, *Imperial Germany 1867–1918*, p. 5. He disagrees however with Wehler and Stürmer: 'it is inappropriate to describe the German Empire of the Bismarck era as a "Bonapartist dictatorial regime" (Wehler) or as an "authoritarian system governed with the aid of extra-constitutional threats of a coup" (Stürmer)'. *Ibid.*

11 *Ibid.*, p. 3.

12 Arthur to Odo, 29.2.72. FO 918 84.

13 Odo to Derby, 20.11.75. Derby Papers, 920 DER (15) 16/1/15.

14 Diary Entry: 5.4.1875. *Derby Diary*, p. 205.

15 Odo to Granville 22.4.73. PRO 30/29 93. Also quoted in Fritz Stern, *Gold and Iron* p. 267.

16 Alfred Milatz (ed.) *Otto von Bismarck. Werke in Auswahl. Reichsgestaltung und Europäische Friedenswahrung*, Vol. 5 (Stuttgart, 1983), p. 201.

17 For a discussion of these see, for example, Büchman, *Geflügelte Worte* (1st edn 1867) (München, 1959), p. 261. See also Stern, *Gold and Iron*, p. 266.

18 See Bernd Sösemann, 'Publizistik in staatlicher Regie. Die Presse und Informationspolitik der Bismarck Ära', in Johannes Kunisch (ed.), *Bismarck und seine Zeit* (Berlin, 1990), p. 291.

19 Sir James Rennell Rodd, *Social and Diplomatic Memories, 1884–1893*, 3 Vols (London, 1926), p. 52.

20 Odo to FO, 16.10.74. FO 64 806.

21 See also Paul Kennedy, *The Rise of the Anglo – German Antagonism* p. 152.

22 Odo to FO, 16.10.74. FO 64 806.

23 *Ibid.*

24 Bismarck feared the 'antagonistic influences of the Empress, the Royal Family, the reigning German Princes and the conservative supporters of the throne, who were alarmed by his "unholy alliance" as an ex-conservative, or Junker with what had hitherto been looked upon by them as a revolutionary party in Germany'. Odo to FO, 16.10.74. FO 64 806.

25 *Ibid.*

26 *Ibid.*

27 *Ibid.*

28 *Ibid.*

29 Bismarck in a conversation with Odo, 20.12.72. FO 64 747.

30 *Ibid.*

31 *Ibid.*

32 22.12.72. FO 64 748.

33 *Ibid.*

34 Odo described in a letter the confusion which prevailed: 'The Ministerial crisis seems a puzzle to many here'. Odo to Morier, January 1873. Morier Papers, Box 8/4.

35 Odo to Derby, 26.12.74. Derby Papers. 920 DER (15). 16/1/15.

36 Odo to Morier, 20.2.75. Morier Papers, Box 37/1.

37 Odo to Derby, 13.2.75. Derby Papers, 920 DER (15) 16/1/15.
38 Odo's source for this was Bleichröder. Odo to Derby, 6.3.75. *Ibid.*
39 See Otto Pflanze, *Bismarck and the Development of Germany. The Period of Consolidation*, p. 78.
40 Odo to Arthur, 6.3.72. FO 918 84. For an examination of the influence the British parliamentary system had on Germany see R. Lamer, *Der englische Parlamentarismus in der deutschen politischen Theorie im Zeitalter Bismarcks. Ein Beitrag zur Vorgeschichte des deutschen Parlamentarismus* (Lübeck, 1963).
41 Rennell Rodd, *Social and Diplomatic*, p. 64.
42 16.10.74. FO 64 806.
43 See Hajo Holborn, *Deutsche Geschichte in der Neuzeit. Das Zeitalter des Imperialismus 1871–1945*, Vol. III (Frankfurt, 1981), p. 21f.
44 Odo to Granville, 19.1.73. PRO 30/29 93.
45 Highlighted by Russell. 13.3.74. FO 64 802.
46 *Ibid.*
47 'They [Bismarck's words] show that he would not more shrink from a violation of the constitution or coup d'état than from a war of aggression to realise the German Empire of his dreams'. *Ibid.*
48 Confidential, 21.3.74. FO 64 803.
49 Lucian Hölscher, 'Politischer Aufbruch in einer Endzeit', in Johannes Kunisch, *Bismarck und seine Zeit* (Berlin, 1990), p. 392.
50 Odo to Derby, 8.5.75. Derby Papers, 920 DER (15) 16/1/15.
51 Odo to Salisbury, 1.12.83. Hatfield Papers.
52 Quoted in Noel Blakiston, *The Roman Question* p. xviii.
53 Plunkett to Granville, 30.7.72. FO 64 745.
54 Odo to Hastings, 4.6.78. Woburn Papers.
55 Odo to Hastings, 29.8.80. Woburn Papers.
56 Odo to Hastings, New Year's Day 1880.
57 Odo to Hastings, 14.1.80. Woburn Papers.

Notes to Chapter 6(b)

1 See Thomas Nipperdey, *Deutsche Geschichte 1866–1918. Machtstaat vor der Demokratie* (München, 1992) and Wolfgang J. Mommsen, *Das Ringen um den nationalen Staat. Die Gründung und der innere Ausbau des Deutschen Reiches unter Otto von Bismarck, 1850–1890*, Propyläen Geschichte Deutschlands, 7/1 (Berlin, 1993). There are also a lot of standard works on the subject: Erich Schmidt-Volkmar, *Der Kulturkampf in Deutschland 1871–1890* (Göttingen, 1962), Manfred Scholle, *Die preußische Strafjustiz im Kulturkampf 1873–1880* (Marburg, 1974) and Ronald J. Ross, 'Enforcing the Kulturkampf in the Bismarckian State and the Limits of Coercion in Imperial Germany', *Journal of Modern History* Vol. 56, (1984).
2 Odo to Hammond. (8.12.70.) Hammond Papers FO 391 22.
3 See Mommsen's comment: '[it] was the first party to rest on a mass popular base'. Mommsen, *Imperial Germany 1867–1918*, p. 11.
4 Winfried Becker, 'Liberale Kulturkampfpositionen und politischer Katholizismus', in Otto Pflanze and Elisabeth Müller-Luckner (eds), *Innenpolitische Probleme des Bismarck-Reiches*, (München, 1983), p. 59ff. See also a similar article by Becker 'Otto von Bismarcks Rolle bei Ausbruch, Verschärfung und Beilegung des preußischen Kulturkampfes', in Rudolf Lil and Francesco Traniello (eds), *Der Kulturkampf in Italien und in den deutschsprachigen Ländern* (Berlin, 1993).
5 See Becker, 'Liberale Kulturkampfpostionen', p. 84. Bismarck referred to them as 'the anti-national, Roman Catholic element in the new Empire'. Odo to Granville, 11.2.73. PRO 30/29 93.

6   Odo to Derby, 18.5.75 920 Derby Papers. DER (15) 16/1/15.

7   Odo wrote to Hammond about this: 'I am surprised because I thought Bismarck knew the spirit of the Church better than he does, and the amount of passive resistance the Roman Clergy can oppose to State interference with clerical concerns'. 17.5.73. FO 391 22.

8   Odo to Lady Salisbury, Rome, 17.3.68. Hatfield Papers.

9   Odo to Lady Salisbury, October 1867. Hatfield Papers.

10   Odo to Hastings, 26.4.74. Woburn Papers.

11   Odo to Arthur, 23.6.75. Odo had already expressed this thought three years earlier to Arthur: 'If you persecute the Clergy of all denominations, you must be prepared to supply some other comfort to satisfy the "besoin religieux" of humanity. The liberals merely want to destroy *krasse Dummheit* and forget that man does not live on bread alone'. 8.4.72. FO 918 84.

12   Odo to Arthur, 8.4.72. FO 918 84.

13   Stürmer claims that the Liberals saw themselves as a *Gegenkirche* [an alternative church]. Michael Stürmer, *Liberalismus und Kirche, 1848–1933, Die Anatomie eines Un-Verhältnisses* (München, 1984), p. 16.

14   Quoted in Edward Crankshaw, *Bismarck* (München, 1986), p. 370.

15   For the latest account of Windthorst's life see Margaret Lavinia Anderson, *Windthorst. A Political Biography* (Oxford, 1981).

16   Golo Mann, *Deutsche Geschichte des 19. und 20. Jahrhunderts*, 15th edn, (Frankfurt, 1985), p. 423.

17   Brandis to Morier, 13.2.72. Morier Papers, Box 55/2.

18   See Winfried Becker, 'Liberale Kulturkampf-Positionen', p. 66.

19   Odo to Arthur, 23.6.75. FO 918 84.

20   Nipperdey, *Deutsche Geschichte*, p. 273.

21   See Leopold v. Ranke, *Deutsche Geschichte im Zeitalter der Reformation* (München, 1925), Vol. 1, p. 7.

22   See Erich Förster, *Adalbert Falk. Sein Leben und Wirken als preußischer Kultusminister* (Gotha, 1927).

23   Crankshaw, *Bismarck*, p. 369.

24   Quoted from Otto Pflanze, *Bismarck and the Development of Germany. The Period of Consolidation 1871–1880*, p. 202.

25   See Hajo Holborn, *Deutsche Geschichte in der Neuzeit*, p. 30.

26   Before the Bill was published, Russell confronted Bismarck with the question whether this was finally cutting the knot between the church and the state. The Chancellor preferred to put it in more euphemistic terms: 'it was more the emancipation than the separation of the Church from the State that he [Bismarck] desired to achieve'. Berlin, 9.3.72. FO 64 743.

27   16.3.72. FO 64 743.

28   *Ibid.*

29   Odo to Morier, 25.3.72. Morier Papers, Box 35/5. Odo wrote to Hammond, in the same vein a year later: 'But the struggle will be deeply interesting for lookers on'. 17.5.73. FO 391 22.

30   Blackbourn describes the methods by 'which major parts of the newly-unified population were treated: not so much as dissident citizens, but effectively as inhabitants of an occupied state'. David Blackbourn, *Class, Religion and Local Politics in Wilhelmine Germany. The Centre Party in Württemberg Before 1914* (Wiesbaden, 1980), p. 9.

31   In a letter to Morier he wrote that 'busy B' was behaving dreadfully to the Bishops. Odo to Morier, 3.3.74. Morier Papers, Box 36/2.

32   Odo to Arthur, 26.4.72. FO 918 84.

33   Odo to Lyons, 25.3.72. Lyons Papers, Box 197.

34 Gelzer to Odo, Berlin December 1872. FO 918 34.
35 Odo's reply to Gelzer, 1.12.72. FO 918 34.
36 Odo to Arthur, 21.4.72. FO 918 84.
37 20.1.74. FO 64 801.
38 22.4.74. FO 64 803.
39 9.3.72. FO 64 743.
40 31.1.74. FO 64 798.
41 29.1.74. FO 64 801.
42 *Ibid.*
43 *Ibid.*
44 Quoted from the German *Provinzial Correspondence*, 15.7.74. See Adam's dispatch 18.7.74. FO 64 805.
45 *Ibid.*
46 1.8.74. FO 64 805.
47 Quoted in Erich Eyck, *Bismarck and the German Empire* (New York, 1958), p. 210.
48 7.12.74. FO 64 807.
49 Odo to Morier, 13.12.74. Morier Papers, Box 36/1.
50 Odo to Derby, 19.12.74. Derby Papers, 920 DER (15) 16/1/15.
51 These laws were mainly enforced in Prussia.
52 Pflanze, *Consolidation*, p. 203.
53 *Ibid.*
54 Odo to Hammond, 17.5.73. FO 391 22.
55 4.3.74. FO 64 802.
56 For these figures see, for example, P. Heinz Wolter (ed.), *Otto von Bismarck, Dokumente seines Lebens. 1815–1898* (Leipzig, 1886), p. 302f.
57 This was seen as a form of passive resistance. Blackbourn lists some further actions, such as for example, hiding priests and church property. See Blackbourn, *Volksfrömmigkeit und Fortschrittsglaube*, p. 28.
58 Odo to Hammond, 31.5.73. FO 391 22.
59 Odo to Arthur, undated, FO 918 84.
60 *Ibid.*
61 Odo to Arthur, 9.12.72. FO 918 84.
62 *Ibid.*
63 See for example, C.B. Ross, *The Old Catholic Movement* (London, 1964).
64 16.10.74. FO 64 806.
65 He was also informed about the provincial branches of their organisation, as for example, in the Catholic Rhineland. J.A. Crowe to Odo Russell, 9.11.72. FO 918 25.
66 Odo to Morier, 19.10.73. Morier Papers, Box 6/1 xiii.
67 *Ibid.*
68 Odo to Arthur, 18.12.72. FO 918 84.
69 16.3.72. FO 64 743.
70 Odo to Hastings, 14.10.74. Woburn Papers.
71 Noel Blakiston, *The Roman Question*, p. xix.
72 Arthur Russell to Lady Derby, 18.10.74. Hatfield Papers.
73 Lord Russell had written to John Murray at the beginning of 1874: 'But I cannot abstain from proclaiming aloud that I will never exchange my Christian Liberty for submission to priestly supremacy'. 1.1.74. PRO 30/22 17 A. John Russell had written, in a similar tone to William I. See also 28.2.74. FO 64 802.
74 Paul Kennedy, *The Rise of the Anglo–German Antagonism 1860–1914*, p. 105
75 Odo to John Russell, 25.2.74. John Russell Papers, PRO 30/22 17A.
76 *Copy Ibid.*
77 Odo to Arthur, 5.3.74. FO 918 84.

78   Odo to FO, 16.10.74. FO 64 806.
79   Lothar Gall, 'Bismarck und England', in Paul Kluke and Peter Alter (eds) *Aspekte der deutsch-britischen Beziehungen im Laufe der Jahrhunderte* (Stuttgart, 1978), p. 50.
80   Odo wrote to Arthur: 'thought was once free in Germany, but now the Germans are like other people and prosecute for religious convictions'. Odo to Arthur, 14.12.72. FO 918 84.
81   Hammond, however, was aware of Bismarck's blunders: 'You will probably have an exciting [time] in German politics for Bismarck's movements however cunningly and skilfully devised ... do not tend to harmony in civil matters, and in religious matters there seem to be plenty of brands, both at home and abroad'. Hammond to Odo, 1.1.73. FO 918 38.
82   Granville to Odo, 27.5.72. PRO 30/29 110.
83   In 1875, Gladstone called Germany 'that land of Luther which still retained her primacy in the domain of conscience'. Quoted in Kennedy, *Antagonism*, p. 27.
84   3.3.74. Gladstone was replying to a letter from Odo about 'the coming struggle between church and state in Germany'. Odo's letter of 23.2.74. Gladstone Papers 44 443ff p. 27, 58.
85   In his article 'Gladstone as Bismarck', Schroeder claims that despite their many differences, the two statesmen were not at 'opposite poles in the history of European International Relations'. Paul W. Schroeder, 'Gladstone as Bismarck', *Canadian Journal of History*, Vol. 15(2), 1980.
86   Gladstone, *The Vatican Decrees in their Bearing on Civil Allegiance* (London, 1874).
87   See Henry Neville, *A Few Comments on Mr Gladstone's Expostulation with Some Remarks on Vaticanism* (London, 1875).
88   Odo to Hastings, 1.4.75. Woburn Papers. Gladstone's critics, especially the Catholics, were outraged about the Vaticanism.
89   29.1.74. FO 64 801.
90   7.2.74. FO 64 802.
91   22.3.73. FO 64 769.
92   *Ibid.*
93   *Ibid.*
94   Odo to Derby, 21.3.74. Derby Papers, 920 DER (15) 16/1/15.
95   Quoted in Kennedy, *Antagonism*, p. 106.
96   See Scott William Murray, 'The German Career of Robert Morier 1853–1876', unpublished PhD thesis, Calgary, 1997.
97   Fulford, *Darling Child. Private Correspondence of Queen Victoria and the Crown Princess of Prussia. 1871-1878* p. 178.
98   31.1.74. FO 64 801.
99   14.5.73. FO 64 770.
100   *Ibid.*
101   *Ibid.*
102   Odo to Derby, 18.5.75. Derby Papers. 920 DER (15) 16/1/15.
103   Odo to Hastings, 23.11.74. Woburn Papers.
104   Crowe to Odo, 26.2.74. FO 918/25.
105   Odo wrote to Granville about this Bismarckian divide: 'It [is] now evident that the strength of Germany [is] in the Protestant North, her weakness is in the Catholic South'. Odo to Granville, 11.2.73. PRO 30/29 93.

Notes to Chapter 7a

1   Otto Pflanze, *Consolidation*, p. 415.
2   Aubrey Leo Kennedy, *Salisbury 1830–1903* (London, 1953), p. 80. Quoted also

in R.T. Shannon, *The Age of Disraeli 1868–1881: the Rise of the Tory Democracy* (London, 1992), p. 279.

3   The most prominent ones are: R.W. Seton-Watson, *Disraeli, Gladstone and the Eastern Question: A Study in Diplomacy and Party Politics* (London, 1935); Richard Shannon, *Gladstone and the Bulgarian Agitation* (London, 1963); Richard Millman, *Britain and the Eastern Question, 1875–1878* (Oxford, 1979); David MacKenzie, *The Serbs and Russian Pan-Slavism, 1875–1878* (Ithaca, 1978); and B.H. Sumner, *Russia and the Balkans 1870–1880* (Oxford, 1937).

4   For an FO viewpoint of the event see: *Analysis by Lord Tenterden of the Whole Series of Parliamentary Papers Showing the Diplomatic History of the War in Turkey From 1875 to 1878*. Among Disraeli Papers, Dep Hughenden, Bodleian Library, Department of Western Manuscripts.

5   Sir Henry Elliot, *Some Revolutions and Other Diplomatic Experiences* (London, 1922), p. 207. Alan Palmer claims that Elliot was rarely in possession of first hand information because he spent most of his time on a Greek island. Alan Palmer, *Verfall und Untergang des Osmanischen Reiches* (München, 1994), p. 207.

6   Elliot speculates that Russia encouraged the exiled 'troublemakers' to return to their homes and cause organised disturbances. Elliot, *Some Revolutions*, p. 207.

7   Odo to Derby, 10.7.75. Derby Papers, 920 DER (15) 16/1/15.

8   Up until then Bülow had expressed hopes that the Porte would 'master the movement'. MacDonnell to FO, 14.8.75. FO 64 829.

9   His source was Count Münster who had been to Varzin to see Bismarck. MacDonnell to Derby, 20.8.75. FO 64 829.

10   Although Bismarck mistrusted the more martial circles in Austria to exploit the situation, he defended Count Andrássy's intentions: 'He [Bismarck] cannot admit that Count Andrássy, for whom he has the greatest respect, would lure himself to such schemes, or follow so suicidal a policy'. *Ibid*.

11   *Ibid*.

12   Derby to Elliot, 24.8.75. Quoted from *Tenterden Analysis*, p. 1.

13   MacDonnell to FO, 9.9.75. FO 64 829.

14   'The joint action of the three Powers, at this early stage, is worth attention'. See *Tenterden Analysis*, p. 1.

15   Although Disraeli became Earl of Beaconsfield in 1876, for the sake of convenience, he will continue to be referred to by his old surname.

16   Grant Duff to Odo, 16.1.84. FO 918 35.

17   28.12.76. George E. Buckle, *The Life of Benjamin Disraeli Earl of Beaconsfield*, Vol. VI (London, 1916), p. 112.

18   *Ibid*. See also Seton-Watson, *Eastern Question*, p. 45.

19   13.9.1877. Buckle, *Disraeli*, Vol. VI., p. 178.

20   Odo to Derby, September 1875. 920 DER (15) 16/1/15.

21   15.10.75. FO 64 830.

22   23.10.75. FO 64 830.

23   Otto von Bismarck, *die Gesammelten Werke*, Friedrichsruher Ausgabe 1924-1935 Vol. 14, p. 630.

24   (Translation) Gustav Rein (ed.), *Bismarck — Werke in Auswahl, Reichsgestaltung und Europäische Friedenswahrung 1871–1876*, Vol. 5 (Stuttgart, 1973), p. 583.

25   1.10.75. FO 64 830.

26   2.1.76. FO 64 850.

27   *Ibid*.

28   As Disraeli wrote to Lady Bedford, he just had 'to face the question, he did not even have to solve it'. Robert Blake, *Disraeli* (Frankfurt, 1980) p. 474.

29   Salisbury's comment that certain politicians used maps with too small scales has

become a classic. See Blake, *ibid*., p. 478. It is ironic that the ardent imperialist Disraeli lacked geographical knowledge, as Blake proves with several entertaining quotes. Although Disraeli claimed to have first-hand experience of the Mediterranean, Blake doubts whether a holiday trip in 1835 could provide a sufficient basis for this.

30 See, for example, Henry Kissinger, *Diplomacy* (London, 1994), p. 149.

31 The fears towards Russia were, according to Kissinger, universal in the Western world: 'To the outside world, Russia was an elemental force — a mysterious, expansionist presence to be feared and contained either by cooperation or confrontation'. *Ibid.*

32 R.W. Seton-Watson, *Britain in Europe. 1789–1914* (Cambridge, 1937), p. 513. For a historical overview of the struggle of Russia to get access to the Black See, Sigrid Wegner-Korfes, *Otto von Bismarck und Rußland* (Berlin, 1990), p. 28.

33 1.12.75. FO 64 83135

34 Derby to Russell, 24.8.75. 920 DER (15) 17/1/6.

35 *Ibid.* Derby to MacDonnell. 1.9.75.

36 Most historians (e.g. Shannon, Millman, Blake and Seton-Watson) are critical of Derby. His trait of being 'over critical with himself' and his 'lack of initiative' (Millman, *Britain*, p. 6), his cautiousness and his tendency of delaying decisions were common knowledge amongst diplomats and duly reported, for example, by Münster to Bismarck.

37 The measures recommended to the Porte were: 'Religious liberty, ... abolition of the taxes on farming; a law to guarantee that the product of the direct taxation of Bosnia and Herzegowina shall be employed for the immediate interests of the province ... lastly, the amelioration of the condition of the rural population'. *Tenterden Analysis*, p. 2.

38 ... and that most of the measures Andrássy had now put forward, had already been included in the Sultan's Imperial Firman of 12 December. See *Tenterden Analysis*, p. 2.

39 8.1.76. FO 64 850.

40 Odo to Derby, 8.1.76. Derby Papers, 950 DER (15) 16/1/16.

41 Derby to Odo: '[the Austrian note] seems moderate both in tone and in substance', 4.1.76. A few days later Derby was less sure and wrote that the Premier was out of town and one could therefore not say anything 'decisive about the note', 12.1.76. 920 DER (15) 17/1/7.

42 See Disraeli's letter to Lord Derby, 9.1.76. Buckle, *Disraeli*, Vol. VI, p. 18f.

43 Odo to Derby, 15.1.76. 950 DER (15) 16/1/16.

44 22.1.76. *Ibid.*

45 Secret 2.1.76. FO 64 850.

46 'Germany could not well afford to let Austria and Russia to become too intimate behind her back — nor could she let them quarrel with safety to herself'. 2.1.76. FO 64 850.

47 *Ibid.*

48 *Ibid.*

49 The ghost of an earlier German overture to Britain, in December 1875, still circulates in some German articles as the 'Bucher mission'. Lothar Bucher was allegedly sent to England in December 1875 to propose an alliance against France and Russia. For this see Felix Rachefahl, *Bismarcks englische Bündnispolitik* (Freiburg, 1922). Friedrich Frahm, however, has shown that there is not enough evidence for this. See Friedrich Frahm, 'England und Rußland in Bismarcks Bündnispolitik', *Politik und Geschichte*. Heft 4 (1927), p. 373.

50 Another reason for Bismarck's yearning for cooperation with England was Gortschakoff's 'boasting' of 'intimate and confidential relations with HMG'. 3.1.76. FO 64 850.

51 7.1.76. FO 918 12.
52 3.1.76. FO 64 850.
53 *Ibid.*
54 Frahm thinks that Bismarck's long-term plan was to ask Britain's support for an alliance against France and Russia. Frahm, 'England und Rußland', p. 377.
55 31.3.76. FO 64 851.
56 *Ibid.*
57 Derby to Odo, 2.2.76. 920 DER (15) 17/1/7.
58 Paul Kennedy, *The Rise of the Anglo–German Antagonism 1860–1914* (London, 1980), p. 32. For Bismarck's overture see also David Harris, 'Bismarck's Advance to England, January 1876', *Journal of Modern History*, Vol. III (3), (Chicago, 1931).
59 Schouvaloff in an interview with Odo. 28.3.76. FO 64 851.
60 5.4.76. FO 64 851.
61 13.5.76. Copy, Dept. Hughenden 79/3.
62 *Ibid.*
63 *Ibid.*
64 *Ibid.*
65 See Seton-Watson, *Eastern Question*, p. 34.
66 Disraeli to Derby. 29. 5.76. Dep. Hughenden 69/2.
67 Odo to Hastings, 18.6.76. Woburn Papers.
68 *Ibid.*
69 See for example, A.L. Macfie, *The Eastern Question, 1774–1923*, p. 37.
70 Written by the Queen's secretary. 16.5.76. Copy, Dep. Hughenden, 79/3. The Prussian Crown Princess tried to portray the memorandum as a chance for England: 'it is a grand moment for England now, it seems to me, to take the initiative and put forward her plans and propositions'. 16.6.76. Copy, Dep. Hughenden 79/3.
71 18.5.76. FO 64 852.
72 Gontaut-Biron wrote that 'Lord Odo did not share his Government's views and had expressed to Lord Derby his readiness to resign his post'. See Seton-Watson, *Disraeli* p. 34.
73 Dep. Hughenden 67 A 1–110. Late at night on May 17, Odo wrote a note to Bismarck, breaking the bad news: 'Dear Prince Bismarck, not to disturb you at this hour by calling I write a private line to say that Lord Derby telegraphs that HMG see grave objections to the plan put forward by the three Imperial Powers and are not prepared to press its adoption on the Porte. HMG however entertain the same desire to act otherwise as far as possible with the Imperial Government'. Copy of letter to Bismarck 17.5.76., FO 918 12.
74 As to why the memorandum was rejected see also *Tenterden Analysis*, Paul Kennedy, *The Rise of the Anglo–German Antagonism* p. 4.
75 A palace revolution on 30th of May, the day the memorandum should have been presented, and the murder of Abdul Aziz completely changed the situation at Constantinople again. See, for example, Seton-Watson, *Eastern Question*, p. 35f. Tenterden could therefore write in a self-congratulatory way that: 'The Berlin memorandum was dropped without presentation to the Porte, and has not since been revived'. *Tenterden Analysis*, p. 5.
76 Disraeli to the Queen, 18.5.76. Quoted from George E. Buckle (ed.), *The Letters of Queen Victoria, a Selection from Her Majesty's Correspondence and Journal Between the Years 1868 and 1878*, Vol. 1 (London, 1926), p. 454. To underline the British commitment to Turkey, a fleet was also sent to Besika Bay.
77 Quoted in Kissinger, *Diplomacy*, p.149.
78 Macfie, *The Eastern Question*, p. 38.

Notes to Chapter 7b

1   Although Disraeli had tried to put out his feelers to Bismarck during the summer, offering in return for the status quo in Turkey the possibility of support in the Alsace–Lorraine question. For this it was now too late. Bismarck believed in a partition of the Ottoman Empire into different spheres of interest and saw Britain's clinging to Turkey as outdated. See Pflanze, *Consolidation*, p. 427 and Heinrich Pösch, 'Ein englischer Bündnisfühler im Jahre 1876', *Historische Vierteljahreszeitschrift* 5. Heft Jahrgang XXIV (Dresden, 1928).

2   Odo to Hastings, 6.11.76. Woburn Papers.

3   Odo to Hastings, 3.12.76. Woburn Papers.

4   Odo to Arthur, undated FO 918 84.

5   Telegram from Odo Russell to FO. 6.6.76. FO 64 852.

6   Despite Russell's assurance that there was no revival of an Anglo-French alliance in sight. See 8.6.76. FO 64 853.

7   William was, according to Bismarck, of the opinion that Turkey would 'go to pieces from want of vital and cohesive power'. Reported to Odo by Count Schouvaloff, 28.3.76. FO 64 851.

8   Odo was confronted with an amalgam of accusations, including ones relating to the British purchase of the Suez Canal. (William obviously did not share his Chancellor's enthusiasm for it) and the title of Empress of India for the Queen. William saw both as further indications for an English–Russian confrontation. Odo to Derby 11.6.76, 920 DER (16) 16/1/16.

9   Odo to Derby 11.6.76, 920 DER (16) 16/1/16.

10 Odo to Hastings, 28.3.76. Woburn Papers.

11 William had made his hatred of Turkey obvious on many occasions. Already on 21.12.75, he had a long conversation with the Turkish ambassador who was 'very upset' afterwards. FO 64 831.

12 *Ibid.*

13 *Ibid.*

14 Extract from Queen's Journal, 5.7.76. Quoted from Buckle (ed.), *Queen Victoria*, p. 467.

15 In one of the few letters by Russell found at the Bismarck archive in Friedrichsruh he notes that: 'I in no way want to disturb you in your rest, if you are not inclined to receive visits — I merely report myself respectfully'. Friedrichsruh Archive, Odo to Bismarck, 9.7.76. FBA B 102–20.

16 Bismarck to Odo, 9.7.76, FO 918 12.

17 Odo to Derby, 10.7.76, 950 DER (15) 16/1/16.

18 *Ibid.*

19 *Ibid.*

20 Bismarck also blamed this on the insensitivity of Count Münster. The German ambassador in London had written a direct despatch about British armaments to William I and the Emperor had concluded from it that England was on the verge of war. Bismarck wrote Münster a warning letter scolding him about the chain reaction his epistle had caused. Kissingen 7.7.76. Rein, *Werke*, p. 704.

21 Odo to Derby, 10.7.76. Derby Papers, 950 DER 16/1/16.

22 *Ibid.*

23 *Ibid.*

24 *Ibid.*

25 *Ibid.*

26 *Ibid.*

27   *Ibid*. Seton-Watson, *Britain in Europe*, p. 518.
28   Odo to Derby: 'He (the Emperor) became more cheerful and entered into general conversation'. 10.7.76. 915 (DER) 16/1/16.
29   *Ibid*.
310 *Ibid*.
31   Bismarck to Münster, 16.7.76. (Translated). Rein, *Werke*, p. 707.
32   Bismarck to the MP von Benda, mid-July 1876, *ibid*. p. 705.
33   Queen's Journal, 21.7.76. Quoted from Buckle, *Queen Victoria*, p. 472.
34   27.10.76. FO 64 855.
35   The pamphlet was written between the 28.8. and 5.9. despite Granville and Hartington thinking it an unnecessary move. See also, John Morley, *The Life of William Ewart Gladstone*, Vol. II (London, 1903), p. 549ff.
36   Public opinion in Britain varied considerably. The spectrum included 'anti-Turkism, order, anti-war, legalism, anti-Russianism and philo-Turkism'. See Geo Carslake Thompson, *Public Opinion and Lord Beaconsfield, 1875–80* (London, 1886).
37   *Reply by Lord Derby to a Deputation of Working Men at the FO on Monday 11.9.1876.* Printed by the FO 15.9.76. Bodleian Library papers.
38   Gladstone to Granville: 'Derby's declarations were well described by Panizzi as a mystification. Under cover of them they may continue to act in the old spirit. There is nothing but the polls'. Ramm, *Correspondence*, p. 7.
39   *Ibid*. p. 10. The news from Bulgaria also influenced German public opinion in a disfavourable way towards England. 2.9.76. FO 64 854.
40   During August, the Russians expected Bismarck to take the lead in a mediation scheme between the Porte and Serbia. 26.8.76. FO 64 854.
41   7.10.76. FO 64 855.
42   *Ibid*.
43   William I to Alexander II, 2.9.76. *Große Politik*, Vol. 2, p. 38.
44   7.10.76. FO 64 855.
45   Bismarck was of a different opinion, but the tide seemed against him. See Russell's report of 11.10.76. FO 64 855.
46   *Ibid*. In his memoirs Bismarck explained this more generally: 'We could indeed endure that our friends should lose or win battles against each other, but not that one of the two should be so severely wounded and injured that its position as an independent great power participating in European affairs would be endangered'. Quoted from Otto von Bismarck, *Gesammelte Werke 15*, p. 388ff.
47   He finally worked out, that: 'The impression of persons in office and at court is that the German Emperor will do nothing in opposition to the Czar's wishes at present'. 17.10.76. FO 64 855.
48   23.10.76. FO 64 855.
49   *Ibid*.
50   Derby to Odo, 31.10.76. 920 DER (15) 17/1/7.
51   *Ibid*.
52   Odo to Hastings, 15.11.76. Woburn Papers.
53   A.L. Kennedy, *Salisbury*, p. 94. This had been suggested by the cosmopolitan Prince of Wales.
54   Odo to Hastings, 19.11.76. Woburn Papers.
55   Arthur Russell to Morier 4.10.77, Morier Papers, BOX 6/7xii.
56   9.11.76. FO 64 856.
57   Odo to Derby, 18.11.76. 920 DER (15) 16/1/16.
58   Blake, *Salisbury*, p. 98.
59   25.11.76. FO 64 856.
60   Odo's summary of the Salisbury visit to Hastings, 26.11.76. Woburn Papers.

61   Odo to Hastings, 26.11.76. Woburn Papers.
62   See, for example, L.M. Penson, *Foreign Affairs Under the Third Marquess of Salisbury* (London, 1962). J.A.S. Greville, *Lord Salisbury and Foreign Policy: the Close of the Nineteenth Century* (London, 1964). C.J. Lowe, *The Reluctant Imperialists: British Foreign Policy 1878–1902*, 2 Vols (London, 1967). Robert Taylor, *Lord Salisbury* (London, 1973).
63   In an essay about her father, Lady Gwendolyn Cecil shows that he often felt uncomfortable in a social situation. Lady Gwendolyn Cecil, 'Lord Salisbury in Private Life', in Blake and Cecil, *Salisbury*, p. 31.
64   The disagreements with Elliot resulted in Salisbury, after having encountered much opposition at home, finally achieving the replacement of the ambassador, a step of which even Hammond approved. Hammond to Derby, 23.1.77. Hammond Papers, 391 22.
65   Odo to FO, 4.1.77. FO 64 876.
66   *Ibid.*
67   11.1.77. FO 64 876.
68   John Lowe, *Rivalry and Accord. International Relations 1870–1914* (London, 1988), p. 23.
69   Odo to Arthur, 28.2.77. FO 918 84.
70   Odo to Hastings, 21.4.78. Woburn Papers.
71   Odo to Hastings, 31.3.78. Woburn Papers.
72   *Ibid.*
73   Odo to Hastings, 12.6.78. Woburn Papers.
74   Odo to Hastings, June 1878. Woburn Papers.
75   Odo to Hastings, 15.7.78. Woburn Papers.
76   See Bismarck letter vom 19.4.76. Rein, *Werke*, p. 673.
77   Quoted in Heinrich von Poschinger, *Fürst Bismarck und die Diplomaten 1852–1890* (Hamburg, 1900).
78   Odo to FO, 26.11.79. FO 64 936.
79   *Die Gegenwart — Wochenschrift für Literatur, Kunst und öffentliches Leben*, 1878, Vol. 14, No. 32. Theodor Fontane used a great portion of this article for his, from a literary point of view, mediocre portrait of Bismarck.
80   Odo to Arthur, 7.3.79. FO 918 84.
81   This was the opinion of the Austrian opposition with regard to Andrássy's policy in the Eastern Question. Andrássy had said about the Berlin memorandum meetings in May 1876, that nothing binding had been decided, but that the powers agreed 'sich über die Haltung im Orient von Fall zu Fall zu verständigen [to consult about their approach to the Eastern Question on a case by case basis]'. *Büchmanns Geflügelte Worte*, p. 264.

Notes to Chapter 8

1   Odo to Lord Salisbury, 27.12.79, Salisbury Papers 3—A9/58.
2   Lord Salisbury to Odo Russell, 14.1.80. Salisbury Papers, 3—A27/27.
3   Odo to Granville, 29.5.80. Quoted in Paul Knaplund, *Letters from the Berlin Embassy 1871–74 and 1880–85*. p. 144.
4   Otto Pflanze, *Bismarck and the Development of Germany. The Period of Consolidation 1871–1880*, p. 5.
5   Odo to Lord Salisbury, 10.1.79. FO 64 940.
6   Odo to Hastings, 27.6.78. Woburn Papers.
7   Odo to Gladstone, 8.10.78. Gladstone Papers, 44.458ff.
8   Gladstone to Odo. 10.10.78. *Ibid.* 44.458ff.

9   Odo to Hastings, 17.10.78. Woburn Papers.
10   *Ibid.*, Odo to Hastings, 14.10.78.
11   *Ibid.*, Odo to Hastings, 26.1.80.
12   *Ibid.*, Odo to Hastings, 25.7.80.
13   Copy of a letter Russell sent to Hastings. 30.11.80. Woburn Papers.
14   Walter Bussmann (ed.), *Staatssekretär Graf Herbert von Bismarck. Aus seiner politischen Privatkorrespondenz* (Göttingen, 1964), p. 253.
15   3.12.80. Gladstone Papers, 44 467.
16   Odo to Arthur, 3.12.82. FO 918 84.
17   Odo to Arthur, 8.8.81. FO 918 84.
18   Quoted in Winifried Taffs, *Ambassador to Bismarck*, p. 315.
19   May 1882, PA England. 69, Gel. Vol. I.
20   Odo to Granville, 30.9.80. Quoted in Paul Knaplund, *Letters, From The British Embassy* p. 14.
21   Odo Russell to Lady Derby, 20.11.80. Salisbury Papers.
22   Odo to Hastings, 20.8.80. Woburn Papers.
23   Sir James Rennell Rodd, *Social and Diplomatic Memories, 1884–1893*, p. 52.
24   Bismarck's most famous comment on the colonies was 'they are like sable coats worn by Polish noblemen who don't have any shirts'. 9.2.71. Moritz Busch, *Tagebuchblätter* (Leipzig, 1899), Vol. II, p. 157.
25   Russell to Granville, 11.2.73. PRO 30/29 93.
26   Odo to Hammond. Hammond Papers 1.3.73. FO 391 22.
27   *Ibid.*
28   Axel T.G. Riehl, *Der 'Tanz um den Äquator'. Bismarcks antienglische Kolonialpolitik und die Erwartung des Thronwechsels in Deutschland 1883 bis 1885* (Berlin, 1993).
29   Quoted also in Paul Kennedy, *The Rise of the Anglo–German Antagonism* p. 171. Kennedy thinks that this utterance cannot be taken seriously because it is a typically self serving retrospective explanation.
30   Quoted in Paul Knaplund, *Letters From The British Embassy, op.cit* 3, p.118–119.
31   *Ibid.*, p. 337.
32   Norman Rich and M.H. Fisher (ed.) Die geheimen Papiere Friedrich von Holsteins. Erinnerungen und politische Denkwürdigkeiten Vol I (Göttingen, 1956) Vol. II, pp. 112–113.
33   Rennell Rodd, *Social and Diplomatic*, p. 64.
34   *Ibid.*
35   Odo to Granville, 28.6.84. Quoted in Knaplund, *Letters From The British Embassy* p. 298.
36   Odo to Granville, 8.4.84. FO 64 1102.
37   Quoted in Knaplund, *Letters From The British Embassy* p. 337.
38   Odo to Granville, 27.6.84. FO 64 1102.
39   See Knaplund, *Letters From The British Embassy* p. 15.
40   On this see Kennedy, *Antagonism*, p. 172.
41   Odo to Granville, 2.8.84. Quoted in Knaplund, *Letters From The British Embassy* p. 338.
42   Odo to Granville, 16.8.84, quoted in Knaplund, *Letters From The British Embassy* p. 339.
43   Bussmann, *Herbert von Bismarck*, p. 252.
44   26.8.84, *The Times.*
45   Scott to Granville, 1.9.84. FO 64 1051.
46   Rennell Rodd, *Social and Diplomatic* p. 53.
47   24.1.83. FO 64 1024.
48   30.8.84. FO 64 1051.

49   Taffs, Ambassador to Bismarck, p. 391.
50   Rennell Rodd, *Social and Diplomatic* p. 53.
51   26.8.84, *The Times.*
52   Rennell Rodd, *Social and Diplomatic* p. 53.

Notes to Chapter 9

1   Queen to Prussian Crown Princess, 12.10.80. Roger Fulford (ed.), *Beloved Mama. Private Correspondence of Queen Victoria and the German Crown Princess, 1878–1885* (London, 1981), p. 90.
2   Odo to Lyons, 14.3.73. Lyons Papers, Box 197. Also quoted in J.C.G. Röhl, *From Bismarck to Hitler. The Problem of Continuity in German History* (London, 1970), p. 25, and in Klaus Hildebrand, 'Großbritannien und die deutsche Reichsgründung', *Historische Zeitschrift,* (1980), p. 45.
3   Quoted from Noel Blakiston, *The Roman Question* p. XXII.
4   Tenterden to Granville, 15.9.80. Granville Papers, PRO 30/29.
5   Walter Bussmann (ed.), *Staatssekretär Graf Herbert von Bismarck*, p. 253.

BIBLIOGRAPHY

Manuscript Sources

British Sources

Public Record Office
Official Correspondence, Germany FO 64, 700–814 and FO 244, 250–300.
Ampthill Papers, FO 918.
Tenterden Papers, FO 363.
Crowe Papers, FO 298/1.
Granville Papers, PRO 30/29 and FO 362/4.
Edmund Hammond Papers, FO 391.
Loftus Papers, FO 519/274 280, 284.
Russell Papers, PRO 30/22.
White Papers, FO 364/1–10.

Balliol College, Oxford
Morier Papers, Box 2/9–75/6.

Bleichröder Archive, Harvard University
Baron Bleichröder, XXIV, 6e–6i.

Bodleian Library, Oxford
Disraeli Papers, Dep. Hughenden.

British Library
Gladstone Papers, 44 093–44 467.
Layard Papers, Add MSS 38931–39164.

Hatfield House
Salisbury, 3M/A27 Papers. Russell to Salisbury.
Lady Derby (formerly Lady Salisbury) Papers. Hatfield/DER.

Hertfordshire Record Office
Bulwer-Lytton Papers, D/EK 030

Liverpool Record Office
Lord Derby Papers, 920 DER (15).

Nottingham University
Buchanan Papers. BU 25/35–BU 32/121.

University Library, Cambridge
Lord Acton Papers, Add 8119 (5)/ R 200–230.

West Sussex Record Office, Chichester
Lyons Papers, Box 197.

Woburn Abbey
9th Duke of Bedford Papers (Woburn Papers).

German Sources

Bismarck Archive, Friedrichsruh
Odo Russell to Bismarck, FBA: B 102–120.
Answärtiges amt Political Archives, Bonn
Bismarck to Bernstorff, 1870–1873. Aktengruppe London 90.
Bernstorff to Bismarck, 1870–1873. R 5362–5368.

Printed Sources (Selection)

Blue Books Concerning the Franco-Prussian War
Correspondence Respecting Negotiations Preliminary to War Between France and Prussia, 1870. 1870 (c.167) LXX. 17 mf 76.666–667, Parliamentary Papers Index).
Further Correspondence Respecting Public Services Rendered by English Subjects in Paris During the Siege. 1871 (C. 413) LXX 1.285–mf 77.654. Parliamentary Papers.

British

Buckle, George E. (ed.), *The Letters of Queen Victoria 1870–1878*, Second Series, Vol. II, London, 1926.
Bourne, Kenneth and Watt, Donald Cameron. (eds), *British Documents on Foreign Affairs*, New York, 1983.
Hansard Parliamentary Debates, 3rd Series, London, 1870–1894.
Report from the Select Committee Appointed to Inquire Into the Diplomatic and Consular Services 1870, (382) VII.
First Report from the Select Committee on Diplomatic and Consular Services 1871 (238), VII.
Second Report from the Select Committee 1871 (380) VII.

German

Otto von Bismarck. Die Gesammelten Werke (Friedrichsruher Ausgabe 1924–1935).
Kohl, Horst (ed.), *Briefe Otto von Bismarcks an Schwester und Schwager Malwine von Arnim, geb. v. Bismarck, und Oskar von Arnim-Kröchlendorff 1843–1897*, Leipzig, 1915.
Lepsius, Johannes, Mendelssohn-Bartholdy, Albrecht and Thimme, Friedrich (eds), *Die Große Politik der europäischen Kabinette 1871–1914*, Sammlung der diplomatischen Akten des Auswärtigen Amtes. Berlin, 1922–1927.

Milatz, Alfred (ed.), *Otto von Bismarck — Werke in Auswahl. Fünfter Band, Reichsgestaltung und Europäische Friedenswahrung*, Stuttgart, 1983.

Rothfels, Hans (ed.), *Bismarck und der Staat — Ausgewählte Dokumente*, Stuttgart 1953.

Rothfels, Hans (ed.), *Otto von Bismarck, Briefe*, Göttingen, 1955.

Wolter, Heinz (ed.), *Otto von Bismarck. Dokumente seines Lebens*, Frankfurt a.M. 1986.

19th Century Newspapers

Allgemeine Zeitung und Beilage, Augsburg, 1870, 1871.

William Gladstone, 'Germany, France and England', *Edinburgh Review*, Vol. cxxxii October 1870

Blackwood's Magazine

Die Gegenwart — Wochenschrift für Literatur, Kunst und Öffentliches Leben, Vol. 14 (32), 1878.

The Times, 1870–1887.

Reference Books

Büchmanns geflügelte Worte.

Burke's Peerage.

The Royal Commission on Historical Manuscripts Guides to Sources for British History 4: Private Papers of British Diplomats 1782–1900, London, 1985.

The Royal Commission of Historical Manuscripts Guides to Sources for British Historical Manuscripts 1. Papers of British Cabinet Ministers, 1782–1900, London, 1982.

The Cambridge Biographical Encyclopedia Cambridge, 1994.

Unpublished Dissertations

Anderson, Mary Adeline, 'Edmund Hammond — Permanent Undersecretary of State for Foreign Affairs 1854–1873' PhD, University of London, 1955.

Bell, Gary, 'The Men and their Rewards in the Elizabethan Diplomatic Service 1558–1585.' PhD University College, London, 1975.

Hilbert, L., 'The Role of Military and Naval Attaches in the British and German Service with Particular Reference to those in Berlin and London, and their Effect on Anglo-German Relations, 1871–1914.' PhD Cambridge University, 1954.

Murray, Scott William, 'The German Career of Robert Morier', PhD Thesis, University of Calgary, 1997.

Unpublished Research Papers

Hogarth, Jennifer, *Lord Odo Russell's Autograph Collection. Working Paper No. 1.* (Held in the MSS and rare books collection of the Library, University College, London.) School of Library and Information Studies. UCL, London 1989.

Hogarth, Jennifer, *Lord Odo Russell Collection, Working Paper No. 2. Lord Arthur John Edward Russell (1825–1892). A Victorian Intellectual.* UCL 1990.

Printed Secondary Works

Articles (selection)

Bartlett, C.J., 'Clarendon, the Foreign Office and the Hohenzollern Candidature,' *English Historical Review,* 75 (1960).

Berger, Stefan, 'Germany's Illiberal Traditions', [review article] *History Today,* 46 (7) (1996).

Bornkamm, Heinrich, 'Die Staatsidee im Kulturkampf,' *Historische Zeitschrift,* 170 (1950).

Dammermann, Bernhard, 'Lothar Bucher in England. Seine Entwicklung vom Achtundvierziger zum Gehilfen Bismarcks,' *Archiv für Politik und Geschichte,* (1927).

Evans, Richard J., 'From Unification to World War,' (review article) *Bulletin of the German Historical Institute,* (1996).

Frahm, F., 'England und Rußland in Bismarcks Bündnispolitik', *Archiv für Politik und Geschichte,* 5 (1927).

Gall, Lothar, 'Zur Frage der Annexion von Elsaß Lothringen 1870,' *Historische Zeitschrift,* 206 (1968).

Gall, Lothar, 'Liberalismus und bürgerliche Gesellschaft. Zu Charakter und Entwicklung der Liberalen Bewegung in Deutschland,' *Historische Zeitschrift,* 220 (1975).

Gall, Lothar, 'Bismarck und der Bonapartismus', *Historische Zeitschrift,* 223 (1976).

Gall, Lothar, 'Die europäischen Mächte und der Balkan im 19. Jahrhundert,' *Historische Zeitschrift,* 228 (1979).

Harris, David, 'Bismarck's Advance to England, January 1876,' *Journal of Modern History,* III (3) (1931).

Hartung, Fritz, 'Bismarck und Graf Harry Arnim,' *Historische Zeitschrift,* 171 (1951).

Harvey, Charles and Press, John, 'Victorian Values. William Morris — Art and Idealism,' *History Today,* 46 (May 1996).

Hildebrand, Klaus, '"British Interests" and "Pax Britannica". Grundfragen englischer Außenpolitik im 19. und 20. Jahrhundert,' *Historische Zeitschrift*, 221 (1975).

Hildebrand, Klaus, 'Geschichte oder Gesellschaftsgeschichte,' *Historische Zeitschrift*, 223 (1976).

Hildebrand, Klaus, 'Die deutsche Reichsgründung im Urteil der britischen Politik,' *Francia. Forschungen zur westeuropäsichen Geschichte*, 5 (1977).

Hildebrand, Klaus, 'Staatskunst oder Systemzwang? Die deutsche Frage als Problem der Weltpolitik,' *Historische Zeitschrift*, 228, (1979).

Hildebrand, Klaus, 'Großbritannien und die deutsche Reichsgründung,' *Historische Zeitschrift*, (1980). Beiheft 6.

Holborn, Hajo, 'Bismarck und Schuvaloff im Jahre 1875 — Aktenstücke zur Geschichte der deutsch-russischen Beziehungen', *Historische Zeitschrift*, 130 (1924).

Holborn, Hajo, 'Die Mission Radowitz nach St. Petersburg im Frühjahr 1875,' *Archiv für Politik und Geschichte*, (1924).

Jackson, Patrick, 'Skittles and the Marquis — a Victorian Love Affair', *History Today*, 45 (1995).

Kolb, Eberhard 'Bismarck und das Aufkommen von Annexionsforderungen 1870,' *Historische Zeitschrift*, 209 (1969).

Langewiesche, Dieter, 'Reich, Nation und Staat,' *Historische Zeitschrift*, 254 (1992).

Langhorne, Richard, 'The Nineteenth Century Foreign Office: a Study in Administrative History,' (review article) *Historical Journal*, XVI (1973).

Lipgens, Walter, 'Bismarck, die öffentliche Meinung und die Annexion von Elsaß und Lothringen 1870,' *Historische Zeitschrift*, 199 (1964).

Mosse, W.E., 'The End of the Crimean System: England, Russia and the Neutrality of the Black Sea, 1870–1871,' *Historical Journal*, IV (1961).

Mosse, W.E., 'Public Opinion and Foreign Policy: the British Public Opinion and the War-Scare of 1870,' *Historical Journal*, VI/I (1963).

Naujoks, Eberhard, 'Rudolf Lindau und die Neuorientierung der auswärtigen Pressepolitik Bismarck 1871/1878,' *Historische Zeitschrift*, 215 (1970).

Philippi, Hans, 'Zur Geschichte des Welfenfonds,' *Nieders. Jahrbücher für Landesgeschichte*, 31 (1959).

Pösch, Heinrich, 'Ein Englischer Bündnisfühler im Jahre 1876,' *Historische Vierteljahresschrift*, 5 (XXIV) (1928).

Randall, Alec, 'Lord Odo Russell and Bismarck,' *History Today*, 27 (1977).

Rich, Norman, 'Holstein and the Arnim Affair,' *Journal of Modern History*, 28 (1958).

Ritter, Gerhard, 'Bismarcks Verhältnis zu England und die Politik des "Neuen Kurses"', *Protestant Germany Through British Eyes: a Complex Victorian Encounter Archiv für Politik und Geschichte,* 2 (1924).

Robbins, Keith, 1992 Annual Lecture held at the German Historical Institute (London, 1992).

Ross, Ronald J., 'Enforcing the Kulturkampf in the Bismarckian State and the Limits of Coercion in Imperial Germany,' *Journal of Modern History,* 56 (1984).

Schmitt, Hans A., 'Bismarck's Unfinished Empire', *South Atlantic Quarterly* (1966).

Schroeder, Paul W., 'Gladstone as Bismarck,' *Canadian Journal of History,* 15 (2) (1980).

Schroeder, Paul W., 'The Lost Intermediaries: The Impact of 1870 on the European System,' *International History Review,* VI (1984).

Schünemann, Karl, 'Die Stellung Österreich-Ungarns in Bismarcks Bündnispolitik,' *Archiv für Geschichte und Politik* (1926).

Schüssler, W., 'Bismarcks Bündnisangebot an Russland "durch dick und dünn" im Herbst 1876,' *Historische Zeitschrift,* 147 (1933).

Talbott, John, 'Combat Trauma in the American Civil War,' *History Today,* 46 (1996).

Taylor, P.M., 'The Foreign Office and British Propaganda During the First World War,' *Historical Journal,* 23 (1980).

Tombs, Robert, 'The Thiers Government and the Outbreak of Civil War in France. February to April 1871,' *Historical Journal,* 23 (1980).

Urbach, Karina, 'Between Saviour and Villain: 100 Years of Bismarck Biographies,' *Historical Journal,* 41 (1998).

Wertheimer, E.v., 'Der Prozeß Arnim,' *Preußische Jahrbücher,* 222 (1930).

Wittram, Reinhard, 'Bismarcks Russlandpolitik Nach der Reichsgründung', *Historische Zeitschrift,* 186 (1958).

Autobiographies and Biographies Containing Primary Material (Selection)

Abeken, Hedwig, (ed.), *Heinrich Abeken, Ein schlichtes Leben in bewegter Zeit,* Berlin, 1898.

Ballhausen, Freiherr Lucius von, *Bismarck Erinnerungen,* Stuttgart, Berlin, 1921.

Blakiston, Georgiana (ed.), *Lord William Russell and His Wife 1815–1846,* London, 1974.

Buckle, George Earle, *The Life of Benjamin Disraeli, Earl of Beaconsfield Vol. IV (1855–1868), V (1868–1876) and VI (1876–1881).* London, 1916–1920.

Buckle, George E. (ed.), *The Letters of Queen Victoria. A Selection from Her Majesty's Correspondence and Journal between the Years 1868 and 1878.* Vol. I. London, 1926.

Busch, Moritz, *Bismarcks große Tage,* Landsberg, 1990.

Duff, Sir Montstuart E. Grant, *Notes from a Diary 1851–1872.* 2 Vols; London, 1897.

Ebeland, Gerhard and Behnen, Michael (eds), *Paul Graf von Hatzfeldt. Botschafter Paul Graf von Hatzfeldt, Nachgelassene Papiere 1838–1901.* 2 Vols; Boppard, 1976.

Elliot, Sir Henry, *Some Revolutions and Other Diplomatic Experiences,* London, 1922.

Hertslet, Sir E., *Recollections of the Old Foreign Office,* London, 1901.

Hohenlohe-Schillingsfürst, Chlodwig zu, *Denkwürdigkeiten des Fürsten Chlodwig zu Hohenlohe-Schillingfürst,* Vol. II, Leipzig, 1907.

Holborn, Hajo, *Josef Maria von Radowitz. Aufzeichnungen und Erinnerungen aus dem Leben des Botschafters 1839–1877,* 1 Vol., Stuttgart, Berlin, Leipzig, 1925.

Malet, Sir Edward, *Shifting Scenes. Or Memories of Many Men in Many Lands,* London, 1901.

Ponsonby, Sir Frederick (ed.), *Briefe an die Kaiserin Friedrich,* Berlin, 1929.

Ramm, Agatha, *The Political Correspondence of Mr Gladstone and Lord Granville 1868–1876,* London, 1952.

Rich, Norman and Fisher, M.H. (eds), *Die Geheimen Papiere Friedrich von Holsteins. Erinnerungen und politische Denkwürdigkeiten,* Vol. 1, Göttingen, 1956.

Ringhoffer, Karl (ed.), *Im Kampfe um Preußens Ehre. Aus dem Nachlasse des Grafen Albrecht von Bernstorff und seiner Gemahlin Anna, geb. Freiin von Koenneritz,* Berlin, 1906.

Robolsky, Hermann, *Aus der Wilhelmstraße. Erinnerungen eines Offiziösen,* Berlin, 1887.

Russell, Bertrand and Patricia, (eds), *The Amberley Papers. The Letters and Diaries of Lord and Lady Amberley,* Vol. I, London, 1937.

Russell, George, *One Look Back,* London, 1911.

Russell, George, *Prime Ministers and Some Others. A Book of Reminiscences,* London, 1918.

Schweinitz, Hans Lothar von, *Denkwürdigkeiten des Botschafters General von Schweinitz,* Vol. 1, Berlin, 1927.

Super, R.H. (ed.), *Matthew Arnold. Schools and Universities on the Continent,* Michigan, 1964.

Vierhaus, Rudolf (ed.), *Das Tagebuch der Baronin Spitzemberg. Aufzeichnungen aus der Hofgesellschaft des Hohenzollernreiches,* 5th edn Göttingen, 1989.

Vincent, John (ed.) *A Selection from the Diaries of Edward Henry Stanley, 15th Earl of Derby (1826–93). Between September 1869 and March 1878.* Camden Fifth Series, Vol. 4, London, 1994.

Wemyss, Rosslyn, *Memoirs and Letters of the Rt Hon. Sir Robert Morier, G.C.B. From 1826 to 1876,* London, 1911.

Secondary Sources (Selection)

Adelman, Paul, *Gladstone, Disraeli and Later Victorian Politics,* London, 1992 (10th impression).

Anderson, Margaret Lavinia, *Windthorst — A Political Biography,* Oxford, 1981.

Annan, Noel., 'The Intellectual Aristocracy' in: J.H. Plumb (ed.), *Social History. A Tribute to G.M. Trevelyan,* London, 1955.

Bassett, Arthur T., *Gladstone and His Wife,* London, 1936.

Baum, E.M., *Bismarcks Urteil über England und die Engländer,* München, 1936.

Beales, Derek, *From Castlereagh to Gladstone,* London, 1969.

Becker, J. and Hillgruber, Andreas, *Die Deutsche Frage im 19. und 20. Jahrhundert,* München, 1983.

Becker, Winfried, 'Liberale Kulturkampf-Positionen und politischer Katholizismus,' in Otto Pflanze and Elisabeth Müller-Luckner (eds), *Innenpolitische Probleme des Bismarck-Reiches,* München, Wien, 1983.

Becker, Winfried, 'Otto von Bismarcks Rolle bei Ausbruch, Verschärfung und Beilegung des preußischen Kulturkampfes,' in Rudolf Lill and Francesco Traniello (eds), *Der Kulturkampf in Italien und in den deutschsprachigen Ländern,* Berlin, 1993.

Bellamy, Richard, (ed.), *Victorian Liberalism — Nineteenth-Century Political Thought and Practice,* London, 1990.

Beust, Ferdinand Graf von, *Aus Dreiviertel Jahrhunderten. Erinnerungen und Aufzeichnungen,* Vol. II, 1866–1885, Stuttgart, 1887.

Birke, Adolf M. and Kettenacker, Lothar (eds.), *Wettlauf in die Moderne. England und Deutschland seit der industriellen Revolution,* München, 1988.

Birke, Adolf M. and Kluxen, Kurt (eds.), *Viktorianisches England in deutscher Perspektive, Prinz-Albert-Studien, Vol. I,* München, 1983.

Birke, Adolf M. and Kluxen, Kurt (eds.), *Staat und Gesellschaft im 19. Jahrhundert — Ein deutsch-englischer Vergleich. Prinz-Albert-Studien Vol. 2,* München, New York, London, Paris, 1984.

Birke, Adolf M. and Kluxen, Kurt (eds.) *Deutscher und Britischer Parlamentarismus,* München, 1985.

Birke, Adolf M. and Recker, Marie-Luise (eds.), *Das gestörte Gleichgewicht — Deutschland als Problem britischer Sicherheit im Neunzehnten und*

Zwanzigsten Jahrhundert. Prinz-Albert — Studien Vol. 8, München, London, New York, Paris, 1990.

Blackbourn, David, *Class, Religion and Local Politics in Wilhelmine Germany. The Centre Party in Württemberg before 1914*, Mainz, Wiesbaden, 1980.

Blackbourn, David, 'Die Zentrumspartei und die deutschen Katholiken während des Kulturkampfes und danach,' in *Innenpolitische Probleme des Bismarck-Reiches*, München, 1983.

Blackbourn, David, *Volksfrömmigkeit und Fortschrittsglaube im Kulturkampf,* Stuttgart, 1988.

Blackbourn, David and Eley, Geoff, *The Pecularities of German History: Bourgeois Society and Politics in the Nineteenth Century*, New York, 1984.

Blake, Robert, *Disraeli — Eine Biographie aus Victorianischer Zeit,* Frankfurt a.M., 1980.

Blake, Robert, *Gladstone, Disraeli and Queen Victoria. The Centenary Romanes Lectures*, Oxford, 1993.

Blake, Robert and Cecil, Hugh (eds), *Salisbury — The Man and His Politics,* New York, 1987.

Blakiston, Georgiana, *Woburn and the Russells,* Suffolk, 1988.

Blakiston, Noel (ed.), *The Roman Question. Extracts from the Despatches of Lord Odo Russell from Rome, 1858–1870*, London, 1962.

Blanning, T.C.W. and Cannadine, David (eds), *History and Biography. Essays in Honour of Derek Beales,* Cambridge, 1996.

Böhme, Helmut (ed.), *Die Reichsgründung*, München, 1967.

Böhme, Helmut (ed.), *Probleme der Reichsgründungszeit, 1848–1879*, Köln, 1968.

Bosbach, Franz (ed.), *Feindbilder. Die Darstellung des Gegners in der politischen Publizistik des Mittelalters und der Neuzeit*, Köln, 1992.

Bourne, Kenneth, *The Foreign Policy of Victorian England 1830–1902*, Oxford, 1970.

Briggs, Asa (ed.), *Lionel Tollemache. Gladstone's Boswell Late Victorian Conversations,* Sussex, 1984.

Brook-Shepard, Gordon, *Edward VII*, Stuttgart, 1975.

Bullen, Roger (ed.), *The Foreign Office 1782–1982*, Maryland, 1984.

Burghclere, W.A., *A Great Lady's Friendships. Letters to Mary, Marchioness of Salisbury, Countess of Derby. 1862–1890*, London, 1933.

Burke, Peter, 'Ranke als Gegenrevolutionär,' in Wolfgang Mommsen (ed.), *Leopold v. Ranke und die moderne Geschichtswissenschaft,* Stuttgart, 1988.

Bussmann, Walter (ed.), *Staatssekretär Graf Herbert von Bismarck. Aus seiner politischen Privatkorrespondenz*, Göttingen, 1964.

Cannadine, David, 'Kaiser William II and the British Monarchy,' in Blanning T.C.W. and Cannadine, David *History and Biography,* Cambrige, 1996.

Cannadine, David, *The Decline and Fall of the British Aristocracy*, New Haven, London, 1990.

Cannadine, David, *The Pleasures of the Past*, London, 1990.

Cannadine, David, *Die Erfindung der britischen Monarchie 1820–1994*, Berlin, 1994.

Cannadine, David, *Aspects of Aristocracy*, London, 1995.

Carr, William, *The Origins of the Wars of German Unification*, London, 1991.

Cecil, Algemon, *The Foreign Office. The Cambridge History of British Foreign Policy*, Vol. III, 1923.

Cecil, Gwendolen, *Life of Robert Marquis of Salisbury*, 4 Vols, London, 1921.

Chamberlain, Muriel E., *Pax Britannica? British Foreign Policy 1789–1914*, London, 1988.

Churchill, Winston S., *A History of the English-Speaking Peoples, Vol. IV. The Great Democracies*, London, 1958 (reprinted 1991).

Clarke, John, *British Diplomacy and Foreign Policy 1782–1865*, London, 1989.

Conacher, J.B., *Britain and the Crimea, 1855–56. Problems of War and Peace*, London, 1987.

Cook, Sir Edward, *Delane of the Times*, London, 1911.

Craig, Gordon A., *Germany 1866–1945*, New York, 1978.

Craig, Gordon A., *Das Ende Preußens. Acht Porträts*, München, 1985.

Crankshaw, Edward, *Bismarck*, München, 1986.

Dawson, W.H., *The German Empire and the Unity Movement*, London, 1966.

Demps, Laurenz, *Berlin-Wilhelmstraße. Eine Topographie preußisch-deutscher Macht*, Berlin, 1994.

Dülffer, Jost and Hühner, Hans (eds): *Otto von Bismarck. Person-Politik-Mythos*, Berlin, 1993.

Duroselle, Jean-Baptiste, 'Die europäischen Staaten und die Gründung des Deutschen Reiches,' in Theodor Schieder and Ernst Deuerlein (eds), *Die Reichsgründung 1870/71. Tatsachen, Kontroversen, Interpretationen*, Stuttgart, 1980.

Ensor, R.C.K., *England 1870–1914* (first published 1936), Oxford, 1988.

Farley, Lawrence T., *Plebiscites and Sovereignty—The Crisis of Political Illegitimacy*, London, 1978.

Fischer-Frauendienst, Irene, *Bismarcks Pressepolitik*, Münster, 1963.

Förster, Erich, *Adalbert Falk. Sein Leben und Wirken als preußischer Kultusminister*, Gotha, 1927.

Friedell, Egon, *Kulturgeschichte der Neuzeit. Die Krisis der Europäischen Seele von der Schwarzen Pest bis zum Ersten Weltkrieg*, München, 1927.

Fulford, Roger, *Darling Child. Private Correspondence of Queen Victoria and the Crown Princess of Prussia. 1871–1878*, London, 1976.

Gall, Lothar, 'Bismarck und England,' in Paul Kluke and Peter Alter (eds), *Aspekte der deutsch-britischen Beziehungen im Laufe der Jahrhunderte. Ansprachen und Vorträge zur Eröffnung des Deutschen Historischen Insitituts London*, Stuttgart, 1978.

Gall, Lothar, *Bismarck — Der weiße Revolutionär,* Berlin, 1980.

Gall, Lothar, *Europa auf dem Weg in die Moderne, 1850 – 1890,* München, 1989.

Gebauer, Fritz, 'Zur Bismarckbiographie Theodor Fontanes,' in Jost Dülffer and G.P. Gooch, (eds), *History and Historians in the Nineteenth Century,* London, 1952.

Gruner, Wolf D., *Die deutsche Frage in Europe 1800–1990.* München, 1993.

Guedalla, P., *The Queen and Mr. Gladstone 1845–97,* 2 Vols., London, 1933–1934.

Haffner, Sebastian and Venohr, Wolfgang, *Preußische Profile*, Frankfurt, a.M. 1986.

Hagen, M. von, *Bismarck und England,* Stuttgart, 1943.

Hare, David, *Plenty*, London, 1978.

Harenberg, Bodo, *Die Chronik Berlins*, Dortmund, 1986.

Hart, Neil, *The Foreign Secretary*, Suffolk, 1984.

Hayes, P., *Modern British Foreign Policy: the Nineteenth Century, 1815–1888.* London, 1975.

Hennock, E.P., *British Social Reform and German Precedents. The Case of Social Insurance 1880–1914,* Oxford, 1987.

Herre, Franz, *Anno 1870/71*, Berlin, 1970.

Herzfeld, Hans, *Deutschland und das geschlagene Frankreich 1871–1873*, Berlin, 1924.

Heydemann, Günther, 'Partner oder Konkurrent? Das britische Deutschland während des Wiedervereinigungsprozesses 1989–1991,' in Franz Bosbach (ed.), *Feindbilder. Die Darstellung des Gegners in der politischen Publizistik des Mittelalters und der Neuzeit,* Köln, 1992.

Hibbert, Christopher, *Queen Victoria in Her Letters and Journals,* London, 1984.

Hiery, Hermann, *Reichstagswahlen im Reichsland,* Düsseldorf, 1986.

Hildebrand, Klaus, 'Von der Reichseinigung zur 'Krieg-in-Sicht' Krise. Preußen-Deutschland als Faktor der britischen Außenpolitik,' in Michael Stürmer (ed.), *Das kaiserliche Deutschland. Politik und Geschichte 1870–1918,* Düsseldorf, 1970.

Hildebrand, Klaus, *Deutsche Außenpolitik 1871–1918,* München, 1989.

Hildebrand, Klaus, *Die britische Europapolitik zwischen imperialen Mandat und innerer Reform 1856–1876,* Düsseldorf, 1993.

Hildebrand, Klaus, *Das vergangene Reich — Deutsche Außenpolitik von Bismarck bis Hitler,* Stuttgart, 1995.

Hill, Christopher, 'The Historical Background — Past and Present in British Foreign Policy' in: Michael Smith, Steve Smith and Brian White (eds) *British Foreign Policy — Tradition, Change and Transformation*, London, 1988.

Hillgruber, Andreas, '"Die-Krieg in-Sicht" Krise 1875. Wegscheide der Politik der europäischen Großmächte in der späten Bismarckzeit,' in Ernst Schulin (ed.) *Gedenkschrift Martin Göhring. Studien zur europäischen Geschichte*, Wiesbaden, 1968.

Hillgruber, Andreas, *Bismarcks Außenpolitik*, Freiburg, 1972.

Hillgruber, Andreas, *Bismarck — Gründer der europäischen Großmacht Deutsches Reich*, Göttingen, 1978.

Hillgruber, Andreas, *Die gescheiterte Großmacht — Eine Skizze des Deutschen Reiches 1871–1945*, Düsseldorf, 1980.

Hobsbawm, Eric J., *Das Imperiale Zeitalter 1875–1914*, Frankfurt, a. M. 1989.

Hobsbawm, Eric J., *Das Zeitalter der Extreme*, München, 1995.

Hofer, W. (ed.), *Europa und die Einheit Deutschlands. Eine Bilanz nach 100 Jahren*, Köln, 1970.

Holborn, Hajo, *Bismarcks europäische Politik zu Beginn der siebziger Jahre und die Mission Radowitz*, Berlin, 1925.

Holborn, Hajo, *Deutsche Geschichte in der Neuzeit. Das Zeitalter des Imperialismus (1871–1945)*, 2nd edn, Vol. 3, Frankfurt a.M. 1981.

Hollet, David, *The Alabama Affair. The British Shipyard Conspiracy in the American Civil War*, Cheshire, 1993.

Horne, Alistair, *The Fall of Paris*, revised, London, 1989.

Hübner, Hans (ed.) *Otto von Bismarck. Person-Politik-Mythos*, Berlin, 1993.

Jenkins, Roy, *Gladstone*, London, 1995.

Joll, James, *Europe Since 1870. An International History*, 4th edn, London, 1990.

Jones, Raymond, *The Nineteenth Century Foreign Office: a Study in Administrative History*, London, 1971.

Jones, Raymond, *The British Diplomatic Service. 1815–1914*, London, 1983.

Kennedy, A.L., *Salisbury 1830–1903*, London, 1953.

Kennedy, Paul, *The Rise of the Anglo-German Antagonism 1860–1914*, London, 1980.

Kennedy, Paul, *Strategy and Diplomacy 1870–1945*, London, 1983.

Kennedy, Paul, *The Realities Behind Diplomacy*, London, 1986.

Kennedy, Paul, *The Rise and Fall of the Great Powers. Economic Change and Military Conflict from 1500 to 2000*, 2nd British edn, London, 1989.

Kent, G.O., *Arnim and Bismarck*, Oxford, 1968.

Kettenacker, Lothar (ed.), *Studien zur geschichte Englands und der Deutsch – Britischen Beziehungen*, München, 1981.

Kinzer, Bruce L., *The Gladstonian Turn of Mind*, Toronto, 1985.

Kissinger, Henry, *Diplomacy*, New York, 1994.

Kißling, Johannes B., *Geschichte des Kulturkampfes im Deutschen Reiche*, 3 Vols, Freiburg i. Br, 1911–1916.

Kleinknecht, Thomas, 'Die Gründung des Deutschen Reiches 1870/ 71 aus der Sicht des britischen Gelehrtenliberalismus,' in Bernd Jürgen Wendt (ed.), *Das britische Deutschlandbild im Wandel des 19. und 20. Jahrhunderts*, Bochum, 1984.

Knaplund, Paul, *Gladstone's Foreign Policy*, London, 1970.

Knaplund, Paul, *Letters from the Berlin Embassy 1871–74 and 1880–85*. Annual Report of the American Historical Association for the Year 1942, Washington, 1942.

Knoepflmacher, V.C., *Nature and the Victorian Imagination*, Berkeley, 1977.

Kohn, Hans, *The Mind of Germany: Education of a Nation*, London, 1961.

Kolb, Eberhard, *Der Kriegsausbruch 1870. Politische Entscheidungensprozesse und Verantwortlichkeit der Julikrise 1870*, Göttingen, 1970.

Kolb, Eberhard (ed.), *Europa und die Reichsgründung. Preußen-Deutschland in der Sicht der großen europäischen Mächte 1860–1880*, München, 1980.

Kolb, Eberhard (ed.), *Europa vor dem Krieg von 1870. Mächtekonstellation — Konfliktfelder — Kriegsausbruch*, München, 1987.

Kollander, Patricia, *Frederick III: Germany's Liberal Emperor*, Westport, 1995.

Kratzsch, G., *Harry von Arnim. Bismarck-Rivale und Frondeur. Die Arnim-Prozesse 1874–1876*, Göttingen, 1974.

Kunisch, Johannes (ed.), *Bismarck und seine Zeit*, Berlin, 1990.

Kutsch, R., *Queen Victoria und die deutsche Einigung*, Berlin, 1937.

Lamar, Cecil, *The German Diplomatic Service 1871–1914*, Princeton, 1976.

Lamer, R., *Der englische Parlamentarismus in der deutschen politischen Theorie im Zeitalter Bismarcks. Ein Beitrag zur Vorgeschichte des deutschen Parlamentarismus*, Lübeck, 1963.

Langer, William L., *European Alliances and Alignments 1871–1890*, 2nd edn, New York, 1950.

Langewiesche, Dieter, *Liberalismus in Deutschland*, Frankfurt, 1988.

Lieven, Dominic, *The Aristocracy in Europe 1815–1914*, London, 1992.

Lill, Rudolf and Traniello, Francesco (eds), *Der Kulturkampf in Italien und den deutschsprachigen Ländern*, Berlin, 1993.

Löhde, Walter, *Das Päpstliche Rom und das Deutsche Reich*, Stuttgart, 1978.

Lowe, John, *Rivalry and Accord. International Relations 1870–1914*, London, 1993.

Ludwig, Emil, *Bismarck*, Berlin, 1932.

Macfie, A.L., *The Eastern Question 1774–1923*, London, 1979.

MacKenzie, David, *The Serbs and Russian Pan-Slavism, 1875–78*, Ithaca, 1978.

Magnus, Philip, *King Edward the Seventh. The Most Edwardian of them all*, London, 1964.

Mander, John, *Our German Cousins. Anglo-German Relations in the Nineteenth and Twentieth Centuries*, London, 1974.

Mann, Golo, *Deutsche Geschichte des 19. und 20. Jahrhunderts*, 15th edn, Frankfurt a.M., 1985.

Matthew, H.C.G., *Gladstone 1875–1898*, Oxford, 1995.

McDonough, Frank, *The British Empire* 1815–1914, London, 1994.

McElrath, Damian, *Lord Acton — The Decision Decade, 1864–1874*, London, 1970.

Meine, Karl, *England und Deutschland in der Zeit des Übergangs vom Manchestertum zum Imperialismus 1871 bis 1876*, Vaduz, 1965.

Melville, Ralph and Schröder, Hans Jürgen (eds), *Der Berliner Kongress von 1878*, Wiesbaden, 1982.

Messerschmidt, Manfred, *Deutschland in englischer Sicht. Die Wandlung des Deutschlandbildes in der englischen Geschichtsschreibung*, Düsseldorf, 1955.

Michael, Horst, *Bismarck, England und Europa*, München, 1930.

Middleton, Charles R., 'The Foundation of the Foreign Office,' in Roger Bullen (ed.), *The Foreign Office 1782–1982*, Maryland, 1984.

Millman, Richard, *British Foreign Policy and the Coming of the Franco-Prussian War*, Oxford, 1965.

Millman, Richard, *Britain and the Eastern Question, 1875–1878*, Oxford, 1979.

Mommsen, Wolfgang J., *Die politsche Rolle des deutschen Liberalismus im 19. Jahrhundert und in der Weimarer Republik*. Tutzing bei/München, 1984.

Mommsen, Wolfgang J., *Imperialismustheorien*, Göttingen, 1987.

Mommsen, Wolfgang J. (ed.), *Leopold von Ranke und die moderne Geschichtswissenschaft*, Stuttgart, 1988.

Mommsen, Wolfgang J., *Das Ringen um den nationalen Staat. Die Gründung und der innere Ausbau des Deutschen Reiches unter Otto von Bismarck 1850 bis 1890*. Berlin, 1993.

Mommsen, Wolfgang J., *Imperial Germany 1867–1918. Politics, Culture and Society in an Authoritarian State*, London, 1995.

Mommsen, Wolfgang J. and Mock, Wolfgang (eds), *Die Entstehung des Wohlfahrtsstaates in Großbritannien und Deutschland 1850–1950*, Stuttgart, 1982.

Morley, John, *The Life of W.E. Gladstone*, Vol. II, London, 1903.

Mosse, Werner Eugen Emil, *The European Powers and the German Question 1848–1871*, Cambridge, 1958.

Mosse, Werner Eugen Emil, *The Rise and Fall of the Crimean War System 1855–71. The Story of a Peace Settlement*, London, 1963.

Müller-Seidel, Walter, 'Fontane und Bismarck,' in *Nationalismus in Germanistik und Dichtung. Dokumentation des Germanistentages in München*, 1966.

Münch, Fritz, *Bismarck's Affäre Arnim. Die Politik des Diplomaten und die Verantwortlichkeit des Staatsmannes*, München, 1990.

Musil, Robert, *Der Mann ohne Eigenschaften* (3 Vols published in 1943), Hamburg, 1978.

Neville, Henry, *A Few Comments on Mr. Gladstone's Expostulation with Some Remarks on Vaticanism*, London, 1875.

Newton, Lord, *Lord Lyons*, 2 Vols, London, 1913.

Nicolson, Harold, *Kleine Geschichte der Diplomatie*, Frankfurt a.M., 1955.

Niedhardt, Gottfried, *Englische Geschichte im 19. und 20. Jahrhundert*, München, 1987.

Nipperdey, Thomas, *Gesellschaft, Kultur, Theorie. Gesammelte Aufsätze zur neueren Geschichte*, Göttingen, 1976.

Nipperdey, Thomas, *Deutsche Geschichte 1866–1918:* Vol. 1, *Arbeitswelt und Bürgergeist*, München, 1990.

Nipperdey, Thomas, *Deutsche Geschichte 1866–1918 Machtstaat vor der Demokratie*, München, 1992.

Pabst, Wilfried, *Das Jahrhundert der deutsch-französichen Konfrontation*, Hannover, 1983.

Pakula, Hannah, *An Uncommon Woman: The Empress Frederick, Daughter of Queen Victoria, Wife of the Crown Prince of Prussia, Mother of Kaiser Wilhelm*, London, 1995.

Palmer, Alan, *Glanz und Niedergang der Diplomatie*, München, 1992.

Palmer, Alan, *Verfall und Untergang des Osmanischen Reiches 1875–78*, München, 1994.

Parry, Jonathan P., *Democracy and Religion, Gladstone and the Liberal Party, 1867–1875*, Cambridge, 1986.

Parry, Jonathan P., *The Rise and Fall of Liberal Government in Victorian Britain*, London, 1993.

Parry, Jonathan P., 'Past and Future in the Later Career of Lord John Russell,' in T.C.W. Blanning and D. Cannadine (eds), *History and Biography*, Cambridge, 1996.

Pflanze, Otto, *Bismarcks Herrschaftstechnik als Problem der gegenwärtigen Historiographie*, Schriften des Historischen Kollegs, München, 1982.

Pflanze, Otto, *Bismarck and the Development of Germany. The Period of Consolidation 1871–1880*, Vol. II, Princeton, 1990.

Pflanze, Otto and Müller-Luckner, Elisabeth (eds.), *Innenpolitische Probleme des Bismarck-Reiches*, München Wien, 1983.

Philipson, Martin, *Das Leben Friedrich III.* Wiesbaden, 1908.

Platt, D.C.M., *Finance, Trade and Politics in British Foreign Policy. 1815–1914*, Oxford, 1971.

Platt, D.C.M., *The Cinderella Service: British Consuls Since 1825*, London, 1971.

Pohl, Heinz-Alfred, *Bismarcks 'Einflußnahme' auf die Staatsform in Frankreich 1871–1877*, Frankfurt a.M., 1983.

Porter, A.N., 'Lord Salisbury. Foreign Policy and Domestic Finance 1860–1900,' in Lord Blake and Hugh Cecil (eds), *Salisbury — the Man and his Policies*, New York, 1987.

Porter, Bernhard, *Britannia's Burden — The Political Evolution of Modern Britain 1851–1990*, London, 1994.

Poschinger, Heinrich von, *Fürst Bismarck und die Diplomaten 1852–1890*, Hamburg, 1900.

Pugh, Martin, *The Making of Modern British Politics. 1967–1939*, Oxford, 1982.

Ramm, Agatha, *Sir Robert Morier, Envoy and Ambassador in the Age of Imperialism 1876–1893*, Oxford, 1973.

Ramm, Agatha, 'Granville', in: Keith M. Wilson (ed.), *British Foreign Secretaries and Foreign Policy: From Crimean War to First World War*, London, 1987.

Raymond, D.N., *British Policy and Public Opinion During the Franco-Prussian War*, New York, 1921.

Reissner, Alexander, *Berlin 1675–1945*, London, 1984.

Rheindorf, Kurt, *Die Schwarzmeer-Pontusfrage*, Berlin, 1925.

Rich, Norman, *The Age of Nationalism and Reform, 1850–1890*, New York, 1977.

Rieder, Heinz, *Napoleon III.*, Gernsbach, 1989.

Ritter, G., *Europa und die deutsche Frage. Betrachtungen über die geschichtliche Eigenart des deutschen Staatsdenkens*, München, 1948.

Ritter, Gerhard A., *Sozialversicherung in Deutschland und England. Entstehung und Grundzüge im Vergleich*, München, 1983.

Robbins, Keith, *Protestant Germany Through English Eyes: A Complex Encounter, The 1992 Annual Lecture*. German Historical Institute, London, 1992.

Robolsky, Hermann, *Bismarck und England*, Berlin, 1889.

Röhl, John., *Kaiser, Hof und Staat. Wilhelm II. und die deutsche Politik*, München, 1987.

Röhl, John, *Wilhelm II. — Die Jugend des Kaisers 1859–1888*, München, 1993.

Ross, C.B., *The Old Catholic Movement*, London, 1964.

Roth, Joseph, *Der Radetzkymarsch*, Berlin, 1932.

Rothfels, Hans, *Bismarcks englische Bündnispolitik*, Berlin, 1924.

Rothfels, Hans, *Bismarck, der Osten und das Reich*, Darmstadt, 1960.

Russell, Bertrand, *Autobiographie II, 1914–1944*, Frankfurt a.M., 1970.

Russell, Bertrand, *Briefe aus den Jahren 1950–1968*, Frankfurt a.M., 1970.

Sandiford, K.A.P., 'Gladstone and Europe,' in Bruce L. Kinzer (ed.), *The Gladstonian Turn of Mind*, Toronto, 1985.

Sasse, Heinz Günther, *100 Jahre Botschaft in London - Aus der Geschichte einer Deutschen Botschaft*, Bonn, 1963.

Satow, Sir Ernest, *A Guide to Diplomatic Practice*, 2 Vols. London, 1917.

Schaarschmidt, Thomas, *Außenpolitik und öffentliche Meinung in Großbritannien während des deutsch-französischen Krieges von 1870/71*, Frankfurt a.M, 1993.

Schieder, Theodor and Deuerlein, Ernst, *Die Reichsgründung 1870/71. Tatsachen, Kontroversen, Interpretationen*, Stuttgart, 1980.

Schipperges, Heinrich, *Rudolf Virchow*, Hamburg, 1994.

Schmidt, Rainer F., *Die gescheiterte Allianz. Österreich-Ungarn, England und das Deutsche Reich in der Ära Andrassy. 1867–1878/79*, Frankfurt a.M., 1992.

Schmidt-Volkmar, Erich, *Der Kulturkampf in Deutschland 1871–1890*, Göttingen, 1962.

Schmitt, Bernadotte Everly, *England and Germany 1740–1914*, Princeton, 1916.

Schramm, Percy Ernst, 'Englands Verhältnis zur deutschen Kultur zwischen der Reichsgründung und der Jahrhundertwende,' in Werner Conze (ed.) *Deutschland und Europa. Historische Studien zur Völker und Staatenordnung des Abendlandes. Festschrift für Hans Rothfels*, Düsseldorf, 1951.

Seton-Watson, R.W., *Disraeli, Gladstone and the Eastern Question: a Study in Diplomacy and Party Politics*, London, 1935.

Seton-Watson, R.W., *Britain in Europe 1789–1914. A Survey of Foreign Policy*, Cambridge, 1937.

Shannon, R.T., *Gladstone and the Bulgarian Agitation 1876*, London, 1963.

Shannon, R.T., *The Crisis of Imperialism 1865–1915*, London, 1976.

Shannon, R.T., *The Age of Disraeli, 1868–1881: the Rise of Tory Democracy*, London, New York, 1992.

Sheehan, James, *German Liberalism in the Nineteenth Century*, Chicago, 1977.

Simon, W.M., *Germany in the Age of Bismarck*, London, 1968.

Smith, Michael, Smith, Steve and White, Brian (eds), *British Foreign Policy. Tradition, Change and Transformation*, London, 1988.

Smith, Woodruff, *The German Colonial Empire*, Chapel Hill, 1978.

Snyder, Louis L., *Diplomacy in Iron. The Life of Herbert von Bismarck*, Miami, 1985.

Sontag, Raymond James, *Germany and England. Background of Conflict 1848–1894*, London, 1938.

Sontag, Raymond James, *European Diplomatic History 1871–1932*, 1st published 1933, New York, 1961.

Sösemann, Bernd, 'Publizistik in staatlicher Regie. Die Presse und Informationspolitik der Bismarck Ära,' in Johannes Kunisch (ed.), *Bismarck und seine Zeit*, Berlin, 1990.

Spiel, Hilde, *Glanz und Untergang. Wien 1866–1938*, München, 1988.

Steinberg, Jonathan, *Yesterday's Deterrent: Tirpitz and the Birth of the German Battle Fleet*, London, 1965.

Stern, Fritz, *Gold and Iron. Bismarck, Bleichröder and the Building of the German Empire*, New York, 1977.

Strachey, Lytton, *Eminent Victorians*, London, 1918.

Studt, Christoph, *Lothar Bucher (1871–1892). Ein politisches Leben zwischen Revolution und Staatsdienst,* Göttingen, 1992.

Stürmer, Michael (ed.), *Das Kaiserliche Deutschland. Politik und Gesellschaft. 1870–1918,* Düsseldorf, 1970.

Stürmer, Michael, *Regierung und Reichstag im Bismarckstaat 1871–1880,* Düsseldorf, 1974.

Stürmer, Michael, *Liberalismus und Kirche 1848–1933. Die Anatomie eines Un-Verhältnisses,* Tutzing: München, 1984.

Stürmer, Michael, *Die Reichsgründung. Deutscher Nationalstaat und europäisches Gleichgewicht im Zeitalter Bismarcks,* München, 1986.

Stürmer, Michael, *Die Grenzen der Macht. Begegnung der Deutschen mit der Geschichte,* Berlin, 1992.

Sumner, B.H., *Russia and the Balkans 1870–1880,* Oxford, 1937.

Swartz, M., *The Politics of British Foreign Policy in the Era of Disraeli and Gladstone,* Oxford, 1985.

Taffs, Winifried, *Ambassador to Bismarck, Lord Odo Russell, First Baron Ampthill,* London, 1938.

Taylor, A.J.P., *Europe: Grandeur and Decline,* London, 1967.

Taylor, A.J.P., *The Struggle for Mastery in Europe 1848–1918,* London, 1972.

Thompson, F.M.L., *English Landed Society in the Nineteenth Century,* London, 1963.

Thompson, G.C., *Public Opinion and Lord Beaconsfield 1875–80,* London, 1886.

Thomson, David, *England in the Nineteenth Century 1815–1914,* revised edn by Derek Beales, London, 1978.

Tilley, John and Gaselee, Stephen, *The Foreign Office,* London, 1933.

Tombs, Robert, *France 1814–1914,* London, 1996.

Trebilcock, Clive, *The Industrialisation of the Continental Powers. 1780–1914,* London, 1981.

Trollope, Anthony, *Phineas Finn,* 1st published 1869, reprinted London, 1985.

Valentin, Veit, *Bismarcks Reichsgründung im Urteil englischer Diplomaten,* Amsterdam, 1937.

Voss, Karl, *Reiseführer für Literaturfreunde — Berlin,* Frankfurt, 1980.

de Vries, Jürgen, *Bismarck und das Herzogtum Lauenburg. Die Eingliederung Lauenburgs in Preußen 1865–1876,* Neumünster, 1989.

Waller, Bruce, *Bismarck,* Oxford, 1985.

Ward, A.W. and Gooch, G.P. (eds), *Cambridge History of British Foreign Policy, 1783–1919,* 3 Vols. Cambridge, 1922–1923.

Ward, W.R., 'Faith and Fallacy: English and German Perspectives in the Nineteenth Century,' in Richard J. Helmstadter and Bernhard Lightman (eds), *Victorian Faith in Crisis. Essays on Continuity and Change in Nineteenth Century Religious Belief,* Stanford, 1990.

Wehler, Hans-Ulrich (ed.), *Bündnis der Eliten. Zur Kontinuität der Machtstrukturen in Deutschland 1871–1945*, Düsseldorf, 1979.

Wehler, Hans-Ulrich, *Das deutsche Kaiserreich. 1871–1918*, 4th edn, Göttingen, 1980.

Wehler, Hans-Ulrich (ed.), *Europäischer Adel 1750–1950*, Göttingen, 1990.

Welchert, Hans-Heinrich (ed.), *Die glückliche Straße — Geschichte und Geschichten Unter den Linden*, Hamburg, 1949.

Conze, Werner (ed.), *Deutschland und Europa. Historische Studien zur Völker und Staatenordnung des Abendlandes. Festschrift für Hans Rothfels*, Düsseldorf, 1951.

Wiegler, Paul, *Wilhelm I. — Sein Leben und seine Zeit*, Dresden, 1927.

Wilson, Keith M. (ed.), *British Foreign Secretaries and Foreign Policy: From Crimean War to First World War*, London, 1987.

Wolff, Arnold, *Der Kölner Dom*, Köln, 1995.

Wolter, Heinz, *Bismarcks Außenpolitik 1871–1881*, East Berlin, 1983.

Zechlin, E., *Die Reichsgründung*, Frankfurt, 1978.

INDEX

Note: Since Prince Otto von Bismarck and Lord Odo Russell, 1st Baron Ampthill, as well as their respective home countries are mentioned throughout the book, they do not appear in the index.